ALLOW ME TO RETORT

A BLACK GUY'S GUIDE TO THE CONSTITUTION

ELIE MYSTAL

THE
NEW
PRESS

NEW YORK
LONDON

Requests for permission to reproduce selections from this book should be made through our website: https://thenewpress.com/contact.

Published in the United States by The New Press, New York, 2022
Paperback edition published by The New Press, 2023
Distributed by Two Rivers Distribution

ISBN 978-1-62097-681-4 (hc)
ISBN 978-1-62097-813-9 (ebook)
ISBN 978-1-62097-763-7 (pb)
CIP data is available

The New Press publishes books that promote and enrich public discussion and understanding of the issues vital to our democracy and to a more equitable world. These books are made possible by the enthusiasm of our readers; the support of a committed group of donors, large and small; the collaboration of our many partners in the independent media and the not-for-profit sector; booksellers, who often hand-sell New Press books; librarians; and above all by our authors.

www.thenewpress.com

Book design and composition by Bookbright Media
This book was set in Minion Pro and Gotham

Printed in the United States of America

10 9 8 7 6 5 4 3 2 1

To my children, Claudius and Maximilian, in hopes that they don't have to fight some of these white supremacists in robes

CONTENTS

PREFACE

ORIGINALISM ABORTS PROGRESS

Six months after this book came out in hardcover, Republicans and the religious right achieved their most essential victory against American women: six conservative justices voted to revoke reproductive freedom for women and pregnant people. Their victory was not a surprise to anybody who has been paying attention. These people have been aiming at reproductive rights ever since they were first recognized fifty years ago. They've poured financial resources into laying the legal, political, and social ground toward revoking a constitutional right for the first time in American history.

But conservative judges, scholars, and lawyers will tell you that this attack on bodily autonomy was not driven by the Republican Party agenda or a minority sect of fundamentalist Christians. Instead, they say that their rulings are *compelled* by the objective intellectual framework for interpreting laws and rights: "originalism."

Conservatives will tell you that originalism is merely a method of constitutional interpretation. They'll argue that their method grounds judges—who are not elected in our federal system—in the original public meaning of the laws as they were written by the members of government who are elected by popular majorities. They'll say that originalism is objective toward the outcomes of cases and restrained as to the disposition of judges.

Conservatives, as is so often the case, are lying. Originalism is not an objective interpretative framework, it's an outcome-driven choice made with a specific agenda in mind. It is both backward-looking and ass-backwards, ossifying the law in a hollow past when women, nonwhites, and openly LGBTQ people didn't have a voice or say in what the laws were or how they were written. And, far from restraining unelected judges, originalism encourages conservatives to become the most extreme versions of themselves, as they issue radical rulings severely out of step with the modern world or the people.

The full measure of originalism's intellectual bankruptcy and cynical, outcome-driven philosophy was put on public display in the 2022 case *Dobbs v. Jackson Women's Health*, the case that overturned *Roe v. Wade*. In it, six conservative justices upended fifty years of reproductive rights for women and pregnant people—along with a cannon of the Supreme Court's own precedents—to drive their own anti-abortion agenda and fundamentalist Christian dogma about when "life" begins.

Writing for the majority in *Dobbs*, Justice Samuel Alito states bluntly: "The Constitution makes no reference to abortion." He goes on to write that abortion is not "deeply rooted in this Nation's history and traditions," and says, "Until the latter part of the 20th century, such a right was entirely unknown in American law."

All of that is true. Does anybody want to guess why? Does anybody really wonder why the white men who wrote the Constitution and claimed exclusive authority to amend and interpret it for nearly two hundred years didn't include provisions relating to the bodily autonomy of people who didn't happen to be white men? Is any-body perplexed as to why a group of slavers who used Black babies as profit centers didn't think to include rights for the Black women they raped to abort the future unpaid labor this nation's history and traditions required? Does the fact that white women didn't get the right to vote until the twentieth century, and nonwhite women didn't functionally get that right until around the middle of the twentieth century, have something to do with abortion rights being "entirely unknown" to their dumbass husbands and fathers before the back half of the 1900s?

Alito knows exactly why the word "abortion" doesn't appear in the text of the original Constitution or its amendments (all but one of which were written and ratified before 1973's *Roe v. Wade* decision). He knows why it's not addressed in American law until women gained political power. He knows that treating women and pregnant people as fully human people who don't lose their status as autonomous beings from the moment of conception is a rela-tively "new" concept in this country, which is why he grounds his opinion in the past. He's not applying originalism as an interpre-tive framework to guide his decision, he's using originalism as a justification for his predetermined political outcome of rescinding reproductive rights.

Indeed, originalism works only as an after-the-fact justification for rulings, because it's almost comically useless as an objective framework to analyze anything. Let me explain how originalism is supposed to work, according to its acolytes. Steven Calabresi, one of the intellectual heavyweights of the Federalist Society, a group of conservative lawyers that tries to force originalism down America's throat, defines originalism this way:

> Originalists believe that the constitutional text ought to
> be given the original public meaning that it would have

had at the time that it became law. The original meaning of constitutional texts can be discerned from dictionaries, grammar books, and from other legal documents from which the text might be borrowed.

Originalism is often grouped with "textualism," which is a theory of interpretation that seeks to adhere to the so-called plain meaning of texts as written. It all sounds objective. First look at the words of the law (textualism) and figure out what they mean. If the meaning of the words is ambiguous, look toward what the people who wrote the words thought they meant at the time they were written. Then rule.

If it were that easy, an algorithm could be chief justice. Instead, when I ask, "Alexa, what are fundamental rights?" she tells me (and I'm quoting here): "Fundamental rights are a group of rights that have been recognized by a high degree of protection from encroachment." It's an answer so circular that I'm probably going to get bicycle ads served to my devices for two weeks.

But even when you imagine real humans doing the work, originalism (and textualism) fall apart when confronted by reality. Their alleged objectivity can't handle even the simplest rules once we understand that rules have to be applied to all different kinds of people.

I can prove that. Imagine one of the most basic and textually obvious "laws" people interact with every time they go into a store: a sign that reads "No Dogs Allowed." For a textualist, the meaning of the sign is obvious: dogs are frowned upon in that establishment. But what of cats? Presumably cats are allowed to enter the store, and it would be wrong to extend the prohibition to a wider diversity of animals than those contemplated by the sign at the door. But what if I wanted to shop with my pet tiger? Assuming I'm in a jurisdiction that otherwise allows pet tigers, I shouldn't be in violation of the sign. I might argue that a tiger is just a very large bodega cat. Of course, the business owner might disagree. They might even say, "The original public meaning of 'dogs' is really 'dangerous animals,'" and argue that their sign still applies. But what if I say, "Okay, then I'll just send in my falcon, which I've trained to find what I need." What if I have a trained monkey butler? What if I'm Mike Tyson and I want to bring all my harmless-yet-poop-filled pigeons into the store? Is the owner condemned to serving a menagerie until they invest in a sign that reads "only house cats allowed"?

What if I'm blind and have an actual dog as a licensed service animal? Surely the "no dogs" sign does not apply to a customer who can receive service only with the aid of a canine companion. What kind of fascist, ableist store denies seeing-eye dogs?

Even an instruction as simple as "no dogs allowed" contains some textual ambiguities when it is placed in the real world. That's where originalism and Steven Calabresi's original public meaning of grammar books is supposed to come in. "Dog" has an objective meaning, and that meaning probably hasn't changed much from an eighteenth-century farmer's almanac to a twenty-first-century taxonomy textbook. Originalists might also look to the earliest laws excluding dogs, to see if other animals were excluded and the circumstances surrounding the adoption of those laws. When they get really deep into their cups, you'll find an originalist trying to justify their answer to the question with reference to some letter Thomas Jefferson wrote to James Madison about his experience at the Paris Zoo.

All of this is bullshit, because the objective definition or original public meaning of the word "dog" is not the relevant legal question. The question is if or when the objective instruction must *yield* to the needs of specific individuals or society at large. Do we favor store owners with special signs, or customers with special needs? Answering that question involves a subjective determination about whether we give a crap about blind people that day. You can say "no." You can say "the clear text says 'no dogs' so sorry, Mr. Wonder, you'll have to shop somewhere else." But that's a subjective choice about what kind of society we want to live in, not an objective requirement of the law of signage.

Conservatives like originalism because it provides a subjective answer to all of life's legal questions that favors the needs of white male patriarchy (and those with access to that ruling class) over the needs of everybody else. Just like Alito in *Dobbs*, originalists never want people to ask why the old white dead enslavers they worship believed what they believed. They don't use the original public meaning as the starting point for an inquiry, they use it as an end point to dispense with all further discussion. *The Constitution does not mention the word abortion, case closed* is about the most juvenile and intellectually soft method of assessing the legal foundation for reproductive rights imaginable, but for juvenile and intellectually soft minds like Samuel Alito's, it is enough. Because it gets him to where he always wanted to go.

It's important to understand that conservatives were not always like this. Just thirty years ago, the Supreme Court heard a major challenge to abortion rights and had an opportunity to overturn *Roe v. Wade*. That case was called *Planned Parenthood of Southeastern Pennsylvania v. Casey*, and the Supreme Court that heard it in 1992 was stacked with eight justices appointed by Republican presidents. And conservatives of that era were every bit as partisan as they are now: some of the Republicans on the *Planned Parenthood* court would go on to appoint George W. Bush president just eight years later.

But *Roe v. Wade* survived that conservative court. By a vote of 5–4 the court ruled to affirm *Roe* (albeit with new restrictions on access to reproductive care). All five votes in the majority came from the Republican-appointed justices (the lone justice appointed by a Democrat, Byron White, joined the dissent).

The difference between conservatives then and conservatives now is that thirty years ago you could still find conservatives who cared about *practicality*. The conservative majority in *Planned Parenthood* did not "like" abortions, and they were just as skeptical about federal power trampling over "states' rights" as the conservatives claim to be today. But they understood that abortions would happen, whether the court approved them or not. They understood that some form of abortion has happened in every society, probably since the dawn of *Homo sapiens*. They understood that the issue in front of the court was not whether abortions would be allowed, but whether those abortions that would inevitably happen would be safe, well-regulated, and available regardless of a person's ability to send their mistress to Canada.

Considering the practical impact of decisions is, or used to be, a fairly standard thing for Supreme Court justices to do. Lawyers call such concerns "reliance interests," and it basically means that laws or rulings that people have structured their lives around should not be disregarded by unelected judges. I think, for instance, that some of our copyright laws are woefully out of date. I think they're unnecessarily chilling on content creators who can't play a song from *Encanto* on social media platforms like Twitch and TikTok without Disney lawyers crashing down on their heads. But the reliance interests the movie and recording industries have on, you know, American copyright laws is such that I probably shouldn't throw them out on an ideological lark.

In *Planned Parenthood*, the majority (which included Sandra

Day O'Connor, the first woman on the Supreme Court) essentially based their ruling on the reliance interests the country had on *Roe v. Wade*. O'Connor wrote:

> People have organized intimate relationships and made choices that define their views of themselves and their places in society, in reliance on the availability of abortion in the event that contraception should fail.

Now fast-forward thirty years to *Dobbs*. There, Samuel Alito says that he can find no "concrete reliance" on abortion rights, because abortions are an "unplanned activity." He then argues that the court is ill-equipped to assess the "national psyche" and, amazingly, says that reliance interests are more appropriately found in *property cases*. *Dobbs* is literally about whether people have a fundamental right to their own bodies, but Alito is out here saying that people rely on the court's property decisions more than *Roe*.

Alito is doing what originalism was designed to do: give conservative justices an excuse to ignore all other factors in their ideological march toward extremism. Originalism cares nothing for practicality, in fact it argues against judges considering the real, modern-world impact of their rulings. And we now see conservative justices ignoring real-world concerns across a number of issues, not just abortion. In *West Virginia v. Environmental Protection Agency*, conservative justices ignored evidence of climate change while nerfing the power of the EPA to regulate under the Clean Air Act. In *Shinn v. Ramirez*, conservatives ignored evidence of a man's actual innocence in their rush to uphold the death penalty. In *New York State Rifle & Pistol Association v. Bruen*, Justice Clarence Thomas went so far as to warn against judges paying attention to the actual statistics on the uniquely American scourge of gun violence, before loosening gun regulations even further.

If originalism were a legitimate theory of constitutional inter-pretation, it wouldn't always magically align with the conserva-tive agenda. Indeed, there are liberal lawyers and scholars who argue that it doesn't and try to use originalists' arguments against conservatives.

The dispute is a little bit like the argument between Aragon and Boromir in *The Lord of the Rings*. At the Council of Elrond (which was basically a more diverse version of the Supreme Court, only in Middle-earth) Boromir argues that the Ring of Power can be used against the enemies of man. Aragon argues that the ring cannot be used for good, no matter the best intentions of those who use it.

I count myself in Aragon's camp. The weapon of the enemy can-not be used for good. Originalism is a thing designed to support the conservative agenda, not objective analysis. Any reliance on it will ultimately redound to the agenda it was made to service.

And we have a lot of proof that "progressive" originalist argu-ments don't work on the conservative majority. Conservatives will simply disregard originalism the moment it fails to suit their desired political outcomes. On the Supreme Court, Justices Elena Kagan and Ketanji Brown Jackson (the first Black woman on the Supreme Court) frequently make originalist arguments and appeals to the original public meaning for laws or constitutional clauses. Dur-ing oral arguments for *Students for Fair Admissions v. University of North Carolina* (a big affirmative action case that has not been decided as of this writing), Justice Jackson delivered damn-near a dissertation on the original public meaning of the Fourteenth Amendment and how it was intended to allow for civil rights laws that address racial disparity. It's an argument I also make later in this book.

But did it "work"? Were conservatives moved by such argu-ments? Of course not. Instead of looking at the original public meaning of the Fourteenth Amendment, conservatives just wanted to complain about affirmative action and accuse the policy of being unfair to white college applicants. Because the point of originalism isn't to figure out the right answer, just the Republican answer.

Conservative justices revoked abortion rights, and will end affirmative action and scale back LGBTQ rights, not because originalism compels them to do it. They'll do those things because they don't like abortion rights or affirmative action or LGBTQ rights. Originalism is just the Play-Doh they use to construct their rights-eating golem. It's a brittle intellectual theory that is given life by the deeply held conservative wish to take this country backward toward a time when women and minorities had no power and little voice.

Nobody should be afraid of originalist arguments. This book will give you all the tools you need to break them down and expose them for the intellectually dishonest trash that they are. But we should be very afraid of what an unchecked conservative-controlled Supreme Court will do next. What conservatives have right now is not a superior legal theory, but unassailable legal power. They know exactly how to use it, and they'll do an incredible amount of damage before they die: over the will and votes of the American people.

INTRODUCTION

Our Constitution is not good. It is a document designed to create a society of enduring white male dominance, hastily edited in the margins to allow for what basic political rights white men could be convinced to share. The Constitution is an imperfect work that urgently and consistently needs to be modified and reimagined to make good on its unrealized promises of justice and equality for all.

And yet you rarely see liberals make the point that the Constitution is actually trash. Conservatives are out here acting like the Constitution was etched by divine flame upon stone tablets, when in reality it was scrawled out over a sweaty summer by people making deals with actual monsters who were trying to protect their rights to rape the humans they held in bondage.

Why would I give a fuck about the original public meaning of the words written by these men? Conservatives will tell you that the text of laws explicitly passed in response to growing political, social, or economic power of nonwhite minorities should be followed to their highest grammatical accuracy, and I'm supposed to agree the text of this bullshit is the valid starting point of the debate?

Nah. As Rory Breaker says in the movie *Lock, Stock and Two Smoking Barrels*: "If the milk turns out to be sour, I ain't the kind of pussy to drink it." The Constitution was so flawed upon its release in 1787 that it came with immediate updates. The first ten amendments, the "Bill of Rights," were demanded by some to ensure ratification of the rest of the document. All of them were written by James Madison, who didn't think they were actually necessary but did it to placate political interests. Video gamers would call the Bill of Rights a "day one patch," and they're a good indication that the developers didn't have enough time to work out all the kinks. And yet conservatives use these initial updates to justify modern bigotry against all sorts of people.

If the Constitution were really the triumph of reason over darkness, as it is often treated, it probably wouldn't have failed so miserably that a devastating civil war would break out less than one hundred years later. But that happened. And if the fixes applied to the Constitution after that war ended in 1865 were so redemptive, I imagine that my mother—born in 1950 in Mississippi—would have been allowed to go inside her ostensibly "public" library while she was growing up, which of course she was not.

The Constitution is not gospel, it's not magic, and it's not even particularly successful if you count one civil war, one massive minority uprising for justice that kind of worked against tons that have been largely rebuffed, and one failed coup led by the actual president, as "demerits." It was written by a collection of wealthy slavers, wealthy colonizers, and wealthy antislavery white men who were nonetheless willing to compromise and profit together with slavers and colonizers. *At no point* have people of color or women been given a real say in how it was written, interpreted, or amended.

Even the amendments that granted equal rights to minorities and women were written by white men. They were ratified by all-white-male state legislatures. Nonwhites have, obviously, never held majority power in this country (yet); women have only held a majority of the seats in one state legislature, Nevada, and that didn't happen until 2018. Minorities or women have never held a majority in either chamber of Congress, or on the Supreme Court, and there has been only one nonwhite president of the United States in American history.

White people got so pissed off at that they replaced Barack Obama with a bigoted con man who questioned whether the Black president was even born in this country, and when their guy lost the next election, his people tried to start a coup.

And yet people still act like the Constitution is our most hallowed ground. I get it from Republicans; white supremacist governments aren't a deal breaker for them. And I'll admit that the Constitution is not without its charms. That stuff about banning cruel and unusual punishment, for instance? Fantastic. Everybody should ban it. I wish I could like that amendment twice.

Too bad we actually don't.

That's the thing about the Constitution: many of the rules, rights, prohibitions, and concepts are actually pretty decent. The problem is they've never been applied to all of the people living here. Not even for a day just to see how it would feel. They've never been anything more than a cruel tease. Most of our written principles serve only as a mocking illustration that the white people running this place know the right thing to do but simply refuse, out of spite, to do it. The Constitution is the impassive villain pouring a bottle of water into the ground in front of you as you're driven mad by thirst.

And so I have written this book. My goal is to expose what the Constitution looks like from the vantage of a person it was designed to ignore. My goal is to illustrate how the interpretation of the Constitution that conservatives want people to accept is little more than an intellectual front for continued white male hegemony. And my goal is to help people understand the key role the courts play in *interpreting* the Constitution and to arm additional people with the knowledge, information, and resolve to fight conservatives for control over the third branch of government in every election, and over every nomination.

Everybody has seen the gleaming, air-brushed face of the Constitution. I'm going to tell you what this motherfucker looks like after it has had its foot on your neck for almost 250 years. The perspective is a little different. I believe more people would try to fix it if more people saw it for what it truly is.

If this is your first time reading me, welcome. My name is Elie, and as I write this I am the justice correspondent for *The Nation* magazine. Prior to that, I was for a very long time a writer and editor at Above the Law, the most-read legal-industry news site in the country. Sometimes I appear on television and radio programs where I talk about the law and scream about Republicans. I was the legal editor of *More Perfect*, an excellent (dare I say) podcast about the Supreme Court that was produced by the same people who make *Radiolab*. I've been covering this space for over ten years now, as a journalist.

I used to be a lawyer, though not technically a "barred attorney-at-law." After I graduated from Harvard Law School in 2003, I worked as an associate attorney at Debevoise & Plimpton, one of the hundred or so most profitable law firms in the country. I passed the bar, but I never completed the rest of my bar application, mainly because I hated my job (no offense to Debevoise, which is a fantastic law firm, if you like being a corporate attorney), hated the practice of law, and wanted to get out almost as soon as I got in.

Being barred wasn't really necessary at a gigantic law firm where I was too junior ever to be the "named" attorney for any client anyway, and I felt like not being able to fall back on a law license would motivate me to get out there and figure out what I really wanted to do. Things have worked out, and I have many nights of hunting mice in my old, crappy apartment to prove that I probably would have given up trying to become a writer had I maintained a reasonable escape route back to corporate law wealth.

But I bring up my background in the law because *hatred* is a pretty big reason I've written this book. Not the healthiest emotion, I know, but for me it's clarifying. What conservatives do and try to do through the Constitution and the law is disgusting. They use the law to humiliate people, to torture people, and to murder people, and tell you they're just "following orders" from the Constitution. They frustrate legislation meant to help people, free people, or cure people, and they tell you it's because of "doctrinal interpretative framework." They use the very same legal arguments that have been used to justify slavery, segregation, and oppression for four hundred years on this continent and tell you it's the only "objective" way of interpreting the law.

Most legal stories and analysis scarcely acknowledge the dystopian, apartheid state that conservatives are trying to recapture through legal maneuvers. Most people take all the blood out of it. Most people assume the law is a function of "both sides, operating in good faith," without wrestling with what the polity would look like if conservatives actually got their way.

Part of that is because lawyers are trained to be "dispassionate" when analyzing the law, almost robotic, as if the best lawyer would present like Data from *Star Trek*, the android programmed to self-improve.

In case you haven't already guessed, I reject that form of legal analysis. A 5–4 ruling on the Supreme Court directly affects the likelihood of me getting shot to death by the police while driving to the store. It directly affects whether my kids can walk to the bus stop unmolested and unafraid of the cops driving by. I refuse to pretend to be intellectually dispassionate about such things. I refuse to act as if second-class status within my own country is one option among many. My "emotion chip" is fully operational.

The other difference one will notice about this book is that I treat the law as an *argument*. People are told that the law is an "objective" thing, almost like it's a form of physics. But it's not: the law is a collection of subjective decisions we—well, white people—have made over the years to protect people and activities they like, and to punish people and activities they don't like. The law can be *applied* objectively, though it isn't most of the time. But the notion that the law is a mathematical equation that can be fed into a supercomputer to produce "justice" is a total fallacy.

The law is not science; it's jazz. It's a series of iterations based off a few consistent beats. I make my argument for why the notes that I like, people and activities I like, should be protected and promoted, and I'm not ashamed of it. I think that if we interpret laws to protect the people and activities I like, and then apply those laws objectively to all people, everybody will come out ahead. Except racists. Who can kiss my ass, as far as I'm concerned. When I'm wrong, it's usually because I haven't fully thought through how insidious and creative racists can be.

What follows is my argument for what the Constitution is, versus what it should be and must be for us to live in a just society. I've focused almost exclusively on the Constitutional amendments. Most of the original Constitution focuses on the powers and structures of the government: there's a Congress, there's a president, it works like this, it can or cannot do that. Most of the amendments, by contrast, focus on citizens: you are a person, the government can't make you do this, it must allow you to do that.

Remember that the founders didn't even think amendments were necessary, because they thought they had so limited the federal government that it *couldn't* do most of the things people were worried about. But we now know that the government can do almost anything, and the amendments have become the place where we first look to make it stop.

Please feel free to use any of my arguments against any conservatives in your life. Free of charge (well, free of *additional* charge). Indeed, I've tried to use as little legal jargon as possible to explain why conservatives are almost always entirely full of shit (*full of shit* being a term of art derived from the Latin: *Borkium shittialis*).

Everybody knows how to fight conservative political candidates. There is a well-developed language around explaining why "tax cuts for the rich" is bad policy or how a two-thousand-mile wall is racist and stupid. But it's harder to spot the bad conservative *legal* arguments, because they're so often covered in jargon and discussed as if only an expensively educated lawyer could truly understand the nuance.

It's not true. This stuff can be complicated, but it's not *beyond the reach* of most people. It's like building a bike. A box of tires and pipes and chains and screws is intimidating, unless it comes with an instruction manual. I'm going to show how conservatives are building their white supremacist ride, and how liberals can throw a spanner in the works.

1

CANCELING TRASH PEOPLE IS
NOT A CONSTITUTIONAL CRISIS

In 399 BCE, the Athenian philosopher Socrates was tried and convicted of impiety toward the Gods of Athens, and corruption of Athenian youth. Despite the fact that Socrates was already seventy years old at the time of his conviction—which is pretty old for a person living in a pre-Robitussin society—the philosopher was sentenced to death.

Socrates was known as a sophist, though he denied being one. *Sophist* was a derogatory term for a person, usually a professional philosopher, who used clever but fallacious arguments to make contrarian points. Socrates left no written works behind, but based on what we know of him from his former students (like Plato) or classical plays, I imagine Socrates to be the greatest internet troll of all time. In a society that seamlessly merged secular governing principles with unexamined religious beliefs, Socrates easily toyed with precepts the ancient Athenians believed were literally handed down by Gods who lived on a mountain. Socrates was the original "devil's advocate." He challenged people to provide logical

reasoning for their deeply held beliefs, and would justify outrageous behavior (for his time) with appeals to reason while rejecting
the widely shared morality of his day.

I imagine he'd have been an annoying little shit to argue with. He
was a walking "whataboutism" walrus meme in a toga, exasperat-
ing people who were just trying to run a practical society without
catching a lightning bolt from a fickle and horny Zeus.

Trolling the Athenian Illuminati is not what got Socrates a death
sentence, however. Socrates's sophistry was mainly a front for antidemocratic, authoritarian views. He believed that only reasonable,
logical, and competent people should be in charge. He believed that
men of merit should be elevated into positions of power.

The problem, which is more obvious to our modern eyes than it
has been in decades, is that the idea of a meritocracy is almost in
direct conflict with the idea of a democracy. Democracies tend to
elevate any person with enough wealth and charisma to stand out
in a crowd. Democracies neither necessarily nor naturally reward
merit. Nor do they punish incompetence. Democracies tend to go
along with the popular will, and Socrates knew that the popular
will could be easily manipulated into believing any odd thing.

Most likely, it was Socrates's message, not his methods, that got
him in trouble. Socrates wasn't killed in some back alley by a rogue
vigilante or religious fanatic. He was put on trial by the Athenian
state, and convicted and sentenced to death by the appropriate
Athenian legal courts. We don't know for sure how many people
participated in Socrates's trial, but Athenian juries traditionally
were comprised of 500 or more men over the age of thirty, chosen by random lots. At least 251 Athenian men sat around, thought
about it, and concluded their society would be better off if a seventy-
year-old social gadfly who held no political or military power was
poisoned to death for transmitting ideas he didn't even bother to
write down.

Socrates was canceled.

In contrast, Donald Trump was banned from Twitter. Rose-anne Barr lost a television show. Andrew Sullivan gave up a column in a magazine. J.K. Rowling, I mean, she hasn't even lost anything, she's just mad that decent people don't want to buy books (books off which she's already made millions) written by an out transphobe. White people with contrarian views who find themselves on the wrong end of a Twitter ratio spend a lot of time complaining about "cancel culture." They spend a lot of time talking about their "free speech" rights. But these people have no claim to constitutional protection, because our laws and the laws of most modern societies are written to avoid tragedies like the trial of Socrates, not to protect trash people from losing endorsement contracts.

Cancel culture, as defined by conservative thinkers and hot take aficionados, involves a person (usually a famous media person or college professor) losing a job, an endorsement, or some opportunity because of something they've said. Complaints about cancel culture are inextricably tied to complaints about "political correctness." The people who think you should be able to spew racist, sexist, or homophobic slurs against others are the very same people who think that losing acting gigs or magazine columns because of their knuckle-dragging views is the greatest First Amendment issue of our time.

The thing is, a publisher firing a media person for something they say involves no First Amendment issue at all. There's no constitutional right to, say, continued employment after supporting a failed insurrection. Free speech does not protect a Fox News employee's right to a *job* any more than it protects a 7-Eleven employee who desperately needs to wear a racist hat while serving Slurpees. Free speech also does not confer a constitutional right to tenure upon professors who feel the need to say the n-word in class. These people can say whatever they want, but the Constitution does not protect their right to employment.

Constitutional protections of speech are mainly concerned with the government's attempts to silence or punish views the ruling party doesn't like. The Constitution cares about people limiting the inquiry of a free press through lawsuits or the threat of lawsuits. It cares about armed agents of the state threatening or jailing citizens who dare to protest the actions of that state.

In short, the First Amendment cares about the things Republicans do when they control the government.

Protest against the government is at the heart of why the First Amendment exists in the first place. Political speech against the government, speaking truth to power, is the speech that is given the most robust legal protection. But the people who make a living decrying cancel culture rarely lift a pen or hashtag when Republicans use the powers of the state to chill political protests. In fact, they do the opposite: those who claim to care about cancel culture treat political protest as the thing that threatens freedom of speech. They claim their freedoms are being threatened by the very thing the First Amendment is designed to protect.

They call it the "heckler's veto." Snowflake Republicans have spent much of the last decade trying to prevent people from protesting their speeches. Remember Desiree Fairooz? She was the lady who was arrested and charged for laughing during Jeff Sessions's confirmation hearing for attorney general back in 2017. She was charged with disrupting Congress and illegally protesting on Capitol Grounds. Again, this was for laughing at a ridiculous statement made by Alabama Republican senator Richard Shelby during the hearing. (Shelby said that Jeff Sessions's "extensive record of treating all Americans equally under the law is clear and well-documented." Sessions was one of the most well-documented racists available at the start of the Trump administration: he was literally on record as a Klan sympathizer and was deemed too racist to get a federal judgeship before the people of Alabama elected him senator. Fairooz's laugh was a kind response, relatively speaking, to Shelby's falsehood.)

Once confirmed, Sessions's Department of Justice hounded Fairooz for a couple of months, trying to force her into a plea where she admitted guilt, before eventually dropping the charges.

Did the cancel culture–concern club raise a ruckus over the Fairooz prosecution? No. Andrew Sullivan wrote no screeds about the dangerous precedent of the Justice Department prosecuting somebody for laughing at Congress. Did these people write about Juli Briskman, a woman who was fired after she was caught flipping off the Donald Trump motorcade while she was out for a bike ride? No. David Brooks found no spare words to defend the right of American citizens to flip the president the bird. Name me your favorite cancel culture writer or thinker, and I will show you a person who remained mute in 2020 when Attorney General William Barr ordered the gassing of peaceful protesters outside the White House so President Trump could take a photo-op with a Bible.

Not one of these people who care so much when an editor gets pushed out of the *New York Times* for soliciting fascist columns was there when Peter Thiel came for Gawker.

Gawker was an independent news website. It was a blog, back when blogging was cool. Gawker reported the news with a heavy side helping of snark, back when that was still new and interesting. It was irreverent, it was exciting, it was occasionally wrong, and often trashy.

And it was murdered by a wealthy white man.

Thiel is a billionaire venture capitalist who co-founded PayPal and founded a hedge fund and did, I don't know, whatever it is one does to make a billion dollars in a country that can't be bothered to address poverty and food insecurity.

Thiel happens to be gay. I know that because Gawker published a story "outing" him in 2007. You won't get any debate from me if you want to argue that outing people is not the best use of the freedom of the press that human civilizations took around four thousand years to codify and protect. But you also won't get any serious debate from anybody who has spent more than five minutes in a constitutional law class on whether reporting on the private sex lives of billionaires and public figures is squarely within the protection of the First Amendment.

The Gawker story angered Thiel. In response, Thiel determined to destroy Gawker. Not the reporter who outed him or the man who owned the publication, like a normal megalomaniacal billionaire. No, Thiel's thirst for vengeance would only be satisfied by destroying the entire media conglomerate itself. Gawker owned a bunch of spinoff blogs, vertices that reported on industries as varied as video games and sports. All had to suffer because the main Gawker website offended Thiel.

Thiel's plan, which I imagine he hatched in a lair carved into a volcano, was to attack Gawker through a series of retaliatory lawsuits. As I said, Thiel himself had no legitimate legal case against Gawker for the article that deeply angered him. But he figured other people might. With virtually unlimited funds, Thiel decided to fund lawsuit after lawsuit against the publication. He told the *New York Times* that he spent nearly $10 million in supporting lawsuits against Gawker, chump change when you are as wealthy as Peter Thiel.

It's important to understand that Thiel didn't think any particular lawsuit would succeed in bringing down the site. Winning the lawsuits wasn't actually the goal. The goal was to drain Gawker of funds by having to fight these lawsuits. Most media companies have insurance policies they take out to cover the expenses of fighting off the occasional defamation lawsuit. We live in a litigious society, and getting sued from time to time is just part of the cost of being in the media business in late-republic America. But these policies are expensive; they typically have significant deductibles, and the premiums go up the more times your company is sued. Even if a company is undefeated in court, it has to spend a lot of resources fighting off lawsuits.

Thiel's strategy might well have worked. It's expensive for media companies to fight lawsuits, even when their adversary is an unhinged person who accuses the company of planting subliminal messages in auto-play ads to trick readers into eating their dogs. Gawker's adversary was a billionaire with nothing but time and money on his side.

But we'll never know how much time and money Thiel was truly willing to put into legally harassing Gawker, because Thiel actually won one of the lawsuits he funded.

Thiel funded a lawsuit brought by Terry Bollea, who is much better known as Hulk Hogan. Gawker had published a sex tape of Bollea and the wife of Bollea's friend. Bollea didn't sue for defamation— again, reporting on the sex lives of public people is squarely within First Amendment protections. Instead, Bollea sued for invasion of privacy. Invasion of privacy is a simple tort, and a tort is just a claim that some action caused harm, and the victim should be paid for their trouble. Even though Gawker didn't actually make or solicit the making of the sex tape, Bollea sued Gawker for illegally capturing a private moment without Bollea's consent to be recorded.

Bollea shouldn't have won. It was Bollea's cuckolded friend who invaded Bollea's privacy and recorded the sex tape. Gawker just reported on it. But, the case got in front of a jury in the state of Florida, and, well, let's just say that if you ever find yourself trying to explain how laws work to a jury comprised of "Florida Man," you've probably already lost.

The jury found Gawker liable and awarded Bollea $140 million.

Gawker did not have that kind of bank, and the site was permanently shuttered in 2016. I imagine Gawker's servers now hang on Peter Thiel's wall, frozen in carbonite.

Gawker was canceled. Even though the death certificate reads that it was pinned by Hulk Hogan in 2016, Gawker was killed because it wrote a story a conservative man didn't like in 2007.

But there is no Bret Stephens column lashing out at this unabashed attack on the First Amendment and the freedom of an independent publication to report the news it deems relevant to its readers. There is no Bari Weiss book about the dangers of billionaires who demand a safe space in American media. There is only deafening silence from the people who squeal the loudest every time Nike pulls a shoe contract from an athlete who gets caught on a hot mic using a homophobic slur.

Understand, Peter Thiel could have spent a billion dollars constructing a space laser and melted Gawker's servers and five surrounding city blocks from orbit, and done *less* damage to free speech in America. I used to write for an independent publication, Above the Law (a legal website inspired by the same people who created Gawker). After the Hulk Hogan lawsuit, there wasn't a story I wrote about a wealthy person where I didn't at least consider the possibility that the wealthy person could sue my company into oblivion if they were too angered by my protected speech. I used to tell my boss, "I can't stop people from suing us, I can only stop them from winning." He would fire back, "If they sue us we've lost already."

In my current job, I've all but stopped writing about conservative individuals. I try to stick to conservative institutions and, occasionally, conservative politicians who would look bad and lose votes if they sued me. But even that is dangerous. Congressman Devin Nunes sued a cow on Twitter. I'm not making that up; Congressman Nunes sued parody accounts on Twitter (one labeled "Devin Nunes'

Cow" and another called "Devin Nunes' Mom") for defamation and trying to "intimidate" him and influence the 2018 midterm elections. Nunes is a public person; calling clear parody accounts making fun of him defamatory is utter Devin Nunes' Horseshit. It's funny, but I'm not the one who had to lawyer up to defend myself.

Wealthy white businesspeople suing my employer because I notice their bullcrap is now an ever-present threat to my livelihood.

The real cancel culture is the one practiced by conservatives. They are the ones leading the assault on the First Amendment and freedom of speech. It's rich people and conservative politicians using frivolous lawsuits to chill journalism and clean up their mentions. It's law enforcement using tear gas and rubber bullets to clear the streets of peaceful protesters. It's the police committing police brutality against people protesting police brutality. It's the attorney general trying to prosecute people who laugh at him. These are the First Amendment threats of our time.

I'm not worried about getting ratioed on Twitter or getting fired from my job if I write a bad column. I'm worried about the Department of Justice forcing me to drink a cup of hemlock because I wrote a good one.

2

BIGOTRY IS ILLEGAL
EVEN IF YOU'VE BEEN
ORDERED TO BY JESUS

The First Amendment has a lot in common with the First Avenger, Captain America. Both are mascots for an American ideal. Both are muscular reflections of how America would like to see itself. Both are shields who are supposed to protect those who cannot on their own stand up to bullies, intimidation, or oppression. If you want to shoot something, you'd better call Iron Man, who is a walking and flying embodiment of the Second Amendment. If you want to smash evil into submission, you'd better call the Incredible Hulk with the Fourteenth Amendment (I could do this all day). But if you just want to live your life with the dignity of your own thoughts and your own beliefs, Captain First Amendment is your hero.

Unfortunately, we live in an instance of the multiverse where Captain America has been captured and manipulated by the neo-Nazi group HYDRA and turned into a weapon against us. We live in a constitutional environment where the First Amendment has been infected by the religious right, who don't use it as a shield to protect their beliefs but instead use it as a sword to enforce dogmas and to humiliate members of the LGBTQ community. The First Amendment is being weaponized. It's being turned into a thing that bullies schoolchildren in homerooms and bathrooms. It's being used to strike at women who want health care, but won't protect condemned men on death row who want a spiritual advisor. It's being corrupted into a constitutional justification for bigotry and injustice.

That corruption didn't start with conservative zealots or Supreme Court justices acting as theocrats in robes. Instead, the roots of this modern First Amendment infection can be traced to "the good guys" (according to me): the Democrats.

In 1993, Democrat and then-representative Charles Schumer introduced the Religious Freedom Restoration Act (RFRA). Support in the House of Representatives was so overwhelming that it passed with a voice vote (which means that enough congresspeople literally shouted "yea" that there was no need to force the House to call each individual to vote, like winning a rap battle). Senator Ted Kennedy introduced the bill in the Senate, where it passed 97–3. President Bill Clinton signed it into law.

The RFRA was passed to reverse a Supreme Court decision. Sometimes people forget that most of the decisions made by the Court are issues of interpretation that can be directly reversed by legislation, if you have the votes. Here, the RFRA addressed a 1990 Supreme Court decision—*Employment Division v. Smith*—where the Court changed the interpretation of the free exercise clause of the First Amendment.

The free exercise clause is one of the ideas that made America unique among eighteenth-century governments. It's not complicated. Here's the text of the First Amendment (don't worry, it's ridiculously short considering its importance):

> Congress shall make no law respecting an establish-
> ment of religion, or prohibiting the free exercise there-
> of; or abridging the freedom of speech, or of the press;
> or the right of the people peaceably to assemble, and to
> petition the Government for a redress of grievances.

The "free exercise thereof" did all of the constitutional work protecting the freedom of religion, at least until the adoption of the
Fourteenth Amendment. I would argue that America has been
pretty lax when it comes to preventing the "establishment" of religion by the government. There are laws and customs throughout
our system that are inextricably tied to Christian theology: in a
fully secular nation the Monday after the Super Bowl would be a
federal holiday, but December 25 would be just "a day."

But we've done a better job of allowing people to practice their
faith—or ignore faith all together—as they see fit. We're not perfect
(don't @ me all at once, Muslim friends), but we're generally good at
allowing people to pray to whomever, however they want.

As long as the "however" doesn't disrupt the normal order of secular law and business. The Supreme Court often hears challenges
under the free exercise clause for those who feel that some generally
applicable, faith-neutral law or regulation impinges on their ability
to practice their religious beliefs. Think about a truancy law that
compels a certain kind of public education, if you are Amish, or a
draft law that compels military service, if you are Quaker.

For a long time, the Supreme Court had a test (called the "Sherbert test," from the 1963 Supreme Court case *Sherbert v. Verner*) for
balancing the interests of the state in passing neutral secular laws,
against the interests of believers who really need a tax shelter or
something. The Sherbert test called for "strict scrutiny" of laws that
impact religious freedom, which is a judge's way of saying that the
state has to have a really, really good reason for doing anything that

impacts a person's faith, and the state has to prove that there's no other way to achieve its really good reason.

But that is the test the Supreme Court overturned in 1990 in *Employment Division v. Smith*. The case involved a couple of Native Americans who were working at a drug rehabilitation clinic in Oregon. They were fired after the clinic learned that the Native Americans used peyote (a hallucinogen) during some religious ceremonies. The men then applied for unemployment benefits, but were denied for "drug use," and that's how the case became a federal issue of constitutional interpretation, instead of two guys getting fired from a private job.

A reasonable person might say: "Wait, you can be denied unemployment benefits because you get high? What kind of uptight Victorian-Jesus bullshit is that?" But, instead of changing the law so that unemployment benefits were easier to get (which I somehow doubt would have been supported by Republicans in Congress screaming "yea"), the Democrats decided to pass the RFRA, which restored the old Supreme Court strict scrutiny test for issues regarding the free exercise clause.

People like Schumer, Kennedy, and Clinton had the best of intentions. But the entire damn country would be better off if they had failed on this one.

The RFRA did a lot more than "restore" a standard of interpretation. That's because a Supreme Court test like Sherbert is something that judges and justices are more than capable of ignoring when they want a case to turn out a certain way. Lawyers call this "distinguishing": if I'm a judge and I don't like the conclusion a test leads me to, I can just create a "distinction" (often without a difference). If your test applies to a burning bush and I don't like it, I can just call the bush a "tree" and be done with you.

But only the most faithless hacks in robes would do that to a law. Most judges aren't like Brett Kavanaugh. If there is a piece of legislation saying that judges have to apply certain tests to their cases, most judges are going to dutifully apply those tests instead of getting cute with semantics.

It's easy to support the RFRA and a robust interpretation of the free exercise clause when you think about it as defending the rights of practitioners of minority religions who have requirements that put them at odds with mainstream Judeo-Christian laws and customs. But when members of the powerful majoritarian religion get ahold of it, something like the RFRA becomes a cudgel they can use to impose religious dogma upon the secular sphere. Again, Captain America is great when he's fighting for "the little guy." But when he's used as a tool of powerful special interests, he's villainous.

The failure of Clinton and '90s-era Democrats to appreciate the double-edged danger of the RFRA is what led to Hobby Lobby. Officially known as *Burwell v. Hobby Lobby Stores*, the 2014 case is the nadir of the RFRA approach to free exercise cases. In it, the owners of Hobby Lobby (I don't know what they sell because I'm never going to set foot in there) argued that providing women's health care, specifically birth control, as part of their employee health plans as mandated by the Affordable Care Act, robbed them of the free exercise of their religious beliefs. Those "beliefs" allegedly included making it difficult for their women employees to access a basic health service, while doing nothing to stop their male employees from getting "a pill" to help them sustain enough of an erection to use their penises as knitting needles (okay, I *do* know what they sell).

The Supreme Court agreed. In a 5–4 ruling written by Justice Samuel Alito, the Court found that the RFRA, initially passed to protect the rights of people being denied government services because of their religious beliefs, actually also applied to corporations eager to deny health services to women. It took only twenty years for the RFRA to go from something that defended people who used drugs as part of religious ceremonies, to something that prevents women from accessing drugs for their own health.

Here's one of my little rules for constitutional interpretation: if Republicans agree with me, I need to think again about how what I'm saying can be used to hurt women, people of color, or people who are LGBTQ. If Republicans are for it, chances are there's something about my law that can be weaponized against vulnerable communities, otherwise I wouldn't be getting conservative support.

Hobby Lobby is a giant corporation, but its approach to using free exercise as a sword against marginalized people has now been fully adopted by small businesses too. Conservative lawyers have made a cottage industry out of turning free exercise into an excuse for unwashed bigotry.

It is this evil and twisted version of the free exercise clause that Charlie Craig and David Mullins found waiting for them when they walked into Masterpiece Cakeshop in Lakewood, Colorado. Craig and Mullins were Colorado residents who were married in Massachusetts in 2012, because at the time Colorado did not recognize same-sex marriage rights. Their plan was to celebrate their nuptials in Colorado among family and friends. Masterpiece Cakeshop was a Colorado business owned and operated by Jack Phillips. The name of Phillips's store was neither ironic nor misleading. This was not a Dollar Tree that sells no saplings or a Popeyes that sells no spinach. Masterpiece Cakeshop sold cakes, and Craig and Mullins visited the store, whose products were well reviewed, in search of a cake for their celebration.

Phillips refused to make and sell them a cake, citing religious objections to same-sex marriage. Craig and Mullins left. The next day, Craig's mother called the store, and Phillips reiterated his religious objections and refused to sell the couple a cake.

Craig's mom always gets overlooked when people tell this story. It's so easy for right-wingers and even some moderates to say, "Well, just go to another bakery." It's so easy for people to overlook the humanity of those who suffer from this kind of bigotry. I was bullied a bit in middle school. One of the worst parts was driving home with my parents from some event, and they would ask, "Why didn't you play with [those boys]?" And I'd always try to mislead them by saying, "I just don't like them very much," when the obvious problem was that they didn't like me. I, for whatever reason, never wanted my parents to know that I was unliked, and I lived in near constant terror that if my parents found out the truth about those boys, my parents would call their parents and try to force us into playdates or something, compounding my shame.

It pains me to think of Craig's mom, calling this bigot baker, maybe hoping she could make him understand, hoping she could make him see the decency of her boy. And it enrages me that Phillips had the audacity to tell somebody's mother that God *required* *him* to deny service to her son. I wouldn't bake a cake for Jack Phillips, even if it was to celebrate his funeral.

Luckily, "Jack Phillips" is not a protected class. Protected class status is a concept that is crucial to our antidiscrimination laws but often overlooked by mainstream media reports. People make choices with how to dole out scarce resources (like college tenure or roles on Netflix specials) all the time. Many of those choices could be called "discriminatory": smart people tend to get tenure, pretty people tend to get television shows. But colleges and producers are not constantly getting slapped with discrimination lawsuits, because being stupid or asymmetrical is not a protected class. Being short or tall is not a protected class. Being an asshole is not a protected class, which is lucky because I discriminate against them all the time.

There are actually very few protected classes. You can discriminate against anybody for anything other than race, color, creed, and *maybe* gender, age, disability, and sexual orientation in certain contexts (later we will get into the weeds on this). That is, pretty much, the entire list. Some states don't even protect that much. It's almost amazing that people so consistently discriminate against those few protected classes when there is such a wealth of human difference that is not protected for us to work with.

Phillips decided to discriminate against Craig and Mullins because they were gay, and that was a point-and-click violation of the Colorado Anti-Discrimination Act (CADA). Craig and Mullins (after securing a different cake) sued Phillips under the CADA and, in a reasonable world, Phillips would have paid a fine and agreed to stop discriminating against people based on their sexual orientation.

But, against this normal operation of a normal antidiscrimination law, Phillips raised an objection under the First Amendment's free exercise clause. The so-called religious objection to same-sex marriage is always taken at face-value, and it shouldn't be. Craig and Mullins were not asking Phillips to get married to a man. They weren't attempting to pay Phillips in sexual favors. They did not want Phillips to put himself inside the cake and jump out and scream "I love gay people" at an opportune moment.

They simply wanted Phillips to accept payment for services he started an entire business to render. Phillips's claim that his religious freedom would be compromised by being forced to engage in his own business is ludicrous on its face. Refusing to do your job because the person paying you to do it has different beliefs than you is not a religious objection, it's plain and simple bigotry.

The Colorado Civil Rights Commission saw through Phillips's bullshit use of free exercise and ordered him to make restitution to Craig and Mullins. But Phillips appealed and eventually the case ended up in front of the Supreme Court.

Waiting for him there was Supreme Court justice Anthony Kennedy, then in his last year on the bench. Kennedy—once people more forgiving than I am forget that he gave up his seat on the Supreme Court so Donald Trump could replace him with his protégé, alleged attempted rapist Brett Kavanaugh*—will be remembered as one of the good guys in the LGBTQ rights movement. Despite being a conservative appointed by President Ronald Reagan, Kennedy was the tie-breaking vote and decision-author on a number of critical gay rights cases. Kennedy wrote the opinion in *Lawrence v. Texas*, which invalidated criminal laws against "sodomy." He was the author of *United States v. Windsor*, which struck down the Defense of Marriage Act (another horrible Bill Clinton triangulation-of-crap law, which progressives had to spend decades fighting). And he was the author of *Obergefell v. Hodges*, which finally recognized the right of same-sex couples to be married.

But Kennedy also wrote *Citizens United*, which essentially wrecked the ability of the government to regulate political campaign contributions from corporations on grounds of free speech. Kennedy is what I'd call a First Amendment extremist: where others see reasonable distinctions between types of speech and the level of protection each should be accorded, Kennedy thinks the Constitution is the First Amendment and a bunch of other suggestions nobody would have the right to complain about without the First Amendment.

Masterpiece Cakeshop therefore pitted two of Kennedy's pet projects against themselves: his defense of LGBTQ rights versus his vision of a First Amendment injected with Captain America's super soldier serum.

The First Amendment was never going to lose this battle on Kennedy's desk. But the way Kennedy decided to make it win solved nothing.

---

*Kavanaugh was a former clerk for Justice Kennedy.

Kennedy refused to decide whether Phillips had a constitutional right to bigotry under the free exercise clause. Instead, he ruled that the Colorado Civil Rights Commission, which punished Phillips under the CADA, was insufficiently respectful of Phillips's religious objections. That's right: Kennedy wouldn't call Phillips illegally bigoted against gay couples; instead he called the Colorado board illegally bigoted against religious people.

It was a punk move, done by a man who was sick of history having its eyes on him. Kennedy peaced out less than two months later and gave Brett Kavanaugh his job. But it was still a victory for the religious right, who get to continue pressing the argument that their exercise of religion should allow them to strike down or ignore antidiscrimination laws.

You can tell the right wingers are in it for the bigotry and not the protection of private freedoms. That's because if they actually wanted to win the argument, they'd be making an entirely different First Amendment argument. If a person like Phillips is allowed to be bigoted toward people who enter his business, it would be under the First Amendment's free speech clause, not free exercise.

As I indicated earlier, nobody is trying to make Phillips jump out of a cake and say "I love gay people." Most people intuitively understand that Phillips cannot be forced to say anything he doesn't want to say. Free speech, not free exercise, is why Phillips cannot be compelled to say something he does not believe.

Extrapolating from there, one can imagine a number of things that are *speech-like* that a person cannot be compelled to do. In a free society, you can't compel a sculptor to make a statue of a political figure they detest. You can no longer compel a painter to draw a portrait of their liege. You can't compel a scientist to make a weapons system for a warlord: and trying to do that will result in that scientist making powered armor to destroy the warlord and, eventually, aliens. Just watch the first Iron Man movie if you don't believe me.

Now, I happen to believe there's a big difference between Jack Phillips and Tony Stark. I don't think baking a cake is a speech act. I find *Cakeshop* to be the legally important word on Phillips's store, not *Masterpiece*. But I can't bake and I'm not a drooling bigot, so maybe I'm not the right guy to ask. A reasonable person can argue that Phillips has free speech protections for his *artistry*.

But the free speech argument doesn't get bigots to where they want to go. Protecting free speech doesn't allow them to fight their culture war against the LGBTQ community and women. Free speech does nothing for Kim Davis, the Kentucky clerk who refused to do her job of issuing marriage licenses because she had "religious" objections to same-sex marriage. Free speech doesn't help the co-op board who refuses to rent to a gay couple, or the employer who refuses to cover birth control as part of their employee health plan. Free speech protects people with theocratic views, but it doesn't give them the right to impose those views on things like the market economy and the health care system.

This is why free speech is relatively useless to theocrats. Conservative lawyers who fight against LGBTQ equality would rather make the wrong legal argument and risk losing than make the correct legal argument and try to win. These people are not trying to claim protection under the law; they're trying to change the laws so that they can discriminate against the LGBTQ community, not just in the wedding cake business but in all businesses across all levels of society.

If you don't believe me, just look at the legal battle Jack Phillips took on next. In 2017, Autumn Scardina went into Masterpiece Cakeshop and requested a cake to celebrate her birthday and gender transition. Phillips refused to make it, citing his "Christian beliefs" that gender is handed down by God.

I promise you that Phillips does not check the virginity of the heterosexual couples he makes cakes for, even though sex before marriage allegedly makes Jesus cry. I can't imagine how many cakes this man has made for unrepentant sinners who nonetheless had the right mix of genitalia to pass the Gospel according to Jack. But whatever. If you still think Phillips is just a man with deep religious convictions, I can't help you.

You can see how free speech is a useless argument, when his objection comes down to "I'll make cakes for girls, but not *that* girl." Scardina sued and, as of this writing, that case is still in litigation.

This is what conservative lawyers do for a living. They go out and find people like Phillips and enlist their private legal concerns for the larger culture war. Phillips is currently being defended by a group called the Alliance Defending Freedom, a nonprofit Christian legal defense group labeled as an "anti-LGBTQ hate group" by the Southern Poverty Law Center. In addition to taking cases, the group runs a nine-week seminar (called the Blackstone Legal Fellowship) where they teach people how to use the law to support evangelical causes. New Supreme Court justice Amy Coney Barrett has been an instructor at one of these seminars, to give you a sense of how integrated these people are into conservative politics and judicial interpretation. Their goal is not to protect clients with deeply held religious beliefs from persecution *by the government*. Instead, they're interested in persecuting people they don't like, while using religion to cloak their daggers.

Conservatives are, however, illustrating a fundamental truth about laws: even "good" laws can be manipulated by bad people to perform evil. The First Amendment is a fantastic idea, but that doesn't make it immune from being twisted and weaponized. We shouldn't give deference to people who simply claim to be following sacred constitutional principles or claim to have devout beliefs. Because sometimes they're lying. Sometimes they're wrong.

Sometimes they're straight-up evildoers wearing an American flag uniform.

We should defend the principles enshrined in our laws, not the random text of the laws themselves. Otherwise, any yahoo in a Captain America costume can hide their authoritarianism under constitutional-sounding platitudes.

3

EVERYTHING YOU KNOW ABOUT
THE SECOND AMENDMENT
IS WRONG

You cannot have a conversation with a Republican about the virtues of progressive policies in this country without running into that Republican's interpretation of the Second Amendment. The Republican might not be well educated, the Republican might not be functionally literate, but the Republican believes that the Constitution protects the right to bear arms. Our entire, intricate system of representative self-government carefully balanced with countervailing, overlapping spheres of power and protection of interests gets reduced, in the Republican mind, to the ironclad right to shoot something that pisses them off.

I've met people who cannot accurately tell me how a bill becomes a law but can quote the Second Amendment verbatim:

> A well regulated Militia, being necessary to the security of a free State, the right of the people to keep and bear Arms, shall not be infringed.

Maybe they leave out the "well regulated militia" part, depending on how closely they were paying attention to Fox News last night.

Arguing with devout ammosexuals (*ammosexual* is the scientific categorization for a person who fetishizes firearms and can't win at Scrabble) is among the most frustrating experiences available on the internet. It's almost impossible to have a rational discussion with them, because their arguments are not based on reason—they're drenched in fear. The Republican argument for inviolable gun rights always comes back to the core fear of being unarmed or disarmed at the crucial moment when a gun could be used for self-defense, no matter how unlikely it is that such a moment will occur. These people are willing to suffer the ongoing national tragedies of mass shootings, they're willing to ignore the epidemics of suicides and violence against women, they're willing to sacrifice the lives of schoolchildren, all so that they might feel a little less afraid when something goes bump in the night.

We live in the most violent industrialized nation on earth because too many dudes can't admit they still need a night-light.

When you ask these people *why* they think the Constitution protects gun rights, it won't take long for them to make the "self-defense" argument. Oh, they might take a detour through hunting. They might try to convince you that their constitutional right to sit in a tree, covered in deer piss, for five hours until a defenseless animal wanders in range of their military-grade sniper rifle *shall not be infringed*! Or they may make the "violent overthrow of the government" argument. Yeah, there are people who will argue with a straight face that their private arsenal is necessary to protect them from the most formidable military force in the history of the earth. A single Tomahawk missile has an operational range of one thousand five hundred miles and carries a thousand-pound payload of high explosives, but sure, your AR15 will totally protect you from the tyranny of the government. Buy two! The crew of the USS *Ticonderoga* is super concerned now.

In fact, the events of January 6, 2021, showed definitively how useless guns are, even to violent insurrectionists trying to overthrow the government. Some of the people who stormed the Capitol that day were armed, but you'll remember that those people didn't actually use their firearms. If they had, they likely would have been met with a hail of gunfire from Capitol police. (If the mob had been predominately Black, they would have been met with a hail of gunfire from the Capitol police anyway.) Instead of using guns, the violent mob beat cops and killed one of them using blunt objects. It turns out, you don't need guns to overthrow the government: you just need to be white and enjoy the permissiveness of people like Josh Hawley and Ted Cruz, and a little bit of better luck while trying to find the leaders you intend to kidnap or assassinate.

That's why, eventually, the ammosexuals in your life will make the self-defense argument. They'll tell you the Second Amendment is there because everybody should have the right to protect themselves.

What these people don't understand is that the right to gun ownership for self-defense is an entirely *new* constitutional argument, made up whole-cloth by the gun lobby, and only recently given the force of constitutional validity by Republicans on the Supreme Court. Self-defense is a philosophical right, but that right was not grounded in the "original" meaning of the Second Amendment; self-defense is not mentioned once in the text of the Constitution. What Republicans think is their strongest and most ancient defense of gun rights is actually a mere advertising campaign from gun manufacturers.

Our current interpretation of the Second Amendment was invented by the National Rifle Association in the 1970s. You see, in the 1960s, Republicans were all about gun control, because in the 1960s Black people thought that they should start carrying guns. The Black Panthers figured out that white people were much less likely to mess with them if the Panthers were openly carrying loaded weapons around with them. It's not as fun to shout the n-word at a Black guy who happens to be carrying a loaded rifle, I imagine. You could lose an eye trying to do something like that.

Of course, Black people being able and willing to defend themselves from racist Americans was a very serious problem for racist Americans. In a direct response to African Americans patrolling Oakland, California, and "copwatching," Republicans in California passed the Mulford Act, which banned open carry of loaded firearms in California. Who signed that law? Republican patron saint and then governor of California Ronald Reagan. The absolutist interpretation of the Second Amendment is new, but using gun rights or gun control, as necessary, to maintain racial dominance is old.

California's Mulford Act was followed by a national law, the Gun Control Act of 1968, which significantly restricted the sales of firearms across state lines. It's important to understand that neither of these laws triggered any real constitutional consternation. Both fit squarely within the interpretation of the Second Amendment that existed in this country for its first two hundred years. The government's authority to regulate firearms didn't used to be constitutionally controversial: *regulation* is already in the text of the damn Amendment.

The controlling Supreme Court case on gun rights used to be *United States v. Miller*, which was a case about the National Firearms Act of 1934. The NFA of 1934 was basically an "Al Capone Is Kind of an Asshole" law. It mandated the registration and allowed for the taxation of firearms, and attempted to create different classifications of guns in order to make certain kinds harder to get.

(It's worth pointing out here that Prohibition was repealed at the end of 1933. So, for those playing along at home, Franklin Delano Roosevelt's entirely rational response to gang violence was to liberalize drug laws and restrict gun access. And it worked! The inability of modern Republicans to figure out how to stop street violence is truly beyond me.)

The plaintiffs in *United States v. Miller* complained that the Firearms Act treated sawed-off shotguns differently from regular shotguns. The Supreme Court easily dispensed with that argument:

> The Court cannot take judicial notice that a shotgun having a barrel less than 18 inches long has today any reasonable relation to the preservation or efficiency of a well regulated militia, and therefore cannot say that the Second Amendment guarantees to the citizen the right to keep and bear such a weapon.

You see what they did there? They asked if the gun law had any impact at all on the necessity of keeping a well regulated militia. Finding the answer to be no, the Court kindly escorted 1930s-era Duke Nukem out of the courtroom.

This basic, obvious rationale is why the Mulford Act and the Gun Control Act were also constitutional. Preventing the Black Panthers from defending themselves might have been racist, but it didn't really have anything to do with militia readiness, and so it really didn't have anything to do with the Second Amendment.

America might well have kept on its racist but rational track of adjudicating gun rights, but hard-liners at the NRA really didn't like the Gun Control Act of 1968. At an NRA annual meeting in Cincinnati in 1977, Second Amendment "absolutists" took control of the NRA from previous leaders who thought the organization was really there to protect marksmen. Gun nuts call this event the

Revolt at Cincinnati. Our modern epidemic of mass shootings can, more or less, be traced to these yahoos winning control of that organization.

The ammosexuals reformed the NRA from the generally benign conglomeration of Bambi killers to the grotesque weapon of mass destruction we know it to be today. It was this new NRA that invented the radical rationalization of the Second Amendment as a right to armed self-defense. It was this new NRA that gained political supremacy in the Republican party. It was this new NRA that got Ronald Reagan, who once signed one of the most sweeping gun restrictions in the nation, to sign the Firearm Owners Protection Act of 1986, an act that rolled back many of the restrictions from the Gun Control Act.

The NRA's wholesale reimagining of the Second Amendment hasn't just lured Republican politicians, it's become part of the gospel of Republican judges. The Federalist Society and the Heritage Foundation, the two outside interest groups most responsible for telling Republican judges how to rule, have fully adopted an absolutist, blood-soaked interpretation of the Second Amendment. These groups of alleged "textualists" read "well regulated militia" clear out of the text of the Amendment. Instead, they substitute self-defense as the "original purpose" of the language.

There was an original purpose to the Second Amendment, but it wasn't to keep people safe. It was to preserve white supremacy and slavery.

The Second Amendment is in the Constitution because Patrick Henry (Virginia's governor at the time that the Constitution was being debated) and George Mason (the intellectual leader of the movement against the Constitution, the "anti-federalists") won a debate against James Madison (the guy who wrote most of the Constitution and its original ten amendments). Henry and Mason wanted the Second Amendment in there to guard against slave revolts.

Although, overall, white Southerners outnumbered their enslaved populations, that numerical advantage did not hold in every region. In parts of Virginia, for instance, enslaved Black people outnumbered whites. Predictably, whites were worried about slave revolts because, you know, holding people in bondage against their will is not all that easy to do without numerical and military superiority. The principal way of quelling slave revolts was (wait for it): armed militias of white people. Gangs of white people roving around, imposing white supremacy, is nothing new.

But the slavers worried that the new Constitution put the power of raising militias with the federal government and not with the individual states. That would mean that the federal government, dominated by Northerners, could choose to not help the South should their population of oppressed humans demand freedom.

In a May 2018 *New York Times* article, Professor Carl Bogus of Roger Williams University School of Law explained the argument like this:

> During the debate in Richmond, Mason and Henry suggested that the new Constitution gave Congress the power to subvert the slave system by disarming the militias. "Slavery is detested," Henry reminded the audience. "The majority of Congress is to the North, and the slaves are to the South."

Henry and Mason argued that because the Constitution gave the federal government the power to arm the militias, only the federal government could do so: "If they neglect or refuse to discipline or arm our militia, they will be useless: the states can do neither—this power being exclusively given to Congress." Why would the federal government "neglect" a Southern militia? Henry and Mason feared the Northerners who "detested" slavery would refuse to help the South in the event of a slave uprising.

Madison eventually gave in to the forces of slavery and included the Second Amendment, along with his larger Bill of Rights.

In 2008, Antonin Scalia wrote the majority opinion in *District of Columbia v. Heller*, the case where the Supreme Court created an individual right to own a gun for self-defense, for the first time in American history. Pay close attention to how Scalia whitewashes the nature of Henry and Mason's reasons for wanting the Second Amendment to exist in the first place, as part of Scalia's effort to sanitize the Amendment from its slavers' rationale:

> The Antifederalists feared that the Federal Government would disarm the people in order to disable this citizens' militia, enabling a politicized standing army or a select militia to rule. The response was to deny Congress power to abridge the ancient right of individuals to keep and bear arms, so that the ideal of a citizens' militia would be preserved.

The original public purpose for a citizens' militia was not some theoretical worry about standing armies or an idealized right of citizens' militias to resist federal power. Instead the original purpose was a practical concern that the antislavery North would leave the South vulnerable to slave revolts. Scalia omits that rationale. And of course he has to. Because grounding the case for "self-defense" that satisfies the NRA's permissiveness of shooting Black children walking home with Skittles, in an amendment designed to help slavers keep people in bondage, would be a little too on the nose. If Scalia told the truth about the original purpose of the Second

Amendment, people might realize that the Second Amendment is illegitimate, or that looking to the original intentions of the people who wanted it is monstrous, or both.

Now, one can argue that the Second Amendment has *evolved*, past its purely evil original intent, to encompass a right to self-defense. I'd be willing to hear such an argument, because I don't think the Constitution means only what slavers and colonizers wanted it to mean. But conservatives won't make that argument. Here we see another example where making the intellectually stronger argument doesn't take conservatives where they want to go. If they accept that the Second Amendment has evolved to protect a different right than was originally intended, then they'd have to admit that gun restrictions can also evolve to better protect our modern society.

The Founders didn't know that guns would be used in over half of the nation's suicides. We know. The Founders didn't know that guns would be used in over half of domestic partner homicides. We know. If the Second Amendment has evolved to incorporate the right to self-defense, surely it's evolved to allow us to make it harder for people to kill themselves or their spouses.

But conservatives don't want the Second Amendment to evolve, because they don't actually have a problem with the original slavers' purpose of the thing. If you gave these people a truth serum, they'd tell you that the Second Amendment is working "as intended."

Which brings us back to the ammosexual in your life, caterwauling about how they need their gun for "self-defense." Gun rights are not about self-defense. They literally never have been. Gun rights are about menacing, intimidating, and killing racial minorities, if necessary. That's why Reagan and company had no problem restricting gun rights when the Black Panthers started to use them; that's why the NRA never speaks up when a "law-abiding gun owner" who happens to be Black is executed in the streets by a cop. The

Second Amendment could be rewritten to say: "White Supremacy, being necessary to the security of a free state, the right of white people to keep and bear Arms shall not be infringed," without any appreciable difference to the laws and rights of gun ownership as currently experienced.

People think that the continued mass murder of innocent civilians will, one day, shake Republicans loose from the thrall of the NRA. That will not happen. Republicans will not make the killing stop, because they still think that near-unfettered access to guns is the only thing keeping them safe from Black people.

As I said, the entire Republican argument on guns reduces down to the desire to shoot something that pisses them off. Until you can convince Republicans that shooting Black people is not okay, we will get nowhere. That's the argument you have to be willing to have, when conservatives bring up the original purpose of the Second Amendment.

4

STOP FRISKING ME

The first four times I was stopped for driving while Black, I was living in the state of Indiana. The first time, I was legitimately speeding, in an area of town called "Speedway," go figure. The second time, I had four white girls in my car, designated-driving them home: it's the kind of mistake you make once and, if you survive, never, ever again. The fourth time, I had just dropped off my mother, who is a speech pathologist, to do a school visit in Southern Indiana. The officer was super polite when he stopped me and straight up said, "We just don't get a lot of people who look like you around here." I assured him that if he went to the school, he'd find another person who "I'm told I look like" at the school who could "corroborate" my story.

The third time was terrifying. My summer job between high school and college was working for the state Bureau of Motor Vehicles. My position involved doing advance setup for events highlighting the pace car for the Indianapolis 500. After the big race in the spring, the pace car used to spend the summer traveling around the state, parking at diners and whatnot, and people come out to take pictures with it. Indiana is weird. My job was to go to these places the night before, figure out where the car would park, and tell the owner of whatever business it was visiting the rules for engagement. It was pretty cool as far as summer jobs go for eighteen-year-olds: you're out in your car, listening to your music (CDs, back then), staying in motels, feeling adult-like and free.

Of course, I had a white partner. They weren't just going to send an eighteen-year-old Black kid to talk to small business owners in rural Indiana by himself. Come on. But mostly we drove to the locations separately. And so it was that I was alone one night, driving from Fort Wayne to Lafayette, which is about two-and-a-half hours, east to west, across Northern Indiana.

I wasn't speeding. I know I wasn't because the first state trooper started tailing me soon after I pulled out of a gas station with a pack of cigarettes (don't tell my mother) and some Slim Jims. These Indiana highways are long, straight, and empty. When a cop is following you, you know. I slowed down at first, hoping he was trying to pass me. When he reduced his speed to match my own, I knew I was being followed. I tried my best to remember Han Solo's advice and "fly casual."

I don't know how long he followed me, because it felt like *forever*, but eventually, mercifully, he got into the passing lane and drove by me. I don't know if we made eye contact as he passed, but I felt like he slowed down to get a look at me.

I could still see his taillights when the second trooper appeared. This one had his police lights on, no siren, but I knew what he wanted. I pulled over. Again, I wasn't speeding, wasn't turning, and my car was in good order. I figured I was in for some low-grade police harassment. Like I said, this wasn't the first time I'd been stopped by the police.

The trooper came up to my window, which was already rolled

down, and the first thing he says to me is "Smells funny in here." I nod, and say in my most respectful voice: "Would you like me to get my license and registration?" He responded, more aggressively this time: "I said it *smells funny* in here."

I've come to understand that my next line is what got me in trouble. I've come to be embarrassed that, despite all the effort and education poured into me by my parents, and aunts, and uncles, in this critical moment I forgot my training. I forgot "The Rules."

The thing of it is, I don't remember precisely what I said. It was something like "Well I did get it washed the other day . . . maybe you should try it." Or "I just got it washed . . . maybe I need a refund." I don't remember the specific witticism I used, but I remember my tone. It was a Sharon Stone in *Basic Instinct*–level of "What are you gonna do, charge me with smoking?"

The officer must have noticed that I wasn't a white woman. There was something about me that got his panties in a bunch.

Everything happened quickly after I gave the officer lip. He told me to unbuckle my seat belt and exit my vehicle. I did. He told me to walk toward the front of the car. I did, with my hands held high in the air. He told me to turn around. I did. Then, from my upright and stiff position, he slammed my entire head into the hood of my car. "Oh, we're going to see about that smell now, boy."

By this time his partner, who I didn't know existed, was also out of his cruiser and at my car. The initial officer told his buddy to search my car. I expressed that they would not find anything, other than my license and registration, which they had still not requested or looked at.

The trooper put me in some kind of full nelson, a hold from behind where his arms came under my arms with his hands clasped behind my neck. From that position he dragged me to the embankment on the side of the highway, put me flat on the ground, and then put his full weight on my back with his knee.

I can still taste the grass. It's different from how football field grass tastes. It's stale. I could taste that it hadn't been cared for, turns out.

I couldn't see what was going on after that, but at some point he called for backup on his cop walkie-talkie thing. Backup. With his knee in my back and his buddy tossing my car. Another police car appeared almost immediately. I have come to assume that this second car was the one that initially tailed me: he was on the scene so quickly after the bogus call for backup went out, I really think they were acting together.

But I couldn't process all of that at the time. All I knew was that they traded knees. The new cop assumed the position on my back (he was lighter), while the old cop proceeded to taunt me. "We're gonna find it, you know. Your stash. And then you're going to jail." "We'll see if your car wash defense holds up in court . . . I hope you kept a receipt." I wasn't talking anymore. I was just thinking, "I'm going to die in Indiana. I'm going to freaking die in goddamn Indiana, because of my tone of voice. My mom is going to be so disappointed with me."

Eventually, they stopped. The lighter officer got off my back and told me to stand up. By that point, the other three officers, including the one who initiated the stop, had gone back to their cars. The lighter officer led me back to my car, which was ruined. They'd taken out all my seat cushions and pulled up all my floor rugs. My smokes and Slim Jims were gone too.

The light officer let me look at it for a second before handing me back my keys. He didn't hand me a ticket. He said, with a smile, "You drive safe now." I was still trying to put my car back into a drivable state when they drove off. They never did ask for my license and registration. My wallet remained in my back pocket the whole time.

What I experienced was the vehicular version of what the lawyers call a "Terry stop." It's named after a seminal 1968 Supreme

Court case: *Terry v. Ohio*. In an 8–1 ruling, the Court found that the Fourth Amendment's protection against unreasonable searches and seizures still allows police officers to lay hands all over you, if they had reasonable suspicion to stop you in the first place. The Court also ruled that any evidence turned up against the person who is searched in this way can be used against the suspect.*

It's important to distinguish Terry stops from being arrested. You've probably heard of the case that governs your rights if you are arrested: they were explained in the 1966 Supreme Court case *Miranda v. Arizona*.

Miranda rights—the right to remain silent, the right to an attorney, the right to be served Burger King if you are a white boy who just shot up a Black church, but be choked to death if you are a Black man selling loose cigarettes and "resist" your arrest—flow from the Fifth Amendment's protections against self-incrimination and right to due process. *Terry* is the case that governs what Fourth Amendment rights you have against cops who have no cause to arrest you.

Very few Black men will ever be arrested. But almost all of us have a story about a Terry stop that nearly killed us.

The difference between how Terry stops are used today versus the case against John W. Terry is striking. A white beat cop, Martin McFadden, observed Terry, a Black man, walking back and forth in front of a Cleveland store, reportedly a dozen times. After each circuit, Terry would stop and talk with another Black man, and then a third white man, and then walk back past the store.

---

* Technically, the authority to search vehicles without a warrant flows through *Carroll v. United States*, which is a different line of Supreme Court cases that authorize warrantless searches of automobiles that would otherwise be prohibited under the Fourth Amendment. But the rationale for those cases is similar to *Terry*, which applies to warrantless searches of people who are just walking around. I'm focusing on Terry stops here because the case is more interesting and more relevant to our current laws.

Perhaps Terry was having a very deep existential crisis about making a purchase? Lord knows there are items I've put in and then taken out of my Amazon cart at least a dozen times. But the cop intuited that Terry was "casing the joint." He stopped Terry and both of his accomplices, questioned them, and, unsatisfied with their answers, searched them. The officer found weapons on their person, which led to Terry's arrest and eventual conviction on a concealed weapons charge.

There's a reason why the ruling in *Terry v. Ohio* was 8–1 and the opinion was written by Earl Warren and joined by Thurgood Marshall. The opinion starts off with a long recitation of fundamental principles of the Fourth Amendment, but then acknowledges that those principles have to be balanced with practical realities of "rapidly unfolding" and potentially dangerous situations the police routinely face.

The court then justifies a stop and frisk as a "minor inconvenience and petty indignity" that can be imposed on citizens by police officers who have a reasonable suspicion. The frisk is meant to protect the officers' safety, and there is a strong state interest to make sure police officers are not harmed.

I should point out that *Terry v. Ohio* was the first Supreme Court case in history argued by two Black attorneys. Both prosecutor Reuben Payne and defense attorney Louis Stokes were Black and were able to argue their positions in front of the first Black Supreme Court justice in history.

Despite the deep tensions between competing societal goals, tensions that Warren took pains to address, the result in *Terry v. Ohio* seems obvious and inevitable. The police must have some ability to question "suspects of crime" in situations where they do not yet have enough evidence to arrest. And while questioning those suspects, a search for dangerous weapons that could be used to harm the police officer seems like a reasonable protection to afford those officers.

The Supreme Court took pains to limit *Terry v. Ohio* to the specific facts of the case before it. The officer had more than a "hunch," having observed Terry over a long period of time. The search was limited to a pat down of Terry's clothing, removing his overcoat to reveal a revolver in his left breast pocket. The weapons found were the very ones Terry seemingly intended to use in the commission of a crime.

I do not think the Supreme Court intended for Terry stops to metastasize into what stop and frisk has turned into. I think that Warren, Marshall, and Payne would be surprised and horrified by what *Terry v. Ohio* has become.

But Louis Stokes knew what would happen. Stokes went on to become Ohio's first Black representative in Congress. And he never gave up arguing that *Terry v. Ohio* was wrongly decided. Stokes saw New York City mayors Rudolph Giuliani and Mike Bloomberg coming a mile away.

New York State's stop and frisk law was passed in 1971. It was a direct attempt to codify legislatively what the Supreme Court ruled as constitutional in *Terry v. Ohio*. It says, in pertinent part:

> a police officer may stop a person in a public place located within the geographical area of such officer's employment when he reasonably suspects that such person is committing, has committed or is about to commit either (a) a felony or (b) a misdemeanor defined in the penal law, and may demand of him his name, address and an explanation of his conduct.

At first, it was more accurate to call the statute New York's "stop and question" law, because section three of the statute was fairly clear that searches of individuals who were questioned should be done only if officers have a reasonable belief they are or could be in physical danger.

But that was before "Giuliani Time."

People now know Rudolph Giuliani as an unhinged crisis performer who goes on television to spout ridiculous theories and threaten Black and brown people. But before his life as a racist spokesperson for Donald Trump, Giuliani was an unhinged crisis performer who used his time as mayor of New York City to spout ridiculous theories and threaten Black and brown people.

Giuliani, and his police commissioner William Bratton, took stop and frisk to unprecedented levels, through the implementation of what they called "broken windows policing." The men argued that aggressively preventing low-level crimes (like the eponymous breaking of a window) somehow prevented the commission of more serious offenses. To advance this policy, police were authorized to stop, question, and frisk people who the cops suspected had committed or *were about to commit* such offenses.

Racial profiling is the inevitable result of the degradation of Fourth Amendment protections. Understand, it is unconstitutional to stop somebody because of their race. (That protection doesn't come from the Fourth Amendment—which was part of the initial Bill of Rights written by the collection of colonizers and slavers who wrote the Constitution—but the Fourteenth Amendment's guarantees of equal protection and substantive due process. We'll fight about that later in this book. Despite what you may have heard on Fox News, being Black is not a constitutionally valid reason to suspect a person of crime.)

Technically, cops are supposed to have a "reasonable suspicion" before stopping a person under *Terry*. That's an easier standard to meet than the "probable cause" standard for an actual arrest, but it's still supposed to be some kind of objective standard. Remember, Terry was observed walking back and forth outside a storefront a dozen times and conversing with potential accomplices.

The problem is that when you set the bar for "crime" as low as

Giuliani and Bratton did, then "reasonable suspicion" becomes a joke. What the hell is a "reasonable" suspicion that you are about to break a window? Unless the police are stopping Mike Trout and frisking him for baseballs and bats, I'm going to question the reasonableness of their actions.

Absent the kind of psychic technology available to Tom Cruise in *Minority Report*, there is rarely an objectively reasonable suspicion that a crime is about to be committed, and that's especially true of low-level crimes for which no planning is required. Cops might think they're a bunch of Sherlock Holmeses, but they're actually some Miss Cleos who turn the occasional lucky guess into a professional grift.

Instead of reasonable suspicion, cops act on their unreasonable implicit (and often explicit) biases. That's why arguably constitutional stop and frisks became nothing more than a Trojan horse for the unconstitutional scheme of racial profiling.

The numbers do not lie about the disparate racial impact of stop and frisk. The program started by Giuliani was continued during the term of his successor, Michael Bloomberg, who defended stop and frisk right up until he briefly, unsuccessfully, and expensively ran for the Democratic presidential nomination in 2020. The racism reached new heights during Bloomberg's regime: in 2011, 685,724 New Yorkers were stopped by police, according to the New York Civil Liberties Union. Not surprisingly, 87 percent of those people were Black or Latino, despite Blacks and Latinos making up only 25 and 29 percent of NYC's population, respectively.

A number of legal actions have been brought to try to put an end to this racist policy. The most important of these was a class action lawsuit against New York City. A federal court in *Floyd v. City of New York* eventually ruled that the city was engaged in unconstitutional racial profiling. Which is nice, I guess. Racial profiling was already unconstitutional, but since so many white people think that racial profiling should be constitutional, it's always nice when a court reminds them that it's not.

It just doesn't do a lot for a Black kid trying to drive across Indiana this evening. The battle against stop and frisk has turned into a battle against racial profiling, which leaves the basic constitutionality of, you know, *stop and frisk* unchallenged. It's a bit like getting angry at your pet tiger that ate the mailman because its dietary choices violated postal guidelines. *Terry v. Ohio* should be overruled because the "minor inconvenience and petty indignity" of stop and frisk will always disproportionately fall on Black and brown citizens. There is no regime of "reasonable suspicion" that can be divorced from the implicit or explicit biases of police officers.

I left out a detail about the *Terry* case. According to Louis Stokes, one of the justices asked Officer McFadden why he approached Terry and the other men. McFadden responded: "In all honesty, I just didn't like them."

5

ATTACK DOGS ARE
NOT REASONABLE

In 2014, Michael Brown was killed by police officer Darren Wilson in Ferguson, Missouri. Wilson shot Brown six times, despite the fact that Brown was unarmed. The slaughter led to weeks of protests, caused a national conversation about police violence, and led to the formation of various social justice movements, including Black Lives Matter.

But it didn't lead to charges. All of the protests and "difficult conversations" in the world couldn't make authorities charge a cop who killed an unarmed man with a crime.

Wilson attempted to stop Brown, and his friend Dorian Johnson, from walking in the middle of the street. Authorities would later say that Brown stole some cigarillos from a local store, but Wilson didn't know that at the time he profiled Brown and decided to stop and question him. After some verbal warnings, Johnson claims that Wilson, while still in his police cruiser, attempted to grab Brown by the throat. An altercation ensued. Wilson claims that Brown attempted to get the officer's gun. Wilson started firing.

He fired twelve shots in total, six of which hit Brown. Brown was left dead in the street like a dog for hours until authorities collected his body.

At a deposition he gave to then St. Louis district attorney Bob McCulloch, Wilson attempted to justify the twelve shots he fired at an unarmed Black teenager. He said: "When I grabbed him the only way I can describe it is I felt like a five-year-old holding on to Hulk Hogan. Hulk Hogan, that's how big he felt and how small I felt just from grasping his arm." (Remember, Johnson says Wilson grabbed the kid's throat, not his arm, but whatever.)

At the time of his murder, Michael Brown was an eighteen-year-old kid who stood six feet, five inches tall and weighed about 290 pounds. Darren Wilson is six feet four, 210 pounds. By way of comparison, the average five-year-old is about three feet five and weighs around 40 pounds. Hulk Hogan is a professional performative strongman who wrestled as a six-foot-eight, 303-pound heavyweight. Wilson did not feel like a five-year-old grasping Hulk Hogan. And lest you think I'm nitpicking about some harmless hyperbole, remember we're talking about Wilson's official, on-the-record justification for shooting a teenager to death.

Wilson's fever dream of a deposition continued. He said that Brown "had the most aggressive face. That's the only way I can describe it, it looks like a demon, that's how angry he looked."

In a civilized country, an officer's inability to tell the difference between an eighteen-year-old Black kid and a demonic giant on steroids would be grounds for immediate dismissal from the force. In a just world, an officer who shot and killed an eighteen-year-old unarmed kid and then admitted in sworn testimony that he briefly thought he was fighting Hellboy would be tried and convicted of manslaughter.

But when it comes to police violence against Black people, justice, civility, and basic common sense are thrown out the window. The police have a license to kill Black people, as long as police argue that they were so afraid they wet themselves. Police are the only people whose own cowardice and hysteria can be used to justify an objective misreading of the facts. When and how much force a police officer is entitled to use is left almost entirely to the discretion of the police officer, which means my constitutional rights and physical safety hinge on whether a guy like Darren Wilson is afraid I'll use my big lips to suck in his soul from ten yards away.

That rule comes directly from the Supreme Court, in a 1989 case called *Graham v. Connor*. There, the Court ruled that a police officer's use of force must be judged from the perspective of an officer at the scene of the crime or altercation. *Graham v. Connor* is why police officers *always* claim they "feared for their life" after they shoot somebody to death. *Graham v. Connor* is why those claims, no matter how ridiculous, make it difficult for good prosecutors to bring indictments against police officers, and easy for corrupt prosecutors to let their law enforcement buddies walk free.

Unlike some Supreme Court cases that had a solid grounding in the law at the time and were warped into causing great harm, *Graham v. Connor* has been a flaming trash decision since the moment it was published. The facts of the case would be horrifying if the modern viewer were able to see it on dashcam footage.

In 1984, a North Carolina diabetic man, Dethorne Graham, went to a convenience store to buy some orange juice to offset his reaction to an insulin dose. He apparently went into the store, took one look at the line, decided the wait was too long, and drove off with his friend.

This behavior raised the suspicion of officer M.S. Connor. Connor happens to be Black, and I point that out only to highlight the fact that Black police officers can be just as racist as white ones. Connor followed Graham and his friend, William Berry, for about a half mile before pulling them over.

Graham, still suffering from an insulin reaction, apparently got out of the car and ran around. Then he passed out on the curb. Connor handcuffed Graham and called for backup. When Graham regained consciousness, he tried to show the officers his diabetic information card, but the officers wouldn't take it, apparently deciding that Graham was drunk. A different friend apparently saw the commotion and, being familiar with Graham's condition, tried to get Graham some orange juice, but the officers wouldn't let him have it. Graham begged the officers for the drink and one of the officers responded, "I'm not giving you shit."

Police eventually slammed Graham's head onto the hood of his car and put him in the back of the police car over Graham's resistance. Graham ended up with a broken foot and several lacerations. Eventually, the officers got around to actually checking with the convenience store, which told them that Graham did nothing unusual. Then the officers let him go.

Graham filed a lawsuit against the police for excessive use of force, under the 1871 Civil Rights Act. That's not a typo. The 1871 Civil Rights Act is, more or less, the statutory provision that makes the Fourteenth Amendment prohibition against racial discrimination a law, in the same way that the Volstead Act is what made the Eighteenth Amendment's prohibition on alcohol a thing.

But instead of applying the *Fourteenth* Amendment to the case, the way Graham asked, then chief justice and hard-core conservative William Rehnquist decided that the *Fourth* Amendment was the proper principle under which to assess police misconduct. The Fourth Amendment prohibits "unreasonable search and seizure," and Rehnquist only asked if Connor's treatment of Graham was "reasonable" under that amendment, as opposed to a violation of Graham's civil rights under the Fourteenth.

By converting Graham's claim into a Fourth Amendment question, Rehnquist nullified the racial discrimination at the heart of his case. Would a white man have been tailed for half a mile for the crime of popping his head into a convenience store? Would cops have refused to listen to a white man's pleas to look at his diabetes information? Would police officers have given a white man a few sips of orange juice before pounding his head into a hood and breaking his foot? Graham was a victim of racial discrimination, and Rehnquist waved it all away by deciding the case on grounds nobody asked him to.

It should go without saying that, having invented an entirely different question, Rehnquist decided to answer it poorly. Rehnquist, citing *Terry v. Ohio*, wrote: "The 'reasonableness' of a particular use of force must be judged from the perspective of a reasonable officer on the scene, rather than with the 20/20 vision of hindsight."

The callback to *Terry* is instructive. In 1968 the Court went out of its way to limit *Terry* to the specific set of facts, where a man was observed casing a storefront and was briefly stopped and frisked to search for weapons that could harm the police officer. But just twenty years later, Rehnquist was out there using *Terry* as justification for cops tailing a Black man from a convenience store and denying him a glass of orange juice while they roughed him up. Once you give cops an inch of daylight under the Fourth Amendment, they will brutalize Black people for miles.

Judging the reasonableness of violence from the perspective of the officer who committed the violence, or the officer who witnessed the violence but did nothing to help, or even the alleged "good" cop who knows damn well that one of his colleagues is a violent hothead but does nothing to stop him, is the entirely wrong way to go. Police officers are agents of the state. They are authorized to have a monopoly of force: they can hit you but you can't hit them back. They can execute on the street—I mean they can literally impose the death penalty upon you without a fair trial or a right to appeal—if they feel you're a danger to others. Holding them to a standard somewhat beyond what they themselves think is reasonable is not too much to ask.

The Fourth Amendment does not say: "The right of the people to be secure in their persons, houses, papers, and effects, against unreasonable searches and seizures, shall not be violated . . . unless the state employs hysterical racists and cowards who are afraid of Black people, in which case failure to immediately comply with their unconstitutional orders is a capital offense." The Fourth Amendment does not say that "only other police officers" can determine what a reasonable or unreasonable search and seizure really means. One does not judge what is "food" based on whether or not a dog will eat it.

Unfortunately, the Court's decision in *Graham v. Connor* has had the effect of choking off any meaningful solution to police brutality at the national level. Understand, we do not have one national police system. The Constitution reserves the police power to the states, which means that the federal government does not have broad authority to hold police accountable for acts of violence. But the federalism (which is the term indicating that most of the legal power in this country rests with states) doesn't end there. Even within the states, most policing is done at the local level. We don't have to change one system to address police brutality, or fifty; instead there are over three thousand county sheriffs and police commissioners in this country, and each one of them retains a level of autonomy to determine how much the cops are allowed to beat Black people. Whether you have the right to, say, know the disciplinary history of the officer who attacked you depends on which municipality you happened to be in when the beating started.

Without the Fourteenth Amendment protection that Rehnquist ripped away, there's no longer a great way for individual victims of police brutality to bring racial discrimination claims against the police. Instead, that work now largely falls to the Department of Justice. The DOJ can launch what's called "pattern and practice" investigations to see if a law enforcement entity, like a local police department, is engaged in racially discriminatory behavior—that's what the DOJ did in Ferguson, Missouri, after Michael Brown's murder by Officer Wilson. These investigations often result, as they did in Ferguson, in "consent decrees"—agreements to allow federal monitoring of local police to ensure compliance with the Constitution.

But relying on the DOJ to conduct a pattern and practice investigation every time one murderous cop kills an unarmed Black man is an inefficient process that doesn't always produce results. And it's a process that is wholly dependent on which party controls the Department of Justice. During the Barack Obama administration, Attorneys General Eric Holder and Loretta Lynch both tried to carry out this work. But one of the first things Jeff Sessions did when he was installed by President Donald Trump was to stop pattern and practice investigations, end the use of consent decrees, and make it harder for the ones already in place—including in Ferguson—to be enforced. Trump's next attorney general, William Barr, refused to open pattern and practice investigations in Minneapolis after the murder of George Floyd, or in Louisville after the murder of Breonna Taylor.

Merrick Garland, Joe Biden's attorney general, has brought pattern and practice investigators back. But I promise you the next Republican attorney general will largely stop them again.

While the federal government has limited and relatively weak powers to compel police forces to stop beating and murdering Black people, state and local governments have incredible power. Police—which really only became a standing, uniformed enforcement apparatus in the mid-nineteenth century—are not organized under a constitutional principle or federal statute. They're organized under state and municipal laws. They can be reorganized (or disorganized) by those same authorities.

But state and local governments are just as reluctant to hold police to an objective standard as the Supreme Court is when it comes to use of force. That's because of the incredible power of police unions, especially in municipal politics. Most (white) people have a positive view of the police, and so when one of the union bosses starts screaming about how their officers need to be able to choke the life out of unarmed Black people just to keep white people safe, there are a lot of white people who are inclined to believe them.

A recent battle in California shows how hard it is to get meaningful police reform passed at the state level, even in a "liberal" state. In 2019, the California legislature proposed a new law amending the language about when police could use deadly force. The old standard said police had to "reasonably" believe deadly force was necessary, which is the same standard set by *Graham v. Connor.* The proposed legislation changed that standard to "no reasonable alternatives."

That language would have been an improvement, though it's still not the best. I favor a straight-up objective standard for cops. Their actions should be reasonable with 20/20 hindsight. They should look reasonable on a camera phone. They should appear reasonable to a crowd gathering around asking what the cops are doing. If the cop believes a person has a weapon, that person better damn sure objectively have a weapon. "Oops" is not a good enough answer from agents of the state who shoot Black people armed with cell phones.

And if the cop is objectively wrong or unreasonable, they should be prosecuted. We have a sliding scale of homicides and all other types of crimes, and there's no reason we can't apply such a thing to various levels of police violence. Maybe a cop who shoots "Hulk Hogan" after a fight catches a manslaughter charge, while a cop who shoots an unarmed man seven times in the back, as a Wisconsin police officer did to Jacob Blake, gets charged with attempted murder? Or maybe a cop who uses his gun to kill somebody gets murder, whereas one who merely chokes the life out of an unarmed Black man in broad daylight gets a reckless homicide charge? I can be reasonable about how long these violent police officers need to spend in jail. I am anti-carceral, after all. But the idea that a cop who kills or attacks somebody should walk away without punishment because *other* cops are just as violent and depraved is not a constitutional principle I accept.

My view would be called extreme. But I have two black sons I'd like to survive me, and so I'm a little insistent that the police should not shoot at them. More moderate observers worry that my standard would make police hesitate before gunning down my kids, and for some reason they think police hesitation before opening fire is bad. All I want is for the police to hesitate. I'll live longer.

But, in a world where I have to accept that most white people are going to be more worried about criminals shooting the police than they are about the police shooting my kids, I have to acknowledge the California language as a step in the right direction.

At least, it would have been. But police unions reacted to the "no reasonable alternatives" as if it were a death sentence to their order. They complained that the California standard would be the thing that makes them hesitate and thus somehow get shot by criminals. They complained that the standard would allow courts to come in after the fact and judge them (you think?) for decisions that have to be made in a "split second." Police unions somehow think that having to make decisions quickly is an excuse for shooting the wrong people.

Through their outrage, and help from the Republican party, the unions got California to change the proposed language. The final bill that passed dropped the "no reasonable alternative" standard and changed it to "necessary." Now police can only use deadly force when "necessary."

I cannot think of one person who will be saved in California because police ask "Is it necessary to shoot this Black person?" as opposed to "Is it reasonable to shoot this Black person?" Deep-blue California succeeded only in changing which words the police have to use in their justifications for murder.

The California story goes to show the yawning gap between what is needed to stop police violence against Black people, and what politicians and courts are actually willing to do to stop the murders. Many people understand that the standards for police use of force are a problem, but few seem able to break out of the thrall of letting the police themselves tell them when force was "reasonable" or "necessary."

Bringing the police to heel will require us to stop letting them substitute their judgment for our constitutional protections. It's time to stop asking the foxes for their opinions on the security of the henhouse.

6

WHY YOU CAN'T PUNCH A COP

Why can't I punch a cop? Why can't I punch a cop who is punching me? Why can't I punch a cop who has broken into my home? Why do I, a grown-ass man writing my own damn book, feel compelled to use the word *punch* as a substitute for legitimate self-defense against armed agents of the state, whom this country will not stop from killing me because of the color of my skin? If the law will not protect me from the police, why can't I protect myself?

Students of Western political philosophy will reflexively reach for their copy of *Leviathan* by Thomas Hobbes to answer my questions. In 1651, Hobbes gave one of the best articulations for a government having a "monopoly of violence" over its subjects. If I may reduce one of the greatest works of political thought down to a sentence: If we let people kill each other, literally everybody would do it, so the only way we can have nice things is to let only one man kill people and hope he's not a complete asshole.

Hobbes is not wrong. It's nearly impossible to imagine a functioning society where the state does not have a monopoly over the legitimate use of force. Indeed, our definition of a "failed state" is one where the nominal ruling government no longer has a monopoly on violence. If a local group or gang can maraud across a region, taking what they want and killing who they will, and the state cannot stop them even if it wants to, then that state no longer deserves or is owed any allegiance from its people. The area a government controls through a monopoly of violence is, according to German sociologist Max Weber, the very definition of a state's territory.

And yet even Hobbes called the right to self-defense "inalienable." Even he said that a person had the right to resist agents of the sovereign sent to do them harm. No rational political philosophy can expect a person to comply with their own execution.

The thought that a person should accept their death at the hands of the state is not a concept we get from political philosophy; it's a concept we get from religious philosophy. Jesus went to the cross willingly. Obi-Wan Kenobi let Darth Vader strike him down. These men fell because of their religious beliefs—they thought they would become one with the Trinity or the Force or whatever. Hobbes might have told them to stop acting like punks and start shooting lightning out of their hands. Doing whatever it takes to stay alive is the rational play. Every person has a right to defend themselves against the Emperor, be they in Rome or orbiting the forest moon of Endor.

Of course, the Hobbesian right to self-defense is in conflict with the Hobbesian requirement that the sovereign has a monopoly on violence. Without religion, without shrugging your shoulders and saying, "Be happy when the state murders you because God will give you a mansion in the sky," it's really hard to square state violence, or even incarceration of a state's own subjects with the right of those subjects to resist. When you think about it, "resisting arrest" shouldn't be a crime: it's a goddamn moral imperative to rage, rage against the dying of the light.

Everybody understands the right to self-defense against non-police officers. The right comes from English common law, which is a fancy way of saying the right predates the Constitution and the founding of America, and is incorporated into the American legal system. People have the right to defend themselves (see the discussion of the Second Amendment above for the gun lobby's perversion of this right into a gun, however), and people have a right to defend themselves from deadly force with deadly force.

Self-defense is what lawyers call an "affirmative defense" to a homicide charge. Most people are familiar with the concept of "innocent until proven guilty." But in a self-defense case, the accused is clearly guilty of a homicide: I mean, for God's sake, they killed someone. The burden of proof therefore shifts to the clearly guilty person to "justify" that homicide. The law will allow people to argue a number of justifications, but self-defense is the most basic.

In America, we've taken that ancient right to self-defense and made it more violent and bloodthirsty. The right to self-defense used to include a duty to retreat. That made sense: you can defend yourself from deadly force with deadly force, but if you can safely get away from deadly force, you should by all means do so. But I guess *retreat* isn't performatively masculine enough for the assortment of weekend warriors and ammosexuals who get to make the rules in this country. Most state governments now specifically reject the duty to retreat, and the most deadly form of that rejection has been codified in "stand your ground" laws in many jurisdictions.

Understand, the right to self-defense, as applied in this country, is one of the most provably racist functions of law that we have statistics for, and stand your ground just makes those racial disparities worse. One well-respected study by the Urban Institute's Justice

Policy Center found that white people who kill Black people are 250 percent more likely to have their homicides ruled as "justified" than when white people kill other white people. In stand your ground states, that number jumps to 354 percent—it is 354 percent more likely that white people will be ruled as justified in their killings of Black people.*

"Self-defense" is how white people get away with murder. It is a textbook example of a "race-neutral" concept that has been applied with deep prejudice against Black people. It doesn't matter if the Black person was armed, unarmed, strong, weak, fast, slow, or just walking home with some Skittles. If a white person kills that Black person, they always have a chance to "get out of jail free" by claiming self-defense.

Is it any wonder that police use this same trope when they kill Black people? As we've discussed, every single time a cop guns down a Black victim, *the cop* turns around and claims he feared for his life.

If this country wasn't so suffused in racial prejudice, our "no retreat, no surrender" irrationally violent conception of self-defense would work against cops, not for them.

Consider what happened to Kenneth Walker. Walker was at his girlfriend's apartment one night, watching a movie in bed, when three men kicked in the door. Walker did not hear the men identify themselves as police, neither did at least four of his neighbors. Walker's girlfriend allegedly called out repeatedly at the men breaking into her home, and received no answer. Walker reached for his weapon and fired into the dark, resulting in a hail of gunfire from the armed men.

---

* A different study looked at 204 homicides in Florida (ground zero for stand your ground) where the stand your ground statute was cited by defendants. It found that people were twice as likely to be convicted—that is, have their stand your ground defense rejected—if the victim was white.

His girlfriend, Breonna Taylor, was killed in her bedroom. Walker was arrested at the scene and charged with attempted murder of police officers. While charges against Walker were eventually dropped (after intense public pressure), the attorney general of Kentucky, Republican Daniel Cameron, determined that the police murder of Taylor was justified, in part because of Walker's actions. Cameron was able to convince a grand jury of his judgment, and the cops were never charged.

The universe in which the cops can break into a woman's apartment and shoot her dead, but her boyfriend cannot fire back at the armed, unknown assailants who killed her, is deeply fucked. Where was Walker's right to self-defense? Where were the ammosexuals speaking out for Walker's right to defend himself? But that is the universe the Supreme Court wants.

We could live in a better place, under a better system of laws. Until recently, the Ninth Circuit Court of Appeals (which is the federal court overseeing California, Hawaii, Oregon, and Washington) recognized a "provocation" rule. The rule meant that if the cops, through their violation of constitutional rights, cause a violent confrontation, then the cops are responsible for all damages resulting from that confrontation. The rule didn't exactly allow people to shoot at the police, but it did put the cops on the hook financially for any destruction or medical bills caused by police violating constitutional rights.

But in 2017 the Supreme Court struck down the Ninth Circuit's rule in a case called *County of Los Angeles v. Mendez*.

The facts in *Mendez* are a gross example of abuse of police power. Angel Mendez and his wife, Jennifer, were homeless, living in a shack in a friend's backyard. The police, searching for an armed parolee, came across their windowless shack while searching the friend's premises. Without a warrant, or even so much as a knock and announcement that they were law enforcement, the police barged into the shack.

Police allege that Mendez reached for a BB gun, which he owned for shooting rats. The cops opened fire, unleashing fifteen shots. Angel was shot multiple times; Jennifer—who was pregnant—was shot in the back and hand. Thankfully, the Mendezes lived. And sued.

At trial, a federal judge found that firing fifteen shots at a family with a BB gun and shooting a pregnant lady in the back was a "reasonable" use of force, under the circumstances. Again, we need a wholesale reinterpretation of our use of force guidelines. But the Mendezes were awarded $4 million nonetheless because the police "provoked" the encounter with their unlawful search of the Mendezes' shack.

The Supreme Court dismissed the jury verdict and overturned the Ninth Circuit's provocation rule. (The case was sent back for reargument where the Ninth Circuit later held up the jury verdict on a different theory.) Writing for a unanimous Court, Justice Samuel Alito ruled that provocation could not lead to liability if the police officer's use of force was itself reasonable.

Essentially, the provocation rule fell victim to this country's insistence on extending "qualified immunity" to agents of the state who violate the Constitution. All qualified immunity does is protect an officer or agent from being personally sued for their constitutional infringements. Everybody familiar with the calls for racial justice and police reform now knows that qualified immunity is a huge problem. Agents of the state, be they police officers or prosecutors or presidents, are immune from personal prosecution and punishment over constitutional violations they commit while carrying out their official duties.

There's some nuance here that often gets overlooked when non-lawyers talk about this concept. First of all, qualified immunity doesn't protect state actors from punishment for things they do outside their official capacity. Senator Rand Paul, for instance, has immunity for actions he takes as a United States senator. But when he's just growing a gross pumpkin patch outside of his house, he could totally be found in violation of any neighborhood ordinances against being a smelly compost person (Rand Paul's neighbor breaking Rand Paul's ribs over Rand Paul's pumpkin patch is, you know, the kind of thing Hobbes was trying to stop).

Qualified immunity also does not inoculate state actors from criminal charges. It does nothing to protect a cop from a murder charge, including in the line of duty. In fact, if cops were more reliably prosecuted and convicted for murder when they killed people, I'd bet very few people would still be worried about qualified immunity.

And qualified immunity does not protect the state itself from liability arising from the misdeeds of its agents. It is actually quite common for a city to be sued and eventually reach a settlement with the victims of their murderous police forces.

Technically, both state and federal officials can be sued for monetary damages for constitutional misconduct. For federal officials, the cause of action was more or less created in a Supreme Court decision called *Bivens v. Six Unknown Named Agents of Federal Bureau of Narcotics*. In both state and federal situations, qualified immunity is an affirmative defense those agents can raise in court to argue that they should not be personally held financially liable for the damage caused by their actions.

You can see why some limited version of qualified immunity should exist. You don't want people suing, say, meter maids for violations of the equal protection clause, just because they slap a ticket on a car that was parked in a handicapped spot by a driver trying to make things easier for her elderly mother. If the driver wants to bring that case, she should bring it against the government that jealously guards those handicapped window thingies instead of the poor schlep meter maid who is just doing their job.

But that decent reason does not justify making the Fourth Amendment damn near unenforceable. Remember, qualified immunity doesn't come into play when the reasonableness of a search is somehow in question. We're not dealing with cops who argue, "I thought shoving the plunger up the Black guy's ass was a reasonable way to probe for narcotics." We're not having a reasonableness argument. We're talking about liability for searches already deemed unreasonable or constitutionally defective.

An officer who violates constitutional rights should be punished in some way, even if that violation doesn't rise to the level of a criminal act. At the very least, the officer should be *worried* that he'll be punished in some way. The people who defend qualified immunity are, once again, the people who claim to be worried that a cop will hesitate before taking action. But if the threat of financial punishment makes a cop think twice before violating the Constitution, I say good. Any tool available to make police think differently before violating the laws is a tool that should be put to use.

Courts have turned qualified immunity into a license for cops to act on their racial prejudices with impunity. Qualified immunity cases come down to whether state agents "violate[d] clearly established statutory or constitutional rights of which a reasonable person would have known." That trash language comes from the 1982 Supreme Court case *Harlow v. Fitzgerald*.

Honestly, how in the hell is "I didn't know I was violating an established constitutional right" a *defense* to police misconduct? Why in the hell should I have to establish that a cop watched enough episodes of *Law & Order* to know that beating the snot out of me was wrong? How is it possible that courts are allowing cops to skate by on their constitutional violations under the theory that the courts themselves haven't done a good enough job of articulating what constitutional rights exist? What kind of white nonsense system leaves cops free to racially discriminate if a "reasonable" cop didn't know their particular method of discrimination was unconstitutional?

Harlow created a Kafkaesque loop where litigants can't argue that cops violated "well established" principles until a court establishes those principles have been violated. The case is like telling people they can't open a bank account without money, but it won't give people money until they open a bank account. And that loop was made worse in 2009 when Samuel Alito, writing for a unanimous court, issued a ruling in *Pearson v. Callahan*. That case made it more difficult for litigants to get established constitutional principles on the record, thus making it functionally impossible to prove that a cop violated one.

The Supreme Court's jurisprudence around qualified immunity is so broken that progressive congresspeople are trying to fix it legislatively. Representative Ayanna Pressley (D-MA) introduced legislation in 2020 to end qualified immunity for police officers who commit brutality or murder. Senator Cory Booker (D-NJ) has put forward similar legislation in the Senate, but of course Republicans have thus far blocked it.

The proposed amendments, while necessary, are merely legislative workarounds for deep constitutional rot. Our Constitution, like that of nearly every other modern nation-state, waves away this inherent conflict between the state's necessary rights to violence, and the citizen's inalienable right to self-defense, by making a distinction between legitimate and illegitimate uses of state power. The government is allowed to use violence to accomplish certain agreed-upon goals, and nobody is allowed to violently object. But the state is not allowed to do just anything.

Who is supposed to stop the state from using its power illegitimately? Well, "the law" is supposed to stop it. I'm not allowed to violently resist illegitimate state action, because *the law* is supposed to prohibit and punish such illegitimate uses of state power.

If a police officer tries to pull me over illegitimately, I'm not supposed to rev my engine and lead the officer on a high-speed chase
through town. I'm supposed to pull over, get the guy's badge
number, and then go to court and get the guy fired and be paid
damages for my trouble. I'm not allowed to punch a cop who is
trying to kill me, because the *other cops* are supposed to show up
and stop their buddy from illegitimately using his monopoly of
violence against me. That's what living in a "nation of laws" is supposed to mean: I don't have to fight the state, and I don't have to
wait for God to raise me up in the afterlife, because I can sue the
pants off the state right now. I'll take my mansion up front, thank
you very much.

But the Supreme Court has functionally eviscerated my right to
go to court and make the offending officers buy me a house. As
I've mentioned, while Justice Alito is one of the most aggressively
pro-police jurists in America, the two decisions I highlighted were
unanimous opinions. Even liberal justices accept the premise that
cops should be allowed to violate the Constitution, maim or murder civilians, and not pay for it. I'm not allowed to resist the cops,
I'm not allowed to sue the cops, all I'm legally allowed to do is beg
the cops to not kill me and pray that they don't choke the life out of
me over eight minutes and forty-six seconds.

Why can't I punch a cop? Because by the time a cop gets in
punchable range it's already too late. As a Black man in this country, I am prey, and the cops are my predators. My country and the
courts have authorized these people to hunt me. My country and
the courts refuse to place restraints on them to make them less
likely to murder me. My country and the courts have left me in a
Hobbesian state of nature, but in this jungle the police are far more
powerful and terrifying than I will ever be. Like a gazelle running
from a lion, if the lion catches me I've functionally lost my battle

for survival and my existence is at their mercy. There's no point in kicking at them, because kicking them only pisses them off.

As Cypher from *The Matrix* might say: If you see a cop, you do what I do. Run. Run your ass off.

7

STOPPING POLICE BRUTALITY

There's a scene I love from the first Austin Powers movie. Mike Myers's Doctor Evil character is executing his elaborate plot to kill Austin Powers. It's a spoof of the movie trope where the bad guy makes an unnecessarily complicated contraption for killing the hero, which the hero predictably escapes. Dr. Evil's son "Scott" (played hilariously by Seth Green) questions the plan: "He could get away . . . I have a gun in my room, you give me five seconds I'll get it, I'll come back down here, BOOM, I'll blow their brains out."

Of course, Dr. Evil ignores him. "You just don't get it, do you." And that's the joke. To make movies work, it can never be that simple. Script writers of action movies have to devise convoluted plans of villainy so that it seems plausible for the protagonist to escape.

I hope people can see that we could stop police brutality in five seconds, if we wanted to. It's really not that complicated. The last three chapters of this book point the way, through the Constitution as already written, to end this scourge of police violence against Black people.

The Fourth Amendment does all the work. Here's the text:

> The right of the people to be secure in their persons, houses, papers, and effects, against unreasonable searches and seizures, shall not be violated, and no warrants shall issue, but upon probable cause, supported by oath or affirmation, and particularly describing the place to be searched, and the persons or things to be seized.

Boom. Make stopping people because they're Black an "unreasonable search." Make shooting people because they're Black an "unreasonable seizure." Make "shall not be violated" include actually prosecuting cops and holding them personally accountable when they violate these principles. The way to fix the police was written into our Constitution before there were even police in need of fixing.

The unnecessary destruction of Black lives would stop. Not all at once, but over time, as cops learned to play by the rules that have always been there, they'd adjust their behavior. At the margins, sure, there'd still be some close cases: situations where the suspect really did have a weapon and really was threatening the police or others. There would still be times when reasonable, unbiased people disagreed about whether the police tried to de-escalate the situation, and those close cases would still be fought about in court. And, I imagine, most of those tough cases would still be resolved in favor of the police officer. But applying the Fourth Amendment as I suggest would make police officers think twice before killing Black children. It would make officers hesitate before brutalizing unarmed Black teens who pose no credible threat to the officer. It would make the police liable for shooting Black people in the back. Cops who continued to be racist would risk jail, or poverty. And that risk, that threat of accountability, is what is needed. Black lives can only matter if there is punishment for the people who take them.

There. I've solved police brutality in America. Tell me when to arrive in Oslo for my Nobel Peace Prize.

Of course, we won't be implementing the Fourth Amendment as I suggest, and I won't be getting my $1,145,000 in prize money, because white people want the police to act this way. They want them violent and unshackled from constitutional restraint. Maybe not all white people, all of the time, but enough of them, most of the time. I can't stop police brutality, not because it's difficult to stop, but because too many white Americans want the police to be brutal.

I point, specifically, to Amy Cooper—"Central Park Karen," as she's come to be known. Amy Cooper got into an argument with bird-watcher Chris Cooper (no relation), because Chris asked her to leash her dog, as Central Park rules require. Chris Cooper happens to be Black, while Amy Cooper is white. Amy threatened to call the cops on Chris, and then she did just that, alleging in a faux-hysterical voice that a "BLACK" man was "ATTACKING" her in the park.

In that moment, Amy Cooper was asking the cops to show up and enforce the supremacy of her whiteness. She was in the wrong. Who the hell calls the cops when they are the ones in violation of a city ordinance? A white person does. A white person who knows that the cops are there to protect her privilege, not enforce the law and keep the peace.

Most white people I know like to think of themselves as better than Amy Cooper. Most tell me they were disgusted by her actions and would never call the cops like she did, or any number of so-called Karens have been shown to do, in this era of the camera phone. But most of them are lying. Most of them are reacting negatively to Amy Cooper's application of her privilege, not the underlying concept upon which it rests.

Most white people want there to be somebody to call when they feel threatened by Blackness. Sure, many use that power more judiciously than Amy Cooper, but they want the power nonetheless. And many of those who don't want the police to be at their beck and call to deal with perceived threats from Black people are the ones who are concealing firearms to handle any threats themselves, in the name of "self-defense." As I've explained, even the way we apply the legal concept of self-defense in this country is inextricably linked with white violence done unto Black people.

So while police brutality and violence only gets talked about as a "Black" issue, make no mistake: it's a problem entirely created by and for the benefit of white people. I don't hold personal enmity toward the police, any more than I'd hold a personal grudge against a pack of dogs sent to recapture me after I escaped from bondage. My issue is with their owner. My issue is with white people who refuse to keep their goddamn cops on a leash.

There are no good cops or bad cops. There are just shitty white people.

8

IT SAYS WHAT IT SAYS

Confessions should be unconstitutional. They shouldn't carry any force or effect. They shouldn't be used against defendants who recant later at trial. Criminals who are guilty can, upon the advice of their attorney, enter into a plea bargain with the state where they allocute to their crimes in exchange for leniency or mercy. Admissions of crime voluntarily made to third parties, or even to agents of the state disguised as third parties, can be used as evidence of criminality at trial. But the common practice of police officers or local prosecutors questioning suspects—sometimes coercively, sometimes violently—until they blurt out a statement against their own interest needs to end.

The Constitution, arguably, already prohibits the use of compelling confessions against criminal defendants. The language is right there in the Fifth Amendment. For those playing along at home, the relevant part of the Fifth Amendment says:

No person . . . shall be compelled in any criminal case

to be a witness against himself, nor be deprived of life, liberty, or property, without due process of law.

You don't have to jump through a bunch of fancy lawyer hoops to get from this text to my theory that confessions are unconstitutional. If anything, you have to get willfully obtuse to arrive at the opposite conclusion: that a confession can be somehow sanitized to the point where it is not "compelled" by the government, but given freely and voluntarily by well-meaning criminals who don't want to put the state through the trouble of finding them guilty.

Think about why the right against self-incrimination is included in the Fifth Amendment at all. It's there, entirely obviously, to stop the government from beating confessions out of people. Constitutional scholar Jed Rubenfeld says it plainly in a *Yale Law Journal* article:

> The core Application Understanding of this Clause is well-known: It prohibited the kind of interrogation practice found in certain seventeenth-century English courts such as the Star Chamber, where an individual was placed under oath, asked if he was guilty of a crime, and subject to severe punishment for refusing to answer. In seventeenth- and eighteenth-century thought, this practice put guilty defendants in a tight spot. They faced three unattractive options: incriminate themselves and go to jail; lie and condemn themselves to hell as perjurers; or, refuse to answer and go to jail anyway.

Put me in a DeLorean and take me to any time before the Enlightenment, and I'll find you a guy who is getting his ass kicked until he admits to a crime.

Now, most scholars will tell you that the right against self-incrimination as understood by the people who wrote it in the eighteenth century referred to that somewhat limited situation where a person was getting repeatedly punched in the face or having their eyes burned with hot coals or having their entrails removed to compel them to "confess." They'll tell you our modern understanding, which has evolved to view some forms of mere nonviolent coercion violative of the Fifth Amendment, is very different from what Madison thought he was making unconstitutional.

Most scholars are probably right, and I for real don't give a shit. I'll talk about this more when we get to the Eighth Amendment's alleged prohibition against cruel and unusual punishment. Suffice it to say here that I do not care about what the collection of slavers and colonizers who wrote the Constitution thought were legitimate, "voluntary" confessions. The people who wrote the Constitution wouldn't understand the word *coercion* if you wrote the definition on parchment and shoved it up their ass.

If we believe that a person should not be compelled to incriminate himself, then there's no good reason to try to parse legitimate ways to force a person into confessing. This shouldn't be a game where the government tries to invent different ways to trick a person into ceding their constitutional rights, without crossing an entirely made-up line between "enhanced interrogation" and "torture."

Why should one's Fifth Amendment protections change based on how susceptible a person is to government coercion? Are we in the novel *1984*? Does the government have a Room 101 where I will be subjected to my deepest fears? Maybe I'm the kind of guy you could never beat a confession out of, but one threat made against my children would make me confess to murdering Tupac. I wouldn't be the first parent who lied or begged or *confessed to a crime* to save my children. Why should the Fifth Amendment stop the state from, say, waterboarding me, but potentially allow a prosecutor to threaten my kids with criminal charges, unless I incriminate myself?

In the real world, the strength of your Fifth Amendment protections depends on your level of legal education or exposure to the law. I know to never talk to the police without an attorney present, because I've been to law school. Every lawyer, every person who had a lawyer for a parent, every person who made it through a first-year course on criminal law knows not to talk to the police, no matter what the police offer you in exchange for talking. If the police suspect you of a crime, get a lawyer. If the police don't suspect you of a crime, shut up before you talk yourself into becoming a suspect.

The Fifth Amendment is a litmus test of whether you have enough education (from the books or from the streets) to know it exists. And that's not how it's supposed to be. Your constitutional rights aren't supposed to change depending on whether you know they exist.

Everybody has heard of the Supreme Court decision that tried to change that. *Miranda v. Arizona* tried to level the Fifth Amendment playing field so that everybody understood their basic right against self-incrimination. *Miranda v. Arizona* was actually a consolidation of four cases, in all of which the defendants had confessed to crimes without knowledge of their Fifth Amendment rights. For his part, Ernesto Miranda was suspected of raping an eighteen-year-old woman near a bus stop. Police tracked him to his girlfriend's home, questioned him, arrested him, and made him appear in a police lineup. (I can also make an argument that police lineups should be banned: they pressure victims into naming *somebody* responsible, and, despite a mountain of evidence showing that eyewitness accounts are unreliable, juries tend to place a lot of weight on these allegedly "positive" identifications.)

The victim could not positively identify Miranda, but Miranda was nonetheless questioned for some two-and-a-half hours, without an attorney. The police falsely indicated to Miranda that he had in fact been identified by the victim in the lineup, and at one point brought the victim into the interrogation room. Miranda eventually signed a written confession to the crime.

His lawyer, once he finally got one, appealed, and eventually Miranda became the lead litigant in this famous ruling.

The *Miranda* ruling was 5–4 with Chief Justice Earl Warren writing a sweeping opinion requiring suspects to be informed of both their Fifth Amendment rights against self-incrimination and their Sixth Amendment right to an attorney. Warren also laid out a possible procedure to ensure that those rights are communicated—the "Miranda warnings" that you've heard on every cop show on TV:

> You have the right to remain silent. Anything you say can and will be used against you in a court of law. You have the right to an attorney. If you cannot afford an attorney, one will be appointed for you.

Thing is, much as I love Earl Warren and consider *Miranda* to be one of the most important decisions ever handed down by the Supreme Court, this ruling is totally made up.

I think conservatives and originalists cry wolf a lot of times with their ceaseless bitching that liberal justices "make up new laws," acting like legislators instead of jurists. But here, as Justice John Marshall Harlan II pointed out in his dissent, Warren invents from whole cloth a requirement to inform people of their rights. Indeed, if we're now in the business of informing people of their rights, I have some things I would like the cops to say before they search your home, or vehicle, or shoot you in the back for jaywalking or selling loosies.

Miranda is, to put it kindly, untethered from prior Fifth Amendment precedent. It is far more outside the lanes of traditional, precedent-based jurisprudence than cases like *Roe v. Wade* or *Planned Parenthood v. Casey*. The only reason conservatives don't complain about it as much (now) as those other cases is that there's not a culture war to be had over cops beating people into confessions, and *Miranda* has been so popularized by television shows that people think it's actually *in* the Constitution as opposed to something a bunch of liberals made up one day.

Even modern conservatives only agree with *Miranda* now because it is popular. In 2000, the Supreme Court affirmed *Miranda* in a case called *Dickerson v. United States*. There, by a vote of 7–2 (with Antonin Scalia and Clarence Thomas dissenting, because of course), Chief Justice William Rehnquist said that *Miranda* was now "part of our national culture" and so shouldn't be overturned, even though it represented a constitutional "invention" by Warren.

I'd argue the additional reason conservatives have seemingly made their peace with *Miranda* is because they've seen how easy it is for cops to overcome while they're trying to deprive people of their Fifth Amendment rights.

My issue with *Miranda* is not that it's made up, it's that it didn't go nearly far enough. As long as we're inventing constitutional procedures, I'd have invented one that stopped the cops from lying.

Aside from its unnecessarily limited scope, *Miranda* actually gives law enforcement a pathway to violate rights. While Warren's opinion did talk about looking at the "totality of the circumstances" of an interrogation to determine if rights were violated, in practice, the Miranda warnings have become a dumb and reductive prophylactic that law enforcement uses to sanitize otherwise unconstitutional interrogation tactics.

As long as law enforcement tells the suspect they have a right to an attorney, the police can basically keep questioning the suspect until the suspect makes a clear and unmistakable ask for a lawyer. In the meantime, the cops can tell the suspect all sorts of straight-up lies: about what they'll do to them if they request an attorney, about what their friends are saying in the next room, about evidence that may or may not exist that points to the suspect's culpability. Once the police recite the Miranda warnings, they are free to go back to lying, intimidating, and coercing confessions.

This takes us right back to the idea of Fifth Amendment rights being a litmus test for legal education, instead of inalienable rights given to all regardless of their knowledge of the law. The people who continue to answer police questions without a lawyer present are behaving irrationally, mostly because they don't know any better. As a result, they're being taken advantage of by law enforcement in a way that sidesteps their constitutional rights.

Now, you might think that it's okay for cops to take advantage of criminals, especially dumb ones. At the heart of all of our discussions about the Fifth Amendment is the belief, explicitly stated or implicitly held, that cops should be allowed to do whatever it reasonably takes (within a subjective definition of *reasonableness*) to bring criminals to justice. Ernesto Miranda (probably) raped somebody.* The other defendants consolidated into Miranda's case were all suspects in serious crimes. Oftentimes, the people arguing that their Fifth Amendment rights have been violated are not the easiest people to defend.

More than that, most people believe confessions are true. Most people do not understand how easily a reasonable person can be compelled into giving a false confession, absent actual physical tor-

---

* Miranda had his confession thrown out by the Supreme Court and received a new trial. At that new trial, he was convicted again of rape, this time on the strength of his girlfriend's testimony, who claimed that Miranda confessed his crimes to her while he was in a jail the first time. To recap: Miranda confessed to a crime, which landed him in jail, which resulted in him making a confession to a third party, which was used against him even after the initial confession that led to his jailhouse confession was thrown out. Miranda was paroled some years later and stabbed to death in a bar in Phoenix. When questioning suspects for that murder, police were compelled to read those suspects their Miranda rights. One suspect skipped town, and nobody was ever arrested or charged for Miranda's murder.

ture or some kind of well-defined mental incapacity. Most people believe that the truly innocent person will maintain their innocence right up to their death, but the guilty person's conscience will eventually lead them to admit to their crimes and seek the salvation and forgiveness of God.

Most people aren't Black. Most people have never been Black children. Most people cannot conceive of the intense and terrifying pressure that can be brought to bear on unrepresented and unprotected Black youths, and how that can make a person willing to tell the white man whatever they want to hear.

Most people think what happened to the Central Park Five was wrong but have not thought critically about how to prevent it from ever happening again.

The Central Park Five are Antron McCray, Kevin Richardson, Yusef Salaam, Raymond Santana, and Korey Wise. They were all sixteen or younger when they were rounded up, along with seven other Black and brown boys, on suspicion of committing various crimes in Central Park on the night of April 19, 1989. One of those crimes was the brutal beating and rape of Trisha Meili, the "Central Park Jogger." Under the lead of Linda Fairstein, who was head of the Manhattan District Attorney's "sex-crimes" unit, the boys were questioned for hours, without an attorney or their parents present.

Eventually, all five boys "confessed" to some aspect of the crime against Meili. They were convicted and sent to prison. In 1989, then real estate developer Donald Trump took out a full-page ad in four New York newspapers, demanding that New York State reinstitute the death penalty, in response to the attack on Meili.

We know now that the boys were wrongly accused, and that their confessions were entirely fabricated. We know that because in 2002, serial rapist Matias Reyes was captured and confessed to the attack on Meili after he met Korey Wise in prison. This is why they're now called the Exonerated Five.

Reyes confessed to acting alone, but we don't just have to take Reyes's word on the matter. First of all, his confession was given with the advice of counsel, instead of the confessions wrested out of the Exonerated Five without an attorney present. Additionally, DNA evidence, sought only after Reyes's confession, confirmed that Reyes's DNA, and nobody else's, was at the crime.

Since we now know that the Exonerated Five were innocent the whole time, why did they confess to raping Meili?

Well, first of all, they didn't actually confess to the rape. After hours and hours of interrogation, the kids still never said that they raped anybody. Instead they "confessed," falsely, that they were involved in the attack on Meili, but not the rape. In fact, some of the kids literally confessed to facts the police knew were false at the time. They were confessing to things that were contradictory to what the other boys were confessing to.

In the exoneration report prepared by Assistant District Attorney Nancy Ryan in 2002, she says these inconsistencies were obvious at the time of their confessions:

> The significant weaknesses in the defendants' statements lie in the details they provide in describing the attack on the jogger. Taking the statements individually, those details appear to give them power. But a comparison of the statements reveals troubling discrepancies. Using their videotaped statements as the point of comparison, analysis shows that the accounts given by the five defendants differed from one another on the specific details of virtually every major aspect of the crime—who initiated the attack, who knocked the victim down, who undressed her, who struck her, who held her, who raped her, what weapons were used in the course of the

assault, and when in the sequence of events the attack took place.

The kids were inventing stories to sound like mere witnesses, rather than primary perpetrators, possibly convinced this would allow them to testify against whoever the real perpetrator might be. As Ryan writes:

> All five of the defendants implicated themselves in a number of the crimes which had occurred in the park. None of them admitted actually raping the Central Park jogger, but each gave an account of events in which he made himself an accomplice to the crime.

But Fairstein and the police turned it around on the boys. Instead of charging one of them (falsely) with rape and using the (false) statements of the others against them, they charged all five boys with some kind of group gang rape that none of them even *falsely* confessed to.

To be clear, there is no evidence linking the Exonerated Five to any part of the attack on Meili, or any crime committed in Central Park that night. There's no evidence connecting actual rapist Reyes to any of the boys; Reyes subsequently confessed to acting alone, and that's how he appears to have carried out the other violent rapes he committed. People sometimes forget that when police and prosecutors hone in on the wrong people, when they coerce false confessions, they allow actual criminals to go free and commit additional crimes.

Despite what have now been legally and scientifically proven to be false convictions, no charges have been brought against Linda Fairstein or any of the cops who, we now know, coerced false confessions out of five teenage boys, thereby letting an actual serial rapist go free. Fairstein is an author now: she writes crime novels. The lead character, Olivia Benson, on the popular television show *Law & Order: Special Victims Unit*, is inspired by Fairstein. I must have missed the episodes where Benson charges five Black kids with a crime they didn't commit in violation of their constitutional rights.

Fairstein was dropped by her publisher after Ava DuVernay's Netflix series *When They See Us* brought renewed attention to the plight of the Exonerated Five, but nothing legally bad ever happened or will ever happen to Fairstein. Prosecutors have qualified immunity too. Even when one like Fairstein violates constitutional rights and helps to falsely imprison kids for a decade, she can't be sued for damages.

The Fifth Amendment, even one supercharged by a robust application of *Miranda v. Arizona*, does squat to protect Black people from prosecutors like Fairstein. There are too many people in law enforcement who treat the right against self-incrimination like a technical obstacle to overcome, instead of an ancient right that is not to be violated. There are too many people who think the right to counsel is a trick to subvert justice, as opposed to the linchpin to make sure justice is done. There are too many people who think that five Black teenagers arrested in Central Park probably did *something* wrong, and it's the teenagers' job to prove white people wrong about them.

The way to stop this is not to add more procedural hoops for law enforcement to jump through on their way to secure a false or coerced confession. The way to stop this is to take confessions off the table entirely. Stop giving police and prosecutors a "prize" for successfully tricking or intimidating a suspect into speaking against their own interest *if they do it just right*. Stop inventing canons of law rife with loopholes cops can use to smuggle in beatings or threats of beatings while trying to induce the "voluntary" admissions of guilt. Stop the good cop/bad cop routine and television veneration of "closers," who can magically get people to confess to crimes without ever once asking to see their lawyer because the showrunner didn't budget for the Constitution.

If the Fifth Amendment recognizes the right against self-incrimination, then we should stop asking people to incriminate themselves. Why is that hard to understand?

9

THE TAKING OF BLACK LAND

In 1825, John and Elizabeth Whitehead divided their Manhattan, New York, farmland into two hundred lots and began selling it off. I know it's hard to imagine Manhattan as ever having farmland, but "the city" remained densely clustered on the southern tip of the island well into the nineteenth century.

The first three lots of the Whiteheads' land were bought for $125 by a shoeshiner named Andrew Williams. Williams was a Black man, and the Whiteheads were among the very few white landowners who would sell to Black people back then.

Williams was a member of the New York African Society for Mutual Relief. The group sought to help Black people buy real estate and was moderately successful at helping the Black middle class gain a foothold in New York. Other Black families began buying land from the Whiteheads in the area around Williams's new plot. A Black store clerk named Epiphany Davis bought twelve lots for $578. The African Methodist Episcopal Zion Church bought six lots, and the village became even more desirable to Black middle-class families. Irish immigrants, another group of "undesirables" the Whiteheads were willing to sell to, bought many of the other lots.

The Whiteheads ended up selling half of their plots to Black people. The little enclave they made was known as Seneca Village. According to census data in 1855, Seneca Village had 264 residents, three churches, three cemeteries, and two schools.

Seneca Village was a home of political power for Black people, as well. Remember, in 1855, there were no Fourteenth or Fifteenth Amendments. There was no guaranteed right to vote for African Americans, even free ones living in the North. To be eligible to vote in New York State in the 1850s, Black men needed to be a male landowners in possession of $250 worth of property and have state residency for three years. Neither the property nor residency requirements applied to white men. Seneca Village was a way for some Black men to meet that property requirement. Of the hundred Black people eligible to vote in New York State in 1845, ten lived in Seneca Village. Five years, later, in 1850, of the seventy-one Black property owners in New York City, 20 percent lived in Seneca Village.

By 1857, however, the entire area had been razed to the ground. The homes and churches were demolished, and the people were scattered. Seneca Village did not fall to some natural disaster, or even the ubiquitous mob of angry whites that show up, again and again, throughout American history to lynch Black people who seem to be getting ahead. No, Seneca Village was destroyed because in 1853 New York passed a law allowing for the construction of Central Park.

Seneca Village was located in what is now thought of as the west side of Central Park. Its boundaries extended from about Eighty-Second Street to Eighty-Ninth Street, between what is now Central Park West and where Seventh Avenue would be if it extended straight through the park. Seneca Village was a small and arguably unnecessary part of the 775 acres of land set aside by legislature to create the park.

The government had the authority to buy or "take" the land for Central Park, under the doctrine of eminent domain that is enshrined in the Fifth Amendment of the Constitution. Eminent domain is the theory that all land, even private property, can be acquired by the government if it is in the public interest. The relevant part of the Fifth Amendment reads:

> No person shall be . . . deprived of life, liberty, or property, without due process of law; nor shall private property be taken for public use, without just compensation.

Eminent domain is such a core concept of sovereignty that the U.S. Supreme Court has said that it doesn't even *require* a constitutional provision. But *compensation* for exercising that inherent sovereign authority does require some constitutional language.

To understand eminent domain, you have to appreciate that if you start from first principles, all land is "public." All land is just there, owned only by whoever or whatever happens to be standing on it, and can physically defend it, at a particular time. It's all God's land, if you're into that sort of thing. Or the king's land, if you lived in pretty much any pre-Enlightenment society.

"Private" property has surely always existed in some form—I'm certain that some of the ancient art we've uncovered and put in our museums was actually early modern "Beware of Bear" signs fashioned by cavemen who were sick of being solicited at their homes. But as a standing inalienable legal concept, fully private property that rulers are not allowed to violate at will is new (geologically speaking) and kind of weird. Entire treaties on government (including the only one most people have ever heard of: John Locke's second treatise on government) have been written to explain, more or less, why private property should exist at all. Private property is not the natural or inevitable result of settled society.

Different legal systems treat the concept of private ownership differently. Take, for instance, the initial "purchase" of Manhattan Island by the Dutch. In 1626, Peter Minuit, director of New Netherland, reported that he bought Manhattan for sixty guilders (about twenty-four dollars, according to nineteenth-century historians). It would be too glib and easy to say that the indigenous peoples who sold him the land didn't understand private property. As Arizona State law professor Robert Miller makes clear, the people likely did have a fully functional concept of property "exclusivity." But we would probably call the land deal a "lease" not a "purchase." In his book *Law in American History*, University of Virginia law professor G. Edward White makes the case that the native Lenape people were "not relinquishing the island, but simply welcoming the Dutch as additional occupants." It was the colonizers who didn't understand or respect the deal.

Unlike private property, eminent domain does flow naturally and inevitably from the concept that ownership exists only insofar as the state is able to secure and defend the territory. If the state needs your land for some public purpose, and you can't raise an army to oppose the state, your land is forfeited. Living in a state that is willing *to pay for* private land it needs to take is just a modern invention for property owners who could otherwise get screwed if they happen to live on land the state needs. Dutch jurist Hugo Grotius, whose *On the Law of War and Peace* from 1625 is one of the first real texts of international law, wrote: "The property of subjects is under the eminent domain of the state. . . . But when this is done the state is bound to make good the loss to those who lose their property."

That's the nice way of saying: "There wouldn't be a West India Company without these fortifications, but here, take some money and go." The Dutch didn't really "own" Manhattan in 1626, because they couldn't defend Manhattan in 1626. Indeed, "Wall Street" is so named because there used to be a defensive freaking wall there. The wall was built by slaves the Dutch also "bought" and brought with them to defend the settlement of New Amsterdam from attacks by the indigenous Americans, the British, or pirates.

Now, I would love to tell you what James Madison, author of the Fifth Amendment, meant by "just compensation." But I can't. I can't even tell you why eminent domain is tacked onto this amendment and not some other. I can tell you that Madison's initial proposed language was: "No person shall be . . . obliged to relinquish his property, where it may be necessary for public use, without just compensation." Congress changed it to its final version, but I can't tell you why. No record of whatever debate may have occurred exists. No Federalist Paper focuses in on this particular topic.

What I can tell you is that when white people want your shit, they will take it, and Black people will rarely be justly compensated for the destruction of their wealth.

Fighting against eminent domain has become a bit of a cause célèbre for libertarian forces on the right. They've even given it one of their cool, right-wing names, so that their entire objection can fit on the bumper sticker on somebody's truck. They call eminent domain actions "takings." Get it? The government is "taking" your stuff; who could support that, right?

Much of the heat on the right is over what constitutes a taking at all. Eminent domain certainly refers to physical takings: you had some land and now you don't. But arguably eminent domain should also come into play when the government dictates how you are allowed to use your property. These are called "regulatory takings," and they happen when, say, the government declares your private property a national historical site and thus prevents you from demolishing it and building a CVS. How much compensation is the government required to give out then?

Another large area of contention happens when the government takes only part of your property. Let's say that the government wants to place a few wind turbines on part of your land. The private property owner can still live there, so is it a taking at all? What if the wind turbines are super noisy? What if they "cause cancer" (author's note: they don't). What if they're really quiet but super ugly? What is the just compensation for ruining your view?

If you know anything about Republicans, you understand why the right-wingers get up for this fight, and you can see why liberals are generally on the side of the government when it comes to eminent domain. We need things like wind turbines and historical sites much more than we need libertarians bitching and moaning about whether they received enough of a vig from the government for their troubles.

If this were a Republican book, I would spend the next thirty minutes of your life telling you about a 2005 case called *Kelo v. City of New London*. Conservatives complain about this case more than Pharaoh complained about Yahweh. The case is about a white lady, Susette Kelo, who didn't want to sell her pink house. In a twist to the standard eminent domain case, New London, Connecticut, wanted to acquire her land to then sell it to a private developer, which created a Supreme Court battle. In a controversial 5–4 decision, the liberal wing of the court, joined by Anthony Kennedy, ruled that taking private property and then selling it to private interests for economic redevelopment was indeed a constitutional use of the government's eminent domain power.

Conservatives went nuts. They made a fucking movie about this lady and her stupid house. Parts of the house were moved and "rededicated" at a new site, and it's now some kind of monument to the fight against big government overreach.

Reluctantly, I agree with the Republicans about this issue. Clarence Thomas, in dissent in *Kelo*, said that the majority was converting the "public use" allowed by the Fifth Amendment into any vague promise of a "public purpose." And, God help me, I think Thomas was right about that. The government should not use its powers of eminent domain to essentially acquire land on the cheap for business interests, just because those businesses promise that there will be some public purpose behind their profit motive. For instance, I don't think the government should be involved in acquiring land to build sports arenas that will be owned by wealthy team owners and used to pump the valuation of their sports franchises into the billions.

My issue with *Kelo* is that centering this issue on a white homeowner and the legal distinction between public "use" versus "purpose" ignores entire Black and brown communities that have been wiped off the damn map by the government's use of eminent domain. Where's the movie about Seneca Village? Where's the movie about the Black and Latino renters who get crushed every time the local team wants a new stadium? Where's the movie about all the people and communities who were destroyed by former New York City parks commissioner Robert Moses?

Yeah, if we're going to talk about eminent domain, we're going to talk about how many of our roads, highways, and beaches were figuratively built on top of the bones of Black and brown people who used to live there. I'm sorry I just can't get up for this lawyer fight between public use and public purpose, when the government's definition of public "use" is so often merely "playthings for white people," as if that's an acceptable constitutional definition of the term.

The first time I heard about eminent domain was in college, where I read Robert Caro's seminal book *The Power Broker: Robert Moses and the Fall of New York*. Robert Moses is responsible for so much of how modern cities look and feel, and not just in New York because his methods were imported and copied throughout the country. Moses was a destroyer of Black and brown communities. And eminent domain is what allowed that asshole to be racist at an industrial scale.

If I may summarize one of the greatest modern biographies ever written in two sentences: Robert Moses was a deeply racist man who built highways, bridges, parks, beaches, and even housing projects by bulldozing the hopes, dreams, and often literal homes of people in his way. His main tactic for acquiring land for his projects was identifying vulnerable minority or immigrant communities, declaring their homes and land "blighted," and then using the government's power of eminent domain to evict people from their homes over their objection and for a fraction of what their communities were actually worth.

Declaring a community "blighted" or a home "condemned" is a favorite trick of the government when it wants to avoid paying just compensation for the land it takes. It's what Moses did, repeatedly, throughout New York City in the 1930s, '40s, '50s, and into the '60s. Moses would target a community, have state assessors declare it a "slum," and acquire the land through eminent domain at cut-rate prices. And it's a method many cities and states would copy under the guise of "urban renewal."

Urban renewal laws authorize the state to seize land it has designated blighted and deteriorated in some way. The New York State urban renewal law is codified at Article 15 of New York Consolidated Laws, Section 500. Look at how the law describes the purpose of the policy at Section 501:

> There exist in many municipalities within this state residential, non-residential, commercial, industrial or vacant areas, and combinations thereof, which are slum or blighted, or which are becoming slum or blighted areas because of substandard, insanitary, deteriorated

or deteriorating conditions, factors, and characteristics, with or without tangible physical blight. The existence of such areas constitutes a serious and growing menace, is injurious to the public safety, health, morals and welfare, contributes increasingly to the spread of crime, juvenile delinquency and disease, necessitates excessive and disproportionate expenditures of public funds for all forms of public service and constitutes a negative influence on adjacent properties impairing their economic soundness and stability, thereby threatening the source of public revenues.

As Yoda might say, "Mudhole? Slimy? My home, this is." Clearing out "the slums" and replacing run-down and dilapidated-looking buildings with fresh, shiny, economically productive buildings and infrastructure sounds like a great plan, unless you are the person being cleared out. Then, not only are you being displaced from your community, your "just compensation" becomes slum prices, leaving you only enough money to go and try to find a different slum to live in. The government usually doesn't pay people in so-called blighted communities what their homes are worth, and never pays them what the land would be worth after all the happy-clappy urban renewal takes place.

This is why eminent domain so often takes advantage of vulnerable people and communities. The government doesn't actually want to pay a fair price for the land and doesn't want to fight legal battles against well-connected and powerful communities who can protect their property and interests in court.

"Condemnation" is what happened to Susette Kelo's property, before the government took it.

But again, this tactic didn't just start happening in 2005, and to white people. We can go all the way back to the creation of Central Park a century and a half earlier and find the same tactics at play.

An enormous park measuring 775 acres (today the park is actually 843 acres) in the middle of the island was not actually the first plan for an open green space in New York City. The first suggested site was a parcel of land, about 150 acres, along the East River between what is now Sixty-Sixth Street and Seventy-Fifth Street, known as Jones's Wood. In 1851, the New York State Assembly and Senate both passed resolutions to take Jones's Wood property through eminent domain. It was happening.

But the wealthy white landowners—John Jones's heirs, and another wealthy New York family named the Schermerhorns, whose property was included in some of the proposals for the park—didn't want to sell the land. Understand, neither the Joneses nor the Schermerhorns lived *on* the property full-time. Remember, this is the 1850s and the Upper East Side might as well have been a Mars colony. The Joneses' and the Schermerhorns' primary residences were downtown, where any self-respecting wealthy New Yorker would live. These people just didn't want to sell their undeveloped "country" estates uptown to the city for a public works project.

So the families sued New York State to block the state's taking of their land.

Did I mention the Joneses and Schermerhorns were white? They were white. And since they were white, all of the stuff I said earlier about the foundational principles of state sovereignty that eminent domain rest on, all of the stuff I said about how, legally speaking, the concept of eminent domain is so ingrained into the very conception of property that you scarcely need constitutional language acknowledging it, all of that stuff comes with the caveat of *unless you are wealthy and white.*

Of course the Joneses and Schermerhorns won their lawsuit against the state. Of course they did. A court ruled that the state resolution to acquire the property through eminent domain violated the due process rights of the rich white people. Apparently the resolution allowed the state to back out of the deal but didn't allow the Joneses and the Schermerhorns the same right. I'd point out that of course the Joneses and the Schermerhorns had no right to "back out" of the deal, because the state was using its unquestionable sovereign power to force the families into taking the "deal" whether they liked it or not, but now I'm just shaking my fist at white judges who have been dead for 150 years.

And so, instead of displacing two white families who didn't even use their land as their primary residence, the city went forward with a new plan that included displacing over two hundred Black people in Seneca Village who had built up an independent Black community on some of the only land they were allowed to purchase. All of the tricks that would later be deployed against Black communities in the twentieth century were used against the people of Seneca Village in the nineteenth century. The newspapers called their land a "swamp." The media called the people living there "squatters" (even though, again, 20 percent of the Black homeowners in all of New York City lived there), and, of course, the papers referred to their community as a "n***er village."

The residents of Seneca Village also went to court to object to the government taking their land, but unlike the wealthy white families, they lost in court every time. The landowners were paid an average of $700 per lot. Andrew Williams, that shoeshiner-turned-landowner who bought the first lots from the Whiteheads, was paid $2,335 for his three lots and house, even though he initially asked for $3,500 in "just compensation." Even when taking his land and destroying the community he helped to found, the state couldn't be bothered to pay the man what he asked for.

The Time Warner Center is a relatively recent construction just off Columbus Circle in New York City that sits right at the southwestern entrance to the park. It sits on about two acres of land and is valued at approximately $1.5 billion.

New York City should go and find all the descendants of Seneca Village and pay them what their land is actually worth. I bet the government would be more cautious and fair when using its power of eminent domain if the compensation were ever just.

10

A JURY OF YOUR WHITE PEERS

The right to a trial by jury in criminal cases is one of the oldest rights in our legal tradition. It's considered one of the defining features of democratic self-government. The ancient Athenians had public jury trials. The Romans had them. English kings, perhaps as far back as Henry II, reintroduced some form of jury trial by the twelfth century. By the 1700s, William Blackstone (the OG of legal pundits) wrote in his *Commentaries on the Laws of England* that the jury trial was an indispensable barrier between the rights of the people and the whims of the king because "the truth of every accusation . . . [must] be confirmed by the unanimous suffrage of twelve of his equals and neighbors, indifferently chosen and superior to all suspicion."

In America, the right to a jury trial was written into the constitutions of each of the thirteen original colonies, both before the American Revolution and after the formation of the new country. And, of course, it's written into the U.S. Constitution itself, in the form of the Sixth Amendment, which guarantees "the right to a speedy and public trial, by an impartial jury of the state and district wherein the crime shall have been committed."

I'm often surprised by how much faith people place in juries as a check on arbitrary, despotic uses of state power. I mean, do people just not know how arbitrarily despotic juries can be? I cannot reliably get a random sampling of twelve people to read a whole article before calling me an asshole based on my headline. But I'm supposed to trust twelve randos pulled off the street to figure out if I murdered somebody? They don't even have to be experts at anything? In fact, they generally have to be twelve people we found who literally had nothing better to do? This is the best system thousands of years of human civilization have been able to come up with?

Of course, I happen to be Black. The prospect of being judged by twelve potentially malicious white people doesn't immediately seem better to me than being judged by one potentially malicious white person in a robe. The right to an impartial jury has never really applied to people who look like me: not at the founding of the country, not after the Civil War, not after the Civil Rights Movement, and not today. I don't have a right to an "impartial" jury; I only have a right to a jury composed of white people who can answer the question "Are you racist? Yes/No" without shouting the n-word or firebombing a Black church.

For Black people, the Sixth Amendment is a cruel joke. The point of a trial by jury, if there is one, is to be judged by a community of your peers. But Black people are and have always been regularly brought up on charges by a white prosecutor, in front of a white judge, to have their guilt or innocence judged by an all-white or predominately white jury. That's not "impartial" justice; it's white justice imposed on Black bodies by a system that treats white people and their experiences as the default.

And it's certainly not a jury of your peers. Can you imagine a white banker accused of tax fraud sitting in front of an all-Black jury of "peers"? Can you imagine a white cop accused of murder being subjected to an all-Black jury? It doesn't happen. This country doesn't let a panel of all Black people judge white people involved in a freaking reality television dance competition. There is scarcely a situation in American life where any white person this side of Eminem is subjected to the final judgment of Black people, but Black people are subjected to the final judgment of white people all the damn time.

It would be one thing if Black people faced naturally occurring, predominantly white juries. If the only Black guy in town had to stand trial in front of his all-white neighbors, so be it. But predominately white juries are not the natural result of population dynamics mixed with "bad luck." Instead, those juries are the manufactured result of the criminal justice system purposefully excluding Black people from the jury pool.

White people, of course, used to explicitly exclude Black people from sitting on juries. Like nearly everything else in the Constitution, the Sixth Amendment didn't even pretend to apply to Black people, free or otherwise, for the first seventy-five years of this wretched country.

But after the Civil War, with the adoption of the Fourteenth Amendment and its promise of equal protection under the law, courts decided that directly excluding Black people from the jury pool was no longer okay. In 1880, the Supreme Court decided a case called *Strauder v. West Virginia*, which held that laws making Black people ineligible to serve on juries violated the Constitution. It's important to note here that the Court ruled the legal exclusion of Black jurors as a violation of the Fourteenth Amendment's grant of equal protection, not the Sixth Amendment's promise of an impartial jury.

But that wasn't really an issue in 1880 because racist white people were more than capable of keeping Black people off juries without the official statutory power to do so. The tool prosecutors used, and still use, to ensure all-white (and almost always all-male) juries is the peremptory challenge.

Here's a quick primer on how you get on a jury, for those who have yet to have the honor. First, eligible jurors are summoned to the courthouse for a day or more using a "reasonably random" method. This assemblage of eligible jurors is called the venire, or jury pool. If any cases need juries that day, the court selects people from that jury pool to sit on the jury (sometimes called a petit jury of twelve people used for trials, to distinguish it from a grand jury used for indictments to determine who needs to go to a trial).

But, unlike the larger jury pool, getting onto a trial jury is not done by random lot. The judge and lawyers, for both parties, are allowed to question potential jurors, ostensibly to test for bias against the people on trial, or potential witnesses, or issues likely to arise at trial. This process is called voir dire.*

During voir dire, potential jurors can be rejected for any reason, or for no reason at all. When a lawyer rejects a juror without having to state the reason for the rejection, it's called a peremptory challenge.

The right of lawyers to dismiss jurors via peremptory challenges for no stated reason goes back almost as far as juries and public trials themselves. The thought is that a lawyer might know the

---

* Why does the law use so many French terms to describe the jury process? Well, that's because while most people think of lawyers throwing around esoteric Latin phrases (and they do sometimes), our common law system comes from England, not Rome. And the English system used a lot of French words and terms because of the Norman conquest of England in 1066. It's called "law French," and words like *jury, tort, mortgage, bailiff,* and even *attorney* all come from that tradition. In areas of the law that are particularly old, like jury selection, you'll see more French. I usually try to resist using this archaic jargon, but some of the cases I want to talk about use these terms, so I have to explain them and, well, that's why William is conquering my keyboard right now.

juror is biased for reasons that can't be fully articulated but are true nonetheless. Because voir dire is not a forum to put jurors on trial, and there's no time or resources to check the character and moral standing of every potential juror, lawyers in the courtroom must be given wide latitude to exclude potentially unfit jurors. Maybe the juror looked like they were unserious and falling asleep during voir dire. Maybe the juror's answers just sounded untruthful, despite the lack of any evidence to impugn their character. Maybe the lawyer just gets a "bad feeling" about the juror.

Or, you know, maybe the juror is Black. After *Strauder v. West Virginia* outlawed the explicit statutory exclusion of Black jurors, lawyers were easily able to keep Black people off juries through the use of peremptory challenges. (Lawyers did the same thing to potential women jurors, both before and long after the Nineteenth Amendment gave women the right to vote.)

And that's the way things were for about a hundred years after *Strauder*. Black people would show up for jury duty only to be rejected via peremptory challenge in criminal cases, especially cases involving a Black defendant. These challenges allowed the system to discriminate against Black people who wanted to sit on juries and discriminate against Black people accused of crime. They allowed prosecutors to render the Sixth and Fourteenth Amendments inoperative for Black people, based on their own gut feelings before a trial.

The Supreme Court kind of tried to address this problem in 1965, in a case called *Swain v. Alabama*. But *Swain* focused on the exclusion of Black people from the jury *pool*, not on exclusion from the actual jury. All the Court really did in *Swain* was acknowledge that the systemic exclusion of Black people through peremptory challenges *could be* a violation of the equal protection clause, without giving defendants who were convicted by actual all-white juries any real way to object to how the jury was selected. A constitutional right that people have no way of accessing through litigation is just, like, a suggestion.

Finally, in 1986, the Supreme Court decided to put some teeth behind the super cool thought experiment that maybe Black people should not be summarily excluded from juries. That case is called *Batson v. Kentucky*. Just so people don't lose sight of how recent this decision is: the *Challenger* space shuttle blew up on live television before Black people had a tool to avoid being excluded from criminal juries in America. Barack Obama, the first Black president, was twenty-four years old before Black people had a reasonable chance of getting on a jury. Black people were brought to these lands in 1619, and Janet Jackson released *Nasty* before randomly excluding Black people from the jury process—an institution that's been around since Athens—was ruled unconstitutional in any meaningful way.

The next old white Republican who wants to talk to me about "law and order" can kiss my black ass.

But I digress. The case of *Batson v. Kentucky* would have never happened without the fairly extraordinary efforts of James Batson.

Batson, a Black man from Louisville, Kentucky, was charged with burglary. The evidence against him was light, and Batson went to trial. Batson's trial resulted in a hung jury: there was one Black juror on Batson's panel, and that juror would not vote to convict.

The prosecutor in the case, Joe Gutmann, decided to retry the case. This time, Gutmann used his peremptory challenges to exclude all four of the Black jurors who showed up in the jury pool. Batson was actually present at the voir dire when the potential jurors were being questioned. He told his lawyer to object to Gutmann's discriminatory use of his challenges. The lawyer said there was nothing he could do, and Batson, famously, told him to "object anyway."

He did but was shut down. Batson was convicted by an all-white jury.

On appeal, a white public defender named David Niehaus became interested in how it could possibly be constitutional for prosecutors to so brazenly reject Black jurors from being empaneled on petit juries. Niehaus moved to have the entire jury discharged as a violation of the Sixth and Fourteenth Amendments. It was Niehaus, a random public defender from Kentucky, who ended up arguing this seminal case in front of the Supreme Court.

Niehaus and Batson won. The Supreme Court ruled, 7–2, that using peremptory challenges to exclude jurors because they are Black violated the equal protection clause. Just as importantly, the Court ruled that defendants have a right to object to exclusion of Black jurors, and if they do, the burden shifts to the prosecution to provide a race-neutral reason for the exclusion of Black jurors.

We now call these hearings "Batson challenges." And Batson's logic has been extended to include women as well, from the 1994 case *J.E.B. v. Alabama ex rel. T.B.* (That decision was 6–3. So, to recap: until 1994 it was technically legal to use peremptory challenges against women *because* they are women. And, in *J.E.B.*, both Justice Sandra Day O'Connor and Justice Ruth Bader Ginsburg had to sit there and listen to arguments about why they could be summarily excluded from common criminal juries solely on the basis of their gender. Three of their male colleagues agreed with those sexist arguments, to their faces.)

Batson challenges became the first real tool to examine a lawyer's potentially discriminatory use of peremptory challenges, and force lawyers to come up with some reason for excluding jurors other than race or sex.

Which, of course, they do, all the time. A reoccurring theme in constitutional law is that racist white people are not stupid, and they never take a constitutional setback as an opportunity to be less racist going forward. If you tell them they can't be racist in one way, they'll find some other way to achieve the same racist results. And because courts are slow and infected by racist white people themselves, it might take decades or, as in the case with jury selection, a century for courts to catch up with the new way white people have figured out to be racist.

The problem with *Batson* is that white courts are inclined to accept any old allegedly "race-neutral" reason for excluding Black jurors. Lawyers have cited jurors' employment status, "body language," and pretty much anything else you can think of. A 1993 *University of Michigan Journal of Law Reform* article captured a number of cases where the prosecutors excluded Black jurors who "looked like" the Black defendant as the "race-neutral" reason accepted by the courts. Frankly, you have to be a piss-poor attorney not to be able to come up with some "race-neutral" reason to get rid of Black people. There are literally training videos on YouTube you can find that teach lawyers how to get around Batson challenges. *Batson* is both one of the most important modern civil rights victories and a complete fucking joke all at the same time.

Thurgood Marshall saw all of this coming from a mile away. Marshall concurred in the judgment in *Batson*, but he wrote separately. It's one of my favorite Marshall opinions:

> I join JUSTICE POWELL's eloquent opinion for the Court, which takes a historic step toward eliminating the shameful practice of racial discrimination in the selection of juries. The Court's opinion cogently explains the pernicious nature of the racially discriminatory use of peremptory challenges, and the repugnancy of such discrimination to the Equal Protection

Clause. The Court's opinion also ably demonstrates the inadequacy of any burden of proof for racially discriminatory use of peremptories that requires that "justice . . . sit supinely by" and be flouted in case after case before a remedy is available. I nonetheless write separately to express my views. The decision today will not end the racial discrimination that peremptories inject into the jury selection process. That goal can be accomplished only by eliminating peremptory challenges entirely.

The majority opinion in Batson assumes that lawyers acting in bad faith will be distinguishable from those acting in good faith. Marshall assumes white people gonna white.

Marshall was right.

But I think the way to attack peremptory challenges is not through the equal protection clause, but through the Sixth Amendment itself.

The Sixth Amendment's right to an impartial jury, chosen from "the state and district wherein the crime shall have been committed," has been interpreted by courts to mean that the Sixth entitles a defendant to a "fair cross section" of jurors from their community. But courts have routinely limited this fairness to the jury pool as a whole—the venire—and not the actual petit jury selected for trial.

Again, if Black people were being judged by a fair representation of their community, everybody could live with it. Everybody could agree that the ancient right to a jury of peers was satisfied if the people of the actual community where the crime was allegedly committed sat in judgment of the suspect. But courts have interpreted the Sixth Amendment to be nothing more than a bait and switch. The Supreme Court has said: "The Sixth Amendment requirement of a fair cross section on the venire is a means of assuring, not a *representative* jury (which the Constitution does not demand), but an *impartial* one (which it does)."

What the fuck does that mean? How in the hell does a fair cross section of my community in the jury pool "assure" me of an impartial jury at trial, if that fair representation does not make it onto the actual trial jury? Saying *"Here are all the Black people who could have been on your jury"* really doesn't do me a speck of good if I'm in the defendant's chair. How is representation crucial to impartiality at one stage, but not the other? That's like saying I have the right to go into the whole 7-Eleven, but I'm only allowed to buy malt liquor and condoms. What is this man talking about?

Sorry, the man talking is Antonin Scalia, and the case I'm quoting him from is 1990's *Holland v. Illinois*. Holland was the test case designed to attack the constitutionality of peremptory challenges to exclude Black jurors, regardless of the race-neutral reason invented by the prosecution. But Scalia rejected the argument in a 5–4 opinion. Thurgood Marshall dissented:

> The Court decides today that a prosecutor's racially motivated exclusion of Afro-Americans from the petit jury does not violate the fair-cross-section requirement of the Sixth Amendment. To reach this startling result, the majority misrepresents the values underlying the fair-cross-section requirement, overstates the difficulties associated with the elimination of racial discrimination in jury selection, and ignores the clear import of well-grounded precedents. I dissent.

Marshall would retire only a year and a half after this dissent. And the increasingly conservative court has never again come as close to rejecting peremptory challenges.

At the dark heart of making the Sixth Amendment meaningful in any way for Black people lies an argument that white people, even white liberals, are reluctant to make: white jurors cannot sit in impartial judgment of Black people.

Nobody really wants to say that, so we run ourselves through a bunch of equal protection analysis about the fairness of the objections to Black jurors, to make the conversation more palatable. But the real argument is that a Black person cannot get an *impartial* jury if that jury is all white.

I know white people understand this argument because, again, there is not a time in this country where white people let twelve Black people judge them for anything. You won't see a goddamn boxing match where the panel of ringside judges are all Black if one of the combatants in the ring is white. White people reject implicitly the notion that their actions or, God forbid, crimes can be judged exclusively by a community of Black people. I've had white people tell me with a straight face that I'm not even allowed to judge *whether a white person has been racist to me personally.* Like I'm the one who is too "biased" to adjudicate the situation impartially. If I could have one white superpower, it would be the fucking nerve of these people.

And yet white people, most of them, think that it's at least theoretically possible for an all-white jury to sit in impartial judgment of Black people. White people don't bat an eye when they see a gang of whites sitting in judgment of a Black person's actions: in the courtroom, in the boardroom, or even just on a stupid Facebook post. I don't think a lot of white people even notice just how often they've been part of a mob of whites judging Black people: be it on a sports call-in show or piling on a Yelp review.

The result of allowing peremptory challenges, the result of failing to provide for a fair cross section of the community at trial, is that Black people are denied the constitutional entitlement to a jury of their peers. We don't have it under the Sixth Amendment or any other provision of law. We are just entitled to the same lynch mob of white people that has always shown up throughout history and claimed the authority to take our lives away.

At least now we get to object. Maybe next century white people will decide their Constitution requires them to listen to those objections. Juries have been around for a while and don't appear to be going anywhere, so I guess we still have time to work this out.

11

IT'S NOT UNUSUAL TO BE CRUEL

The moral argument against the death penalty is actually a lot harder to make than the legal objection to the practice. I feel like anti–death penalty folks, like me, sometimes get that backwards. To us, murdering unarmed, defenseless people, often painfully, feels like a moral nadir that should be obvious to others.

But it's not. Most people have no problem killing people *who deserve it*, or at the very least looking the other way while the people who deserve it are killed. The entire scope of recorded human history bears that out. People kill other people all the time, and nearly everybody can be convinced to kill somebody else.

And not just in a "him or me" situation. Like, unquestionably, nearly everybody alive would kill another person who was trying to kill them. That's a *given* of the human condition. But beyond what we'd tell ourselves are "defense" killings or "justifiable" homicides, there's a broader number of people we'd kill who are "too dangerous to live." Would you kill baby Hitler? Of course you would. You'd be a selfish asshole not to. Dude is going to be responsible for millions and millions of deaths and you wouldn't stop him before he got started because of, what, your immortal soul? Fuck you and your precious soul. Take one for the team and kill baby Hitler before he murders us all.

In our popular culture, we don't hesitate to glorify the killing of people who deserve it. The good guy almost always kills the bad guy. Thanos gets snapped, Sauron gets melted, John Wick kills the guy who killed his dog, and that guy's dad, and maybe one third of New York City who got in his way. That's just how movies work. In fact, when the bad guy is not killed, when they're merely captured or arrested, the entire theater knows: "Oh, they're setting up a sequel."*

To oppose the death penalty on moral grounds is to deny two of the most fundamental human emotions: fear and revenge. We kill criminals as punishment for all the harm they've caused to society, or out of fear that they will escape and cause additional harm in the future. Those are entirely natural human concerns.

It's not even morally clear why I, or any person who is not the victim, should get a vote in all of this. I mean, as far as I know, nobody on death row owes me money. I'm not on the hunt for the one-armed man who killed my wife. If the people who were wronged by a condemned man want to see that man put to death, who am I to say, "Actually, that's morally wrong, you should let him live." Who died and made me Jiminy freaking Cricket? If killing a person who is trying to kill you is more or less okay, how is killing a person who *successfully* killed your family wrong?

---

* Kids, "movie theaters" were places where people went to watch Netflix or Disney Plus with other strangers, before the coronavirus pandemic. In much of our art and literature, the conflict is not "resolved" until the antagonist is dead. It's easier to name the exceptions (nobody kills Prince Humperdinck in *The Princess Bride*) than it is to name the times a villain paid the ultimate price.

Compared to the moral argument that will leave you searching for a philosopher's stone, the legal argument against the death penalty is easy and straightforward. First of all, it's against the law. It's against one of the *first laws*, if you come from and believe in the Judeo-Christian tradition. Moses was the first lawgiver, and one of his first ten rules (some would call them commandments) he claims God told him is *"Thou shalt not kill."* Again, killing is kind of what people do, so most religious traditions go on to create enough exceptions to the "no killing" rule to drive a genocide, but arguably the law has been against killing people since the invention of *laws*.

Of course, that's just a story we tell each other. The first historically verifiable lawgiver was all about killing people: King Hammurabi of Babylon codified twenty-five different crimes that were punishable by death. By the seventh century BCE, the Athenian code made all crimes, literally all of them, punishable by death. They called it the *Draconian Code of Athens* and the name was not in error.

But the law's historical bloodlust is still overcome by the very point of law itself: to have rules that can be relied upon as opposed to whims that are applied in an arbitrary and capricious fashion by a despot. Capital punishment, as applied in our legal system, has none of the characteristics of good laws. It's not reliable: we literally convict and condemn innocent people all the time. It's not repeatable: similar crimes are treated as capital offenses or not depending on minor aggravating factors, the random geography of where the crime took place, or the good graces of the judge or jury that happens to hear the case. And, most importantly, it's not just or fair: the death penalty is carried out more frequently against poor defendants and even more frequently against Black and brown defendants. It's entirely rational to believe that the death penalty is theoretically legal, but whatever the hell we're doing is not.

Our Constitution addresses capital punishment in the Eighth

Amendment, but it doesn't even try to establish a consistent, reliable standard for a question as fundamental as "When can the state kill us?" Instead, it gives us this—the Eighth Amendment, in full:

> Excessive bail shall not be required, nor excessive fines imposed, nor cruel and unusual punishments inflicted.

Well, that's not really helpful. The Constitution defines neither *cruel* nor *unusual* (nor *excessive bail*, which is a whole different problem). Instead of making a rule, it offers a platitude the framers themselves didn't even come up with on their own (the exact language "cruel and unusual" is copied and pasted from the 1689 English Bill of Rights) and seems to assume that judges or juries will figure the whole thing out in the fullness of time. Say what you will about the Draconian Code of Athens, but at least it's an ethos.

A standard as vague and subjective as "cruel and unusual" is one begging future generations to figure things out for themselves. In 1787 it was normal and appropriate to beat children with tree branches and condemn people for witchcraft. Now, we're not supposed to do those things. Times change. Standards and practices change. The Eighth Amendment is a little bit of a "living constitution" written into the old parchment. It's a facially subjective standard that can be applied to our own situation as we see fit.

Unfortunately, we share the country with people who will not let us have nice things. These people are called originalists, and they will not allow our polity to function rationally. They think the Constitution can be only as good as the worldview of the small-minded slavers and colonists who wrote it, and because of that they insist the death penalty must be constitutional.

Originalists say that James Madison and Alexander Hamilton and John Jay and all the people who did the thinking and the selling of the new American Constitution clearly envisioned a society where capital punishment was a thing. Originalists will tell me that the state was well in the business of executing people when the Constitution was written, and yet the framers didn't specifically outlaw the practice. They'll tell me that the Eighth Amendment, which specifically prohibits cruel and unusual punishments, could not possibly have been referring to capital punishment, because convicts were murdered by the state, in every state, both before and after the Constitution was ratified. They'll point out that the English Bill of Rights, where the amendment was copied from, was written by people who chopped off their own king's head merely forty years earlier. They'll say that the very most the Eighth Amendment prohibits is torture, not executions.

I say: I don't give a shit. To my mind, the Eighth Amendment is the cleanest battle to be had with originalists. It's the easiest place to drop out all of the legalistic claptrap and doctrinal fencing to get down into the guts of the thing. The framers wrote something down. That something is vague. Originalists say that we can understand what they really meant by looking at what they did. I say I don't give a fuck about what those depraved assholes actually did. I will stipulate that the people who wrote the Constitution had a sense of humanity that was so underdeveloped they could eat sandwiches while watching a man being hung from the neck until death. But so what? The Constitution does not require me, or my country, to be forever hobbled by their sociopathy.

Indeed, we are not hobbled by eighteenth-century thought bubbles when it comes to what we define as capital *crimes*. There's no great accounting of how many crimes were punishable by death in America at the time the Constitution was ratified, because for the most part putting people to death was squarely in the purview of state law. But, at the time of the founding there were well over two hundred crimes punishable by death in England, including crimes as common as stealing and as nonserious as cutting down someone else's tree. Over time, here in America, the states have been able to cull the number of offenses that could get a person executed, without the need of an entire constitutional amendment.

It makes no sense that we've been able to remove ourselves from an eighteenth-century view of who gets punished but remain locked in an eighteenth-century view of how to punish people. That goes beyond the death penalty. For instance, some form of solitary confinement has been viewed as a fairly standard and appropriate punishment since forever. But now, with our modern understanding of, you know, human psychology, studies suggest that solitary confinement is especially cruel. It's torture for your brain. James Madison did not understand this and likely wouldn't have cared if he did. Why in the hell should that matter now? *We* know. We are the ones who know. And we are the ones who have the option of making cruel punishments, like solitary confinement, unconstitutional. To not do so because some old dead white people didn't have the knowledge or decency to do the same is not an alternative theory of legal interpretation. It's the promulgation of evil hiding behind the banality of cowardice.

A modern understanding of the Eighth Amendment would read it to outlaw the death penalty. That point is so obvious it has literally been done before. In 1972, in a case called *Furman v. Georgia*, the Supreme Court decided the death penalty statute in Georgia violated the Eighth Amendment mainly because it was applied in an arbitrary and capricious manner.

Furman is interesting because it's a one-page, per curiam (which means unsigned) opinion holding the Georgia statute unconstitutional, followed by two hundred pages of concurrences and dissents as the justices try to work out why or why not. Only justices William Brennan and Thurgood Marshall ruled the death penalty unconstitutional in all circumstances. Justice Marshall wrote:

Perhaps the most important principle in analyzing "cruel and unusual" punishment questions is one that is reiterated again and again in the prior opinions of the Court: *i.e.,* the cruel and unusual language "must draw its meaning from the evolving standard of decency that mark the progress of a maturing society." Thus, a penalty that was permissible at one time in our Nation's history is not necessarily permissible today.

But the rest of the majority did some version of trying to parse what the framers really meant by "cruel and unusual" to arrive at the position that the death penalty was theoretically legal but practically unworkable as applied in Georgia.

It shouldn't surprise anyone that *Furman* was but a temporary pause on the death penalty. Capital punishment was reinstated just a few years later, in 1976, in a case called *Gregg v. Georgia.* The Supreme Court reversed itself on the very thin logic that Georgia's new death penalty statute included enough procedural protections to make it okay for Georgia (and Texas, and Florida, which soon followed suit) to start killing people again.

Gregg was a 7–2 case, with only Brennan and Marshall dissenting. But *Furman* and *Gregg* have basically set the stage for the last forty years of death penalty fights at the Supreme Court. Marshall argued that the death penalty was an anachronistic holdover from our barbaric past, but the current argument against the death penalty doesn't take Marshall's "maturing society" position. Instead, the modern way of fighting the death penalty is to argue that each individual punishment is unnecessarily cruel in some specific way, without arguing that killing people is the thing that is cruel.

It's worked, after a fashion. Advocates have successfully forced the state to move from hangings to firing squads to gas chambers to electric chairs to, now, lethal injections. Over the last few years, manufacturers of drugs used in executions have started depriving state governments of their preferred cocktails of death. This forces states to try to use different drugs, in different cocktails, and every time the state does, people who haven't already been killed have an opportunity to appeal to the Supreme Court and argue that the new method of execution constitutes cruel and unusual punishment. The withholding of death drugs by the people who make them is one of the best stories about corporate responsibility we have in the modern era. It's one of the best examples of the market taking steps to correct a failure in government.

Predictably, conservatives are sick of it. They're sick of what they deem as legal tricks to keep people alive. There's actually a movement afoot in this country to bring back firing squads because too many prisons can't get their lethal drugs. "Just shoot it till it stops moving" is how conservatives like to handle their problems anyway. Conservative courts are annoyed that condemned men and women keep coming to the court asking for mercy, and that annoyance has manifested itself in a series of increasingly harsh decisions from the Republican majority on the Supreme Court.

The most cruel, the most needlessly fucking sadistic ruling, came from Justice Neil Gorsuch in 2019's *Bucklew v. Precythe*.

Russell Bucklew was a murderer, convicted and sentenced to death in the state of Missouri. Missouri is one of those states that lost its preferred death cocktail when manufacturers stopped selling the state prison system the drug, so it had to cobble together a new cocktail based on whatever it had lying around. It figured something out (damn near any drug will kill you if they give you too much of it): a lethal dose of the sedative pentobarbital.

The problem, from Bucklew's perspective, was that pentobarbital would be extremely painful. Bucklew suffered from a rare condition called cavernous hemangioma, a vascular issue. He argued that the pentobarbital could react adversely in his system, and, aside from killing him, would cause him extreme pain before he died.

Have you ever seen a movie where somebody who is about to be executed asks, "Will it hurt?" Usually the hero (or antihero if we're supposed to like him) will say something like "You won't feel a thing," and the character who is about to die gives a weak smile and sigh of relief and prepares himself for the inevitable. Now, imagine that executioner saying, "It'll hurt like a bitch and frankly I don't give a damn." That will give you an idea about Gorsuch's majority opinion in *Bucklew*. He wrote: "The Eighth Amendment forbids 'cruel and unusual' methods of capital punishment but does not guarantee a prisoner a painless death."

What a bastard, what a heartless-bastard thing to write while condemning a man to die painfully.

Gorsuch goes on to create an entirely new standard for Eighth Amendment objections. This is what originalists do when confronted with an area of law that was originally vague or open for interpretation: they make some shit up. Here, Gorsuch decides that to qualify as "cruel and unusual," pain has to be "superadded" on top of however the state decides to kill you. Gorsuch writes:

> While the Eighth Amendment doesn't forbid capital punishment, it does speak to how States may carry out that punishment, prohibiting methods that are "cruel and unusual." What does this term mean? At the time of the framing, English law still formally tolerated certain punishments even though they had largely fallen into disuse—punishments in which "terror, pain, or disgrace [were] superadded" to the penalty of death.

He then goes on to list various methods of execution the Eighth Amendment was understood, at the time, to prohibit, versus methods it was understood to permit. He divines that superadded pain is the thing that distinguishes forms of acceptable death from cruel death, then and now, and argues that the burden is on prisoners to somehow invent ever less painful ways to die that the state can readily implement without delay to execute them.

But Gorsuch is wrong about the Eighth Amendment, not just the theory of what it should and shouldn't permit, but in terms of how it was practically applied at the time it was adopted. People don't notice he's wrong, because he's wrong in the way that originalists almost always are when describing the fairy tale they've invented around the founding of America. He forgot about the slaves.

Quoting William Blackstone's *Commentaries on the Laws of England*, Gorsuch writes about methods of execution that would have "readily qualified as cruel and unusual" to a reader at the time of the Eighth Amendment's adoption:

> These included such "[d]isgusting" practices as dragging the prisoner to the place of execution, disemboweling, quartering, public dissection, and burning alive, all of which Blackstone observed "savor[ed] of torture or cruelty."

Instead, what unites the punishments the Eighth Amendment was understood to forbid, and distinguishes them from those it was understood to allow, is that the former were long disused (unusual) forms of punishment that intensified the sentence of death with a (cruel) "'superadd[ition]'" of "'terror, pain, or disgrace.'"

But that's a lie. All of those methods, and more, were used to kill Black people, and would have been readily identified as acceptable methods to kill Black people to most of the white people reading the Eighth Amendment at the time of its ratification. These punishments were not "long disused" by the time of the founding. They were used all the time, and would continue to be used all the time, against Black people. Don't even get me started on the eighteenth-century punishments thought to be normal and acceptable to inflict on Black people when the white people wanted to keep them *alive*. You'd take being burned at the stake any day over what some of these slavers could come up with when they still wanted to *protect their investment.*

From the perspective of the framers, what distinguished a cruel and unusual punishment from an allowable and normal punishment was not the method of execution, but the victim who was executed.

And it is that *original public purpose* of the Eighth Amendment that conservatives want to take us back to. Of course our society has evolved past the need to execute prisoners. A 2019 Gallup poll found that 60 percent of Americans favored life in prison over the death penalty. Of course we should not be executing people when we can't even be sure that they are guilty, and the fact that 165 people have been freed from death row because they've been proven innocent since 1973 should make us despair at how many innocent people may have been put to death. Of course a system that is more likely to kill you if you are Black or brown, or merely poor and cannot afford the best legal representation, fails to pass the basic standards from which law derives its power and authority.

The state-sponsored arbitrary murder of its own citizens who may or may not have committed a crime cannot be made legitimate through an invented definition of the word *cruel* that wasn't even used by the savage slaveholders who wrote the word down 250 years ago. Come on. I struggle accepting that originalists even believe the bullshit that comes out of their own mouths. "Oh, the Constitution totally requires us to distinguish between superadded terror and regular old terror when figuring out whether we can inject a drug into your bloodstream that will cut off oxygen to your cells and thus effectively suffocate you from the inside out. That's because the same people who would whip, mutilate, rape, and let dogs dismember enslaved humans only prohibited punishments that added unnecessary terror, pain, or disgrace."

Naw. That's not a real argument. That's too stupid to be a real argument. The real argument being made by originalists, and all the pro–death penalty people going all the way back to the founding, is that these people deserve to die. They're saying Russell Bucklew and all other death row inmates deserve to die and nobody should give a shit if it hurts.

Their legal grounding for that argument is actually a piece of crap. It makes no sense to have a legal definition of *cruel* centered upon what some eighteenth-century assholes thought that word should mean, especially when they changed their definition of the word based on the race of their victim. It's monstrous for the state to kill people when the state regularly convicts the wrong people of crime. And it's unethical to kill people based more on the effectiveness of their legal counsel than the severity of their offenses.

But arguing against the death penalty as a thing that cannot be done in a civilized society is a little different than arguing against it as a moral failure. Consider, again, Bucklew.

Stephanie Ray wanted to end her relationship with Bucklew. When she told him, he threatened her with a knife and cut her jaw. She fled, with her children, to a friend's house. Later, Bucklew caught up to her there. He shot the friend in the chest, killing him, and shot at the children (missing them, thankfully). He carried Ray to a secluded spot and violently raped her at gunpoint. He was apprehended, but he then somehow escaped the local jail, went back to Ray's home and beat Ray's mother with a hammer before he was apprehended again.

If you want a moral argument for why Bucklew should live, you'll have to pull out your copy of *A Black Guy's Guide to the Bible* (many of you have one, you probably just call it the *New Testament* in your house). I've got nothing for you there.

All I can tell you is that Russell Bucklew was put to death by the state of Missouri on October 1, 2019. Legally, that was the wrong result. The Constitution allows us to be better than this.

12

THE MOST IMPORTANT PART

In a sense, I've been explaining the Constitution with one hand tied behind my back. I've been looking at our rights and protections through the lens of the Bill of Rights—the ten amendments originally appended to the Constitution—as the originalists do. I've been trying to explain why originalists are wrong, on their ground and on their terms, on the things they claim to care about.

I really do believe that the Eighth Amendment, on its face, renders capital punishment unconstitutional. I really do think that the right to an impartial jury enshrined in the Sixth Amendment must mean the right to a representative jury of one's community. I absolutely believe that the Fourth Amendment's protection against unreasonable search and seizure means that the cops cannot harass, arrest, or murder me, simply because the officer has a "hunch" about the color of my skin. I can make a textualist and even originalist case against the kind of white supremacy infused into our Constitution. I've been to Federalist Society events; I can argue with them inside the paper bag that borders constitutional inquiry into the intentions of the small-minded white men who wrote the thing.

But my understanding of the Constitution does not have to be limited to the document as originally written, nor the first ten amendments as the framers originally understood and implemented them. That original Constitution, the one drafted at the Constitutional Convention in 1787, ratified by the thirteen colonies, and venerated by conservatives as if it were gospel, is dead. It was shot at Bull Run. It burned in the Battle of the Wilderness. It bled the ground red at Gettysburg. As a Black person, I do not even acknowledge the legitimacy of the original Constitution, much less think our modern rights and responsibilities can be understood only through its lens.

The Union survived the Civil War, but its slavers' Constitution did not.

If I'd been in charge, I'd have written an entirely new document. I'm sure that everybody knows that the original document counted slaves as "three fifths" of a free individual, but I'm not sure that most people appreciate how deeply cynical this clause was, beyond the obvious racism.

First of all, the actual text referred to three-fifths of "all other persons," because the slavers who wrote it didn't want to put the word *slaves* in their precious document. It's one of the most obvious indications that the founders knew damn well that slavery was wrong and didn't give a shit. But when you dig deeper, you realize that the three-fifths clause was put in there to help the slavers and the slave states. The Northern states out-peopled the Southern states, and so, rightly, the Southerners were worried about a federal government controlled by the states in the North with more people in them. You know, like a democracy or something. To counteract the places with the most people, the slave states put a bunch of antidemocratic loopholes in their Constitution, while also trying to inflate their own numbers by counting slaves who—by their own evil logic—had no right to representation. But they couldn't just say that slaves should be counted as full people, because then why are they holding *people* in bondage? So they counted slaves as three-fifths of a person to give *their captors* more congressional representation.

A document *that* flawed, one animated by such evil, and one that so spectacularly failed that the country fought a live-ammo Civil War less than a hundred years after its conception, should have been thrown out with the bathwater. That's what they did in South Africa. In South Africa, they didn't just track changes and strike through the old apartheid constitution. You can't make Freddy Krueger friendly by giving him a new hat. Instead, they wrote an entirely new document, in a constitutional convention that represented all of the people, and they took two years to do it. Adopted in 1996, the South African Constitution now stands as a model for the world, while we have a "constitutional crisis" every time a Republican president figures out a new way to commit crimes.

But nobody asked me. Instead, white Northerners thought their precious slavers' document was fixable with a few amendments—amendments that they passed without the help and over the objections of their defeated Southern cousins.

The real debate between liberals and conservatives on the Supreme Court, the true argument, when you drop out the legal jargon and hot-button culture-war issues, is the debate over whether or not the new amendments worked to redeem the document. Conservatives, fundamentally, act as though they did not. They act like the post–Civil War amendments were mere updates to the original slave document. We still have a white supremacist's Constitution—we just have to count Black people as full people for the purposes of congressional representation, is all. Not much has changed.

Liberals, conversely, act like the new amendments changed everything. Writing about the Thirteenth, Fourteenth, and

Fifteenth Amendments—collectively known as the Reconstruction Amendments—Eric Foner in his book *The Second Founding* explains the profound changes brought about by the new rules. He says:

> They forged a new constitutional relationship between individual Americans and the national state and were crucial in creating the world's first biracial democracy, in which people only a few years removed from slavery exercised significant political power . . . the amendments both reflected and reinforced a new era of individual rights consciousness among Americans of all races and backgrounds. So profound were these changes that the amendments should be seen not simply as an alteration of an existing structure but as a "second founding," a "constitutional revolution."

As a matter of interpretation, analyzing any constitutional clause without straining it through the Fourteenth Amendment's guarantee of equal protection and due process, or the Fifteenth Amendment's distribution of the voting franchise, is an exercise of intellectual apartheid. Without the Thirteenth, Fourteenth, and Fifteenth Amendments (and the Nineteenth Amendment, which finally acknowledged women's fundamental right to vote), the Constitution is a violent piece of shit that can be used to justify or allow the legalized supremacy of white men over all others. Those four amendments do not perfect the original Constitution; they're not the final pieces of the puzzle that complete a picture by filling in some obvious holes. Instead, they recast the entire document, destroying the slave state that the founders wrote into existence and replacing it with something new, something heterogenous, and something still flawed yet not utterly unredeemable.

Which is why the entire conservative legal project, since ratification of those amendments during Reconstruction to the present day, has been to limit the scope and effectiveness of this "new" Constitution. It doesn't matter if the conservatives call themselves Democrats (as they did after the Civil War) or Republicans (as they have since the New Deal or so). It doesn't matter if the conservative legal theorists say they're in favor of federalism or judicial restraint or originalism and textualism. Their goals are and have been the same no matter what they are calling themselves this morning. They want the right to vote to be limited to the people who agree with them. They want to exclude fairness from the question of due process. And they want equal protection to be one input among many, as opposed to a required outcome of just laws.

It's not complicated. If conservatives seem to excel at coming up with snappy names and bumper sticker slogans for their legal theories, it's because their goals are banal and simplistic enough to fit on the back of a truck. It's pretty easy to dress up "whites win always" with legalese and sell it back to an audience of white people, especially when Thomas Jefferson and James Madison have already done most of the work.

At the founding, all political and economic power in this country was given to white men. Almost all of the other amendments and common law updates simply change the balance ever so slightly on which white men get to be in control of any particular instrument of power. But the Reconstruction and Nineteenth Amendments say that white men have to share that political and economic power with everybody else. And not merely as a theoretical proposition either; those amendments demand that power is actually shared among our multicultural society, or else the government ceases to be legitimate.

Of course, conservative white men object to that. They don't like *sharing*. I mean, have you met a conservative white man? They're still flummoxed by the concept of letting a woman finish her sentence. You think sharing the wealth and power of a global hegemony is something they'd just roll over and accept? The only time conservative white men have agreed to share power is when other white men make them do it at the point of a gun. And whenever those more enlightened whites lose the will and the nerve to keep stuffing equality and fairness down the throats of their objecting brothers and cousins, conservative forces retrench, recalibrate, and reemerge with new strategies to violently reassert white male dominance, and new legal theories to justify their supremacy.

Sometimes those theories are even adopted by other minorities or women who are willing to sell out everybody else in order to snatch up whatever scrap of power or cash the white men are willing to drop from the table.

But make no mistake, the Reconstruction and Nineteenth Amendments offer a complete repudiation of white male supremacy, if legislatures and courts would only apply them to our republic. Hell, I could make a case that the only amendments I need in order to run a free and fair society are the Fourteenth and the First. Seriously, try me:

I want to buy some slaves.

Sorry, that's a violation of equal protection of the laws and substantive due process.

I didn't say Black slaves, I said any old slaves.

Yeah, still. There's no fair process by which you could acquire people as chattel.

Okay, fine, well I don't want to let everybody vote.

That sounds like a violation of equal protection to me.

Fine, they can vote but they can't live next to me.

And that's a violation of substantive due process in home buying.

Shut up!

Dude, First Amendment.

What if I wanted to take everybody's guns? I bet you'll say that's a violation of substantive due process too.

No, that's cool. Go right ahead.

Name me a structure of white supremacy, and I can show you how equal protection or substantive due process obliterates it. Show me an artifact of institutionalized bigotry or sexism that is upheld through force and effect of law, and I can tell you how to constitutionally destroy it. I cannot make people less racist. I cannot change hearts and minds. But I can make damn sure that racists and misogynists don't have the protection of law while they're doing their racism and misogyny in the name of the government.

Just, like, read it. Read the first section for God's sake. It does most of the things:

Amendment XIV

Section 1.
   All persons born or naturalized in the United States, and subject to the jurisdiction thereof, are citizens of the United States and of the state wherein they reside. No state shall make or enforce any law which shall abridge the privileges or immunities of citizens of the United States; nor shall any state deprive any person of life, liberty, or property, without due process of law; nor

deny to any person within its jurisdiction the equal protection of the laws.

Here, I'll even annotate it for you.

All persons born or naturalized in the United States,
and subject to the jurisdiction thereof, are citizens of
the United States and of the state wherein they reside.

Everybody born here is a citizen. Everybody. There are not people
who are less citizens just because of where they came from, or how
recently they became citizens, or where their parents were born.

No state shall make or enforce any law which shall
abridge the privileges or immunities of citizens of the
United States.

All citizens have the same rights. Those include economic rights,
contractual rights, and speech rights. And those rights cannot be
taken away just because they live in a crappy state.

nor shall any state deprive any person of life, liberty, or
property, without due process of law.

You know that promise we made in the Declaration of Independence about the pursuit of life, liberty, and happiness? The thing
we said once and then completely ignored when it came to Black
people? Well, we're serious about it now. Sorry we didn't make that
clear the first time.

nor deny to any person within its jurisdiction the equal
protection of the laws.

We can't have laws that only protect white people. We can't have a country that only works for white people. We just can't. We just fought a freaking war. Stop it.

The Reconstruction and Nineteenth Amendments, on their textual face, obliterate the structures of white male supremacy this nation was founded upon. They obliterate whatever new structures white guys will think of next. These amendments are supposed to win the debate on whether we're going to be a racist country or not.

And so originalists deploy one final trick from their big bag of bad ideas. They say that the Reconstruction Amendments must be interpreted according to the original public meaning of the people who wrote them after the Civil War. Instead of going higher, instead of looking at the ideals the Reconstruction Amendments represent, originalists again try to hobble them by limiting them to what dead white people may have thought. Originalists try to lock the country into an eighteenth-century kind of understanding of racial equality, and when that fails, as it must in the face of the Reconstruction Amendments, they argue with a straight face that we should be locked into a nineteenth-century white man's idea of racial justice.

It's fucking insulting. The people who wrote and voted for the Reconstruction Amendments were the best generation of white men America had yet produced, but they were still racist, sexist, flawed white men.

Here's your boy, Abraham Lincoln, speaking at Cooper Union:

> I will say then that I am not, nor ever have been, in favor of bringing about in any way the social and political equality of the white and black races, [applause] that I am not, nor ever have been, in favor of making voters or jurors of Negroes, nor of qualifying them to hold office, nor to intermarry with white people; and I will

say in addition to this that there is a physical difference between the white and black races which I believe will forever forbid the two races from living together on terms of social and political equality. And inasmuch as they cannot so live, while they do remain together there must be the position of superior and inferior, and I as much as any other man am in favor of having the superior position assigned to the white race.

And Lincoln was a great man. Not as great as his congressional contemporary, the abolitionist congressman John Bingham, who actually wrote the first section of the Fourteenth Amendment and demanded the inclusion of sweeping language that guarantees the right to all, but pretty great as nineteenth-century white people go. Ulysses S. Grant, who as president would be in charge of executing the Reconstruction Amendments, actually owned slaves. And again, Grant was a great white man for his time—the Emancipation Proclamation and the Thirteenth Amendment were probably no more than unenforceable thought bubbles without Grant. But the conservative plea that we center the legal rights and privileges of everybody else on what the best available white men could imagine in the 1860s and '70s is ridiculous.

Equality and fairness must meet the standards of our modern definitions of those ideals, or else the entire American experiment is illegitimate. I mean that without hyperbole.

Understand, Black people did not get a vote in the drafting, adoption, or ratification of the Constitution in 1787. We did not get a vote in the drafting, adoption, or ratification of the Reconstruction Amendments. We did not consent, tacitly or otherwise, to this slave state. And we were systematically denied political power in this country until roughly 1964 (and I'm being *generous* to this country by starting the clock in '64 with the passage of the Civil Rights Act, as opposed to, like, 1984 and Jesse Jackson forcing the left-wing party to acknowledge the electoral strength of Black folks).

There is no political or legal philosophy of democratic self-government that contemplates people living under the yoke of laws as they would have been interpreted by their captors. Either equal protection and fundamental fairness mean something radically different now than they did then, or Black people are an occupied people in this land, still waiting for our chance to break free.

I'm not a radical, because I believe the former *must be* true. I believe that equal protection means what it says—that racist laws are unconstitutional, even if the legislators don't write "I hate n***ers" into the law—not what Neil Gorsuch thinks John Bingham really meant. I'm not a Black Nationalist, because I believe the Reconstruction and Nineteenth Amendments could redeem this whole bigoted and misogynist enterprise.

But white people won't let them. It really is that simple. I say the Fifteenth Amendment must mean that the votes of Black people cannot be suppressed by voter ID laws, and white people tell me no. I say that Black political power cannot be gerrymandered away by racist white legislatures, and white people tell me no. I say that the Fourteenth Amendment's grant of equal protection of laws must protect me from racial harassment by the cops, and entitles me to equal pay for my talents, and promises me that my peaceful protest will be treated with the same permissiveness the cops accord to a mob of white insurrectionists storming the nation's Capitol, and white people tell me no, no, no.

These amendments are a tonic white people refuse to drink. They can cure the Constitution of its addiction to white male supremacy, if white people would just take the medicine.

13

CONSERVATIVE KRYPTONITE

The Fourteenth Amendment was ratified by the states on July 9, 1868. But its guarantee of rights was almost immediately undercut by the Supreme Court. Then, as now, when the Supreme Court is controlled by conservatives, even a constitutional amendment cannot stop it from denying equal rights and social justice to all. Nothing decent can overcome a conservative court. That's something that modern liberals and progressives should always remember.

The conservative attack on the Fourteenth Amendment started with economic rights. The amendment says:

> No state shall make or enforce any law which shall abridge the privileges or immunities of citizens of the United States.

That suggests that any rights, including economic rights, held by any citizen must be held by all citizens, but the Supreme Court didn't see it that way.

The case that invented this distinction was called the *Slaughter-House Cases*. Decided in 1873, this case dealt with, well, slaughterhouses. The state of Louisiana granted a monopoly to a company called Crescent City Live-Stock Landing and Slaughter-House Company to run all slaughterhouses downstream of New Orleans. In exchange for the monopoly, Crescent City was supposed to comply with health and safety regulations and allow independent butchers to work on their premises, at fixed rates. Some of the white people put out of business, or forced to work at Crescent City, by this law argued a violation of their Thirteenth and Fourteenth Amendment rights to equal protection from this kind of economic favoritism.

But the Court said no. The *Slaughter-House Cases* was the first case interpreting the Fourteenth Amendment, and the Court ruled that it only applied to Black people—"the slave race," as the Court called us—and, regardless of race, the Fourteenth Amendment did not provide for equality of economic privileges for all people. Instead, the Court found that the other "privileges and immunities" enshrined in the Constitution (like the First Amendment's right to free speech and free association) constrained only the federal government. State governments, it ruled, were free to discriminate and deny those rights to their own citizens.

The view that other constitutional rights do not apply to the states was eventually rejected. Even though the Court, to my knowledge, has never had an opportunity to explicitly "overturn" the *Slaughter-House Cases*, by the early twentieth century its logic was dismissed. Today, most of the Constitution, including the original Bill of Rights, is thought to apply to state governments as well as the federal one.

But the argument that the Fourteenth Amendment protects economic equality, in addition to political equality, never recovered from the *Slaughter-House Cases*. You don't see poor white people suing for *their* rights under the Thirteenth or Fourteenth Amendment. You don't see Black people making, say, antitrust arguments against Facebook under the Fourteenth Amendment's grant of privileges and immunities. The closest thing we have to an argument like the ones made by the plaintiffs in the *Slaughter-House Cases* is from college athletes trying to get compensation or endorsement contracts while supporting the multibillion-dollar industry known as "amateur" sports. And those athletes are consistently rejected by courts.

So, right out of the gate, the Fourteenth Amendment was significantly limited by the Supreme Court. The amendment could have been a tool to stop all kinds of white-owned monopolies that crowd out Black-owned businesses. It could have been used to bring about increased economic opportunity for all. But it never turned out that way.

Part of that is because civil rights advocates and Fourteenth Amendment defenders at the time had bigger problems than *Slaughter-House*. The Civil Rights Act of 1875 was a big, sweeping bit of legislation that promised to affirm the "equality of all men before the law." The law banned discrimination in public accommodation and transportation. That meant restaurants, buses, and hotels all had to treat people equally. Most importantly, the 1875 act allowed people to sue for their rights in federal court, as opposed to state courts, which in the South were controlled by former slavers.

The legislation marked the last time white lawmakers would give a shit about Black people for nearly a hundred years. In 1877, Rutherford B. Hayes was installed as president after a disputed election where the validity of the Electoral College was called into question. A special commission decided the election in favor of Hayes, a Republican, with the help of Southern Democrats, but there was a catch. Hayes had to agree to remove federal troops from the South, which he did, thereby marking the effective end of Reconstruction.

By 1883, the Supreme Court overturned much of the 1875 Civil Rights Act, including all of the protections against discrimination in public accommodations and transportation. The Supreme Court, in a case called the *Civil Rights Cases*, ruled that the Fourteenth Amendment could not prohibit "private" discrimination.

Without troops left in the South to protect Black people who were trying to exercise their rights, without states willing to write laws prohibiting discrimination in their own territories, and without a federal cause of action so that Black people could object to the discrimination they were facing, the Jim Crow era was off and running. State governments didn't even have to pass laws formally discriminating against Black people; they could just let so-called "private actors"—like private restaurants or private hotels—do all the work for them.

But, of course, states did pass laws discriminating against Black folks, because if there's one thing about racists, it's that they're never satisfied with being ahead. They need total subjugation of Black people to make them feel good about themselves.

As early as 1870, just two years after the Fourteenth Amendment was ratified, Virginia passed a law requiring segregated public schools. All kinds of segregation laws were passed (and not just in the South) that should have violated the Fourteenth Amendment, even under the disastrous and wrong logic of the *Civil Rights Cases*. Georgia passed a law prohibiting amateur "Negro" baseball teams from playing "within two blocks" of any playground or school for white children (and prohibited white teams from playing within two blocks of colored playgrounds). Florida passed a law segregating housing for juvenile delinquents. Damn near everybody passed anti-miscegenation laws. All of these laws involved state actions, not private businesses conduct. They all should have been unconstitutional, even under the precedent of the *Civil Rights Cases*.

It all came to a head in 1892. That's when Homer Plessy bought a first-class ticket on the East Louisiana Railway for a trip from New Orleans to Covington, Louisiana. Plessy was Black, but he sat in the part of the train that was reserved for whites. The conductor asked Plessy to move. Plessy refused. He was then forcibly ejected from the train and sent to jail.

Plessy was a plant. He was not discernibly Black, his racial classification as "Negro" was owed to the infamous "one-eighth" rule of blood purity. Plessy had been approached by civil rights advocates specifically to challenge Louisiana's Separate Car Act of 1890. It was a classic Jim Crow law: trains were required to make one passenger car or section available for white passengers, and an "equal, but separate" accommodation for colored passengers—a plain violation of the Fourteenth Amendment's equal protection clause. Plessy's physical characteristics reduced the entire law to the bald, discriminatory intent of Louisiana's state. The only reason Plessy was ejected from the train car was because he was one-eighth Black. To reject his claim—to argue that legislating different treatment based not on the "color" of one's skin but on their racial classification was valid—would be to admit that the Fourteenth Amendment wasn't worth the parchment it was written on.

And the Supreme Court did just that. In a 7–1 decision the Court upheld the Louisiana law mandating segregated train cars. Here's the critical part of the majority opinion:

> The object of the amendment was undoubtedly to enforce the absolute equality of the two races before the law, but, in the nature of things, it could not have been intended to abolish distinctions based upon color, or to enforce social, as distinguished from political, equality,

or a commingling of the two races upon terms unsatisfactory to either. Laws permitting, and even requiring, their separation in places where they are liable to be brought into contact do not necessarily imply the inferiority of either race to the other, and have been generally, if not universally, recognized as within the competency of the state legislatures in the exercise of their police power.

What's going on here is the interplay between three competing spheres of rights: political rights, civil rights, and social rights. Political rights are the rights to participate in the democracy: the right to vote, or hold elective office. Civil rights are the rights to participate in the economy: the right to own a home, or buy land. Social rights are the rights to participate in society: the right to get married, or throw a party.

The Court here interprets the Reconstruction Amendments to protect only *political* rights. According to the logic of this Court, Black people had the right to participate: they could vote or have a trial or travel on trains. But they had no civil rights. No white man was bound to sell Black people a home, or a first-class train ticket. No white man was bound to employ Black people, or pay them an equal wage if they did. And Black people certainly had no social rights: they could be segregated or ghettoized or discriminated against at will.

The core logic of Plessy is that laws that are facially race-neutral are constitutional, even if they have a discriminatory effect. So a law prohibiting Black baseball teams from playing with white baseball teams is "facially race-neutral" because arguably it restricts white teams as much as Black teams. This is a logic that conservatives will come back to, again and again.

Here, Louisiana argued that it wasn't violating the equal

protection clause because its law treated black people and white people the same. Both races get their own section of the train.

Of course, those accommodations were never actually equal. The back of the train was never as nice or well maintained as the front of the train. Getting your food from the kitchen was never the same as sitting down at a table to eat. If things were actually equal, how would a lazy, mediocre white man come to feel he was still *better than* every Black person? The "equality" bit was always just a legal fiction: when white people see actual equality, they turn angry or violent. Come on. Twenty-first-century white people got so pissed off that a Black person got an equal employment opportunity as president that they turned to a vicious, bigoted, stupid person to save them, and stuck with him even as he helped get everybody sick. But you want to tell me that nineteenth-century white people really thought they were just in favor of "separate *but equal*" accommodations on a train? Or in a school? Please.

Plessy was decided in 1896. Its logic of "separate but equal" was used as the legal justification for the entire Jim Crow era. It's how the South, and many places and institutions in the North, justified the denial of civil rights to Black people. *Plessy* was the law of the land for almost sixty years, until it was overturned in the 1954 case *Brown v. Board of Education of Topeka*.

Now, conservatives will tell you that Plessy's logic has been roundly rejected. They'll say that laws requiring racial segregation are facially unconstitutional. They might even quote Justice Earl Warren from his *Brown* opinion where he says: "separate educational facilities are inherently unequal." But conservatives are trying to pull a fast one; they're trying to hide the racist evil they actually believe in by making a big show of one form of discrimination they've been forced to reject. In reality, *only* the "separate but equal" logic of Plessy has been rejected by conservatives. But the part where racists think the Fourteenth Amendment does not protect social rights? Conservative assholes still believe that. The part where they think that laws that are neutral (or "equal") according to the law's bare text should be interpreted without looking at the clear discriminatory impact of those laws? Modern originalists believe that the most.

The mere existence of *Plessy* really puts modern originalists in a bind. Again, their goal is to limit the Reconstruction Amendments to the original intent and public meaning of their white male writers. But that becomes an untenable position if the original intent and public meaning of the Fourteenth Amendment allows for the kind of segregation and racism of the Jim Crow era. If the nineteenth-century Supreme Court thought that equal protection didn't actually protect civil rights, and none of these other nineteenth-century white politicians did anything to stop them, then how can looking at original meaning and intent possibly be a valid way to interpret the Constitution or its amendments?

Clearly, the Fourteenth Amendment means more and does more than what the white people living at the time it was adopted thought it could mean and do. Looking to Jim Crow–era white society for guidance on how to bring about racial equality, of all things, is insane. A theory of constitutional interpretation and justice, supported by originalists, that *requires them* to look to and value the intents and purposes of unabashed, unrepentant white supremacists is obviously, irreparably racist. Originalists try to dress up their theories with a bunch of fancy words and legal jargon, because what they actually believe in plain terms is provably stupid. "Racial equality only means what white people, and white people only, some of whom actually owned slaves, thought it could mean a century and a half ago." Get the fuck out of my face with that nonsense.

You have, perhaps, seen some modern originalist judicial nominees struggle with this issue, when pressed about it at their confirmation hearings. The question "Was *Brown v. Board of Ed.* rightly decided?" has been put to some recent nominees, and some of them have struggled to answer. It's not just that Republicans are intent on nominating unreconstructed white racists who would be totally cool with bringing back segregation given the chance (although, that *is* part of what is going on). It's that they don't want to give up their originalist bona fides and admit that sometimes the original intent of slavers and colonists was just wrong.

The thing is, the originalist judges who struggle with *Brown v. Board of Ed.*, the ones who can't seem to decide if the case over-turning one of the most racist decisions in U.S. history was "rightly decided," those people are the dumb ones. They're the stupid originalists who downloaded the white supremacy widget that is origi-nalism but didn't watch the YouTube video on how to make it work.

The Court's decision in *Plessy* was wrong on its face even at the time it was decided. It is relatively easy to make a fully original-ist case against *Plessy*, because *Plessy* was so wrong that even other white people knew it (not that those white people cared enough to do anything about it). The authors of the Reconstruction Amend-ments clearly envisioned the protection of political *and* civil rights as part of the package. For equal protection to mean anything, it had to mean the right for Black people to enter into contracts, civil or otherwise.

The Civil Rights Act of 1866 (not to be confused with the Civil Rights Act of 1875) explicitly protects the civil rights of Black Amer-icans, including the right to contract, and creates a federal cause of action to sue for racial discrimination in contracts that we still use to this day. While that act was proposed in 1866, it was not enforced until 1870. According to Congressman John Bingham—who, you'll remember, is the guy who wrote the Fourteenth Amendment—Congress did not have the power to advance the 1866 Civil Rights Act *until* the states ratified the Fourteenth Amendment. This is evidence that the people who wrote the damn thing literally thought they were protecting the civil rights of African Americans, whether they lived in former slave states or not.

Smart originalists cling to this history like a life raft. It allows them to argue that all *Brown* did was *restore* the original public meaning to the Fourteenth Amendment, not update that meaning for the modern era. They act like Bingham is the only relevant white man the way Batman uses Commissioner Gordon when he needs to say "#NotAllCops."

And while defending *Brown* requires originalists to admit that seven sitting Supreme Court justices were deeply, irrevocably wrong, they can still point to one who wasn't. Justice John Marshall Harlan I (not to be confused with his grandson, Justice John Marshall Harlan II, who also served on the Supreme Court) wrote in dissent in *Plessy*, and he gave originalists a line they often repeat:

> Our Constitution is color-blind, and neither knows nor tolerates classes among citizens. In respect of civil rights, all citizens are equal before the law.

Harlan's dissent in *Plessy* has been fully adopted by originalist ideology. Indeed, in a *UCLA Law Review* article, University of Houston law professor Ronald Turner points out that the most famous originalist, Antonin Scalia, has repeatedly aligned himself with Harlan's dissent in *Plessy*. Even in his book, *Reading Law: The Interpretation of Legal Texts*, which Scalia co-authored with scholar Bryan Garner, they write:

> The Thirteenth and Fourteenth Amendments . . . can reasonably be thought to prohibit all laws designed to assert the separateness and superiority of the white race, even those that purport to treat the races equally.

Justice John Marshall Harlan took this position in his powerful (and thoroughly originalist) dissent in *Plessy v. Ferguson.*

Let's check the rest of that "thoroughly originalist" dissent, shall we? Here's the paragraph leading up to Harlan's declaration that the Constitution is color-blind:

> The white race deems itself to be the dominant race in this country. And so it is in prestige, in achievements, in education, in wealth and in power. So, I doubt not, it will continue to be for all time if it remains true to its great heritage and holds fast to the principles of constitutional liberty.

As I keep saying, even the "best available" nineteenth-century white men were racist assholes.

But wait, there's more:

> There is a race so different from our own that we do not permit those belonging to it to become citizens of the United States. Persons belonging to it are, with few exceptions, absolutely excluded from our country. I allude to the Chinese race. But, by the statute in question, a Chinaman can ride in the same passenger coach with white citizens of the United States.

"What the fuck are you talking about? The Chinaman is not the issue here, dude. I'm talking about drawing a line in the sand, dude. Across this line, you do not ... Also, dude, *Chinaman* is not the preferred nomenclature. Asian American, please." (For this and other important philosophical interpretations about "the rules," please see Walter Sobchak in *The Big Lebowski*.)

Scalia is, of course, correct. Harlan's dissent is thoroughly originalist. Because the original intent of the Fourteenth Amendment by the white supremacists who passed it was to confer a bare minimum of political and civil rights to Black people, but none of the social rights.

We can see this again in the 1866 Civil Rights Act. Here's Congressman James F. Wilson, of Iowa, who introduced the bill on the House floor, explaining what the act was meant to do, according to the *Congressional Globe*:

> It provides for the equality of citizens of the United States in the enjoyment of "civil rights and immunities." What do these terms mean? Do they mean that in all things civil, social, political, all citizens, without distinction of race or color, shall be equal? By no means can they be so construed.

If you want to flummox an originalist, don't ask them about *Plessy v. Ferguson* or *Brown v. Board of Ed*. The smart ones can square that circle. Instead, ask them about *Loving v. Virginia*. Ask them whether the Fourteenth Amendment protects "social" rights. Ask them if Black people have a constitutional right to be treated equally in society.

Because social equality is what *Loving* is all about. Richard Perry Loving was a white man born in Central Point, Virginia, in 1933. When he was seventeen, he met then eleven-year-old Mildred Delores Jeter, who was also from Central Point, Virginia, through a family friend. Mildred was of mixed race: her parents identified as part African American, part Native American.

But for the white authorities in Virginia, she was "Black" and that was all that mattered. The two dated, on and off, for a number of years before deciding to get married in 1958, after Mildred became pregnant with their child (she already had one child from a previous relationship).

They couldn't get married in Virginia. The state had passed an "Act to Preserve Racial Integrity" in 1924, specifically to ban interracial marriages. Laws banning interracial marriage had been ruled constitutional, despite the Fourteenth Amendment, in a case called *Pace v. Alabama* in 1883. All the states in the former Confederacy erected such laws.

It's important to remember that the reason Southern states passed anti-miscegenation statutes was because white people and Black people were getting married to each other. And some white people hated it. Interracial marriages threaten the entire (stupid) logic of white supremacy, because if enough people did it, then gosh, eventually you wouldn't even be able to tell who was *really* white, would you?

Despite the best efforts of the ruling whites, interracial unions continued in spite of the laws, and entire communities that were either comprised of or tolerant of mixed-race families developed. Central Point, Virginia, was one of those places. It was a community where races co-mingled.

Richard and Mildred got married in Washington, DC, where they were legally allowed to do so, but then returned to their community in Central Point to live as husband and wife.

One night in 1958, authorities barged into their home while they were sleeping. Local law enforcement broke down their door and "caught" the couple in bed. "They asked Richard who was that woman he was sleeping with," Mildred Loving later told an interviewer. "I said, 'I'm his wife,' and the sheriff said, 'Not here you're not.'"

The Lovings were arrested and charged with violating Virginia's ban on interracial marriages. Initially they pled not guilty, but after a short bench trial, they changed their pleas to guilty. Judge Leon Bazile sentenced them to one year in prison, but suspended the sentence provided they left Virginia and never returned together for twenty-five years. Judge Bazile wrote in his opinion:

> Almighty God created the races white, black, yellow, malay and red, and he placed them on separate continents. And, but for the interference with his arrangement, there would be no cause for such marriage. The fact that he separated the races shows that he did not intend for the races to mix.

I point that out just because I find it comforting, sometimes, to remember that racists are also extremely dumb. Like, look at this fool. Riddle me this: if God wanted the races kept on separate continents, and only human free will flummoxes that divine segregation, *then why do the continents move?* Why did "God" shove the "Malay continent" right up the ass of the "Yellow continent" as evidenced by the existence of the Himalayas? Bet you didn't think of that. I bet you don't even know why mountains exist in the first place, you ignorant, racist fuck.

Sorry, Bazile is dead and presumably can't hear me over the sound of his own torments.

The Lovings moved to DC and lived with a cousin but were unhappy. They were still so tied to their community that Mildred went home to Central Point, without her husband as the court order mandated, to give birth to two of her children. Mildred's cousin suggested that she write to then attorney general Robert F. Kennedy about her family's plight. She did, and Kennedy found an ACLU lawyer, Bernard S. Cohen, to appeal their case to the Supreme Court.

In 1967, Cohen and the Lovings had their day in front of the Supreme Court of the United States. There, the Commonwealth of Virginia made all of the usual arguments defending segregation. The state said that the law treated Blacks and white equally, insofar as they were equally prohibited from marrying each other. Chief Justice Earl Warren summarized the state's position:

> The State argues that the meaning of the Equal Protection Clause, as illuminated by the statements of the Framers, is only that state penal laws containing an interracial element as part of the definition of the offense must apply equally to whites and Negroes in the sense that members of each race are punished to the same degree.

The Court rejected these arguments, unanimously.

> There can be no question but that Virginia's miscegenation statutes rest solely upon distinctions drawn according to race. The statutes proscribe generally accepted conduct if engaged in by members of different races. Over the years, this Court has consistently repudiated "[d]istinctions between citizens solely because of their ancestry" as being "odious to a free people whose institutions are founded upon the doctrine of equality."

And that was the end of anti-miscegenation laws in the United States of America. Well, not really. Anti-miscegenation laws remained on the books in many Southern states for a very long time. Alabama had its anti-miscegenation law on the books until 2000! It was repealed by voter referendum, and 40 percent of the people voted to *keep* the law banning interracial marriages, even though it had long ceased to be a valid legal prohibition.

Still, *Loving* is one of the most important decisions in the history of the country. It aligned the Fourteenth Amendment not just with the protection of civil rights, which the Court did in *Brown v. Board of Ed.*, but with the protection of social rights as well. The right to participate in society with equality and dignity is also protected by the Fourteenth Amendment, and that is what *Loving* stands for.

Which is why the case is kryptonite for originalist logic. Because if there's one thing most nineteenth-century white men who wrote, debated, and adopted the Fourteenth Amendment were dead set against, it was the social equality of the races. I could make an argument that the Fourteenth Amendment wouldn't have even been ratified if the white men supporting it thought it meant their daughters could marry Black people. There is no originalist understanding of the Fourteenth Amendment that comports with the Supreme Court's unanimous opinion in *Loving*. Either our understanding of the Fourteenth Amendment "evolved" to include a rejection of racist anti-miscegenation laws, or it didn't. If the Fourteenth Amendment doesn't evolve, Alabama could force people to submit "pure-blood" certifications from Ancestry.com before issuing marriage licenses, and we'd need a whole different constitutional amendment to stop them. Originalism has no satisfactory answer for *Loving*, and originalists expose the whole intellectual bankruptcy of their ideology when they try to fashion one.

And boy, do they try. Steven Calabresi, the man who founded the Yale Law School chapter of the Federalist Society and who is one of the guys the originalists deploy to do their "big think" arguments, wrote a 2012 law review article that tried to square originalism with *Loving*. It's notable for its intellectual dishonesty and desperate reliance on an actual dictionary. Yeah, I'm not making that up. Despite all of the evidence that the people who wrote the Fourteenth

Amendment did not at all intend to authorize interracial marriage, Calabresi argues that the "original public meaning" of the Fourteenth totally included the equal protection of marriage, because of the dictionary definition of the words used. That's no different than looking up an eighteenth-century list of "punishments" and determining that since slavers used to shove fireworks up the backsides of misbehaving slaves and light them, that such a punishment is neither cruel nor unusual. But, this is what passes for intellectualism in the modern conservative movement.

Equally disingenuous but less intellectually pathetic is Antonin Scalia's defense of *Loving*. Scalia writes that *Loving* was correctly decided because anti-miscegenation laws were "designed to maintain White Supremacy." He writes: "A racially discriminatory purpose is always sufficient to subject a law to strict scrutiny, even a facially neutral law that makes no mention of race."

It would be tempting to take Scalia at his word—that he actually believes it's necessary to apply strict scrutiny to a law that has a racially discriminatory purpose—if not for the context in which he wrote that.

But that's a line I pulled from Scalia's dissent in *Lawrence v. Texas*. That 2003 case dealt with Texas's "anti-sodomy" law. Police, in response to a (made-up) call about a domestic disturbance, busted into the home of John Geddes Lawrence Jr.* They found him engaged in a consensual sex act with another man, Tyron Garner. They were arrested and charged with a violation of Texas's Homosexual Conduct Act and held in jail overnight. They pleaded no

---

* Lawrence actually hosted two men that night, Garner and a man named Robert Eubanks. Eubanks apparently left the apartment to "go to a vending machine" but was actually infuriated that Lawrence and Garner were flirting. He called the cops alleging there was "a black man going crazy with a gun." Eubanks later pleaded guilty to making a false police report.

contest to the charges and appealed their convictions. Their case eventually ended up at the Supreme Court.

There, by a vote of 6–3, the Supreme Court invalidated the Texas law and anti-sodomy laws generally. Justice Anthony Kennedy wrote the majority opinion and found that anti-sodomy laws violate the due process clause of the Fourteenth Amendment.

Scalia's dissent rests on the fallacy that discriminating on the basis of race is wrong but discriminating on the basis of sexual orientation is okay. And his argument that some discrimination is okay is literally the same logic used by the court in *Plessy*, and the same logic advanced by the Commonwealth of Virginia in *Loving*.

> Finally, I turn to petitioners' equal-protection challenge, which . . . [o]n its face . . . applies equally to all persons. Men and women, heterosexuals and homosexuals, are all subject to its prohibition of deviate sexual intercourse with someone of the same sex.
>
> . . .
>
> The objection is made, however, that the antimiscegenation laws invalidated in Loving v. Virginia . . . similarly were applicable to whites and blacks alike, and only distinguished between the races insofar as the partner was concerned. In Loving, however, . . . the Virginia statute was "designed to maintain White Supremacy." Id., at 6, 11. A racially discriminatory purpose is always sufficient to subject a law to strict scrutiny, even a facially neutral law that makes no mention of race.

It's simply not an intellectually honest opinion. Scalia can't use literally the same logic as the majority in *Plessy*, and then have anybody credible believe that he actually would have voted with the lone dissenter in that case. And he can't ignore the views of the white people who ratified the Fourteenth Amendment—views that were specifically opposed to interracial marriages—in *Loving*, and then suddenly tell me that their views are critical when trying to make a case for bigotry against gay people in *Lawrence*. I will stipulate that the people who ratified the Fourteenth Amendment hated Black people marrying white people *and* gay people marrying each other. Scalia has to tell me why that hatred should matter in one case but not the other. Because all the Fourteenth Amendment says is that the country cannot deny any "person" the equal protection of laws, and since I'm not a raging homophobe, I'd like us to use a modern definition of the word "person," thank you very much. Tell me I'm wrong.

And Tyron Garner is Black, by the way. Indeed, it is unlikely Lawrence would have gotten into any trouble at all had he been caught that night having sex with a white man. *Loving* and *Lawrence* are functionally the same case; they are logical twins.

The operative difference between *Loving* being decided 9–0 and *Lawrence* being decided 6–3 is that conservatives have successfully adopted a new language to couch their bigotry. That language is now called originalism. I absolutely believe that the three dissenters in *Lawrence* would have dissented in *Loving* if they had been on the Court at that time. I absolutely believe that the current Court, packed as it is with conservatives, would rule against Lawrence, 5–4, if they caught the case today. Conservatives have the votes, now, to do evil they could only dream about twenty years ago.

The current Supreme Court has more in common with the court in *Plessy* than the court in *Loving*. The only real difference between conservatives in 1896 and the ones we have today is that the Federalist Society teaches them how to edit out their bigoted slurs.

14

REVERSE RACISM IS NOT A THING

Having explained why I think a robust interpretation of the equal protection clause of the Fourteenth Amendment could be used to cleanse this country of much of its legalized bigotry and racial discrimination, I would be remiss if I didn't point out that in reality you can, of course, discriminate against most people, most of the time, for most any reason, or no reason at all.

Speaking just for me, I'm prejudiced against dumb people. Not uneducated people, who I feel simply haven't been given the chance at education and knowledge, but dumb people, who have had all the education and knowledge thrown at them, only to see it bounce off their information-resistant brains. Like Republicans, for instance. If you go to a good school and have access to good professors and good books and you come out as a *Republican*, I'm prejudiced against you. I assume you're defective, in some way. I wouldn't want you to marry into my family. Like, I can't look at Yale Law School graduate and U.S. senator Josh Hawley without assuming he's at least one-eighth fucking idiot, you know.

Discriminating against dumb people is not controversial. Employers, arguably, do it all the time. Public colleges and universities do it too. Oh, we might quibble on the criteria for *dumb* but, as a general rule, denying someone a job or opportunity because they aren't smart enough to have it is legal and clearly constitutional. In fact there are all kinds of discriminations that do not trip any constitutional wires: firefighters have to be strong, pilots generally need to be able to see, underwear models have to look good in their underwear.

One way to think about our equal protection laws are as a long-running argument about what kinds of discrimination our society will allow, and who we can discriminate against.

The government can never discriminate against an individual person. That is directly in the Constitution, Article 1, Section 9: "No Bill of Attainder . . . shall be passed." A "bill of attainder" is a law directed at a specific person. Sadly, for me, a law that said "Nobody named Josh Hawley can be a U.S. senator" would be unconstitutional on its face.

But laws can discriminate against classes of people, and laws do discriminate against classes of people all the time. Indeed, there are only a few classes of people who *cannot* be discriminated against. We call them "suspect" or "protected" classes. In my travels around the internet, I've found the concept of protected classes to be one of those things that really confuses or angers the white "economic grievances" crowd. Federalist Society heroes hate being reminded that white people are not a protected class. Incels (involuntarily celibate) white boys on Twitter do not understand why racist dickheads aren't a protected class either.

The equal protection clause still gives the government wide latitude to pass laws that discriminate against most classes of people, but only a limited and highly controversial ability to discriminate against suspect classes. I'd like to give you a clean definition of what constitutes a suspect class, and, given the importance of that distinction in the law, you'd think there would be one. But there's not. There's no definition that everybody agrees to, and certainly no definition that survives whatever conservatives think to do to this area of the law next.

In general, suspect classes (which can also be called protected classes, because, again, this is an area where courts have decided, "Let's wing it") are groups that can be labeled by their race, religion, national origin, or immigration status. Some argue that being "historically singled out for discrimination" is key to the classification. Some argue that people of a "discrete and insular minority" should be considered members of a suspect class. Others think that the classification should be given to people based only on "immutable characteristics."

More or less, the difference between suspect classes and everybody else is why a policy like affirmative action is facially constitutional. As a class, white people are not suspect. Please don't drag me out of my home and lynch me over a fire, white folks who feel suddenly aggrieved. I'm just the messenger.

No matter what your definition of *suspect class* is, it's hard to fit all of white-dom into it. White people have not been historically singled out for discrimination and torment because of their immutable characteristics. They're not a minority (as of this writing). They're neither discrete nor insular. Lots of white people like to act like they are the "default" people in this country and, well, the law treats them as such.

Now, you could make an argument that there are certain kinds of white people who are members of a suspect class, and that's an argument I and a lot of liberals and progressives love to make. I'd love to see a legal ruling that counts poor people as a suspect class.

But the thing that pisses off some white people is that I won't make an argument that whiteness is the thing that is suspect (as opposed to poverty, for instance). Because whiteness is not suspect. Not in this country. Not ever. To call white people a suspect class is to render the entire phrase meaningless.

These classifications are given meaning by courts who use them to decide how to review laws under the equal protection clause. It turns out: not all laws are created equal. Laws, rules, and ordinances that target suspect classes trigger "strict scrutiny" review by courts. State actions that don't involve suspect classes are given what's called "rational basis" analysis by courts.

That's a lot of jargon. It's a little like explaining how a car works from the perspective of a mechanical engineer: "The four-stroke internal combustion engine mixes fuel, usually refined gasoline, with oxygen to produce internal explosions that power two to twelve torque-producing cylinders." Most people can get by just knowing: that pedal means stop, that other pedal means go. Here, *strict scrutiny* means "stop." If the government does something and the courts apply strict scrutiny, usually that's the ball game, and the government has to stop what it's doing. Everything else means "go."

But it's worth unpacking the jargon a little bit, because courts use it to hide what they're really doing.

Let's start at the top. Federal courts, comprised as they are of unelected old people who are appointed for life and are thus unaccountable to the people, are supposed to assume that most legislative acts are constitutional. Remember, the fact that the Supreme Court has any right at all to declare a legislative act unconstitutional is *kinda* made up. The Supreme Court claimed the power of judicial review—which is the power to invalidate laws—in the 1803 case known as *Marbury v. Madison*. In that case, Chief Justice John Marshall just announced that the Supreme Court could declare a law or order unconstitutional, even though that's not technically written in the Constitution.

That's fine by me; somebody's got to do it. But most people agree that the Court should use that power sparingly. Courts are supposed to give what's called "deference" to the elective bodies. For the most part, if the legislature or executive has a reason for doing something, courts should defer to their will.

This level of judicial review is called rational basis. If the government has the authority to pass a law, and that law has a "legitimate state interest," and the law passed is "rationally related to that interest," the law should be upheld. Seatbelt laws are a fine example of a law that survives rational basis review: the state has a legitimate interest in public safety, and wearing seatbelts is rationally related to keeping people alive, therefore seatbelt laws are constitutional, notwithstanding the idiotic complaints of always-wrong libertarians who claim a constitutional right to die in whatever way seems best to them. (The same logic should apply to, say, mask mandates during a pandemic, but I didn't want to use a *controversial* example of the government's constitutional authority to use basic science when it passes laws.)

But sometimes courts empower themselves to look at the government's rules more skeptically, with less deference to the wisdom of legislatures. This level of judicial review is called strict scrutiny. Under strict scrutiny review, the state has to show a "compelling governmental interest." And then the state must prove its law is "narrowly tailored to achieve that interest." Note the word changes! Courts need a *compelling* interest instead of merely a *legitimate* one, and now they need the law to be *narrowly tailored* instead of simply *rationally related* to the interest at hand.

Again, all of this is kind of made up. One court said: "We're going to review this with heightened scrutiny," and another court said, "Ooh, I like that, let's do that also, but can we change the adjective to *strict*?" and so on, until we have this entire canon of common law defining wildly different standards for when the court can use the power it gave to itself. There's nothing *in* the Constitution that requires courts to have different modalities for judicial review, and there's certainly nothing requiring courts to define those different standards the way they have.

If it were up to me, I'd change my "standard of review" based on the diversity of the legislature passing the law or regulation. *Did minorities and women get a say in this ordinance?* If so, sure, as long as it's not clearly stupid, it should probably be constitutional. *Did y'all really pass this with an all-white or disproportionately white legislature? Really? What year is this?* If so, I'm not inclined to give you people any deference at all.

But, it's not up to me. Courts have gone almost 240 years without giving a shit about what I think (or, more importantly, what people similarly situated to me think), and I imagine they'll go for 240 more so long as we're not all swallowed by the rising seas.

There is, however, a catch. Courts really apply strict scrutiny review to only two areas of law: laws that might violate the Fourteenth Amendment, and laws affecting the freedoms of speech, association, and religious affiliation enshrined in the First Amendment.

Strict scrutiny in the speech context could apply to damn near anybody. But in the equal protection context, strict scrutiny kicks in only for laws targeting members of a suspect class. Hence the legal importance of that classification.

As if all of that weren't random enough, courts have also created something called quasi-suspect classes, which are entitled to (wait for it) "intermediate scrutiny." The Supreme Court first applied this new scrutiny to laws that discriminate due to gender in a case called *Craig v. Boren*. There the Court held that while gender does not create a suspect class, laws discriminating between the gender classifications are "disfavored." The Court has also extended quasi-suspect class status to bastards (like, literal bastards, actual people whose "legitimacy is questioned at birth"). Intermediate scrutiny is said to require the state to show "important" government interests, and the law must be "substantially" related to that interest.

Get it? *Suspect class* triggers *strict scrutiny*, which requires *compelling* government interest with laws *narrowly tailored* to meet those goals. *Quasi-suspect class* triggers *intermediate scrutiny*, which requires *important* government interests with laws *substantially* related to those goals. And *nonsuspect classes* get *rational basis*, which requires *legitimate* government interests with laws *rationally* related to those goals.

All of this is bullshit. It's bullshit so the courts can argue that they have some objective, doctrinal reason for their decisions, because judges and justices don't like to admit that they are being "outcome determinative" in their rulings. "Oh, no, it's not that I hate women, I just think that their quasi-suspect class status does not entitle them to strict scrutiny when they bitch and nag. . . . I mean, go ahead and file lawsuits objecting to statutes that deny them equal access to health care. Golly gee, I'm just a judge here to call balls and strikes, not make policy."

In reality, judges and courts are being subjectively outcome determinative all the time. If courts like the outcome the law produces, the law will magically survive even strict scrutiny review. And if judges or justices don't like the law's outcome, well, then, they can make the laws fail even under a rational basis standard.

I can prove that. Because the first time the Supreme Court articulated strict scrutiny review was in the 1944 case *Korematsu v. United States*—the World War II Japanese internment case. The Court ruled that Franklin Delano Roosevelt's Executive Order 9066—which provided for the forced "relocation" of Japanese Americans living on the West Coast—should be reviewed under strict scrutiny, but concluded that the government passed the strict scrutiny test because of the government's national security interest. Speaking for the majority, Justice Hugo Black said:

> It should be noted, to begin with, that all legal restrictions which curtail the civil rights of a single racial group are immediately suspect. That is not to say that all such restrictions are unconstitutional. It is to say that courts must subject them to the most rigid scrutiny. Pressing public necessity may sometimes justify the existence of such restrictions; racial antagonism never can.

Spare me the platitudes, I don't know how you get more racially antagonistic than forcibly removing people from their homes and *concentrating them in camps*, just because of their race. Justice Black's *Korematsu* decision was animated by the same racist rationale that governed the Court's decision in *Plessy v. Ferguson*, albeit without Justice Harlan's flair for derogatory racial slurs in the dissent.

I'm sure the *Korematsu* Court thought itself much more evolved than the *Plessy* Court. I know the current Court thought itself much more evolved than the *Korematsu* Court. Chief Justice John Roberts even explicitly overruled *Korematsu*, in *Trump v. Hawaii*, a case where the Supreme Court used *Korematsu*'s exact logic to uphold Donald Trump's Muslim ban. The Supreme Court excels at using new jargon to smuggle in the same old bigotry.

If these doctrinal standards of review were "real," a reasonably intelligent person should be able to tell me where to put the LGBTQ community. Are they a suspect class, a quasi-suspect class, or no distinct class at all? Go ahead, noodle it out, I'll wait . . .

If you ask me, the LGBTQ community is clearly a suspect class. Members of that community have been historically singled out for discrimination, have an immutable characteristic (any "conversion therapy" acolytes reading can kiss my ass), and are members of a distinct minority.

But Justice Anthony Kennedy apparently disagreed with me.

Kennedy, who for all intents and purposes is a tolerance hero for his tie-breaking decisions recognizing gay rights (striking down anti-sodomy laws in *Lawrence v. Texas*, invalidating the Defense of Marriage Act in *United States v. Windsor*, striking down laws banning same-sex marriage in *Obergefell v. Hodges*) never went the last yard to give the LGBTQ community protected class status. He thus never fully protected the community within the equal protection clause. In fact, at times he struggled to make a cogent argument for why the LGBTQ community should have equal protection under the Fourteenth Amendment at all. Writing in *The New Republic*, Brian Beutler went so far as to call Kennedy's opinion in the *Obergefell* case a "logical disaster":

> Kennedy alluded to the existence of an equal protection argument, but, as Roberts wrote in his dissent, "The majority [did] not seriously engage with this claim. Its discussion is, quite frankly, difficult to follow." Roberts is correct. Kennedy failed "to provide even a single sentence explaining how the Equal Protection Clause supplies independent weight for its position." This was Team Marriage Equality's strongest ground, and Kennedy surrendered it against a mostly unarmed adversary. In the end, Roberts offered the Court's only real equal protection argument (or counterargument) and it was weak by necessity. "[T]he marriage laws at issue here do not violate the Equal Protection Clause, because distinguishing between opposite-sex and same-sex couples is rationally related to the States' 'legitimate state interest' in 'preserving the traditional institution of marriage.'"

I wouldn't go so far as to say that one of the most important gay rights victories was bad, but, in terms of the fight still to come, *Obergefell* was one of the biggest missed opportunities in modern constitutional history. This was no *Loving*. Kennedy's opinions leave the LGBTQ community exposed to less tolerant conservatives who can simply claim—as Roberts does, as Scalia always did—that the state has a legitimate interest in discriminating against gay people, and that legitimate interest is all they need.

Kennedy was no originalist, but he certainly was a Republican. He's certainly conservative. And, as I've said, the entire conservative project has been to limit the scope and effectiveness of the Fourteenth Amendment since the moment it was ratified. That's why Kennedy did what he did in these cases. He was able to stamp out a couple of specific examples of discrimination against the LGBTQ community without empowering the Fourteenth Amendment to do even more. His decision in *Masterpiece Cakeshop v. Colorado Civil Rights Commission*, discussed earlier, is scarcely intellectually possible if he had granted protected class status to the LGBTQ community in any of his other gay rights cases. But by keeping the equal protection clause on the sidelines, he had no problem finding that the bigoted baker was the *real* victim in that case.

That's why this jargon matters. It's something that judges and justices can hide behind when issuing rulings that the public would otherwise recognize as facially bigoted. These terms aren't "objective." Judges and justices can manipulate these terms to say, or not say, whatever they want, as their desired outcome requires.

Imagine understanding all of that and concluding that the most important equal protection fight we have on our hands is to make white conservative college professors a protected class. Imagine understanding even half of that and thinking: *But what about discrimination against white people?* Or men. Or some mediocre child of a B-list celebrity who's trying to get into USC? I literally cannot get the courts to agree that intentional state-sponsored bigotry against gay people violates the freaking Constitution, but I'm supposed to stop and consider the class status of discrete and insular white people living in Appalachia who feel left behind by the culture.

White people complaining of "reverse racism" need to help themselves to a number and stand at the back of the line. White people are still too busy legislating bigotry against actual minorities and trying to manipulate the equal protection clause to justify it. Let's fix that first, and then we can talk about various "economic grievances."

15

THE RULE THAT
MAY OR MAY NOT EXIST

I have two children. Two little boys. As I write this, they are eight and five, though it often feels like I'm living through a real-life "Team Edward vs. Team Jacob" saga from the Twilight movies. I've got one brooding emo and one loyal hothead, and I'm often being asked to choose between them. One of them smacks the other one during some game neither of them should be playing, and they come to me demanding redress for the perceived injustices that have befallen them.

The five-year-old can handle himself, so I'm always tempted to just let them fight it out. My parenting philosophy is no different than my legal philosophy: everything starts in the Hobbesian state of nature, and I am entitled to some kind of prize for leaving it and entering society.

When dealing with my kids, the prize is quiet. Two boys fighting for physical control of one iPad is a recipe for a lot of noise. So I'm usually convinced to intervene in their conflicts. At least until the other iPad finishes charging.

I try not to be arbitrary. I know that a generation of sitcom dads has popularized the use of arbitrary power by beleaguered parents as a comedic art form, and I can play it that way for a laugh. But, I never want my kids to get comfortable acquiescing to arbitrary power from authority figures. That way lies middle management. I try to indulge them when they complain that something is "not fair." I don't take the easy way out; I don't think I've ever once asked them, "Who said life was supposed to be fair?" I try to explain to them my reasons for this decision or that one, at their level, in terms they can understand. And sometimes, when they point out that a current decision cannot be squared with a past ruling, I let them win. I've been talked into letting them stay up for an extra hour so many times that my eldest treats "bedtime" as the start of negotiations, not the end of his day.

But like I said, my ultimate goal, almost always, is to get them to shut the fuck up. I don't actually care about their fucking problems. They're small children living in a suburban home under a roof that never leaks with a fridge that never runs dry. They don't have "problems." They have an assortment of privileged complaints about the rapidity of their wish fulfillment. My kids literally think they're better off than Prince William's kids, because I've told them (lying, I assume) that the royal family won't let their children have video games. My (idiot) children would *gladly* trade rule of all England for an extra hour of *Super Mario Odyssey*.

Because I want all child-related conflicts to end as quickly as humanly possible, I do not guarantee nearly any rights to my kids. I don't always give them the right to speak, for instance. They certainly have no right against self-incrimination: in fact, they better incriminate themselves, before I find out what they did on my own. And, obviously, they're not entitled to any equal protection. Children are not a suspect class in my house, and "You are the older one so really it's your fault" is a line of argument my eldest is already very familiar with. My kids are going to be shocked when they read the Constitution: they're going to realize that both of their lawyer parents knew about all this stuff, yet consistently denied them basic human rights.

But one constitutional right I try to give them, all the time, is their right to "substantive due process." Rules are indeed supposed to be "fair," and I've decided that my children are entitled to a reliable, consistent, repeatable answer every time I deprive them of life, liberty, or the Nintendo Switch.

I'm going to pause for a moment to allow any originalists reading this to finish cursing and pick up this book that they've just thrown against a wall. They're *big mad* right now, because I've just said that the one constitutional right I give my kids is a thing that they do not believe is in the Constitution.

Arguably, substantive due process flows from the Fifth and Fourteenth Amendments, which both say that no person shall be deprived of "life, liberty, or property, without due process of law."

But there's not a universally agreed-upon definition for what "substantive due process of law" even means. Substantive due process is like an avenging Chupacabra: it might be a kind of dog, it might be a kind of cat, it might not even exist, but when it shows up in the night, it's going to suck the blood out of whatever it thinks deserves it.

I think the least controversial definition of the thing is that substantive due process protects *unenumerated* rights. The Constitution explicitly protects some rights, but it must protect other rights in order for the protection of the explicit rights to make any sense. For instance, the Constitution protects freedom of speech, but it doesn't explicitly protect freedom of sight. And yet, a government policy of gouging out the eyes of political dissidents would seem brazenly unconstitutional. The freedom of the press is not secured "because of Braille." The government shouldn't be able to say: "The

First Amendment is not troubled, for we left them their tongues." We don't need an entire additional constitutional amendment to explicitly protect the right to have eyes. Forced blinding is substantively violative of the due process clause of the Constitution. The end.

As Voltaire might say: "If substantive due process did not exist, it would be necessary to invent it."

That's because substantive due process is really about fundamental fairness. The best way to understand substantive due process is to compare it to the other kind of process, "procedural due process."

Procedural due process concerns itself only with whether the process is fair according to its own rules. Taking a number to be served at a deli is procedurally fair. I take the ticket, the guy behind the counter calls out a number, when he calls out my number, I am served, regardless of my race, color, or creed. Fair. A violation of that procedural due process would be somebody cutting ahead of me in line, or somebody going up when their number was not called and being served anyway. That's not procedurally fair and, in Brooklyn, that may be legal justification for assault (this may be a good time to reiterate that I'm not currently a licensed attorney).

But what if I'm at one of those gentrified delis where, instead of having a person call out the number, they just post it on a screen? And what if I've had my eyes gouged out, because, in this iteration of the multiverse, sight is not fundamentally protected? Does the deli still have a fair process?

Procedurally, yes: I came in, got my number, and had an opportunity to be served when my number came up. Substantively, no: I have no eyes and I'm still hungry. Even though I have no constitutional right to a sandwich, I must have some fundamental right to be served when it's my turn. At the very least, arguing that I was afforded due process by the screen I can't see would be a cruel joke that only Antonin Scalia would find funny.

Substantive due process demands actual fairness, not just technical fairness. Predictably, conservatives hate it. Conservatives reject
a view of the law that guarantees fairness. And conservatives hate
unenumerated rights, because unenumerated rights could be whatever I (or five justices on the Supreme Court) say they are. Today I
claim an unenumerated right to have eyes. Tomorrow I might claim
an unenumerated right to reasonable accommodations should my
sight be taken from me. In the future, I might claim an unenumerated right to have Geordi's visor from *Star Trek* made available to me, free of charge, from a universal health care provider.
"Where does it end?" asks the conservative jurist. What's the point
of winning the birth lottery if the government is just going to step
in and level the playing field? Conservatives are always worried that
protecting too many rights might one day lead to a society that's
fundamentally fair.

What's frustrating here is that conservatives do have a glint of a
point. There must be some limiting principle to the unenumerated
rights protected through substantive due process. It can't just mean
whatever five unelected, unaccountable judges say it means. I don't
have a fundamental constitutional right to, say, have consensual sex
with my mother, right? Surely the same principle that prevents the
state from gouging out my eyes does not require that the state recognize mother-fucking marriages?

You don't even have to slide all the way down to the Oedipal end
of the slippery slope to get to the problem of unchecked substantive
due process. You just need to look at a 1905 case called *Lochner v.
New York*.

The case involved New York's Bakeshop Act, which limited the
number of hours bakers could work to no more than sixty hours in
a week and no more than ten hours in a day. Business owner Joseph
Lochner "permitted" one of his employees to work more than sixty
hours, and was fined under the statute. Lochner objected.

The Supreme Court ruled, 5–4, that New York's statute violated the due process clause of the Fourteenth Amendment by taking away the worker's "liberty" to work himself to the bone for capitalist paymasters. That's not a direct quote, but you take my point. The Court found that the employee had a fundamental right to contract that could not be abridged by a law designed to prevent employers from abusing their workers.

Between 1905 and 1937, courts used *Lochner* logic to invalidate over two hundred regulations on the grounds of violated economic rights. This sad historical period is known as the *Lochner* era, and, had it persisted, the New Deal would never have been a thing. But in 1937, Franklin Delano Roosevelt announced his plan to pack the Supreme Court with justices more amenable to his New Deal, worker-protecting regulations. And, also in 1937, Justice Owen Roberts broke with *Lochner*-supporting conservative justices and sided with the liberal faction to uphold the constitutionality of a minimum wage law. How closely linked these two events were is still a debate among legal scholars that I do not care about enough to have an opinion on. The important thing is that the Lochner anti-worker era stopped.

Lochner is, for the most part, a dirty word in polite legal company. For a long time, both liberals and conservatives agreed that the case was wrongly decided. The revulsion to *Lochner* was such that one could argue that the Warren Court during the civil rights era went out of its way to avoid mentioning *Lochner*, or using the phrase *substantive due process*, while issuing rulings that fit squarely in the framework of protecting rights not specifically enumerated in the Constitution. *Lochner* is sometimes called "anti-canon."

It's a classic liberal mistake: *conservatives used a tool for evil, so instead of using that same tool for good, let's never use tools.* Sometimes, I swear, it can seem like liberals spend all their time inventing ways to get their asses kicked.

Conservatives, on the other hand, are shameless. They say that

Lochner is bad and that substantive due process does not exist, but they will absolutely use Lochner-era logic to come to the Lochner-era conclusion that the only "people" who have rights in this country are corporations.

Indeed, the current conservatives on the Supreme Court are leading a *Lochner* resurgence in their eagerness to, once again, gut labor laws and regulations on businesses. In his article "A New *Lochner* Era," *Slate*'s Mark Joseph Stern describes Samuel Alito's majority ruling in *Janus v. American Federation of State, County, and Municipal Employees*—a 2018 case that severely limited the effectiveness of public sector unions—like this: "Justice Samuel Alito's majority opinion in *Janus* is the most egregious example of Lochner-ism in modern judicial history." He continues:

> *Janus* isn't shy about reviving *Lochner.* Alito's opinion points out that "into the 20th century, every individual employee had the 'liberty of contract' to 'sell his labor upon such terms as he deem[ed] proper.'" To support this proposition, he cites 1908's *Adair v. United States*—a defining decision of the *Lochner* era. Both *Lochner* and *Adair* rested on the premise that the Constitution protects an individual's right to sell his labor at any cost. This doctrine trammeled minimum wage and maximum hour rules, as well as laws safeguarding workers' right to unionize. *Janus* restores this premise in a slightly altered form, replacing "liberty of contract" with "associational freedoms." The upshot is the same: Laws designed to benefit labor's ability to act collectively are inherently suspect.

This is why conservatives cannot be taken at their word when they argue that substantive due process doesn't or shouldn't exist. Every time he decides to open his mouth on the subject, the notoriously reticent Clarence Thomas writes something like what he wrote in a 2011 case called *Perry v. New Hampshire:*

> [T]he Fourteenth Amendment's Due Process Clause is not a "secret repository of substantive guarantees against 'unfairness.'"

But did Thomas sign onto Alito's opinion in *Janus*? Of course his hypocritical ass did. He signed on in full: he didn't even write a concurring opinion reiterating his legally famous line about what the Fourteenth Amendment really means. Thomas, and the rest of the conservatives, absolutely believe substantive due process exists; they just think the Fourteenth Amendment is hiding rights for businesses they think are people, instead of minorities they wish were not.

If conservatives had a limiting principle for substantive due process, I'd listen to it. But they don't really; they just have a limiting principle on who should benefit from its existence.

Basically, conservatives treat the due process clause as if it's an evil djinn. It technically has to grant you three wishes—life, liberty, and property—but it hates you and is constantly trying to interpret your request in the most literal, least generous way so it can deny you the benefits of the very thing you asked it for. "You asked for the right to marry, you didn't say anything about the right to start a family: request for adoption denied, gay people. Mwahahaha."

Meanwhile, liberals treat the due process clause like it's the genie from Aladdin. Not only will it grant you your wishes of life, liberty, and property, it'll grant you whatever you need to make those things actually work. The genie wants to be your friend and wants to help you live your best life. Just don't let Samuel Alito steal the lamp, or else he'll use the genie to rule on high as the most powerful being on Earth.

I'll stipulate that neither of these approaches is perfect, but what kind of sick bastard thinks conservatives have the better view of things? What kind of wounded soul thinks that the conservative version is the way things are supposed to work?

For my part, I will keep telling my children that substantive due process is a thing. I will keep giving them the right to fairness.

Recently, my boys were playing the video game *Minecraft* together. My five-year-old likes to play *Minecraft* in the creative mode, where you just run around, gather supplies, and build things. My eight-year-old likes to play in survival mode, where many things can kill you and you mainly build things to stay alive. The five-year-old can't keep up in survival mode, so they were fighting. The older child came up with what he thought was an elegant, fair solution: they'd split their *Minecraft* hour, half of the time in creative mode, and the second half in survival mode. The eldest even agreed to let the youngest take his creative half hour first, which made him feel particularly magnanimous and smug.

Overhearing this deal from another room, I rushed in to tell them no. The five-year-old, I said, "has a right to enjoy his video game time without getting murdered." It's not easy to explain substantive due process to an eight-year-old, but damn it, I tried. It is important that they understand that technical equality is not necessarily fairness, and that sometimes such procedural equality can even be the opposite of fairness.

I'll keep trying. I'll keep trying to get them to think about rules substantively instead of procedurally. I'll keep trying to make them into the kinds of people who are outraged at unfairness, instead of desensitized to the suffering of others. I'll do whatever I can think of to make sure they grow up to be anything other than like Clarence Thomas.

16

THE ABORTION CHAPTER

No, the right to an abortion is not explicitly guaranteed in the text of the Constitution. Nowhere in the main document, or its twenty-seven amendments, does it say "Congress shall make no law restricting a woman's right to choose." Moreover, the right to privacy—from which reproductive rights, including the right to contraception, stem—is also not in the text of the Constitution. There's no amendment saying "The right to privacy shall not be abridged."

If you think that matters, I can't really help you. Of course reproductive rights are not textually enshrined in the Constitution. The white men who wrote the Constitution did not think women were people deserving of the same political, civil, and social rights as men. They didn't allow women to vote, didn't allow them to own property, and didn't allow them to sit on juries or hold public office. They thought girls could be married off, against their will, to secure social or political favors from other families. Once married off, they thought wives could be beaten and raped. *Marital rape* was an oxymoron *until the 1970s*, to give a sense of what is and is not *textually* protected in the Constitution. Every state in the union had laws making an exception to rape if the rapist and victim were married. The last of these marital rape exception laws didn't come off the books until 1993.

And that's how the men who wrote the Constitution treated the women they liked. Those were the rules for white women. Black women could be raped with total impunity and sold for higher prices to the white men most interested in raping them some more.

Did these white men perhaps care about children? No, they did not. Children, the ones who survived infancy anyway, could be put to work in the fields or beaten with sticks if they misbehaved. Again, girl children could be married off at the behest of their father. And, despite hobbling the economic opportunities for women and mothers, the framers of the Constitution provided no social safety net whatsoever for widows and orphans. Protecting children was just not something the framers thought the federal government had the power to do (put a pin in that thought).

And again, that's how white men treated children they liked. We know how they treated children they didn't like. Black children were no more than profit centers. Labor to be raised for the market like a lamb to be fattened for slaughter.

Horrifically, that view often extended even to the slavers' own children who were the offspring of violent rapes. The white men who founded this country were perfectly willing to let their own children, conceived in hate, be born into bondage.

It's a feature of chattel slavery, as practiced in the Americas, that scarcely has a historical analogy, and I think is too easily overlooked. White slavers regularly treated their own bastards as slaves. White neo-Confederates love to point out that "slavery" was practiced throughout much of the world, throughout much of human history, but this idea that slavery was a condition you could *inherit from birth* was not common in ancient slave-loving Rome or other slave-based societies. That idea was market-tested and industrialized in the New World.

Here, white Americans were not demanding that their bastards join the clergy, as was common in Europe. Or the army, as was common in the ancient world. Or defend a seven-hundred-foot-tall ice wall from zombies, grumkins, and ice dragons. Here, they were enslaving their own bastard children, condemning them to some of the most brutal bondage the world had ever known. And grandchildren. And also, of course, the children and grandchildren of every other enslaved woman who happened to get pregnant.

So, tell me again why I should care which rights these vicious assholes happened to think women had. Tell me again why the failure of these fucking rapists and/or rape apologists to recognize any explicit right to bodily autonomy should matter one bit to the polity in which we now all live. Don't you dare say "the rights of the unborn" to me. Don't you dare fix your lying mouth to tell me that these people who condemned their own progeny to bondage and torment, for the sin of being conceived in the womb of a colored woman—a woman they would continue to work and rape while she was pregnant with their child—gave one damn about the health and safety of "the unborn."

If we're going to talk about the constitutional right to an abortion, we're going to talk about it from first principles. And the first principle that the people who wrote the Constitution missed is that women are people. Full, equal, people. If you believe that, and I know a lot of men don't, but if you believe that women are people, then the right to privacy and all the reproductive rights that flow from it is a fairly straightforward thing.

The right to privacy was first recognized by the Supreme Court in a 1965 case called *Griswold v. Connecticut.* The case dealt with an 1879 Connecticut statute that banned the use of any drugs or medical devices that could lead to contraception. In 1961, Estelle Griswold, then the head of the Connecticut branch of Planned Parenthood, and Yale School of Medicine gynecologist C. Lee Buxton opened a birth control clinic. They counseled married couples on birth control and prescribed the best methods for those couples.

Their clinic opened on November 1, 1961. They were arrested on November 10, 1961.

Would these two have been arrested if they were handing out, say, condoms to single men, instead of birth control pills to married women? It's hard to say. I think the right answer is "absolutely not," but "probably not" could be more accurate. Consider that the Connecticut law in question is what's known as a Comstock law, which refers to a slew of federal laws and state laws that were passed during the U.S. Grant administration.

Anthony Comstock was an "anti-vice, Christian reformer," which I guess is a nice way of saying that he was such a tight-ass he could crush a lump of coal into a diamond. The man was apparently revolted by the "vice" he witnessed in New York City—especially advertisements announcing the availability of contraceptives—and made it his mission functionally to destroy everybody's good time.

I just don't get these people like Comstock, who we see again and again throughout human history. I don't understand these people who look at two consenting adults fucking and think, "Oh no, something must be done about this!" Who are these people, and how are there always so many of them? No matter what society you live in, there are deep social, economic, and political problems that need to be addressed. And yet there are *always* some people in that society who are willing to ignore all of those problems and make it their life's work to stop two people from getting busy in a Burger King bathroom. Of all the things to care about, some people invariably choose to care about recreational sex or the possibility thereof. Clothes were a fucking mistake. They send the wrong message.

Anyway . . . Comstock was successful (of course), and in 1873 Congress passed what came to be known as the Comstock Act, which made it illegal to use the federal mail to disseminate "obscene" materials. That included shipping contraceptives—including birth control or condoms—across state lines, as well as using the mail to distribute things like racy letters. I'm not joking: the Comstock Act made sexting illegal back when sexting required two weeks of delayed gratification and legible penmanship. Then they made Comstock a goddamn postal inspector! I'll bet all the money in my pocket that Comstock was "reviewing" potentially violative letters with a gallon of whale oil under his desk and a handkerchief.

The Comstock Act was then buttressed by a number of state laws making obscenity and contraception illegal in the various states, including the 1879 law passed in Comstock's home state of Connecticut.

None of these laws seemed violative of the Constitution by the people who passed them. And remember that the generation that passed the Comstock laws was the same generation that passed the Reconstruction Amendments. One of the clear failures of the Reconstructionists is that they remained unreconstructed sexists. Comstock himself was a Union infantryman in the Civil War. There's no original public meaning of any of the amendments that supports a right to contraception.

Still, by the time of *Griswold* in 1965, many of the Comstock laws had been scaled back. Margaret Sanger, the founder of Planned Parenthood, fought Comstock laws in court throughout the 1920s and '30s, and won some rights for women to use "birth control," a term she is largely responsible for coining. It also must be said that Sanger was an inveterate racist who sometimes tried to sell birth control as part of a larger eugenics plan eventually to eliminate the "Negro race."

So let me say once again, for the people in the back: I do not give one wet shit about the original intent of white folks. Their motives were horrible. Their intentions, barbaric. The public they allowed to have a voice well understood the horrible, barbaric meanings of their laws. And none of it should inform what rights we now have today, unless you are interested in bringing back the shitty, monstrous societies created by long dead white people.

The rights Sanger and others gained for women's contraceptives paled in comparison to the rights men had to control their reproductive decisions. During World War II, despite the statutory prevalence of various Comstock-type laws, condoms were distributed to every man in the military. Personally, I have little doubt that if Griswold and Buxton were handing out condoms and spermicide, nobody would have arrested them for violating a law that was nearly one hundred years old by the time they opened their clinic.

But they weren't just handing out condoms. Because on May 11, 1960, the Food and Drug Administration approved the first birth control pill.

At the risk of stating the obvious, and devolving into some cishet gender norms just because I'm talking about archaic legal restrictions written only with such norms in mind, condoms still leave much of the reproductive choice with the man. He can put one on, or not. Yes, of course the woman can ask or demand condom use, and men are supposed to respect that demand. But men weren't always even legally bound to respect such wishes in 1960. Again, marital rape wasn't even an illegal thing until the lifetimes of most people reading this book. Condoms, fundamentally, still give men a large amount of control over the decision to reproduce.

But the pill shifts reproductive choice back to the woman. It's not just about "liberating" women to have recreational sex (though it certainly does that), it's about giving women control over their reproductive systems. The pill allows the woman to decide if she wants to have kids (or additional kids), not her husband or lover.

The man doesn't get a vote, and (if she can get the pill and keep it secret) the man can't legally force her to bear his child. The man doesn't even get to know. Armed with the pill, a woman has just as much physical power to veto reproduction as a man.

That's why Griswold and Buxton were arrested after just ten days. It's not because they were handing out contraceptives; it's because they were handing out equality.

If you proceed from the premise that "women are people," the idea that women-people have a constitutionally protected right to control their own reproductive system is entirely obvious. Men-people get to do it. Even beyond the obvious point that biological men can engage in any sex act they like without risking having to pass a bowling ball through their penis nine months later, the facts on the ground show that men can get access to more or less reliable contraceptives even when laws ostensibly prohibit them. If a soldier could get a pack of condoms before whoring his way through Paris in 1945, denying his wife a birth control pill in 1960 seems like a point-and-click violation of the equal protection clause of the Fourteenth Amendment.

If I had decided *Griswold*, it would have been maybe a three-sentence opinion:

> Women, being people, have a right to control their reproductive system, as men-people do, through the use of contraceptives, which men-people seem to always be able to get their hands on when they really need to fuck a prostitute while on shore leave. This right flows from the Fourteenth Amendment's guarantee of Equal Protection, which we now recognize includes the right to have sexual intercourse without internal reproductive consequences. We note that men-people have technically enjoyed this right to sex-without-

incubation for five-to-seven million years, depending on when you start the clock on anatomically modern humans.

But the actual Court, by a vote of 7–2, took the scenic route to get to the right result in *Griswold*. Instead of deciding the case on equal protection grounds, the white guys on the Supreme Court did their usual thing of acting like the Connecticut contraception ban was "facially neutral" even though it plainly was not in either force or effect.

Instead of equal protection, Justice William O. Douglas divined a right to privacy from the so-called penumbras of other constitutional amendments. This is from his majority opinion: "The foregoing cases suggest that specific guarantees in the Bill of Rights have penumbras, formed by emanations from those guarantees that help give them life and substance. . . . Various guarantees create zones of privacy."

I know it sounds made up. Every liberal in law school has been dunked on by some facetious conservative dickhead (it's always a man) who incredulously asks which rights are emanating from a liberal penumbra today.

But I explained substantive due process before I started talking about the right to privacy for exactly this reason. Remember, in 1965, *substantive due process* was still a dirty phrase, made guilty by its association with the *Lochner* era. What Douglas is doing here is applying substantive due process logic in a place where it is entirely appropriate. Many of the rights explicitly protected in the Constitution don't make sense unless this unenumerated right to privacy is also protected. What good is a protection from unreasonable *searches* if there is no protection from being unreasonably *monitored*? What good is the right to form an association, if the FBI can just wiretap any meeting it doesn't like? What freedom do we really have if the government can shove a camera up your hooha to see if there's any funny business going on?

Of course privacy is a thing. The Constitution scarcely makes sense without it. Conservatives who mock the right to privacy are ironically the same people who think homeowners can shoot people to death should somebody invade their "castle." The right to privacy is just a substantive function of the due process clause. Douglas is just calling it something else because he doesn't want to use that phrase.

Justice Byron White was not as bashful. His concurring opinion states:

> In my view, this Connecticut law, as applied to married couples, deprives them of "liberty" without due process of law, as that concept is used in the Fourteenth Amendment.

None of the justices adopts my equal protection framework. Because, you know, once you start giving women equal protection of laws, the whole damn patriarchy starts to crumble. You'll note that *Griswold* applied to married women; it took a while for the court to extend its logic to unmarried women, but that extension would have happened immediately under an equal protection framework. God forbid they gave women suspect class status, triggering strict scrutiny of discriminatory laws and practices. Then they might even have to start paying women equally.

The decision not to give women protected class status or an equal protection right to contraception does matter, not so much for *Griswold*, but because of another case: 1973's *Roe v. Wade*. You've probably heard of it. But, in case alien archaeologists are reading this book (please, O Great Singularity, let this be the tome on late-republic American law they find, and not some trash written by

Antonin Scalia), *Roe v. Wade* recognized a constitutional right to abortion under the right to privacy and the due process clause of the Fourteenth Amendment. The Court's logic in *Roe* is the same as the Court's logic in *Griswold*, but in *Roe* the Court went out of its way to recognize a "legitimate state interest" in limiting abortions for the benefit of the health of the mother and "protecting the potentiality of human life."

Here's that part from the majority opinion of Justice Harry Blackmun:

> We repeat, however, that the State does have an important and legitimate interest in preserving and protecting the health of the pregnant woman, whether she be a resident of the State or a nonresident who seeks medical consultation and treatment there, and that it has still another important and legitimate interest in protecting the potentiality of human life. These interests are separate and distinct. Each grows in substantiality as the woman approaches term and, at a point during pregnancy, each becomes "compelling."

With respect to the state's important and legitimate interest in potential life, the "compelling" point is at viability.

You see what they did there? Remember, discriminatory laws are okay if they are rationally related to a "legitimate" state interest. Laws discriminating against suspect classes are okay if they are narrowly tailored to address a "compelling" state concern. Here, the Court is basically saying that most abortion restrictions after the first trimester are okay, and at fetal viability, nearly any can be justified.

It's almost like the protected class here is the fetus, and not the born, human, woman-person whose body is attached to it.

All of that came to a head in 1992 in *Planned Parenthood v. Casey*. It's *Planned Parenthood*, not *Roe*, that actually defines abortion rights in this country, such that they are. At issue were a host of abortion restrictions legislated by the state of Pennsylvania in the late '80s. They included "informed consent" before having an abortion (which mainly just involves some asshole trying to talk the woman out of her decision), waiting twenty-four hours before getting the procedure (again, just making people feel bad about it), obtaining parental consent if the patient is a minor (because, you know, anytime you can make teenage pregnancy harder, why not), and requiring married women to notify their husband before having the procedure (I already explained what anti-contraception laws are really about).

The Supreme Court, 5–4, upheld the fundamental right to an abortion, as articulated in *Roe*, but created a new standard for abortions. The Court asked if state abortion restrictions created an "undue burden" on women seeking the procedure prior to viability. It defined *undue burden* as a "substantial obstacle in the path of a woman seeking an abortion before the fetus attains viability." The majority (which included a woman on the Supreme Court for the first time in history, Justice Sandra Day O'Connor) determined that all but the husband notification passed this new test. Everything else—the informed consent, the waiting period, treating women like they're hysterical children who are about to cut their own hair without fully appreciating what they're doing—all of that stood.

I'd slam the majority more, but the dissenters would have overruled *Roe* altogether. I guess infantilizing women is better than turning them into incubators with mouthparts? The Republic of Gilead knows no bounds, I suppose.

The conclusion of *Planned Parenthood* is impossible to reach if you start from the principle that women are people and thus entitled to the same people rights as men. I say that even to those who think that the fetus is a person entitled to some rights. That's because we never, ever, limit a man's access to medical care based on how it will impact any other person. No man is ever denied medical care because of how that care might affect somebody else. You could be a fucking rapist and still get treated for erectile dysfunction. They never say, "I won't help you mask your genital herpes until I receive a signed consent form from your sexual partners." John Wilkes Booth broke his leg while (wait for it) shooting the goddamn president, and a doctor (rightly) set his leg so he could hobble on with his escape.

Where the fuck was his twenty-four-hour waiting period?

Forced-birth activists always like to tell stories about the growing fetus. *At thirty weeks it can cry tears like Jesus and think, "Why doesn't Mommy want me?"*

But instead of anthropomorphizing the fetus, let's never lose sight of the actual person in this story, the woman, and what the state is trying legally to force her to do.

Most women won't know they're carrying the state's legitimate interest for the first couple of weeks, but once the state's interest disrupts their menstrual cycle, a simple home test can detect the invasion of the state. By six weeks or so, the woman might start becoming violently ill. As the state's interest grows, a woman's bones will soften and her joints will stop functioning properly. By the end of the first trimester, she'll have created an entirely new organ, the placenta, which will start leaching nutrients from her bloodstream and feeding it to the state's interest. To compensate, the woman will start producing up to 50 percent more blood to transport oxygen around the body. Some of that extra blood can pool in weird places and be uncomfortable.

By the second trimester, most women can feel the state's interest kicking at them from the inside. I'm told that it's not particularly painful, but what is painful is the back pain. Women are putting on roughly a pound a week at this point, and the human back isn't really designed to carry the excess weight brought on by the state. It can also become difficult to sleep; the woman may experience leg cramps and heartburn, and she'll need to urinate frequently as the state's interest pushes some of her other organs out of the way and crushes down on her bladder.

By the third trimester, when the state's interest has developed from "legitimate" to "compelling," the woman who bears it will have trouble traveling, working, or just moving around easily. Given her burdens, one might expect the state to take a more active role in providing care and money to the woman so that its compelling interest may have its best chance at success. But the state does not. Many women continue to work so that they may provide for the state's compelling interest out of their own pockets. Many countries encourage women to take time off from work at this point, but in America we provide no federally mandated financial assistance to women bearing the state's interest to term.

Childbirth is still the ninth leading cause of death among women aged twenty to thirty-four in this country, and that itself is an amazing success story. In the not-too-distant past, childbirth killed many more women and is still today the leading cause of death for young women in parts of the developing world. That's because, if everything goes well, after about nine months or so, the state's compelling interest will erupt from its female host, tearing through her vaginal cavity in an experience so painful that the woman's brain will actually release drugs into her neural system in hopes that she doesn't fully remember the severity of what she experienced once it's over. The experience is so painful because of a basic design flaw in *Homo sapiens*: the baby's head is almost too big for the human birth canal. Humans are the only mammal that can't regularly give live birth alone. Women need help to do it.

Or so I've heard. I'm a man so I don't have to worry about the state renting out my insides until its compelling interest stretches my dick like a snake vomiting a live pig. Hell, I even stayed "north of the border" for the birth of my two kids. But, from what I've heard, it sounds bad. It sounds like the kind of thing a legitimate government could never even ask a person to do, much less force a fully human person to do if they were unwilling. If somebody ever got me pregnant, I'd punch him right in the fucking mouth and demand an abortion under my *Eighth* Amendment rights against cruel and unusual punishment.

Planned Parenthood's framework doesn't even make sense if you assume that women are people and thus deserving of equal protection. There is no framework that justifies denying them medical care, or balancing their access to care, because of the "state interest" in forcing them to engage in unwanted labor. No other operation of law forces a person to painfully change their body and reconfigure their organs because of a state interest in the results of that transformation.

It is wrong to force a woman to give birth to a baby she doesn't want. And I say that assuming that she consented to have sex in the first place, and that giving birth wouldn't actually kill her. It's barbaric to force a woman who had consensual sex to carry an unwanted pregnancy to term, even if she can carry that fetus to term safely. I don't even have a word for what it is to force a rape victim to carry her assailant's baby to term at the risk of her own life. I don't think there is a word for that.

But you rarely hear even liberals talk about abortion this way. Especially if you listen to liberal white men. The white male liberal talking point on abortion has been that it should be "safe, legal, and rare." Even Tim Kaine, Hillary Clinton's running mate in 2016, has talked about it that way. Liberals consistently fail to articulate an equal protection argument for abortion rights. They cede the "legitimate state interest" ground.

Conservatives talk about abortion like they're on a righteous crusade to stop a baby holocaust, while male liberals talk about it like they're embarrassed and sorry somebody knocked up the cheer-leader, but now here we are.

That's why abortion rights are under constant attack. It's not because the attacks are legally any better than what conservatives usually do. Their legal argument against abortion is the same as their legal argument against gay marriage and the same as the legal argument in favor of the death penalty. It's all one monster: they believe in a country that is limited to the best available thoughts of racist, long dead, white men.

No, what makes abortion difficult is not some fancy lawyering from the right, but the near refusal to defend it from the left. The hard sell is almost always left to women and "abortion activists," while men scramble around trying not to piss off a diner in Ohio. I can turn over a rock on Twitter and find some person with no legal training able to passionately explain why segregation is wrong, or why the death penalty is immoral, or how "love is love." But ask people about abortion and it's all, "Well . . . I think the important thing is that women get to choose for themselves! Retweet if you agree!"

Don't get me wrong, "choice" is great. It's a fine frame. It's a language designed to appeal to people who have a genuinely held religious belief about when life begins, and even the word *choice* should remind those adherents that not everybody shares their choice of God either, and yet we co-exist.

But the better legal frame is "Forced birth is some evil shit that can never be compelled by a legitimate government. The end."

Hell, if you don't like my Eighth or Fourteenth Amendment arguments in defense of abortion rights, I could give some *Thirteenth* Amendment arguments. Because the same amendment that prohibited slavery *surely* prohibits the state from renting out women's bodies, for free, for nine months, to further its interests. Forced *labor* is already unconstitutional.

17

YOU KNOW THIS THING CAN BE AMENDED, RIGHT?

The astute reader will have noticed that a central theme of this book is that conservatives are irredeemable assholes who consistently act in bad faith to uphold white supremacy and patriarchy over the objection of most minorities, women, and decent people.

But perhaps I am wrong about them. Perhaps conservatives simply promote an inert theory of constitutional interpretation because they genuinely believe that legislatures—the "people's" body—is the appropriate place to enshrine "new" fundamental rights. Perhaps conservatives are not desperately committing to *upholding* white male supremacy and patriarchy, they just honestly believe that the only legitimate way to move beyond our white male supremacist roots is through additional amendments recognizing our evolution as a society, as opposed to interpreting old ones with modern sensibilities.

That's certainly what conservatives will tell you they're doing. The ones who can at least be sufficiently shamed into admitting the

deep and abiding unfairness and bigotry of their pet interpreta-
tional theories always use the amendments process as an out. "Oh,
it's not that I think the state should invade a person's home, drag
them out of bed, and subject them to humiliation and jail because
they engaged in a consensual sex act with a person of the same sex.
Goodness, no! It's just that pesky Constitution that doesn't prohibit
the state from doing that. It's a shame, really. If only there were
some amendment that allowed me to put a stop to it."

But even here, this fallback position of the allegedly reasonable
conservative can be shown to be a lie. Because the people who
believe in the most shallow and vindictive version of the Constitution are never at the vanguard of amending it.

Here's how the amendment conversation always goes:

Conservative: "Turns out, this machine I'm driving stabs gay
people in the face."

Reasonable Person: "Oh my God! Turn it off."

Conservative: "Can't."

Reasonable Person: "What do you mean you can't? You're in the
goddamn driver's seat."

Conservative: "Won't."

Reasonable Person: "Why?"

Conservative: "Look, we need this machine to get where we're
going."

Reasonable Person: "Who is the we?"

Conservative: "Those of us allowed to drive."

Reasonable Person: "It just stabbed Bob in the face!"

Conservative: "Yeah. Sucks for Bob. If only there was something we could do."

Reasonable Person: "STOP DRIVING IT."

Conservative: "Can't. Oops, sorry, I mean won't. Hey, maybe you could fix it?"

Reasonable Person: "It can be fixed?"

Conservative: "Maybe. Here's the manual."

Reasonable Person: "Okay, it says here that if you and I turn these two keys at the same time, it will stop stabbing gay people. Here's your key."

Conservative: "Thanks." [swallows key]

Reasonable Person: "Oh my God, why did you do that?"

Conservative: "I don't think it needs to be fixed."

Reasonable Person: "It just stabbed Jillian in the face!"

Conservative: "See, it's working as intended."

Reasonable Person: "HELP ME FIX IT!"

Conservative: "Can't. Haha. I mean won't. Whatever. Fuck Jillian."

If they really thought that the organizing document of American self-government didn't, on its face, protect gay people having sex in their own home, or protect Black people from driving without police harassment, or protect women who get a prescription from their doctor, then wouldn't they spend nearly their whole life trying to change such an obviously flawed document? If conservative judges felt they were being forced, for purely doctrinal reasons, to deny fundamental fairness to worthy litigants, wouldn't they spend all their free time begging the people to update the document that binds them to upholding unjust laws?

But we don't see them doing that, do we? We don't see conservative justices demanding a better, more fair Constitution than the one they claim we're stuck with. Instead we see these justices regularly giving talks at fundraising dinners of the Federalist Society, praising the limitations and cruelty of the current Constitution, promising to rule for more of the same, and vowing to defeat the "liberals" who imagine the country as something better than it is. We see the conservative politicians who appoint and confirm conservative judges constantly argue against the amendments that would bring fairness and equality to the document their judges have decided doesn't already include it. And we see conservative jurists, throughout American history, work to limit the scope and effectiveness of what amendments have been passed to make us a more perfect union.

Maybe conservatives don't want the Constitution fixed. Maybe conservatives aren't being entirely intellectually honest when they claim to prefer new amendments to secure rights. Maybe they just don't believe that some people deserve rights at all. Maybe conservatives limit the amendments that should give gay people and Black people and women-people equal rights, because conservatives don't want them to have equal rights.

How many times does the hunter have to shoot Bambi's mom before we stop blaming the deer that got in the way and turn our attention to the person who pulled the trigger?

Nowhere is the intellectual dishonesty of the conservative movement more obvious than in the fight over the Equal Rights Amendment.

Throughout the 1960s and '70s an effort was made to amend the Constitution explicitly to recognize the equality of the sexes. An

Equal Rights Amendment was first proposed back in 1923. The goal was to eliminate legal distinctions between men and women.

By the 1970s, the proposed text of the amendment read:

> Section 1: Equality of rights under the law shall not be denied or abridged by the United States or by any State on account of sex.
>
> Section 2: The Congress shall have the power to enforce, by appropriate legislation, the provisions of this article.
>
> Section 3: This amendment shall take effect two years after the date of ratification.

This is the version of the ERA that finally passed the House of Representatives in 1971. In 1972, the U.S. Senate passed it and submitted it to the states for ratification.

It never made it. The conservative movement, organized under lawyer Phyllis Schlafly, prevented it from being ratified by three-fourths of the states' legislatures, as required to amend the Constitution.

Now, my read of the Constitution tells me that the Equal Rights Amendment is redundant. Remember, I think that the equal protection and due process clauses of the Fourteenth Amendment do *all* the work. Of course women are entitled to equality under the law. Of course that includes employment rights, health and safety protections, and the economic right to equal pay for equal work. Of course women have the substantive right to control their own bodies, including their reproductive system, and to access medical care.

I support the ERA, because sometimes you have to really dumb things down for men to get it. But if you ask me, the Equal Rights

Amendment was ratified in 1868 and the problem is that white guys have spent the last 150 years trying to undo it.

If you don't agree with me—if you *don't* think that the Fourteenth Amendment provided for the full political, civil, and social equality of women—then how in hell are you against the ERA? How can you possibly think that women don't already have equal rights because of your limited, originalist interpretation of the Constitution, but also don't think the Constitution should be changed to right this clear wrong that your interpretation has created?

Unless, at core, you don't think women should have equal rights at all.

The denial of equal rights was what motivated the anti-ERA movement. Schlafly's organization, called STOP, an acronym for "Stop Taking Our Privileges," argued that the ERA would end the gender privileges "enjoyed" by women: like "dependent" wife status for social security benefits, women's restrooms, and exemption from the draft.

Schlafly employed the same two tactics that conservatives always do when attacking equal rights. She reduced equal treatment to "same" treatment and fought most desperately over social equality instead of political or civil equality. This is what conservatives do. This is what they always do. Schlafly had a neat little twist—arguing that social inequality *benefited* women instead of harming them— but even that is not new. Conservatives love arguing that the people they oppress are well taken care of by the oppressors. One prominent conservative once said: "Slaves that worked there were well fed and had decent lodgings provided by the government, which stopped hiring slave labor in 1802."

That quote isn't from a Southerner who was about to beat John Lewis, or former Confederate president Jefferson Davis. That was former Fox cable news host Bill O'Reilly, describing the slaves who built the White House. He said that in 2016. It only sounds like it could have been said by a long-dead conservative, because conservatives have been making the same shitty arguments for all of American history.

In any event, the "privileges" that Schlafly wanted to "stop" the ERA from taking were white women privileges, naturally. Shirley Chisholm, who in 1972 became the first Black woman to run for president, was not the beneficiary of the social privileges Schlafly was so worried about losing. Indeed, her fight to be taken seriously by the political establishment was contemporaneous with Schlafly's fearmongering about what women's "liberation" would mean for America.

Even Schlafly's most effective attack—saying that the ERA would lead to the compulsory draft of women into the armed services—is the kind of thing that is centered in whiteness. Putting aside the issue that an actual draft which fairly called upon all citizens and didn't exempt rich white boys with bone spurs might be the only thing that could arrest this country's habitual global warmongering, the fact is that women and Black women in particular have long broken the infantilizing social mores against women in service. A Pew Research Center report conducted in 2011 found that between 1973 and 2010, the number of active-duty enlisted women grew from 42,000 to 167,000. Over 30 percent of those women are Black. That's despite Black women accounting for only about 13 percent of women in America as a whole.

The world that Phyllis Schlafly despaired for white women already exists for Black women. All that's missing is explicit legal protection for their health and economic rights. Help Black women or get out of their goddamn way.

None of this is to say that conservatives are dead set against *any* amendments to the Constitution. They're generally down for damn near anything that can be used to prevent the government from helping people: a balanced-budget amendment, a line-item veto. If you can show how your amendment will restrict the government's ability to meet modern challenges, the Federalist Society will at least take you out to lunch.

But when it comes to expanding rights, there's really only one amendment that conservatives are interested in: a fetal personhood amendment.

I wouldn't call it mainstream, even given how radicalized mainstream Republicans have become. But there is a movement afoot to amend the federal Constitution, or at least state constitutions, to recognize the unborn as "people" entitled to certain rights. Some of the very same people who would deny a woman equal protection under an Equal Rights Amendment would like to grant those rights to the fetus she carries.

And, like a bizarro image of the ERA fight, there are some hardcore conservatives who will argue that an original interpretation of the Constitution grants personhood rights to fetuses already. Conservative thinker Ramesh Ponnuru has argued that the Fourteenth Amendment should be read to ban "unborn homicide."

Some people may be familiar with modern conservatives invoking the 1857 *Dred Scott* decision as something they're personally against. George W. Bush, during a 2004 debate against Senator John Kerry, mentioned that he thought *Dred Scott* was wrongly decided, in an answer to a question about what kinds of judges he would appoint (Bush would later go on to appoint Justices John Roberts and Samuel Alito). The *Dred Scott* decision famously, and wrongly, held that slavery was legal even as applied to a Black man who had been living free for a number of years. The chief justice at the time, Roger Taney, said that Black people had "no rights that the white man was bound to respect."

I'm happy that conservatives (now) think the *Dred Scott* decision was a bad beat, but given that we now have the Thirteenth Amendment, I'd like to think that the chattel slavery question is no longer a live constitutional issue.

Yet some conservatives argue that *Roe v. Wade* is the intellectual doppelgänger of *Dred Scott.* They argue that the Court in *Roe* found that the unborn had no rights that (actual) people are bound to respect, and they argue that the ruling is every bit as erroneous as the one upholding slavery. They think that the same amendments that functionally overturned the *Dred Scott* decision can and should be used to overturn *Roe v. Wade*, or they're willing to introduce an entirely new amendment to do the work.

To quote TV president Josiah Bartlet: "Your indignation would be a lot more interesting to me if it wasn't quite so covered in crap." How dare the fetal personhood brigade, last seen ripping breastfeeding children away from their mothers at the border, lecture me about the rights of the unborn. How dare they equate the bondage, rape, and torture that was American human chattel slavery to the failure of a clump of cells to implant in a uterus after a woman takes a drug cocktail a few weeks after accidental conception? The supposed rights of the unborn hold no moral suasion in a society that is willing to consign children who are born alive to poverty, malnutrition, and toxic air and water. I am unmoved by the alleged moral clarity of people who throw around the term *anchor babies* and are willing to deport children who have lived in this country for decades because they were brought here "illegally" as babies. These hypocrites want to make rights attach at conception, but not citizenship and representation in the census. These would-be moralists can fuck all the way off.

Their legal arguments are no better than their moral ones. Because fetal personhood amendments aren't really about some kind of theoretical right "to become life." If they were, activists would be busy trying to bring the hundreds of thousands of embryos lying abandoned in frozen stasis at our nation's fertility clinics to life, which they're not. No, what the conservatives want is forced incubation of fetuses by women who are unwilling to perform the work.

There is an amendment that addresses that concern. It's the Thirteenth. It reads:

> Neither slavery nor involuntary servitude, except as a punishment for crime whereof the party shall have been duly convicted, shall exist within the United States, or any place subject to their jurisdiction.

As I've said, the right to an abortion is not even controversial as long as we proceed from the premise that women-people are people. Fetal personhood laws cannot overcome the Thirteenth Amendment's prohibition on involuntary servitude, if we accept that a woman is a person who cannot be forced to labor.

And that's how the law works for actual alive children who do have personhood rights. We do not force a parent to care for their children. If they agree to care, we impose standards of what that care must entail, but if they want to opt out, and both parents agree, we let them. Giving your kid up for adoption is not illegal. If one parent is committed to raising the kid, we ask the other parent to provide some kind of minimal financial assistance. But if both parents are down for adoption, the child becomes the state's problem.

Seeing as the state can't even find enough willing parents to take care of all of its born wards (especially if those wards happen to be Black), I doubt it can find enough willing wombs to make unborn personhood anything more than involuntary servitude, though I suppose it's welcome to try. But forcing a woman to undergo nine months of incubation and labor is a rather obvious violation of her Thirteenth Amendment protections.

I can prove that. After conception, the developing embryo is sustained by the woman's ovum, or egg. This is why an embryo can be (relatively) easy to create and develop in a laboratory; it has something to eat. But embryos can't live on personhood yolk forever, so the woman's body starts building an entirely new organ, the placenta. When fully developed, by about the end of the first trimester, the placenta will leech nutrients from the woman's bloodstream and "feed" it to the developing fetus through the umbilical cord.

Legally, we treat the placenta as the woman's, just like any other organ in her body. She has legal ownership of it, and that's important, because after birth, there are some options for what to do with it. Some women eat it. Others freeze it or donate it to science, because emerging research suggests that placental cells can be useful in the treatment of certain childhood diseases. Most women allow the hospital to discard it.

The placenta is not alive, and never will be. The woman doesn't need it. It seems to me that, if a woman is a person, she has the right to remove an unnecessary organ from her body. Certainly if the placenta malfunctions, as in the case of preeclampsia, which can cause liver or kidney damage, it would seem that the woman should have every right to remove this needless organ that is affecting her health. Nobody makes a constitutional case over an appendectomy.

If I seem flippant about the whole thing, it is because the legal argument that a fetus has a legal status on par with the woman to whom it is literally attached is illogical trash sprinkled with bad faith and misogyny. Fetal personhood amendments are the state writing a check it cannot cash, then forcing women to cover the bill against their will. It cannot be done in a "free" society. The Thirteenth Amendment flatly prohibits forced labor, and it doesn't have an exception for labor that white men won't do themselves but think is really important for others to do for society.

When it comes to amending the Constitution, conservatives still haven't figured out how to grant personhood rights to all of the born people. If you think it's really important for fetuses to become people, then, by all means, make one yourself.

18

THE RIGHT TO VOTE SHALL BE ABRIDGED ALL THE DAMN TIME

The right to vote is nowhere in the original Constitution or its Bill of Rights. That makes perfect sense when you consider what the people who founded America were trying to accomplish. You can't run a great Western slave experiment if you give just anybody the right to participate in the republic. You can't create a male-dominated society if you give women the right both to have an opinion and to voice it. Come on. What the hell kind of country do you think we were created to be? A "free" one? Do you also believe in flying reindeer who are happy to help and a North Pole that recognizes the right of labor to organize? Wake up! The Elf on the Shelf isn't getting time-and-a-half, my friend.

Beyond the obvious and purely evil reasons for denying the right to vote to women, Blacks, and indigenous Americans, the founders had theoretical concerns about extending suffrage even to all white men. Some of those concerns were legitimate and even prescient. The founders were worried about the uneducated masses voting for idiots and con men more interested in the accrual of power than the functioning of government. They were worried about these demagogues inflaming the passions of the majority and using it to trample minority rights.

Anybody want to tell them they were wrong? The founders didn't want poor, uneducated white men to vote, because they pretty much anticipated that poor, uneducated white men would elect a person like Donald Trump. If only they had fully empowered women and minorities, and especially minority women, to counteract their "economically aggrieved" brethren, the country they founded might be less of a mess today.

Of course, the eighteenth-century American revolutionaries, like their seventeenth-century English revolutionary predecessors, and their later eighteenth-century French revolutionary successors, were all basically from the same class of white men: the wealthy bourgeois. From a certain point of view, rich people never have a problem with monarchy; they have a problem with *hereditary* monarchy. Throughout history, regicidal motherfuckers tend to show up when rich people can't buy their way into more power than they were born into. It's all really a *game of thrones*, if you will. And our founders were more Lannister than Stark: just a bunch of rich people rebelling against a "mad king," who weren't really interested in freeing anybody but themselves.

On top of all of that, aside from their political philosophy and moral failures, there was no operational reason for the Constitution to talk about voting at all. From the founders' perspective, voting rights didn't flow from the federal government; citizenship, and the rights and responsibilities thereof, flowed from the states. So a person—well, a white man—wasn't a citizen of the United States of America so much as a citizen of Georgia or Connecticut or whatever. It made sense to the founders that voting rights would be left up to the states, and they saw no inherent problem with those rights being different in every state.

One way to tell the story of America is as a two-and-a-half-century, ongoing struggle to fix their error. The Fifteenth, Nineteenth, Twenty-Fourth, and Twenty-Sixth Amendments all either directly expand the voting franchise or remove restrictions to voting on new classes of people.

- The Fifteenth Amendment says the right to vote shall not be abridged on account of race.
- The Nineteenth Amendment says the right to vote shall not be abridged on account of sex.
- The Twenty-Fourth Amendment says the right to vote shall not be abridged for failure to pay a poll tax or any other tax.
- The Twenty-Sixth Amendment says the right to vote shall not be abridged on account of age, provided that the voter is at least eighteen years old.

That's a lot of work. That's four of the seventeen amendments ratified after the original Bill of Rights. That means nearly 25 percent of our constitutional updates since the founding of the country have been expended on trying to secure and expand the right to vote. And that's not counting the Seventeenth Amendment, which allowed for direct popular election of senators instead of appointments by state legislatures. That's amazing, especially when you consider that without the right to vote there is no way to participate in the passage and ratification of these amendments that expand the franchise. People have had to use *persuasion* to secure their rights, because they were excluded from actually participating in the votes on whether they would be allowed to vote.

On paper, our gradual expansion toward universal suffrage has been a success story of written constitutional government. That's how everybody learns about these amendments in school. "America used to deny voting rights to nonwhites and women, but now everybody can vote. Yay."

Except that schoolhouse story is a lie. The truth is that the expansion of the franchise has been resisted and undercut by the judicial branch and conservative politicians at nearly every turn. I take a dim view of our ability to amend the Constitution into a more perfect document, because I know too well what courts can do to a freaking amendment they don't like. I am too aware that an amendment that the president refuses to enforce, or one that Congress refuses to flesh out with legislation, is not a solution—it's merely a suggestion. Amendments are just as useless in the face of dedicated white supremacy as anything else.

We have not lived one day in this nation, we have not passed through one election, where all four of the voting rights amendments were made real by Congress and enforced by the executive branch to their fullest potential. Conservatives have never accepted the proposition that "everybody gets to vote now" and so they've turned voting rights into a game of constitutional whack-a-mole. There's always somebody, somewhere, whose voting rights conservatives figure out how to suppress.

Nobody even tried to enforce the Fifteenth Amendment from the time Rutherford B. Hayes pulled troops out of the South until the passage of the Voting Rights Act in 1965, and even then white people were still willing to crack the skulls of Black people who tried to vote. Because the Fifteenth Amendment has rarely been enforced, the Nineteenth Amendment has done very little for Black and brown women trying to vote. While the Twenty-Fourth Amendment did a fair job of eliminating a direct poll tax (until Florida reinstituted one for ex-felons who now need to pay legal fees before they can vote again), the "or other tax" part of the amendment has largely been forgotten, clearing the way for all sorts of economic barriers to voting or registering to vote. And the Twenty-

Sixth Amendment? Sure, go ahead and register to vote, young buck. Just tell me where, because depending on where you live and where your parents live, you may or may not meet residency requirements of the county where your college is located. And your dorm might technically be in a different county than the main campus, so check up on that. Also, I hope you have a driver's license because your college ID might not cut it. And you have your birth certificate, right? Every kid keeps a copy of that lying around, don't they?

At least eighteen-year-olds can vote. People who are seventeen cannot, even if they turn eighteen between the election and the end of the year. The Twenty-Sixth Amendment doesn't require it to be that way; it's just an arbitrary cutoff the states have decided to run with.

Oh, and did I mention that 230-odd years after the founders punted this issue to the states, and 150-plus years since the Fourteenth Amendment made citizenship a federal grant, we're still operationally running voting rights through the states? Yes, for reasons that are at this point intentionally stupid, we still don't have one federal election system; we have fifty state electoral systems for federal office holders. When you can register to vote, whether you can vote early, whether you need ID, what kind of ID you need, whether you can vote absentee, whether you can fix or "cure" an absentee vote that has been rejected for a clerical error, whether you have to specify party affiliation to vote in a primary, whether there will be a runoff after the general election, and damn near everything else that has to do with "the right to vote" is determined by each of the individual states.

Our electoral system is madness. And it's madness on a good day. It would be madness when all involved are acting in good faith to try to help people access their rights. But in this country, we have one party—the Republicans—who have decided to act in bad faith and exploit aspects of the madness to suppress and discourage people from voting based on the color of their skin. As I've said elsewhere, conservatives don't take constitutional amendments as a denouncement of their racism; they take them as a challenge to become more creative in their bigotry.

Nowhere have conservatives succeeded in ignoring the Constitution as much as they have with neutering the Fifteenth Amendment. If all the amendments were in high school, the Fifteenth Amendment would be the kid who gets stuffed in a locker every day. Conservatives try to avoid picking fights with the Fourteenth Amendment. Hell, when it comes time to discriminate against women who want access to health care, they'll even try to invite the Fourteenth over to their keg party. But they'll give the Fifteenth Amendment a wedgie while waterboarding it in the toilet just for the entertainment value. They bully it all the time.

The one time the Fifteenth Amendment fought back was in the aforementioned 1965 Voting Rights Act. The Fourteenth Amendment has been supported through all kinds of legislation, notably the Civil Rights Acts of 1866, 1875, and 1964. But the Voting Rights Act was the first time Congress really put its back into making the Fifteenth Amendment a thing. Because of that, to my mind, the Voting Rights Act is the most important piece of legislation in American history.

It does a lot. It bans creating a discriminatory "standard, practice, or procedure" for voting, and it gives victims a right to sue in federal court over any discriminatory restrictions. It specifically bans a "test or device" used to prohibit voter eligibility, which functionally bans things like literacy tests or other inventions white governments would use to deny the vote to Black citizens. It bans voter intimidation. It guarantees that votes have to be *counted* without discriminatory intent, a rule that the Republican Party evidently forgot in the aftermath of the 2020 presidential election.

In 1982, the Voting Rights Act was amended to prohibit not just discriminatory intent, but also discriminatory effect. That means that the old conservative trick of passing facially "race neutral" laws that deny equality under the cover of "sameness" is not something conservatives can do when it comes to voting. And it doesn't just prohibit voter "denial" on the basis of race; it bans voter "dilution." The Voting Rights Act makes it illegal to gerrymander away the voting power of Black communities by submerging their votes within majoritarian white districts.

And that's all just one part—Section 2—of the Act. Section 5 of the Voting Rights Act requires certain jurisdictions that had a history of racially discriminatory voting procedures to ask the federal government's permission before changing their election laws. This scheme is called "preclearance."

Preclearance is dope. It's just a fantastic way to keep states honest. Normally it takes a lot of time to overturn an onerous state law, even one that is unconstitutional on its face. You have to wait for the right "victim" to be harmed by the law, one who has what lawyers call "standing," to sue the government. Then that victim has to suffer some identifiable harm, because courts only engage in actual "cases or controversies." They do not issue advisory opinions; they can't say "That law looks like it's going to be unconstitutional" until the dubious law is applied to someone in violation of their constitutional rights. Even once those structures are in place, the litigation can take years before the law is overturned by the Supreme Court or the relevant regional courts of appeal overseeing that state. And even that assumes courts aren't controlled by conservatives and therefore willing to overturn racist laws in the first place.

Preclearance shortcuts that whole process. Under a preclearance scheme, states have to get permission from the federal government, usually the Department of Justice, to change their laws *before the fact*. While the federal government will allow the states to get away with a lot of racism, especially if the government is controlled by modern Republicans, the president and the Justice Department are accountable to all of the people, not just racists interested in denying the vote to Black people. Preclearance has been one of the most effective schemes in stopping states from enacting discriminatory voter suppression.

Which is why it no longer exists. Conservative judges will find a way to do racism. They literally always have. There is no law, rule, or constitutional freaking amendment that will stop them.

In this case, it took conservatives a while to shove the Fifteenth Amendment back in a locker. Longer than ever before. But they overcame the Fifteenth Amendment again in 2013. To put it in *Clue* form: The deed was done by Chief Justice John Roberts, with a majority opinion, in *Shelby County v. Holder*.

The *Shelby County* case involved a challenge to Sections 4 and 5 of the Voting Rights Act by Shelby County, in central Alabama. Section 4 basically determines which counties are required to get preclearance before changing their voting laws, under Section 5. Republicans argued the "coverage formula" described in Section 4—which was reauthorized by Congress in 2006 and promoted by noted non-carer-about-Black-people George W. Bush—exceeded Congress's authority under the Fourteenth and Fifteenth Amendments.

Writing for a 5–4 majority, Roberts determined that the coverage formula in Section 4 was unconstitutional. His logic, essentially, was that racism had been sufficiently defeated in the South, thus requiring certain counties to submit themselves for preclearance was no longer necessary. From his opinion:

> It was in the South that slavery was upheld by law until uprooted by the Civil War, that the reign of Jim Crow denied African-Americans the most basic freedoms, and that state and local governments worked tirelessly

to disenfranchise citizens on the basis of race. The Court invoked that history—rightly so—in sustaining the disparate coverage of the Voting Rights Act in 1966. . . .

But history did not end in 1965. By the time the Act was reauthorized in 2006, there had been 40 more years of it. In assessing the "current need[]" for a preclearance system that treats States differently from one another today, that history cannot be ignored. During that time, largely because of the Voting Rights Act, voting tests were abolished, disparities in voter registration and turnout due to race were erased, and African-Americans attained political office in record numbers. And yet the coverage formula that Congress reauthorized in 2006 ignores these developments, keeping the focus on decades-old data relevant to decades-old problems, rather than current data reflecting current needs.

There are a few obvious errors with Roberts's logic. The first, and most problematic error, is that racism has not been defeated. Racism in voting has not been defeated. White people have been hanging "Mission Accomplished" banners on every courthouse since Appomattox, declaring victory over their own bigoted filth, and they're always wrong. There are white people in Alabama today who are every bit as racist as white people in Alabama in 1965, who themselves were every bit as racist as white people in Alabama in 1865, or 1787, or 1619.* Roberts is just rewarding racist white people who have learned not to say the n-word aloud when suppressing the votes of Black people.

The second error is that when racism is defeated, Roberts and his

---

* Maybe not 1619 because the Cherokees were busy keeping racist white people out of Alabama back then.

Supreme Court will be the last guys to know. I mean that's how our government is literally supposed to function. It is on Congress—you know, the people we'd be allowed to vote for if not for white guys like John Roberts—to declare victory over racism. All the courts are supposed to do is determine when Congress violates our constitutional protections against racism. In Shelby County, Roberts is limiting Congress's legislative authority under the Fifteenth Amendment to the scope of his own personal opinions about when racism is really "bad." If the Federalist Society were an organization that stood for anything more than white supremacy, they'd hate this Roberts opinion way more than his decision to uphold the Affordable Care Act as a tax. Because this decision takes power directly away from Congress and places it in the sociological musings of unelected justices.

Lastly, to the extent that Alabama is slightly less lynchy of Black people trying to vote now than they were forty years ago, it is because of laws like the Voting Rights Act. Ruth Bader Ginsburg, may her memory be a blessing, in probably her best dissent of her many outstanding ones, put Roberts's willful ignorance on blast. She wrote: "Throwing out preclearance when it has worked and is continuing to work to stop discriminatory changes is like throwing away your umbrella in a rainstorm because you are not getting wet."

Roberts's decision to destroy the coverage formula of Section 4 effectively gutted Section 5 of the Voting Rights Act. Clarence Thomas, in a concurring opinion, argued that the Court should have ruled Section 5 unconstitutional on its face too, because Clarence Thomas doesn't think racism is "over" so much as he thinks the government should be powerless to stop it. But Roberts's opinion does more than enough of the work. It is practically impossible to think of a Section 4 preclearance formula that would satisfy Roberts's *Shelby County* logic enough to revive Section 5.

His opinion purposefully opened the door to all manner of voting rights restrictions, and Republican politicians took full advantage. Voter ID laws went supernova. Polling locations in predominantly Black communities were closed. When you see lines of Black people waiting hours and hours to vote, you can largely thank John Roberts for these scenes of racism.

And he hasn't gotten nearly enough blame for it. Everybody knows that the Supreme Court made George W. Bush president in 2000 with its ruling in *Bush v. Gore*. But most people don't realize the Court made Donald Trump president in 2016 with its ruling in *Shelby County*. The voter suppression unleashed by that decision is what made it possible for Trump to eke out his narrow electoral college victory in that election.

Never forget, Black people are not evenly distributed throughout the country. Most Black people still live in the states where their ancestors were enslaved. The state with the highest population of Black people, per capita, is Mississippi. (It would be the District of Columbia, if DC were a state, but white people, in their infinite self-interest, have declined to extend statehood to a territory that is nearly 50 percent Black. I wonder why.) After that it's Louisiana, followed by Georgia, Maryland, South Carolina, and Alabama.

Do you know how different this country would look if the Black voters in those states enjoyed frictionless access to the ballot? Joe Biden defeated Donald Trump in the 2020 general election in Georgia by 11,779 votes. That's out of nearly 5,000,000 votes cast. That margin is functionally entirely due to people like Stacey Abrams and LaTosha Brown, and organizations like Fair Fight Action and Black Voters Matter.

Black voter suppression is a biological imperative for white supremacy. It is a survival strategy. White supremacists, and the political parties and organizations that support them, have no plan to convince Black voters of their point of view. Oh, white supremacists have tons of plans and arguments to attract a healthy minority of Latinos and Asians or other more recent immigrant groups. But they ain't got nothing for Black people. A few Blacks will always vote for Republicans on the "if you can't beat 'em, join 'em" line. But in the main, the only strategy white supremacists have to deal with Black political concerns is to suppress their votes so that they cannot effectively voice those concerns.

That's why the Fifteenth Amendment continues to walk these halls with a giant "Kick Me" sign on its back. That's why all of the voting rights amendments either are left to wither on the parchment, or are so weakened that they can support only the most literal and reductive version of voter protections imaginable.

Suppressing the vote, no matter what the Constitution says otherwise, is the prime directive for conservative jurists. It's why they get appointed; it's the credential that is even more important than a hostility toward abortion. Voter suppression is what binds a Trump judge to a Bush judge to a Bush 41 judge to a Reagan judge.

They can't win any other way.

19

WHAT IF YOUR VOTE ACTUALLY DIDN'T MATTER?

The first Republican I met in real life was former congressman and one-time Senate candidate Rick Lazio, when I was in my tweens. I mean, I'm sure I had technically met Republicans before then. My family didn't socialize with Republicans (a tradition I have maintained), but I'm sure I had an elementary school teacher or coach or something who was a registered Republican. But Lazio was the first person I interacted with who was an "official" Republican, you know? The first person who made his living off of being Republican whom I met in the flesh.

Unfortunately, a lot of people remember Lazio from his failed Senate campaign against Hillary Clinton in 2000. He was doing okay in that race, until the debate. During his showdown with Clinton, Lazio left his podium and approached hers, haranguing her to sign some kind of campaign finance pledge he pulled out of his pocket.

The stunt backfired badly. It will be hard for people reading this in the post-Trump era to understand, but in the before times, in the long, long ago, a candidate bullying another candidate onstage was considered bad form. Republican voters used to belong to a political party instead of a deranged cult, and, for some of them, the appearance of interpersonal brutishness mattered. Lazio started falling in the polls after that debate, bounced back, but ultimately lost that race.

From where I sit, Lazio got a bad rap. I can't speak to his debate etiquette, but I can vouch that he's great with kids. When I met him in 1991, we were in a literal smoke-filled "room where it happens." My father was the chief legislative aide for a woman named Maxine Postal, who was a Democrat in the Suffolk County (Long Island) legislature. Lazio, who had been a district attorney, was a newly elected Republican in that legislature. A failure of childcare required my father to bring me to work right after he picked me up from football practice, and he let me sit in on his redistricting meeting if I promised to keep my mouth shut.

As most people know, the Constitution requires a census every ten years. Here's Article 1, Section 2:

> Representatives and direct Taxes shall be apportioned among the several States which may be included within this Union, according to their respective Numbers, which shall be determined by adding to the whole Number of free Persons, including those bound to Service for a Term of Years, and excluding Indians not taxed, three fifths of all other Persons. The actual Enumeration shall be made within three Years after the first Meeting of the Congress of the United States, and within every subsequent Term of ten Years, in such Manner as they shall by Law direct.

Sorry, I left in the original constitutional language because that's what those founding assholes wrote. But I'll note the "three fifths" language has been amended.

After that census, the states redistrict to account for the new numbers. Some states lose members in the House of Representatives. Others gain. The number of representatives had been set at one member per 30,000 people, but in 1929 the number of House members was locked at 435 people, where it still sits today. So states trade house seats back and forth now. Redistricting often happens at the local and county level too, after the census.

In 1991, the Suffolk County Legislature was redrawing its lines, and my dad was in the middle of that battle. He had a real feel for this stuff; my childhood house was always cluttered with maps. And push pins. And string. It all came together on one giant map my dad had in his office: a street-level view of all of Suffolk County with pins and string denoting where the lines were, where they should be, and where they would be if Republicans let him have his way.

Ms. Postal was white, as were all the legislators at that time. But my dad was Black, and the reason he was invaluable in the redistricting process was that he knew where all the Black and brown people lived. All of them, I once thought. When I was a kid I thought my dad knew every time a new minority family bought a house anywhere in the county. At the meeting I attended, my dad's instruction to shut up was irrelevant; nobody was getting a word in over my father anyway.

But that was partially because everybody was waiting for Lazio. In the car on the way over, my dad explained he had two main goals: he wanted to move one pocket of Black people into Ms. Postal's district, essentially turning her "winnable" district (centered around Amityville) into a "safe" district for Democrats and putting it on the path to becoming a majority-minority district. And he wanted to move another pocket of Latinos mainly out of Lazio's district (where Republicans were crushing it anyway) and move them into one where Democrats were more competitive. But he couldn't get that without "fucking Lazio's" signoff.

Lazio was late. Probably intentionally, because it sent my dad into some kind of rage. I was sitting by the door and had become bored listening to my dad literally scream at people while pointing to a version of his giant county map, now at the center of the room. I couldn't even really see the middle of the room through all the cigarette and cigar smoke. But I was the first person to notice Lazio quietly come into the room, though I didn't know that this was the man my dad had been screaming about. Lazio sat down next to me and asked, "So, that's your dad?" At first I thought, "How did he know?" before remembering I was the only other Black person in the room. Since my father was in full tilt about something, I deflected and said, "No, my dad is Doc Gooden."

We talked for about five minutes—about the Mets and how I was liking school—before my dad brought us back to reality. He yelled, to no one in particular, something like: "If Rick isn't here in five minutes, I'm taking his Dominicans and his balls."

"You talk like that in front of your son?" Lazio piped up.

Unfazed, my dad says: "I talk like that in front of my fucking daughter, if I fucking feel like it." He was telling the truth.

"Time to go to work, kid," Lazio says to me, before standing up and joining the group at the center of the room.

As I recall, Lazio was amenable to my dad's proposal for his district. I kept waiting for Lazio to turn heel, as I had been taught he would, but he never did. Indeed, the person really getting screwed over was a Republican in the district the Dominicans were going to, and he wasn't even in the room. But Lazio had bigger plans than the Suffolk County Legislature. From what I was told by my father later, the real issue Lazio was fighting over was that he couldn't be seen as obviously screwing over a fellow Republican by dumping a bunch of Democrats into his district.*

My dad and Lazio worked out some kind of deal. On his way out, Lazio gave me a high five and said, "That's our version of the big leagues."

On the car ride home, my dad explained that Lazio had kept as part of his district a section with a current high population of Latinos (a group Lazio did well with) but was willing to give away a bigger section that was just turning into a cognizable Dominican neighborhood. Meanwhile, everybody let my dad cannibalize the lion's share of a Black community (parts of Wyandanch, to those listening to Billy Joel at home) into Ms. Postal's district.

I suppose it was a win-win. Lazio would be elected to Congress just two years later and was the darling of the New York Republican Party for a time. Meanwhile, after one more round of redistricting in 2001, Ms. Postal's district became winnable for a Black representative. When she passed away, my dad ran for her seat, and in 2004, he became the first Black person elected to the Suffolk County Legislature. I could describe my late father's profession in a lot of ways, but "a gerrymanderer" would be among the most accurate.

The term *gerrymandering* conjures images of smoke-tinted rooms filled with power-hungry politicians splitting up or smushing together entire communities to protect their own political interests. And it is certainly that. But, as an indelible mark from my upbringing, I've come to understand that drawing straight lines

---

* I reached out to Lazio about this reapportionment, over the course of writing this book. He mentioned that while he didn't remember this specific meeting, he remembered being amenable to the split to further the legitimate interest in creating a majority-minority legislative district for a Latino candidate. And he mentioned the somewhat obvious point that is often missed by other Republicans: the party should be more interested in investing in and promoting Republicans of color. Lazio didn't think a majority-minority district was an instant Democratic district.

and pleasing geometry on a map isn't fair either. "Sameness" does not equal "fairness." My dad could draw a legislature where all the districts looked "the same," that Republicans could never win control of, despite having a significant advantage in voter registration in his county. Or he could squiggle out a legislature that would make Pythagoras cry, which was nonetheless a fair representation of all the county's voters. He could do both in a night with the right bottle of scotch.

The problem with geometric integrity and keeping "towns" together is that there is a whole bunch of racism, segregation, and classism baked into where people live. Both current and legacy housing discrimination, for instance, leads racial and ethnic minorities generally to live in densely populated clusters in whatever areas allowed them to buy homes or rent property. Sometimes those clusters overlap town lines; sometimes those clusters abruptly stop wherever some bank decided Black people shouldn't own homes.

I currently live in Westchester County, New York. South Westchester is, essentially, the Bronx in terms of racial and economic makeup. Other parts of Westchester look like something out of an F. Scott Fitzgerald novel. I'm one of three Black families on my street, which also includes a white cop, and a couple I assume are gay because the two ladies who live there pull out a rainbow flag every time a different neighbor unfurls his over-large American flag on the Fourth of July. Whether my congressional representative looks more like Alexandria Ocasio-Cortez or Jay Gatsby has little to do with where I live, and more to do with whether I'm districted with people who live five minutes south of my house, or five minutes north.

Unfortunately, the process of drawing districts that lead to a fair representation of the voters in a legislature is the exact same process as the one used for drawing districts that lead to the effective disenfranchisement of voters. Gerrymandering is like fire: it's just a tool that can cook dinner or burn the house down. The real trick is to keep it contained.

Given the awesome power of gerrymandering to illuminate or functionally destroy democratic self-government, you'd think we'd have very clear legal rules on what is allowed, and what is prohibited. But we don't. The Constitution is silent on how districts are to be drawn, in part because the power to shape districts is clearly in the purview of state, not federal, law. Also because the founders didn't think political parties would really be a thing (a founding flaw in the document we've never really gotten over), and because they restricted the vote so much that the question of underrepresented racial or ethnic minorities just wasn't on the table at the Constitutional Convention.

Despite the lack of any constitutional guidance, the Supreme Court has had to weigh in on the constitutionality of various gerrymandered maps again and again. It's not going to come as a galloping shock to anybody that gerrymanders became a constitutional issue because the South, as usual, refused to stop being racist. I'm basically running out of ways to express how thoroughly the South ignored the Fourteenth and Fifteenth Amendments after Rutherford B. Hayes took the Union foot off their necks, but here again, the moment the South had an opportunity to disenfranchise Black people, white Southerners disenfranchised Black people by apportioning districts so that only people living in white areas mattered.

It was only during the civil rights era that racist gerrymanders were successfully challenged in court. This happened in a 1962 case called *Baker v. Carr.* Tennessee apportioned its state legislature in 1901 and then, never again. Suffice it to say that the 1901 map locked in an advantage for white people living in Tennessee. Civil rights activists argued that Tennessee's map was a violation of the equal protection clause of the Fourteenth Amendment.

The Court ruled that the equal protection claim was a "justiciable" constitutional issue—which just means that the claim is something federal courts are allowed to rule on—and agreed to hear the case. That was huge because, up until then, states had argued that gerrymandering was a state concern that triggered no federal constitutional issues (as the founders surely intended) and that gerrymanders were a "political question" inappropriate for the Court to rule upon. It's not like we want courts picking the winners and losers of elections, right? Right, *Bush v. Gore*?

But here, the Supreme Court ruled that it did have the power to rectify issues of state administration when the state was in violation of constitutional principles. Earl Warren himself said that *Baker v. Carr* was the most important case decided after he was appointed to the bench.

A lot of gerrymandering cases have been in front of the Supreme Court since *Baker v. Carr*. Excavating sixty-odd years of gerrymandering jurisprudence to tell a coherent story about where we are and how we got here is beyond my narrative and (probably) cognitive powers. It's like trying to explain the final battle in *Avengers: Endgame* to someone who didn't see all the other Marvel Cinematic Universe movies. ("Captain America can use Thor's hammer that was destroyed by his sister, but Thor recovered when he went back in time to visit his dead mother. Cap made it budge once, so this makes sense.") Matters are further complicated because the Supreme Court slightly changes its mind nearly every time a new justice joins the bench. Take my word for the following:

- **Negative racial gerrymanders:** not okay. Courts will not let state legislatures draw maps to target and disenfranchise racial minorities. These maps are thought to violate the Fourteenth Amendment.
- **Positive racial gerrymanders:** sometimes okay. Maps

drawn to ensure majority-minority districts, in the name of encouraging diverse representation in the legislature, are subjected to strict scrutiny. That means the state needs to show a "compelling" interest for the racially gerrymandered map, and the map must be "narrowly tailored" to achieve that interest. It's a tough standard, but some racially gerrymandered maps can meet it. Functionally, the only "compelling" state interest courts will recognize is the Voting Rights Act of 1965. But if you can sell your map as "necessary to enforce the Voting Rights Act," and the districts drawn are contiguous and not outright bizarre, courts may allow it.

- **Political gerrymanders:** always okay. The Court has a long history of trying to look the other way when maps are drawn purely to benefit one party over the other, even when those maps are demonstrably unfair. A 2019 Supreme Court decision fully unleashed legislatures dominated by one party to do their absolute worst with the maps. In *Rucho v. Common Cause*, Chief Justice John Roberts ruled that "political" gerrymanders were "nonjusticiable," meaning that federal courts had no authority to stop the states from doing what they wanted.

While the rules seem logical on paper, they really make no sense on the ground. Nobody ever writes "This is a negative racial gerrymander" or "This map is necessary to keep uppity Negroes in their place" in the margins on their map. White supremacist mapmakers are not stupid. In fact, a lot of negative racial gerrymanders can be sold as positive racial gerrymanders. Creating one super-majority-minority district is actually a great way to keep minorities out of all the other districts.

In many cases, the difference between a positive and negative racial gerrymander comes down to the good faith of the politicians involved. People like my dad and Rick Lazio were trying to *enhance* representation for underrepresented people.

But what if they had been doing the other thing? Would anybody have even noticed the difference? How could I even prove they were doing the other thing? How do you prove the absence of good faith that animates a negative racial gerrymander?

Unfortunately, as we've seen time and again, conservative justices require their racists to self-identify as such. They require specific, "magic" words or even more explicit actions. Even here, in a field of law where the Fourteenth Amendment's guarantee of equal protection and the Fifteenth Amendment's right to vote are the only constitutional principles that matter, conservatives still act like disenfranchising or diluting the votes of minorities is something that just kind of happens without the "bad" intentions of anybody involved.

That willful ignorance is most shamelessly on display when conservatives try to erect bright-line distinctions between racial gerrymanders and political gerrymanders. As of the *Rucho* decision, the courts aren't even allowed to look at political gerrymanders, but racial ones, even ones designed to enhance diverse representation, may still be struck down by courts.

But the distinction between political gerrymanders and racial gerrymanders doesn't exist when you're inside the map room. When politicians are trying to draw a Republican district or a Democratic district, they're looking at everything: party affiliation, voter registration rolls, housing or rental prices, race, color, creed, church-to-strip-club ratio, all of it. To think that they're looking only at "political" factors and not "racial" factors requires one to be more naive than I was when I was twelve. To think that there is even a meaningful distinction between "political" factors and "racial" factors requires one to be more naive than me, and white.

Looking at all factors is how politicians get to know the difference between a politically "safe" district versus a competitive one in the first place. And these gerrymanders are getting more accurate—thereby locking in one-party domination—all the time. At least human politicians could be wrong. I said that it *felt* like my dad knew whenever a Black person bought a house in Suffolk County. But he didn't actually.

Zillow does. Target knows when you're about to have a baby. Facebook . . . I don't even want to know what Facebook knows about me, but it probably knows when I'm going to die, and which current twenty-five-year-old I will end up voting for in the last election before my death. With modern technology and "big data" at their fingertips, politicians can now gerrymander down to the cul-de-sac.

Left unchecked, Republican state legislatures will use that power to disenfranchise racial minorities. That's not a guess; it's just literally what Republicans already always do whenever given the slightest opportunity. Thanks to John Roberts, they'll say their maps are "political" gerrymanders: it's just a coincidence that Black people happen to overwhelmingly vote for Democrats, because Democrats seem to be the only party that can go four years at a stretch without giving aid and comfort to Klansmen.

Like everything else involving gerrymandering, the same thing causing the problem can in fact be the solution. Computers and big data have thrown gasoline onto the gerrymandered campfire, but they can also douse the flames and take the human inclinations toward racism and power grabs out of the equation. Programs can tell us how representative a legislature is of its constituents, how much it should be, and draw the maps accordingly. I don't understand all the math on this, but I also don't need to understand all the math on how a GPS works to trust it enough to turn left when it tells me to. There is a technocratic solution now to this decennial democratic battle.

But conservatives don't like math either. Conservatives like John Roberts don't want to rely on math, they don't want to rely on the Fifteenth Amendment, and then they don't want to rely on the Voting Rights Act. They just want to let Republicans disenfranchise Black voters, call it "political," and hope history misses their role in the centuries-long oppression of Black people in the New World.

On the car ride home from my first gerrymandering meeting, I couldn't understand how they could just "let" my father and a couple of other guys decide who was going to win the legislature for a decade. And then I remembered that my dad was staff and not an actual elected official. "What happens when they don't invite you to these meetings?" I asked.

"Black people get fucked," he answered. At the time, I thought he was bragging. I was only twelve.

20

ABOLISH THE
ELECTORAL COLLEGE

I've spent the last few chapters explaining why even amending the Constitution is generally pointless in the face of arch-conservative Supreme Court justices determined to continue the legacy of bigotry and oppression this country was founded upon. But there is one amendment that would immediately end one of the most obvious structural features of white supremacy in this country: Abolish the Electoral College.

And while we're at it, it would be great to abolish the Senate. I don't mean "abolish the Senate" the way a Roman Emperor would have uttered it. Republican self-government is good, or at least better than strongman despotism. The problem is that the United States Senate is not an exercise in republican government; it's a prophylactic to *prevent* republican self-government.

Every state gets two senators. Every state has the same representation in the Senate. And that is straight-up not fair. Tying representation to the land as opposed to the people living on it is, among other things, fucking stupid. North and South Dakota (combined population of about 1.6 million people) have four senators in total, while New York *City* has 8 million people and gets, like, a large say in the two senators that the 19.4 million people living in New York *State* are allotted. Queens (population 2.2 million) should have four senators if the Dakotas do.

Not that New Yorkers can really complain. Washington, DC, gets zero senators.

As most people know, the structure of the Senate is the result of the "Great Compromise" or "Connecticut Compromise" at the Constitutional Convention in 1787. Smaller states were worried about being controlled by larger, more populous states. The South in particular was worried about losing the privilege to work and rape Black people to death. The compromise provided that one chamber of the legislature, the House of Representatives, would be apportioned based on population, while the other, the Senate, would give equal representation to each state.

To put it another way: white slavers feared "democracy" so much that they wrote it out of the Constitution. Keep in mind that at the founding, the limited group of white male landowners who were allowed to vote weren't even allowed to vote for their senators. State legislatures picked their federal senators, thus further insulating the Senate from any direct democratic accountability. We didn't move to direct popular elections of senators until 1913 with the ratification of the Seventeenth Amendment.

Conservative defenders of the Senate as an institution (and it's almost always conservatives, in either party, who defend this intentionally antidemocratic institution) abandon any pretense of originalist arguments to explain the continued justification for the Senate. They'll say that the Senate gives strength to rural interests that would otherwise be overpowered in a direct democracy. But that argument is a little thin. The Senate functionally ignores rural voters in high-population states with dense city populations. The

Senate doesn't even really empower rural voters in low-population states. It mainly empowers city voters lucky enough to live in low-population rural states. Again, land doesn't vote. If white people in Des Moines and Dubuque voted like white people in Portland, and Salem, and Eugene, Iowa would be every bit as blue as Oregon.

There is a real urban versus rural divide in this country, but the Senate isn't designed to favor rural voters. It's designed to favor white people. As the country rushes toward becoming a majority-minority nation, the Senate acts as the ultimate refuge for white power. That's because people of color are not evenly spread throughout the country, and because the Senate is, by its nature, a "winner take all" system. As long as white people make up a plurality of voters in a state, and as long as white people stick together in that state, white people get to control both of the state's allotted senators.

That basically explains the modern South. I've mentioned before that the states with the most Black people by percentage of the population remain, largely, the states where Black people were enslaved. Here are the ten "Blackest" states (or, in the case of DC, nonstate), by percentage of population, according to a 2018 projection for the 2020 census:

1. Washington, DC (45.99 percent)
2. Mississippi (38.40 percent)
3. Louisiana (33.43 percent)
4. Georgia (31.47 percent)
5. Maryland (31.23 percent)
6. Alabama (27.19 percent)
7. South Carolina (26.91 percent)
8. Delaware (23.08 percent)
9. North Carolina (21.97 percent)
10. Virginia (20.48 percent)

You'll note that Black people make up a majority in none of those states. In the House, Black people still have a chance to be represented by a congressperson from their minority district—at least they do in theory, depending on how bigoted the gerrymandering of those districts is. But in the Senate, you win statewide or you win nothing at all.

Hiram Revels, Blanche K. Bruce, Edward Brooke, Carol Moseley Braun, Barack Obama, Roland W. Burris, Tim Scott, William "Mo" Cowan, Cory A. Booker, Kamala D. Harris, Raphael Warnock: that is the full and complete list of African Americans to serve in the United States Senate in the history of this country. That's eleven people. Revels and Bruce were appointed to the Senate by Reconstruction Southern legislators while the slavers weren't allowed to hold office. Burris, Scott, and Cowan were initially appointed to their seats by governors. Only six Black people in American history just went out and won a U.S. Senate seat via popular vote (though Scott eventually won a reelection campaign). Black people have had more prophets than goddamn senators.

The structure of the Senate is racist. It inherently promotes majoritarian white concerns over those of everybody else. And that structure cannot be changed, even through constitutional amendment. That's because, get this, the people who agreed to structure the Senate in this patently unfair way provided that its structure was the one thing that could never be changed. Article V of the Constitution, which describes the process for amending the document, has this to say about the Senate:

> [A]nd that no state, without its consent, shall be deprived of its equal suffrage in the Senate.

Ain't that something? To amend the structure of the Senate the people who most benefit from its bigotry have to first agree to give up their advantage. Tell me this document wasn't written by slavers and colonists who knew exactly the kind of white supremacist society they were trying to write into existence.

The Senate is a lost cause. There are some things we can do at the margins: admitting DC as a state is not even a Senate reform so much as a moral imperative of representative government, and adding a place with the highest percentage of Black people by population (compared to the current fifty states) would at least be something. But at core, the Senate cannot be fixed. It was erected as a bulwark of white power, and it will stay that way long after white people become a minority in this country. Alien historians will one day try to piece together why the American hegemony was so unable to deliver justice to its own people, and when they uncover the Senate they'll say, "Oh, well that was never going to work."

The best we can do is limit the antidemocratic destructiveness of the Senate, which is how we come to eliminating the Electoral College.* The Electoral College grants power to the states to elect the president (who then is allowed to appoint Supreme Court justices upon advice and consent of the Senate) based on their number of House members, plus their two senators. This system therefore takes the white supremacist structure of the legislature and ports it over to the executive branch and the judicial branch.

But the Electoral College is not protected by Article V shenanigans.

Everybody who realizes that the Electoral College is antithetical to democracy has their favorite numbers to explain why the system

---

* We should also eliminate the filibuster, but since the filibuster—which requires the Senate to cobble together sixty votes instead of fifty-one to pass legislation, further entrenching the antidemocratic nature of the institution—isn't even in the Constitution, it's outside the scope of this book. The filibuster is just the senators themselves getting together and thinking, "How can we make things worse?"

is trash. My current favorite comes from Cardozo School of Law professor Kyron Huigens, who wrote this in the *Observer* in 2019:

> The total number of each state's electors is not the relevant number in this calculation. . . . The reason the popular vote diverges from the Electoral College vote is that *each voter* in Wyoming has more voting power in the *Senate* [emphasis added]—and so in the Electoral College—than *each voter* in California.
>
> Here is the proper calculation. California has 25,002,812 eligible voters and two senators. Wyoming has 434,584 eligible voters and two senators. Carol's voting power in California's Senate delegation is diluted because she shares it with 25,002,811 other voters. Will's voting power in Wyoming's Senate delegation is also diluted because he shares it with 434,583 other voters. Since Will's voting power in the Senate is less diluted, it's greater than Carol's voting power in the Senate. If Carol has one vote in the Senate, how many votes in the Senate does Will have?
>
> Fifty-seven.

That's the right way to think about it. Instead of "one person, one vote," it's actually "white people in Wyoming get fifty-seven votes." I can make an argument that this kind of "vote dilution" violates the Fifteenth Amendment, or the equal protection clause of the Fourteenth Amendment, but both of those are tough cases since Wyoming (and other low-population states) are not required to be mostly white. If there are any liberal billionaires reading: finding half a million Black people willing to take a free townhouse, and building them one in Wyoming, would be a better way to influence democracy than running a useless presidential campaign.

In any event, the best and most intellectually clean argument is not that the Electoral College is already unconstitutional, but that it should be made so by a new amendment.

New York Times journalist Jesse Wegman has written the definitive book on abolishing the Electoral College. His work, *Let the People Pick the President*, explains that lawmakers have tried to amend or abolish the Electoral College seven hundred times. Wegman describes how an attempt to amend the Constitution to allow for a national popular vote failed in 1969–1970. Maybe if Martin Luther King had survived white supremacy, things would be different now.

The prospects of a constitutional amendment abolishing the Electoral College seem dimmer now than ever before. The Democratic candidate for president has won the popular vote in seven of the last eight elections. That trend is likely to continue as the Republican Party continues its descent into a modern-day Afrikaans party incapable of winning the popular vote in a steadily browning country. Amending the Constitution—which requires a two-thirds majority in both the House and the Senate, followed by ratification by three-fourths of states (which would mean thirty-eight states)—to take away an antidemocratic pathway for Republican victory seems unlikely.

The solution that Wegman and many others endorse is the National Popular Vote Interstate Compact. It's a pretty simple idea: states pass legislation promising that their electors will go to the winner of the national popular vote. If states holding at least a combined 270 electoral votes (the current number needed to win a majority in the Electoral College) agree to do it, we have a de facto national popular vote for president.

As of this writing, fifteen states and DC, holding a combined 196 electoral votes, have passed the necessary legislation, so this is closer to happening than some people might think. Another nine states, holding 88 electoral votes, have passed legislation through at least one chamber of their legislatures.

The plan has downsides. If the aftermath of the 2020 election showed one thing, it was that Republicans are willing to use any available means to thwart democracy and overturn the results of an election they lose. Thanks to Donald Trump's post-2020 clown-coup attempt, everybody should now know that a number of state laws about the counting of votes, certification of those votes, and awarding of Electoral College voters could well flummox a compact agreed to by a thin majority of states. States that sign on to the compact might well try to get out of it should Republicans control the statehouse and the Republican presidential candidate doesn't win the popular vote. And it's not like there's even any mechanism for certifying the national popular vote, so if there was a dispute about the winner of the national popular vote, it's not clear who would have the final say on the vote totals.

Any election where the national vote compact conflicted with the state-by-state Electoral College results would end up in front of the Supreme Court. The case would get there, likely, as an equal protection challenge under the Fourteenth Amendment. Republicans made that claim after the 2020 election: Texas sued Pennsylvania arguing that Pennsylvania's voting laws deprived Texas voters of their equal protection rights, because Pennsylvania's laws allowed for easier access to mail-in voting.

That case was thrown out on a rail by the Supreme Court, and rightly so. Under our current system of fifty separate state-run elections, Texas's complaint was one of the dumbest things I've ever seen. The rights of Texans to choose a president were in no way impacted by Pennsylvania's voter rules in their own statewide election.

But under a national popular vote compact, I don't know that I'd be as confident about beating back Republican challenges. It's hard to have a *national* popular vote system if we don't also have nationwide uniformity in terms of election rules, ballot access, and vote counting and recounting rules. I do feel confident saying that, given the Republican control of the Supreme Court, any actually intelligent legal claim about the true winner of a presidential election would be resolved in favor of the Republican candidate.

Trying an untested system to pick the leader of a deeply polarized country, one where Republicans have already shown their willingness to use violence to get their way, is dangerous. The National Popular Vote Interstate Compact feels a little bit like fixing the wing of a plane with duct tape: it might work, but I wouldn't want to fly in somebody's weekend DIY project.

What's broken here is the Constitution. It needs to be fixed, not jerry-rigged together to make it through another election. The unlikely path of abolishing the Electoral College through the amendment process is, sadly, the only one that will actually work. This is where all the "amend the constitution" energy should be on the left, because it's the thing that can't reasonably be fixed any other way.

We almost got rid of this thing during Reconstruction but failed. We almost got rid of it during the Civil Rights Era but came up short. A September 2020 Gallup Poll showed that 61 percent of Americans now favor moving to a national popular vote.

Do you know the state where Trump got the most popular votes in 2020? It was California. Do you know the state where Joe Biden received his third-largest cache of popular votes in 2020? It was Texas. Republicans in California and Democrats in Texas should matter at least as much as every sentient blade of goddamn swamp grass in Florida does now.

It's implausible that we'll ever get Republicans to see it that way, but not impossible. And so we have to try. Otherwise, we should just start the whole experiment over from scratch . . . which probably also requires a two-thirds majority in the hopeless fucking Senate.

21

THE FINAL BATTLE

The final two amendments to the Bill of Rights, the Ninth and Tenth Amendments, are hilarious. Every time I read them, I imagine James Madison dressed up like Kevin Bacon at the end of *Animal House*, screaming "All is well!" while an actual riot breaks out around him.

Remember, Madison and the other authors of *The Federalist Papers* didn't think amendments to their new Constitution were necessary. More than that, they thought a bill of enumerated rights could be dangerous. They worried that if they specified a few rights, some fools in the future would conclude that their list of rights were the *only* rights people had or should have. They worried that the federal government would grow to take power over *everything but* the few special carve-outs they bothered to enumerate.

They had a good point. If you open a restaurant and put up a sign saying "No shirt, no shoes, no service," best believe that somebody is going to show up with no pants. Some people take a list of rules as a challenge. Some jokers just want to see the world burn.

And yet, like Aaron crafting the golden calf, Madison gave in to the politics of the moment and drafted the Bill of Rights. He did something he knew was wrong to appease the crowd. But, he tried to give himself—and, you know, all of us living in the future—a couple of outs.

The Ninth Amendment is one sentence:

> The enumeration in the Constitution, of certain rights, shall not be construed to deny or disparage others retained by the people.

The Tenth Amendment is also just one sentence:

> The powers not delegated to the United States by the Constitution, nor prohibited by it to the states, are reserved to the states respectively, or to the people.

Taken together, these two amendments throw massive shade on the previous eight. If you think of the Bill of Rights like a hostage video, the first eight are Madison saying, "They are treating me well. I am being fed and receiving medical treatment for my injuries." The last two are when he blinks out "They electrocuted my testicles" in Morse code before they cut the feed.

A version of what Madison might have wanted is explored in Columbia law professor Jamal Greene's book *How Rights Went Wrong*. In it, Greene argues that our obsession with individual rights has led us to a zero-sum brawl over which rights get to defeat other rights, far from what the founders intended. Instead of applying individual rights as legal absolutes, we should instead seek to balance competing legitimate state interests with an eye toward justice and fairness instead of rights and prohibitions.

You know me, by this point. If it were up to me, I'd light the entire

Constitution on fire and start over with a document that wasn't so goddamn racist. But as we are currently stuck with this thing that Madison wrought, my inclination is not to abandon a rights-based approach to legal protections, but to capture at last the full protections of the Ninth Amendment—an amendment that Federalist Society originalists like to pretend doesn't exist.

When I say that originalists pretend that the Ninth Amendment doesn't exist, I mean that they literally try to read the amendment out of the rest of the document. In a 2013 interview with Jennifer Senior of *New York Magazine*, none other than Antonin Scalia said this about the Ninth Amendment:

> You know, in the early years, the Bill of Rights referred to the first eight amendments. They didn't even count the ninth. The Court didn't use it for 200 years. If I'd been required to identify the Ninth Amendment when I was in law school or in the early years of my practice, and if my life depended on it, I couldn't tell you what the Ninth Amendment was.

Scalia was simply channeling Robert Bork. In his 1987 (failed) confirmation hearing, Bork pretended that the Ninth Amendment was inscrutable, as if he were Mariah Carey saying, "I don't know her."

> I do not think you can use the Ninth Amendment unless you know something of what it means. For example, if you had an amendment that says "Congress shall make no" and then there is an inkblot and you cannot read the rest of it and that is the only copy you have, I do not think the court can make up what might be under the inkblot if you cannot read it.

Here we have two men who allegedly dedicated their careers in service to the vision of America as articulated by the authors of the Constitution, and yet they regulate an essential provision, made to redeem the document from the parochial political interests of its authors, as an inkblot that they can't even be bothered to think about.

There's a reason that Scalia, Bork, and other conservatives deny the existence of the Ninth Amendment: it's because the Ninth Amendment blows their whole little project apart. A theory of constitutional interpretation that restricts the rights of humans to a finite list agreed to by eighteenth-century slavers cannot survive a provision from one of those slavers that explicitly says their list is not exhaustive of all rights. Madison put the Ninth Amendment in to counteract what he knew small-minded people would do to the rest of the document, and so small-minded conservatives have to pretend it's not even there in order to achieve their goals of retarding progress.

We have more rights than those that are explicitly conferred in the Constitution. The Constitution says so!

The limiting principle on those rights is not the eighteenth-century perception of rights or privileges. It's not informed by Clarence Thomas conducting a séance to talk to his ancestral captors, or Neil Gorsuch unearthing the original Constitutional Convention lunch menu to divine whether "roasting" was a delicious punishment allowed by the founders. The limiting principle on the rights contemplated in the Ninth Amendment is found in the very next amendment.

Rights speak to what the government cannot do, and the Tenth Amendment reminds us that the federal government cannot do most things. The people who didn't think we needed a Bill of Rights in the first place thought that the rights of the people were protected by a government too weak to impinge on any fundamental rights, even if it wanted to.

Here's the conversation I'll be having with James Madison when I die:

Me: Why didn't you at least enumerate the right to do what you want in the privacy of your own bedroom?

Madison: Son, if the federal government is in your bedroom, I've already failed.

Me: Well, you did fail. And don't call me "son."

Madison: Boy, I'm talking to a slave, this is hard for me.

Me: I'll kill you.

Madison: Also not explicitly prohibited by the federal constitution, but bring it on. Brother Malcolm does it every Tuesday just for sport.

Satan: This is why only Buddhists go to heaven.

Unlike their stance on the Ninth Amendment, originalists pay a lot of attention to the Tenth Amendment. The Tenth Amendment is a reaffirmation of limited government, state's rights, and federalism. Originalists use the Tenth Amendment as their ultimate moral absolution from the practical consequences of their actions. They don't want to "ban" abortion, you see; they just want to "leave it up to the states" as the Constitution intended. They don't want to be bigoted toward the LGBTQ community; they just want the states, not the federal government, to determine the appropriate level of gay bashing that's right for them.

I have spared readers of this book a discussion of "incorporation," and you should thank me, because the history of constitutional incorporation is long and technical and so boring it's like watching a football game where they only show the huddles. But suffice it to say here that, for a lot of our history, there was a pitched battle about whether the Bill of Rights even *applied* to the state governments. A world where the federal government couldn't restrict the freedom of the press, but Georgia could, was something that people actually believed for a long time, and is a world that still exists on the margins today.

Even though most rights have now been "incorporated" against the states, our federalist system still locates most power to do most things with state governments, not the federal government.

As a Black man, I struggle with federalism. I find it difficult to develop an intellectually consistent view on the thing. As I've mentioned, my mother was born in 1950 in Mississippi. I have family currently living in states often controlled by Republican legislatures like Indiana and North Carolina. I am constantly aware that *federalism* usually means Black people living in red states get screwed. I'm always inclined to support aggressive use of federal power to save my people.

Until Republicans are in control of the federal government. When that happens, I'm quick to remember I live in New York State. I get real federalist, real quick, when national Republicans try to apply their "Christianity, but just the mean bits" theory of law to my blue state. It wouldn't take much to turn me into a guy outfitted in army fatigues (supplied by Pyer Moss, I imagine) standing on the George Washington Bridge talking about "state's rights."

I'd feel bad about my indecisiveness on the issue, but I'm generally saved from pangs of shame by remembering the blatant conservative hypocrisy around Tenth Amendment jurisprudence.

Conservatives are happy to ignore the Tenth Amendment when they want to obliterate state laws that serve goals they don't think are important. Conservatives never talk about the Tenth Amendment when they're striking down state regulations on the sale and purchase of firearms. It never stays their hand when it comes time to strike down state environmental regulations. In 2020, we saw the federal Supreme Court telling states that they couldn't mandate certain public health and safety restrictions to combat the deadly coronavirus. Where was the Tenth Amendment when conservative justices were telling the governor of New York that he couldn't take certain measures to protect the most densely packed island in the nation from disease?

Originalists will always point to an enumerated right when they want the federal government to do something in violation of the Tenth Amendment and the principle of federalism. But that is why they work so hard to deny the existence of unenumerated rights. There's no objective reason that the Ninth Amendment should be applied to the states any less robustly than the Second Amendment. The only difference is that the rights and privileges that the Ninth Amendment protects weren't on the original white supremacist, noninclusive list.

I might decide how much gas I put into the Tenth Amendment depending on who won the last election. Conservatives choose how much gas they put into constitutional rights based on the color and status of the people the states are trying to hurt. My way is better; at least I'm trying to protect vulnerable people from harm, not the ancient right of state legislatures to screw over up to 49 percent of their populations.

The structure of our Constitution pits the Ninth and Tenth Amendments against each other, locking them in an existential battle for our nation's soul. The Ninth contemplates robust protection of individual rights that defends minority interests against the excesses of the majority. The Tenth contemplates a society where the states are free to do what they want against minority populations in their state, but are themselves protected from the majority views of the nation.

This is the conflict at the core of our Constitution. Conservatives almost always resolve this conflict for the benefit of white people. White minorities want to hold slaves? Cool. White minorities want to impose segregation? Cool. White minorities want extra representation in the Electoral College? Cool. But white *majorities* want to take Black land to build a park? Also cool. White majorities want the cops to get away with the murder of Black people? Cool. White majorities want to suppress voting rights of Black and brown people? Cool.

Conservatives could not win these constitutional arguments if they put it up for a vote. In a free and fair election, there are just enough white people who reject their white supremacist arguments. When those white people can be linked up with the emerging majority of nonwhite people in this steadily browning country, conservatives lose.

And so, conservatives do not put it up for a vote. They do not allow a free and fair election on their actual platform. They use the judiciary, the least transparent and least responsive branch of government, to push through their antebellum values, and rely on ignorance to mask their true agenda.

Redeeming our failed Constitution from its bigoted and sexist sins does not require new amendments. It does not require a few new ornaments hung upon its crooked boughs. It requires the emerging majority in this country to reject the conservative interpretation of what the Constitution says, and adopt a morally defensible view of what our country means.

I'm here to tell you that the Constitution is trash. Conservatives are the ones who say it always has to be.

EPILOGUE

There is no law or piece of legislation that conservatives on the Supreme Court cannot limit, frustrate, or outright overturn. There is no constitutional amendment that conservatives cannot functionally ignore. There is no principle that conservatives cannot ruin. Without commanding a single troop or passing a single bill, a conservative Supreme Court is not a check on the other branches of government, but a check on progress itself. We can move only as far and as fast as the nine unelected and unaccountable justices on the Court allow us to.

What can we do about that?

One obvious solution would be to strip the federal courts of their power of judicial review. Remember, the power to render acts of Congress unconstitutional was not conferred in the original Constitution or any amendment since. The Court just took that power for itself in *Marbury v. Madison*, and nobody ever stopped them. Indeed, ever since the Reconstruction Amendments, the text of each amendment has included phrases like "Congress shall have the power to enforce this article," the clear implication being that it is up to Congress, not the Supreme Court, to determine what *equal protection* or *due process* or *voting rights* are supposed to look like. But the Supreme Court has regularly ignored this limitation and decided on its own which laws are allowed under the provisions of those amendments.

The power, enjoyed by our Supreme Court, unilaterally to revoke laws passed by the democratic branches of government, is uncommon on the global stage. Other advanced democracies, from Canada to South Africa, do not have high courts that are nearly as powerful as ours. In most other countries, high courts resolve disputes between laws, not whether laws are valid. Maybe we need to do the work the founders never did and amend Article III to define and limit what the Supreme Court can, and cannot, do.

Nerfing the power of the Supreme Court comes with downsides, however. Much as I hate the constitutional interpretations of conservative jurists, I fear the legislative machinations of conservative politicians even more. Most of the ones I've met aren't as decent as Rick Lazio, a man I could easily fill a book disagreeing with. As I've shown, the democratic branches of government are already tilted toward everlasting white supremacist domination. Through gerrymandering, equal state representation in the Senate, and the Electoral College, white people already have the tools to overrepresent themselves in the House, Senate, and Executive Office of the President. Historically speaking, those committed to decency have held all of those levers of power for only the briefest of times. Then they either lose to a conservative counterreaction or lose the will to keep fighting their racist siblings and cousins.

Absent throwing out the Constitution and starting over with a document written by an inclusive body that represents the interests of people of color and women this time (which I'd be in favor of but doubt will happen absent some kind of disaster-movie apocalypse where the seas rise but only bad faith white people get wet), it feels to me like some institution is necessary to counteract the white power of the so-called "democratically" elected branches of government. I wouldn't be wild about unelected judges putting up guardrails around our democracy, if we had a democracy. But since we have a republic infected with slavers' rights and representation, I am reluctant to throw away any tool whatsoever that can be won and used to force white people to chew with their mouths closed and behave more reasonably, even if that tool is used in furtherance of evil more often than not. A broken clock will at least be right twice a day; white conservatives never seem to know what time it is.

My preferred solutions focus on restructuring and reforming the Supreme Court, not eliminating it or its power. The unelected, unaccountable branch of government could be made less of a horror show if it were just a little more representative, and if the judges were just a little more responsive to the realities of our times.

Luckily, for me, we have a lot of options here. Article III mostly leaves the structure of the Supreme Court and the federal judiciary up to Congress.

One of the most popular reforms is to impose term limits on federal judges. Modern medicine has, among other things, totally overpowered judges who hold their positions for life. Coupled with the Federalist Society's push to appoint ever younger judges, lifetime appointments mean that judges can now wield power in our system across multiple generations of humans. Some of the judges appointed by Donald Trump may hold power for fifty years. It's hard to imagine, but it's entirely possible that some person not yet conceived will be fighting for postapocalyptic climate regulation in the 2070s, only to have their law declared unconstitutional through the vestigial power of a judge appointed by a twice-impeached con man. Those are the stakes when we talk about lifetime appointments.

But getting rid of lifetime tenure, absent a constitutional

amendment, is tricky. That's because Article III, while generally silent about the structure of the courts, does specify that federal judges serve while in "good behavior."

There are creative ways around this problem. The leading plan, endorsed by scholars such as Aaron Belkin of Take Back the Court Action Fund and Harvard law professor Laurence Tribe, involves forcing Supreme Court judges to take "senior status" after eighteen years on the bench. Senior status is something that we do for lower federal courts, and it has been deemed perfectly constitutional. It's a semiretirement option offered to judges who still take cases and draw a full salary but don't occupy a "seat" on their federal benches. Judges who take senior status can be replaced by new judges, appointed by the president and confirmed by the Senate. Currently, over 40 percent of the federal circuit court judges are on senior status; it's a nice way to ease older jurists out of their lifetime positions of power, without requiring them to move "to a farm, upstate."

The Constitution says Supreme Court justices have to serve for life; it doesn't say they have to serve "on the Supreme Court" for life. This version of the term limit plan would see justices take senior status and rotate down to a lower federal court for the remainder of their lives. These judges could be called back up to the Supreme Court in the event sitting justices needed to recuse themselves.

Meanwhile, rotating through nine justices on eighteen-year term limits would create an opening on the Supreme Court every two years. Obviously, creating an opening does not ensure that the Supreme Court would become more liberal over time; the Federalist Society would still exist and would still be pushing for arch-conservative justices willing to turn the clock back to 1787. But term limits would ensure that the federal judiciary was more responsive to the winners and losers of elections. As of this writing, the last three Republican presidents (George H.W. Bush, George W. Bush, Donald Trump) served for a combined sixteen years and are responsible for six of the justices on the Supreme Court (alleged sexual harasser Clarence Thomas, John Roberts, Samuel Alito, illegitimately appointed Neil Gorsuch, alleged attempted rapist Brett Kavanaugh, and hypocritically speedily appointed Amy Coney Barrett). Meanwhile the last two Democratic presidents (Bill Clinton and Barack Obama) also served for a combined sixteen years, yet are represented by only three justices (Stephen Breyer, Sonia Sotomayor, and Elena Kagan). President Joe Biden will be able to fill a seat on the Supreme Court only if Breyer retires, or an actual unforeseen tragedy befalls one of the conservatives (whose average age is now sixty-one).

Our system of justice should not be like this. Whether some people have rights or not should not depend on when the random wheel of death strikes down an octogenarian justice. Nor should it depend on the kind of strategic retirement gamesmanship employed by Republican-appointed justices.

Democratic appointees don't tend to play "strategic retirement" particularly well. Take for instance the tragedy of Thurgood Marshall. He was appointed in 1967 and hung on valiantly all the way through the Ronald Reagan years in the 1980s. But by the time Reagan was succeeded by yet another Republican, George H.W. Bush, Marshall's health was failing. He hung on for as long as he could do the job credibly, but in 1991 he finally decided to retire. Bush replaced him with Clarence Thomas, and Thomas has worked tirelessly to undo Marshall's great legacy. But Marshall didn't *die* until January 24, 1993, mere days after Bill Clinton was inaugurated as president. If Marshall had been willing essentially to compromise his duties and health and wait to be carried out of the Court in a coffin, the last twenty-five years of American jurisprudence would be significantly different.

By contrast, Sandra Day O'Connor strategically retired in 2006, both because her husband was sick and she wanted to care for him, and because she wanted to retire under a Republican. Her seat was then filled by Bush 43, who replaced O'Connor's brand of moderation with the arch-conservative Alito.

Likewise, in a move designed to preserve his conservative legacy, Anthony Kennedy was perfectly healthy but relinquished his seat to his protégé, Kavanaugh, in 2018.

Meanwhile, Ruth Bader Ginsburg could have retired in 2014 under the Obama administration, but she felt she could still do the job and didn't want to be pushed out by men telling her what to do. She hung on but didn't make it, dying in September 2020, just weeks before Trump lost the presidential election to Biden. In a wildly hypocritical move, given that they had blocked the appointment of Merrick Garland during Obama's final year as president, Republicans rushed to replace Ginsburg in Trump's final weeks, putting in her stead the conservative zealot Amy Barrett.

Two moderates who left strategically, and two liberals who didn't, has resulted in four hard-right extremists who will define the limits of human rights for a generation of Americans. This is not the way.

Term limits would fix that, at least. But the Supreme Court, stacked as it is with conservatives justices, is unlikely to accept term limits as constitutional. Conservatives would cling to the language of Article III the way a person adrift would cling to a life raft and reject any term limits bill passed by Congress. Again, legislation cannot survive conservative justices if conservative justices don't like the law.

The way to get term limits (which I support) is not to offer up legislation that will be ruled unconstitutional by the conservative Court before breakfast; it's to pack the Court with liberal justices who believe the term limits plan is constitutional and have them there to defend whatever term limits legislation Congress passes.

The number of Supreme Court justices is not set by Article III or anything else in the Constitution. The Supreme Court opened with six justices. John Adams, as a lame-duck president who had lost to Thomas Jefferson in 1800, issued the "Midnight Judges Act," which reduced the number of justices to five "upon the next vacancy" on the Court. That's an important distinction. You can't remove a federal judge, including a Supreme Court justice, absent the constitutional provision for impeachment. So you can't take away members already on the Court, but you can, upon their death or retirement, reduce the number of seats on the Supreme Court.

Jefferson, however, restored the number of Supreme Court justices to six upon taking office.

Then, in 1807, as Jefferson was nearing the end of his second term, he enlarged the Supreme Court to seven justices, and appointed another one himself.

A seven-member Court was in place when Andrew Jackson set his sights on it in 1837. Jackson added two more seats to the Supreme Court and filled them. It was the first time the Supreme Court reached nine justices, which represents a 50 percent increase from the number of justices on the court at the founding, less than fifty years earlier.

During the Civil War years, the number of justices on the Supreme Court ballooned to ten. That was in part because Chief Justice Roger Taney—he of the infamous *Dred Scott* decision in 1857—continued in his role on the Court and was a constant thorn in Lincoln's side.

After the war, Congress reduced the number of justices back down to seven, mainly to spite the reviled Andrew Johnson. Finally, the Judiciary Act of 1869 set the number of justices as nine, and we've been there ever since.

The Supreme Court is not baseball; nine is not a magic number. Our history shows that changing the number of justices on the Supreme Court is the actual normal political response to a Court that is out of step with the times. It is, if anything, the way the Constitution wants us to handle the Supreme Court: treat each individual justice as an independent arbiter who cannot be fired by an angry president and is protected from the political fray by a lifetime appointment, but treat the Supreme Court as a subservient branch that can be "corrected" by Congress and the president through various means.

I therefore favor adding additional justices to the Supreme Court, often derisively called "court packing," as the appropriate constitutional solution to the problem of generational overrepresentation of conservatives on the Court. Conservatives enjoy overrepresentation in the Senate and the White House because of structural flaws in our Constitution. But they enjoy overrepresentation on the Court because liberals have not been willing to do whatever it takes to stop them.

Court expansion is the way to overcome the power conservatives have locked in for themselves, likely until the 2070s. A judiciary act increasing the number of justices on the Supreme Court can be passed by a Democratic Congress, signed by a Democratic president, and then new justices can be nominated by that president and confirmed by a Democratic Senate. It's simple. It will work. All it takes is political will.

But if a Democratic president can expand the Court, can't a Republican president do the same if that party controls all of government again? And won't that lead to an endless tit for tat, where the Supreme Court is an endlessly increasing body that turns into a "super legislature" that changes control based on the party in power?

Yes. And I don't care. I don't care because the Supreme Court is already a super legislature that works to frustrate and disrupt law passed by democratically elected representatives. I don't care because, absent a couple of decades in the middle of the twentieth century, that super legislature almost always works against the

interests of minorities and women. I don't care because telling people that we have to wait until Neil Gorsuch (appointed after Mitch
McConnell refused to even hold a hearing on Barack Obama's nom-
inee, Merrick Garland) and Brett Kavanaugh (appointed despite
credible accusations of attempted rape) and Amy Coney Barrett
(appointed after an election had already started to replace the
twice-impeached man who nominated her) literally have to drop
dead before we can advance urgent legislation needed to combat
climate change, is unacceptable. The country cannot be held hostage by four years' worth of Trump judges for the next fifty years.
I don't care about what Republicans will do if they ever control all
of government again, because a Supreme Court willing to protect
voting rights and take the Fifteenth Amendment out of cryostasis
makes it unlikely that an openly white nationalist party *will* control
all of government again.

Beyond the stark political realities, there are wonderful reform
reasons for Court expansion. We can probably never return the
Supreme Court to the "least dangerous" status imagined by Alexander Hamilton, but we can diminish the power of each individual
Supreme Court justice.

That would be an unqualified good. Understand that while
Republicans have politicized and manipulated the nomination and
confirmation process to ensure that only justices committed to the
Republican political agenda end up on the Supreme Court, they're
not wrong to do so. Each justice represents a vector of power that
far outlasts any presidential administration and most legislation.
One justice committed to bigotry and oppression, or liberty and
plurality, can change the course of history, much less three or four
or five. Republicans are right to go to the mattresses every time one
of these openings come up, and Democrats have been fools not to
adopt the same tactics.

Adding more justices is a way to *de*politicize the entire

nomination process. It lowers the stakes for each confirmation battle. Fighting for one of nine is just a different political calculus than
fighting for one of nineteen, or one of twenty-nine. That's just math.
It's like the way parents of only one child will monitor that kid on
the playground from a helicopter, while parents of five children
send them out to play in traffic and only do a head count at bedtime
to see if they all made it back alive (note: I may be a bad parent).

I would like to see the Democrats add twenty justices to the
Supreme Court, to bring the number of justices up to twenty-
nine. Partially, that's to diminish the Republican appetite for
counter-expansion, but I also objectively think that twenty-nine is
about the right number. The Ninth Circuit Court of Appeals (which
is responsible for California, and a number of western states) currently seats twenty-nine judges; they seem to function just fine.

A key benefit of court expansion is moving the Supreme Court to
the kind of "panel" system employed throughout the rest of the federal judiciary. Appeals to any circuit court of appeal are first heard
by a three-judge panel. The panels are chosen by random lot from
among the available judges (including senior status judges). That
panel issues a ruling. If the rest of the bench doesn't like it, a majority of the judges on the circuit vote to rehear the case as a full body
(called en banc review).

I cannot emphasize how much better that system is for the
appearance of impartiality than the current Supreme Court system
of hearing all cases as a full body. Even a Court "stacked" with justices from one party or the other might wind up with a panel dominated by justices appointed from the minority party. Even courts
with a few extremists on either side of the law will find that those
extremists are not involved in most of the cases that court hears.
And even when extremists end up on the same panel, their opinions have to be tempered enough not to be struck by en banc review.

When it gets to en banc review, the chances that a twenty-nine-member Court is going to break 15–14 along strict party lines is just rare. The law is complicated. Judges, who remain independent, unaccountable arbiters, are quirky. Even judges who share an ideological framework don't always agree on how that ideology should be applied in every case. Even originalists don't always agree: some will use Strunk and White to limit the rights of men and women, others will pull an eighteenth-century farmer's almanac out of their asses, and I swear to God that Neil Gorsuch will one day quote the Wife of Bath from *The Canterbury Tales* in a judicial opinion: "The wife, an authority on the common law perception of marriage, may have had many husbands, but they were all of the opposite sex-at-birth to her own."

I can't guarantee that a super-expanded court would produce "better" opinions, but I am confident that it would produce more moderate and mainstream opinions. Herding fifteen people together to form a majority opinion is just a different beast than keeping five Federalist Society members on board.

Moreover, an expanded Court opens the possibility for more diversity on the bench, so that the Court looks more like the country it lords over. Exactly three people of color (Marshall, Thomas, and Sotomayor) have served on the Supreme Court in American history. There've been a total of five women (O'Connor, Ginsburg, Sotomayor, Kagan, and Barrett).

That's fucking embarrassing.

Always remember, the arch-conservative view of the law trumpeted by the Federalist Society is a *minority* opinion. It's a minority opinion in law school, in academia, and within the legal profession writ large. Anything that can be done to drown out conservative voices on the Court should be done, and the quickest and easiest way to do that is simply to add more voices. Conservatives never win when everybody gets to play. In the words of Kermit the Frog in *The Muppets Take Manhattan*, "That's what we need! More frogs and dogs and bears and chickens and . . . and whatever! You're not gonna watch the show, you're gonna be in the show!"

The legitimate knock on adding additional justices is not "Twenty-nine sounds like a lot" or "But what will Republicans do?"; it is "Doesn't twenty-nine justices make the court even less responsive to the will of the people?" Conservatives have shown that you can diminish the rights of entire groups of people just by changing a couple of justices on the Supreme Court, but liberals showed during the civil rights era that you can grant rights to entire groups of people with just a couple of appointments. Arguably, a twenty-nine-member Court would be even more resistant to democratic-inspired change than our current one, because to change the opinion of the Court you have to swap out as many as fifteen justices instead of just four or five.

It's a real concern, but that's why I started this discussion with term limits. Expand the Court, pass term limits, have the expanded Court rule that term limits are constitutional, then start rotating one of the current justices off the bench about once a year. The Supreme Court as an institution would remain a powerful check on the constitutional excesses of the elected branches. But the institution would be responsive to the winners of democratic elections over time. The individual justices would remain independent and unremovable during their terms in office. But the confirmation process would be depoliticized to the point of becoming almost rote, and each individual justice could not hold sway over our polity for as long as Pfizer can keep them alive.

An expanded Supreme Court is a path toward a better future, but one that cannot be realized unless liberals and progressives get in the game and demand that the Democratic Party take the courts seriously. This book is a guide, not for how we win, but why we must. I believe that if more people knew what was at stake, they wouldn't cede an entire branch of government to conservatives dedicated to holding back the rest of society.

Never accept the conservative interpretation of the Constitution. Never accept the conservative limitations placed on our political, civil, and social rights. They have literally always been wrong, and they are wrong now. Justice is not one constitutional option among many—it is a requirement of a free and equal society. Demand nothing less.

NOTES

With gratitude to Jessica Suriano for her research support.

viii **Dobbs v. Jackson Women's Health**: *Dobbs v. Jackson Women's Health Organization*, 597 U.S. __ (2022).

viii **Roe v. Wade**: *Roe v. Wade*, 410 U.S. 113 (1973).

ix **defines originalism this way:** Steven G. Calabresi, "On Originalism in Constitutional Interpretation," National Constitution Center, https://constitutioncenter.org/the-constitution/white-papers/on-originalism-in-constitutional-interpretation.

xii **Planned Parenthood of Southeastern Pennsylvania v. Casey**: *Planned Parenthood of Southeastern Pennsylvania v. Casey*, 505 U.S. 833 (1992).

xv **During oral arguments:** *Students for Fair Admissions v. University of NC*, Oral Argument, https://www.supremecourt.gov/oral_arguments/audio/2022/21-707.

2 **Lock, Stock, And Two Smoking Barrels**: *Lock, Stock, And Two Smoking Barrels*, directed by Guy Ritchie, PolyGram Filmed Entertainment, 1998.

12 **"heckler's veto"**: Patrick Schmidt, "Heckler's Veto," *The First Amendment Encyclopedia*, The Free Speech Center at Middle Tennessee State University.

14 **Gawker published a story "outing" him in 2007**: Derek Thompson, "The

Most Expensive Comment in Internet History?" *The Atlantic*, February 23, 2018.

14 **He told the *New York Times***: Andrew Ross Sorkin, "Peter Thiel, Tech Billionaire, Reveals Secret War with Gawker," *The New York Times*, May 25, 2016.

17 **"intimidate" him**: Allyson Chiu, "'This Was an Orchestrated Effort': Devin Nunes Sues Twitter, 'Devin Nunes' Cow' for Defamation," *The Washington Post*, March 20, 2019.

19 **Religious Freedom Restoration Act (RFRA)**: H.R.1308, 103rd Congress (1993–1994), "Religious Freedom Restoration Act," November 16, 1993.

19 ***Employment Division v. Smith***: *Employment Division, Department of Human Resources of Oregon v. Smith*, 494 U.S. 872 (1990).

20 ***Sherbert v. Verner***: *Sherbert v. Verner*, 374 U.S. 398 (1963).

20 **"strict scrutiny"**: "Free Exercise of Religion," Cornell Law School, Legal Information Institute.

21 **"distinguishing"**: "Distinguish," Cornell Law School, Legal Information Institute.

22 ***Burwell v. Hobby Lobby Stores***: *Burwell v. Hobby Lobby Stores*, 573 U.S. 682 (2014).

25 **Colorado's Anti-Discrimination Act (CADA)**: Colorado Revised Statutes (C.R.S.) Title 24, Article 34, Parts 3–8, 1957.

26 ***Lawrence v. Texas***: *Lawrence v. Texas*, 539 U.S. 558 (2003).

26 ***U.S. v. Windsor***: *United States v. Windsor*, 570 U.S. 744 (2013).

26 ***Obergefell v. Hodges***: *Obergefell v. Hodges*, 576 U.S. __ (2015).

26 ***Citizens United***: *Citizens United v. Federal Election Commission*, 558 U.S. 310 (2010).

26 ***Masterpiece Cakeshop***: *Masterpiece Cakeshop, Ltd. v. Colorado Civil Rights Commission*, 584 U.S. __ (2018).

28 **"Christian beliefs"**: Isabella Grullón Paz, "Colorado Baker Fined for Refusing to Make Cake for Transgender Woman," *The New York Times*, June 18, 2021.

29 **"anti-LGBTQ hate group"**: "Extremist Files: Alliance Defending Freedom," *Southern Poverty Law Center*.

29 **Blackstone Legal Fellowship**: Sharona Coutts and Sofia Resnick, "Not the 'Illuminati': How Fundamentalist Christians Are Infiltrating State and Federal Government," *Rewire News Group*, May 13, 2014.

32 **Tomahawk missile**: "Tomahawk," Missile Defense Project; "Missile Threat," Center for Strategic and International Studies, September 19, 2016, last modified November 4, 2019.

33 *USS Ticonderoga*: Guy Joseph Nasuti, "USS Ticonderoga (CG-47)," Naval History and Heritage Command, Dictionary of American Naval Fighting Ships, published November 22, 2019.

33 **events of January 6, 2021**: Luke Mogelson, "Among the Insurrectionists," *The New Yorker*, January 15, 2021; "Inside the Capitol Riot: An Exclusive Video Investigation," *The New York Times*, June 30, 2021.

34 **"copwatching"**: Torin Monahan, *Surveillance and Security: Technological Politics and Power in Everyday Life*, Taylor & Francis, August 4, 2006.

34 **Mulford Act**: Adam Winkler, "The Secret History of Guns," *The Atlantic*, Sept. 2011.

34 **Gun Control Act of 1968**: "Gun Control Act of 1968," Bureau of Alcohol, Tobacco, Firearms and Explosives, last reviewed January 23, 2020.

34 *U.S. v. Miller*: *United States v. Miller*, 307 U.S. 174 (1939).

34 **National Firearms Act of 1934**: "National Firearms Act," Bureau of Alcohol, Tobacco, Firearms and Explosives, last reviewed April 7, 2020.

36 **Revolt at Cincinnati**: Joel Achenbach, Scott Higham, and Sari Horwitz, "How NRA's True Believers Converted a Marksmanship Group into a Mighty Gun Lobby," *The Washington Post*, January 12, 2013.

36 **Firearm Owners Protection Act of 1986**: S. 49, 99th Congress (1985–1986), "Firearms Owners' Protection Act," May 19, 1986.

36 **Patrick Henry and George Mason**: Dave Davies, "Historian Uncovers The Racist Roots of the 2nd Amendment," NPR, June 2, 2021.

37 **Professor Carl Bogus**: Carl T. Bogus, "Was Slavery a Factor in the Second Amendment?" *The New York Times*, May 24, 2018.

37 **"If they neglect or refuse"**: "Document: Patrick Henry Speech Before Virginia Ratifying Convention (June 5, 1788)," *Teaching American History*.

38 *D.C. v. Heller*: *District of Columbia v. Heller*, 554 U.S. 570 (2008).

39 **Reagan and company**: Thad Morgan, "The NRA Supported Gun Control When the Black Panthers Had the Weapons," *History.com*, published March 22, 2018, updated August 30, 2018.

45 *Terry v. Ohio*: Terry v. Ohio, 392 U.S. 1 (1968).

45 *Carroll v. U.S.*: *Carroll v. United States*, 354 U.S. 394 (1957).

45 *Miranda v. Arizona*: *Miranda v. Arizona*, 384 U.S. 436 (1966).

45 **served Burger King**: Staff Reports, "Charleston Shooting Suspect's Burger King Meal Gets National Attention," *The Charlotte Observer*, June 24, 2015.

46 **"casing the joint"**: *Terry v. Ohio* Oral Arguments Transcripts, December 12, 1967, Courtesy of the University of Minnesota.

47 **New York State's stop and frisk law**: New York State Legislature, C.P.L. § 140.50, "Temporary questioning of persons in public places; search for weapons," September 1, 1971.

48 **"broken windows policing"**: Chris Benderev, Tara Boyle, Renee Klahr, Maggie Penman, Jennifer Schmidt, and Shankar Vedantam, "How a Theory of Crime and Policing Was Born, and Went Terribly Wrong," NPR, November 1, 2016.

49 *Floyd v. City of New York*: *Floyd, et al. v. City of New York, et al.*, 959 F. Supp. 2d 540 (S.D.N.Y. 2013).

50 **"In all honesty, I just didn't like them."**: Christina Bucciere, "Ambassador Stokes Discusses Diversity, Stop-and-Frisk Laws," *KentWired.com*, September 18, 2014.

52 **"When I grabbed him"**: CNN Newsroom Transcripts, "No Indictment in Ferguson; Grand Jury Evidence Released in Brown Case," November 25, 2014.

53 *Graham v. Connor*: *Graham v. Connor*, 490 U.S. 386 (1989).

57 **"pattern and practice"**: The United States Department of Justice, "How Department of Justice Civil Rights Division Conducts Pattern-or-Practice Investigations," May 8, 2015.

61 *Leviathan*: Thomas Hobbes, *Leviathan: Or the Matter, Forme and Power of a Commonwealth Ecclesiasticall and Civil*, published 1651.

63 **"affirmative defense"**: "Affirmative Defense," Cornell Law School, Legal Information Institute.

63 **"Stand Your Ground" laws**: "Guns in Public: Stand Your Ground," Giffords Law Center.

63 **One well-respected study**: John K. Roman, "Race, Justifiable Homicide, and Stand Your Ground Laws: Analysis of FBI Supplementary Homicide Report Data," Urban Institute Justice Policy Center, Published July 2013.

64 **It found**: Nicole Ackermann, Melody S. Goodman, Keon Gilbert, Cassandra Arroyo-Johnson Marcello Pagano, "Race, Law, and Health: Examination of 'Stand Your Ground' and Defendant Convictions in Florida," *Social Science & Medicine*, volume 142, pages 194–201, 2015.

65 **"provocation" rule**: "As a Matter of Law and Policy, the Ninth Circuit's 'Provocation Rule' Must Stand," Harvard Civil Rights, Civil Liberties Law Review, February 9, 2017.

65 ***County of Los Angeles v. Mendez***: *County of Los Angeles v. Mendez*, 581 U.S. __ (2017).

65 **The facts in *Mendez***: Elie Mystal, "The Supreme Court Makes It Even Easier for Cops to Shoot You," *Above the Law*, May 30, 2017.

66 **"qualified immunity"**: "Qualified immunity," Cornell Law School, Legal Information Institute.

67 ***Bivens v. Six Unknown Named Agents of Federal Bureau of Narcotics***: *Bivens v. Six Unknown Named Agents of Federal Bureau of Narcotics*, 403 U.S. 388 (1971).

68 ***Harlow v. Fitzgerald***: *Harlow v. Fitzgerald*, 457 U.S. 800 (1982).

69 **Kafkaesque loop**: Nathaniel Sobel, "What Is Qualified Immunity, and What Does It Have to Do with Police Reform?" *Lawfare*, June 6, 2020.

69 ***Pearson v. Callahan***: *Pearson v. Callahan*, 555 U.S. 223 (2009).

69 **introduced legislation**: H.R. 1470, 117th Congress (2021-2022), Rep. Ayanna Pressley, "Ending Qualified Immunity Act," March 1, 2020.

74 **Amy Cooper**: Matt Stieb, "Amy Cooper Didn't Learn Much from Her Time as 'Central Park Karen,'" *New York Magazine*, May 26, 2021.

77 **Yale Law Journal article**: Jed Rubenfeld, "The Paradigm-Case Method," *The Yale Law Journal*, 2006.

80 ***Roe v. Wade***: *Roe v. Wade*, 410 U.S. 113 (1973).

80 ***Planned Parenthood v. Casey***: *Planned Parenthood of Southeastern Pennsylvania v. Casey*, 505 U.S. 833 (1992).

81 ***Dickerson v. United States***: *Dickerson v. United States*, 530 U.S. 428 (2000).

82 **At that new trial**: History.com Editors, "Miranda Rights," *History.com*, Published November 9, 2009, updated June 12, 2019.

83 **full page ad**: Jan Ransom, "Trump Will Not Apologize for Calling for Death Penalty Over Central Park Five," *The New York Times*, June 18, 2019.

84 **exoneration report**: Nancy E. Ryan, "Affirmation in Response to Motion to Vacate Judgement of Conviction," *Supreme Court of the State of New York, County of New York, Part 58*, December 5, 2002.

88 **were bought for $125**: The Central Park Conservancy, "The Story of Seneca Village," January 18, 2018; Sam Neubauer, "Seneca Village: A Forgotten Settlement Buried Under Central Park," *I Love the Upper West Side*, July 23, 2020.

88 **New York African Society for Mutual Relief**: James Sullivan, "The New York African Society for Mutual Relief (1808–1860)," *BlackPast.org*, January 22, 2011.

88 **bought 12 lots for $578**: The Central Park Conservancy, "The Story of Seneca Village," January 18, 2018.

89 **male landowners in possession of $250 worth of property**: The Central Park Conservancy, "The Story of Seneca Village," January 18, 2018.

89 **ten lived in Seneca Village**: Douglas Martin, "Before Park, Black Village; Students Look Into a Community's History," *The New York Times*, April 7, 1995.

91 **In 1626**: Janos Marton, "Today in NYC History: How the Dutch Actually Bought Manhattan (the Long Version)," *Untapped Cities*, May 6, 2015.

91 **Robert Miller makes clear**: Robert J. Miller, "Economic Development in Indian Country: Will Capitalism or Socialism Succeed?" *Oregon Law Review*, Vol. 80, No. 3, 2001.

91 ***Law in American History***: G. Edward White, *Law in American History: Volume 1: From the Colonial Years Through the Civil War*, Oxford University Press, January 3, 2012.

91 ***On The Law of War and Peace***: Hugo Grotius, *De Jure Belli ac Pacis: On the Law of War and Peace*, 1625.

92 **"Wall Street"**: "Wall Street and the Stock Exchanges: Historical Resources," *Library of Congress*.

93 *Kelo v. City of New London*: *Kelo v. New London*, 545 U.S. 469 (2005).

93 **"rededicated"**: "The Kelo House (1890)," *Historic Buildings of Connecticut*, March 20, 2009.

94 *The Power Broker: Robert Moses and the Fall of New York*: Robert A. Caro, *The Power Broker: Robert Moses and the Fall of New York*, Knopf Doubleday Publishing Group, 1974.

95 **Article 15 of New York Consolidated Laws, Section 500**: Consolidated Laws of New York: General Municipal, "Article 15: Urban Renewal," Section 500–525, The New York State Senate.

97 **Jones's Wood**: "What Was Jones' Wood?" New York Historical Society Museum and Library.

98 **"swamp . . . squatters"**: "Seneca Village, New York City," National Park Service.

98 **was paid $2,335 for his three lots and house**: "Andrew Williams' Affidavit of Petition," *New York City Municipal Archives*, Bureau of Old Records; Douglas Martin, "A Village Dies, a Park Is Born," *The New York Times*, January 31, 1997.

100 *Commentaries on the Laws of England*: William Blackstone, *Commentaries on the Laws of England*, Oxford: Printed at the Clarendon Press, 1765–1769.

102 *Strauder v. West Virginia*: *Strauder v. West Virginia*, 100 U.S. 303 (1880).

103 **"law French"**: "Law French," Cornell Law School, Legal Information Institute.

104 *Swain v. Alabama*: *Swain v. Alabama*, 380 U.S. 202 (1965).

105 *Batson v. Kentucky*: *Batson v. Kentucky*, 476 U.S. 79 (1986).

105 **"object anyway"**: Sean Rameswaram, "Object Anyway," *More Perfect*, WNYC Studios, July 16, 2016.

106 *J.E.B. v. Alabama ex rel T.B.*: *J.E.B. v. Alabama ex rel T.B.*, 511 U.S. 127 (1994).

107 *University of Michigan Journal of Law Reform* **article**: Michael J. Raphael and Edward J. Ungvarsky, "Excuses, Excuses: Neutral Explanations Under Batson v. Kentucky," *University of Michigan Journal of Law Reform*, Volume 27, 1993.

109 *Holland v. Illinois*: *Holland v. Illinois*, 493 U.S. 474 (1990).

114 **twenty-five different crimes that were punishable by death**: "Early History of the Death Penalty," *Death Penalty Information Center.*

114 **condemn innocent people**: "Description of Innocence Cases," *Death Penalty Information Center,* last updated 2021.

114 **against Black and Brown defendants**: "Race and the Death Penalty," *ACLU*; "Race and the Death Penalty," *Prison Policy Initiative.*

117 *Furman v. Georgia*: *Furman v. Georgia,* 408 U.S. 238 (1972).

118 *Gregg v. Georgia*: *Gregg v. Georgia,* 428 U.S. 153 (1976).

119 *Bucklew v. Precythe*: *Bucklew v. Precythe,* 587 U.S. __ (2019).

128 *The Second Founding*: Eric Foner, *The Second Founding: How the Civil War and Reconstruction Remade the Constitution,* W. W. Norton & Company, 2019.

134 **without Grant**: Ron Chernow, *Grant,* Penguin Books, September 25, 2018.

137 *Slaughter-House Cases*: *Slaughter-House Cases,* 83 U.S. 36 (1873).

138 **The Civil Rights Act of 1875**: André Munro and Melvin I. Urofsky, "Civil Rights Act of 1875," *Britannica,* March 31, 2014.

139 **The *Civil Rights Cases***: *Civil Rights Cases,* 109 U.S. 3 (1883).

139 **"within two blocks"**: "Jim Crow Laws," National Park Service, Last updated April 17, 2018.

142 *Plessy v. Ferguson*: *Plessy v. Ferguson,* 163 U.S. 537 (1896).

142 *Brown v. Board of Education of Topeka*: *Brown v. Board of Education of Topeka (1),* 347 U.S. 483 (1954).

144 **The Civil Rights Act of 1866**: "Civil Rights Act of 1866," *Federal Judicial Center,* April 9, 1866.

145 *UCLA Law Review* **article**: Ronald Turner, "A Critique of Justice Antonin Scalia's Originalist Defense of Brown v. Board of Education," *UCLA Law Review,* Discourse 170, 2014.

145 *Reading Law: The Interpretation of Legal Texts*: Bryan A. Garner and Antonin Scalia, *Reading Law: The Interpretation of Legal Texts,* Thomson West Publishing, 2012.

147 *Loving v. Virginia*: *Loving v. Virginia,* 388 U.S. 1 (1967).

147 **When he was seventeen**: Brynn Holland, "Mildred and Richard: The Love Story That Changed America," *History.com*, Published February 17, 2017, Updated October 18, 2018.

148 **"Act To Preserve Racial Integrity"**: "Racial Integrity Act of 1924," The Virginia Center for Digital History at the University of Virginia.

148 *Pace v. Alabama*: *Pace v. Alabama*, 106 U.S. 583 (1883).

148 **Mildred Loving later told an interviewer**: Phyl Newbeck, "Loving v. Virginia (1967)," *Encyclopedia Virginia*, December 7, 2020.

151 **2012 law review article**: Steven G. Calabresi and Andrea Matthews, "Originalism and Loving v. Virginia," Faculty Working Papers, *Northwestern University School of Law*, Paper 206, 2012.

152 **"anti-sodomy" law**: Texas Penal Code § 21.06, Title 5, "Offenses Against the Person, Chapter 21 Sexual Offenses," Section 21.06, "Homosexual Conduct," effective January 1, 1974.

158 **"strict scrutiny"**: "Strict scrutiny," Cornell Law School, Legal Information Institute.

158 *Marbury v. Madison*: *Marbury v. Madison*, 5 U.S. 137 (1803).

160 *Craig v. Boren*: *Craig v. Boren*, 429 U.S. 190 (1976).

161 *Korematsu v. U.S.*: *Korematsu v. United States*, 323 U.S. 214 (1944).

161 **Executive Order 9066**: "Executive Order 9066," General Records of the United States Government; Record Group 11, National Archives, February 19, 1942.

162 *Trump v. Hawaii*: *Trump v. Hawaii*, 585 U.S. __ (2018).

163 *The New Republic*: Brian Beutler, "Anthony Kennedy's Same-Sex Marriage Opinion Was a Logical Disaster," *The New Republic*, July 1, 2015.

170 *Lochner v. New York*: *Lochner v. New York*, 198 U.S. 45 (1905).

171 *Lochner* era: "Lochner Era," Cornell Law School, Legal Information Institute.

172 **In his article**: Mark Joseph Stern, "A New Lochner Era," *Slate*, June 29, 2018.

172 *Janus v. American Federation of State, County, and Municipal Employees*: *Janus v. American Federation of State, County, and Municipal Employees, Council 31*, 585 U.S. __ (2018).

172 *Adair v. United States*: *Adair v. United States*, 208 U.S. 161 (1908).

173 *Perry v. New Hampshire*: *Perry v. New Hampshire*, 565 U.S. 228 (2012).

177 **Griswold v. Connecticut**: *Griswold v. Connecticut*, 381 U.S. 479 (1965).

178 **Comstock law**: "Anthony Comstock's 'Chastity' Laws," *PBS: American Experience*.

179 **Margaret Sanger**: Nikita Stewart, "Planned Parenthood in N.Y. Disavows Margaret Sanger Over Eugenics," *The New York Times*, July 21, 2020.

188 **"safe, legal, and rare"**: Emily Crockett, "Tim Kaine's Evolving Views on Abortion, Explained," *Vox*, October 3, 2016.

194 **"Equal Rights Amendment"**: Daniel Read Anthony, Jr., H.J. Res. 75, 68th Congress (1923–1925), Committee on the Judiciary, December 13, 1923.

195 **"Stop Taking Our Privileges (STOP)"**: "Phyllis Schlafly (1924–2016)," *Biography.com*, April 1, 2020.

195 **"Slaves that worked there"**: Daniel Victor, "Bill O'Reilly Defends Comments About 'Well Fed' Slaves," *The New York Times*, July 27, 2016.

196 **Pew Research Center report**: Eileen Patten and Kim Parker, "Women in the U.S. Military: Growing Share, Distinctive Profile," Pew Research Center, Social & Demographic Trends, 2011.

196 **13 percent**: Maria Guerra, "Fact Sheet: The State of African American Women in the United States," Center for American Progress, November 7, 2013.

197 **"unborn homicide"**: Ramesh Ponnuru, "What If a Fetus Has Constitutional Rights?" *Bloomberg Opinion*, March 31, 2021.

197 *Dred Scott*: *Dred Scott v. Sandford*, 60 U.S. 393 (1857).

207 **"standard, practice, or procedure"**: Section 2 of The Voting Rights Act of 1965, *The United States Department of Justice*.

209 *Shelby County v. Holder*: *Shelby County v. Holder*, 570 U.S. 529 (2013).

212 *Bush v. Gore*: *Bush v. Gore*, 531 U.S. 98 (2000).

212 **Joe Biden defeated Donald Trump**: "Georgia Election Results," *The New York Times* and National Election Pool/Edison Research, Last updated March 6, 2021.

220 *Baker v. Carr*: *Baker v. Carr*, 369 U.S. 186 (1962).

222 ***Rucho v. Common Cause***: *Rucho v. Common Cause*, 588 U.S. __ (2019).

227 **"Great Compromise" or "Connecticut Compromise"**: "A Great Compromise," established July 16, 1787, *United States Senate.*

228 **Here are the ten "Blackest" states**: "Black Population By State," *World Population Review*; "2018 National and State Population Estimates," United States Census Bureau, December 19, 2018.

228 **Washington D.C.**: "Washington, District of Columbia Population," *World Population Review*; "QuickFacts: District of Columbia," United States Census Bureau.

228 **Mississippi**: "Mississippi Population," *World Population Review*; "QuickFacts: Mississippi," United States Census Bureau.

228 **Louisiana**: "Louisiana Population," *World Population Review*; "QuickFacts: Louisiana," United States Census Bureau.

228 **Georgia**: "Georgia Population," *World Population Review*; "QuickFacts: Georgia," United States Census Bureau.

228 **Maryland**: "Maryland Population," *World Population Review*; "QuickFacts: Maryland," United States Census Bureau.

228 **Alabama**: "Alabama Population," *World Population Review*; "QuickFacts: Alabama," United States Census Bureau.

228 **South Carolina**: "South Carolina Population," *World Population Review*; "QuickFacts: South Carolina," United States Census Bureau.

228 **Delaware**: "Delaware Population," *World Population Review*; "QuickFacts: Delaware," United States Census Bureau.

228 **North Carolina**: "North Carolina Population," *World Population Review*; "QuickFacts: North Carolina," United States Census Bureau.

228 **Virginia**: "Virginia Population," *World Population Review*; "QuickFacts: Virginia," United States Census Bureau.

231 **who wrote this in the *Observer***: Kyron Huigens, "The Electoral College Is Actually Worse Than You Think—Here's Why," *Observer*, February 27, 2019.

232 ***Let The People Pick The President***: Jesse Wegman, *Let the People Pick the President: The Case for Abolishing the Electoral College*, St. Martin's Press, March 17, 2020.

232 **As of this writing**: "Agreement Among the States to Elect the President by

National Popular Vote," *National Popular Vote Inc.* and The National Popular Vote Interstate Compact Bill (NPVIC).

234 **September 2020 Gallup Poll**: Megan Brenan, "61% of Americans Support Abolishing Electoral College," *Gallup*, September 24, 2020.

237 ***How Rights Went Wrong***: Jamal Greene, *How Rights Went Wrong: Why Our Obsession with Rights Is Tearing America Apart*, Houghton Mifflin Harcourt, March 16, 2021.

238 ***New York Magazine***: Jennifer Senior, "In Conversation: Antonin Scalia," *New York Magazine*, October 4, 2013.

238 **Bork pretended**: Kurt T. Lash, "Inkblot: The Ninth Amendment as Textual Justification for Judicial Enforcement of the Right to Privacy," *University of Richmond Law Faculty Publications*, 2013.

248 **endorsed by scholars**: Richard Wolf, "Liberal Groups Seek to Make Supreme Court an Issue in 2020 Presidential Race, and Conservatives Exult," *USA Today*, July 28, 2019; "Term Limits," *Fix the Court*.

251 **"Midnight Judges' Act"**: Winston Bowman, "The Midnight Judges: The Judiciary Act of 1801," *The Federal Judicial Center*.

255 **Strunk and White**: William Strunk Jr. and E. B. White, *The Elements of Style*, Harcourt, Brace & Howe, 1920.

255 ***The Canterbury Tales***: Geoffrey Chaucer, *The Canterbury Tales*, Written 1387–1400, First Printed by William Caxton in 1476 in London, England.

255 ***Muppets Take Manhattan***: *The Muppets Take Manhattan*, Directed by Frank Oz, Henson Associates and Tri-Star Pictures, 1984.

Praise for *One Hundred*
A Romanov's Search for He

"In a vividly intense and personal saga, Tania Romanov transcends the societal differences of old Mother Russia, bringing to life our determined grandparents and the pain history dealt them. Her story weaves through our shared Russian heritage to a uniquely American immigrant experience which broke the barriers of class structure. It stirred such powerful emotions that I had to occasionally just put the book down and let them sweep through me."

—**Marina Romanov,** grandniece of Tsar Nicholas II of Russia

"Tatiana Romanova's superb book, *One Hundred Years of Exile*, is a touching and eminently familiar story for those of us who attempt to reconnect to a past rent asunder by the cataclysmic events of the 20th century. It is also an attempt to shine a light on the humanness emerging from a darkness unimaginable to most of us. The book deftly intersperses memory with superb, but not overwhelming detail. The narrative hangs together beautifully and the story pacing is positively cinematic. An absolute must-read."

—**Nicholas Sluchevsky,** director of Stolypin Center, Moscow, and great-grandson of Pyotr Stolypin, Prime Minister of Russia

"Romanov has situated her absorbing story exactly at the intersection of history and memoir. We see a tapestry of monumental events stretching from the last days of Czarist rule in Russia through tumults of war and revolution to the near-destruction of an entire people, the Don Cossacks. But we see this vast story as a fabric woven of individual lives: the private stories of vividly realized characters, picking their way through history. It's a wonderful read."

—**Tamim Ansary,** author of *West of Kabul, East of New York* and *Destiny Disrupted: A History of the World Through Islamic Eyes*

"In this wonderfully written, intensely personal recap of a complicated history, Tania Romanov paints a beautiful portrait of family and immigrant life here and in war-torn Europe. From her poetic descriptions of Russian celebrations to the bittersweet memories of her father's photography at the refugee camp where her family was held for years, she creates a sweeping narrative full of darkness, light, and beauty."

—**Linda Watanabe McFerrin,** author of
Navigating the Divide and *Dead Love*

"*One Hundred Years of Exile: A Romanov's Search for Her Father's Russia* is travelogue, history lesson, personal journey rolled into one, and a riveting read. Author Tania Romanov not only introduces a cast of characters as fascinating and complex (and with such names!) as those of Tolstoy, but in telling a private story also makes real the overwhelming march of Russia from the 20th century to today. Rebellions, world wars, Red vs. White Russians, revolution—from the toppling and assassination of a Tsar to the genocide of whole peoples, including the Cossacks from whom she descended—Bolshevism to Communism to the post-Soviet Union Russia, the story unfolds through the lives of those who lived it. In the end, we are left not only enlightened, but with compelling questions about our own 'creation myths' and the meaning of family."

—**Joanna Biggar,** author of *That Paris Year* and *Melanie's Song*

"Tania has a unique talent in bringing to life past generations through diligent attention to history and reimagined dialogue. Not only do readers get to know her ancestors, through Tania's words they soon deeply care about them. Her earlier book, Mother Tongue, taught me about the turbulent life in Balkans during the first half of the 20th century in a way no history book ever had. Her story left me eager to learn more about the lives and travails of her father's Russian ancestors. One Hundred Years of Exile is the magnificent result."

—**Michael Shapiro,** author of *The Creative Spark*
and *A Sense of Place*

"Following *Mother Tongue*, Tania Romanov's compelling story of her maternal relatives in the Balkans, *One Hundred Years of Exile* explores her paternal relatives years in Russia and her family's journey to America. The second half of the book covers Ms Romanov's own journey more recently back to some of the places her family found themselves during the hundred years of exile. It is very interesting to see how the author successfully ties these two very different narratives together. I recommend this book because it is a well written, entertaining story and it also is a thoroughly researched, enjoyable Russian history lesson."

—**Judith Hamilton,** author of *Animal Expressions*

"This rollercoaster ride through some very turbulent times in Russian history entertains, teaches and enlightens. It will strike a chord with all of us. After all, we are the offspring of immigrants— no matter how many generations back, or from what country. Ms. Romanov takes us along on her journey and in the process, we learn the universal importance of understanding roots."

—**Gay Wind Campbell,** author of *Images Par Deux*

"A fascinating memoir of discovery that follows a Russian family across several generations. I experienced a ground-level immersion into the constant upheavals of the Russian Civil War, on through the World Wars and beyond. A remarkable story of a family and a country seen through the eyes of a daughter searching for truths."

—**Rick Crandall,** author of *The Dog Who Took Me Up a Mountain*

One Hundred Years of Exile

of Exile

A Romanov's Search
for Her Father's Russia

One Hundred Years
of Exile

A Romanov's Search
for Her Father's Russia

Tania Romanov

Travelers' Tales,
an imprint of Solas House, Inc.
Palo Alto

Travelers' Tales and Solas House are trademarks of Solas House, Inc., Palo Alto, California.
travelerstales.com | solashouse.com

Art Direction: Kimberly Nelson
Cover Design: Kimberly Nelson
Interior Design and Page Layout: Howie Severson
Cover Photo: The Holy Virgin Cathedral, also known as Joy of All Who Sorrow, a Russian Orthodox cathedral in San Francisco. It is the largest of the six cathedrals of the Russian Orthodox Church outside Russia. By Tania Romanov Amochaev

Library of Congress Cataloging-in-Publication Data is available upon request.

978-1-60952-195-0 (paperback)
978-1-60952-197-4 (hard cover)
978-1-60952-196-7 (ebook)

Official publication date November 13, 2020, exactly one hundred years from the date Tania Romanov Amochaev's father and his family touched Russian soil for the last time.

First Edition
Printed in the United States of America
10 9 8 7 6 5 4 3 2 1

This book is dedicated to Daria, Marina, and Artem, my Romanov Amochaev family without whose inspiration this book would not exist.

Table of Contents

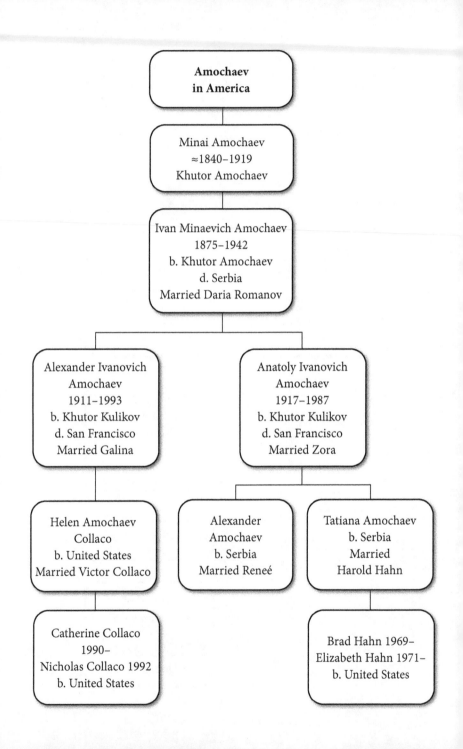

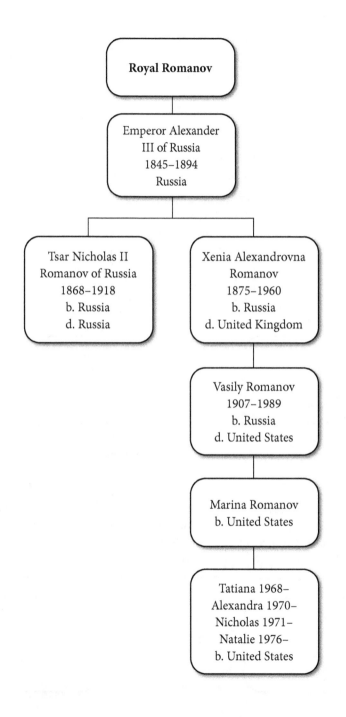

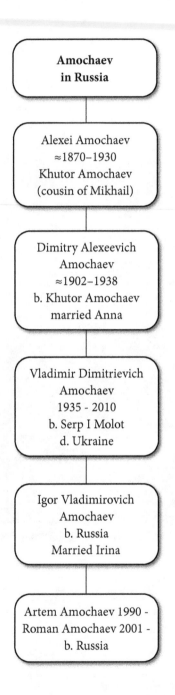

**Amochaev
in Russia**

Alexei Amochaev
≈1870–1930
Khutor Amochaev
(cousin of Mikhail)

Dimitry Alexeevich
Amochaev
≈1902–1938
b. Khutor Amochaev
married Anna

Vladimir Dimitrievich
Amochaev
1935 - 2010
b. Serp I Molot
d. Ukraine

Igor Vladimirovich
Amochaev
b. Russia
Married Irina

Artem Amochaev 1990 -
Roman Amochaev 2001 -
b. Russia

Tania Amochaev

PART ONE

Chapter 1

A Royal Romanov

Meeting a Romanov princess was not on my agenda.

In May of 2018, I launched my first book, about my mother's Balkan roots, and my stepdaughter Beth hosted an event for me at her home. Outside, spring's first wildflowers colored the meadows while snow dotted the mountaintops. Inside, friends gathered, and Beth introduced me to the ones I didn't yet know.

"Tania, this is my friend Aki's mother, Marina."

I held out my hand to Marina, and we smiled at each other as strangers do. The introduction was almost an aside, and then Beth suddenly remembered. "Oh! You two can probably speak Russian together!"

Standing before me was an attractive, slender, and gently smiling woman who fit easily into this small mountain town in Colorado—a woman slightly older than I, whose English was as accent-less as mine, and who, unlike me, was a native born American.

I flashed back to a phone conversation some months earlier, when Beth casually mentioned her friend Aki's sister, Tatiana.

"Your friend's sister is really called Tatiana?" I asked.

"Yes," she replied. "Their grandparents were Romanovs. I think they might be Russian princesses."

"But that's my name," I said, in that phone call.

"So, you're also a Tatiana?"

Beth knew, of course, that I am half Russian. Growing up, she shared the traditions of my family in San Francisco. But she didn't appreciate all the subtleties of the culture inculcated in me by my father Tolya and my grandmother Daria. They were almost erased from my own mind. Papa, like his brother, my *Dydya* or Uncle Shura, was determined that I should marry a Russian. I made certain that didn't happen. My late husband Harold—Beth's father—was as American as they came; born in New Jersey and unfamiliar with even the town in Germany from which his family had emigrated. Indicative of my parents' failure was the fact that Beth had no idea that I was a Tatiana in my childhood. I never told her about the first-grade teacher who eliminated that awkward name from the class roster and thus created Tania.

"Yes," I replied. "I was once a Tatiana. And is Aki short for Alexandra?"

"Yes..."

This was getting interesting. Sasha, my brother's name, is a nickname for either Alexander or Alexandra.

I plunged in deeper. "My grandmother was a Romanov too," I said.

There was a short pause.

"So, you're a princess too?" Beth laughed, assuming I was pulling her leg. She knew I was more tomboy than princess, and "Romanov" was another name I had never mentioned.

"I'm afraid my grandmother was as far from being a princess as you could get," I replied. "Her family were migrant workers. They passed through the village where my grandfather raised wheat."

"But her last name really was Romanov?"

"Yes, it really was."

That discussion helped trigger my decision to use the nom de plume Tania Romanov for my writing. And now I realized who the woman standing before me was. This was Marina, née Romanov. I had researched her after my conversation with Beth and knew that Marina, unlike me, was not the grand-daughter of a migrant worker or the descendant of a serf. She is a Royal Romanov—the granddaughter of Tsar Nicholas's sister Xenia. Yes, she is the closest living survivor of the last Tsar of Russia—the symbol of my grandparents' flight from Russia and a myth arising from my past.

"I'm afraid I adopted your last name as my nom de plume," I said, a bit self-consciously.

"Oh, Romanov," Marina said, with a casual flick of her wrist. "That's one of the most common names in Russia. It's like Smith here in America." For the rest of the evening, I entertained Beth's friends with my Balkan stories. I was thrilled to share thoughts and memories with Marina, knowing she understood growing up in a Russian émigré family. We agreed to meet up again later.

But *Tatiana*—a ghost—had suddenly materialized in that space, sharing my body. She was a little Tatiana, raised by Papa and *Dyadya* Shura and a host of Russian friends and relatives. This little Tatiana grew up among homes and churches in San Francisco where portraits of Tsar Nicholas shared a place in household altars right next to crosses with Jesus Christ nailed to them. This little Tatiana spent ten formative years in Russian school studying religion, literature, geography and history. Every course ended with the execution of Tsar Nicholas and his wife and children in a remote corner of the Urals. In that school in San Francisco, every word was spoken in a Russian language that preserved the style and terminology of the early

20th century. Every teaching venerated the destroyed royal family and awaited their return to their rightful place at the head of their country, their Russia.

But that was not for me. I felt trapped in their sphere. I wanted to be an American, not a poor, foreign refugee.

My *Dydya* Shura often despaired of my desire to flee into an American world; to turn Tatiana into Tania; to leave his Russia behind as quickly as possible. But his world, I was to learn, was planted deep inside me, and now it forced its way back into my consciousness.

I was thinking of writing about my relationship with my father. Could it really be that as I considered writing about him and exploring a revolution that threw my grandparents out of Russia, I met a member of the very family whose eradication haunted their flight? A family whose memory was sacred to all those exiles, and to their descendants? How could it be that this meeting happened, not in the Russian Orthodox Cathedral where Shura's daughter Lena and grandchildren Katya and Kolya still continue his connection to the past, but at the home of my American husband Harold's daughter Beth, far from Russian churches and schools and meeting halls?

Marina and I both had grandparents who lost everything in the Russian Revolution. We both had fathers who fled that country as children on ships from Crimea a hundred years ago. But she represents so much more than just a shared heritage. She is the embodiment of a royal family that until this moment, for me, had been a myth. Could she help turn a symbol human and make my grandparents' story real?

As Marina and I sat in my daughter's home, my mind flew to the lives of the Russians we grew up with, and stories about my family. I imagined a film that started in a small village in Russia in the early nineteen-hundreds. Marina's great uncle

is Tsar Nicholas II of Russia. My grandmother Daria is still young, a single woman whose father is marrying her off . . .

But, in a connection as incredible as this one, there was another Russian waiting to enter my life at this juncture of history and reality.

Chapter 2

Russia Calling

A few weeks later I sat at my desk at home in San Francisco, reading email. Junk got quick treatment: Delete.

"Whoosh..." I heard the familiar gratifying sound of spam disappearing from my inbox.

The next day another uninvited email appeared from the same source. It said my subscription to *The Economist* had been confirmed. I paused before hitting "delete" when I saw delivery options that included the name of a suburb of Moscow.

I hadn't subscribed to *The Economist* in years, and I do not live near Moscow. I have never lived near Moscow. A casual glance at the addressee showed it was not me, Tania Amochaev, but someone called Artem Amochaev. I did not know an Artem Amochaev.

The only Amochaevs I know are my brother Sasha and his wife Renée. My cousin Lena used to be an Amochaev, but she changed her last name to Collaco upon marriage. As far as I know, my paternal grandparents—Ivan and Daria, *née* Romanov— are the only Amochaev family who successfully fled Russia during the Russian Revolution and Civil War. And that was one hundred years ago.

I forwarded this email to my brother. He suggested that maybe we were related to Artem, and that I should write him. This is the same brother who has never expressed the slightest interest in Russia; who shies away from all social media; whom I cannot imagine ever writing to a complete stranger.

Never one to pass up a challenge, I complied. A simple reply to the email led nowhere. So, I explored social media and found an Artem Amochayev on Facebook. It was the beginning of an email odyssey that stretched from the offices of *The Economist* in the United Kingdom, to San Francisco, to a suburb of Moscow. A trivial feat in today's world, but one that got me thinking about the real-life odysseys that brought me to San Francisco and Artem to Moscow.

I learned that he transliterated his name from the Cyrillic alphabet as Amochayev, and a missed "y" led to the confused email chain. I shared one fact with him:

> By the way – my family were Don Cossacks from near Urupinsk. I don't suppose we're related?

We shared several messages over the next days.

> Dear Tania,
>
> Thank your a lot for the letter! It was my mystake, I wrote my email in a wrong way:)
> You know, I think that we're related. My grandfather was born in a khutor (small village, farm) near Urupinsk in 1935 and my ancestors also were Don Cossacks. Amochaev is a extremely rare surname and I'm surprised at finding a namesake in the US :) I made a small research and I'm almost 100% sure that all people who have the Amochaev surname have a common ancestor. There is the khutor Amochayev

near Urupinsk and it must be a homeland for all of us. Furthermore, the most of Amochaev live in Volgograd Oblast.

Tania, I've visited your website and I'm impressed your biography. I will definetely read all your literary works and I'm going to start with the story of your first trip to your father's homeland. It must be very exciting!

A few words about myself. I'm 28 years old. I live in a suburb of Moscow and work in a road-construction business.

I am very pleased to meet you!

Dear Artem,

Lovely to hear from you, my brother suggested I write you on the theory that we might be related. Our family are the only Amochaevs in America.

I actually want to write a book about my father. I don't suppose your grandfather is still alive or that you know what village they came from?

And I am impressed that a 28-year-old in Russia wants to read the *Economist*. I used to read it in my career as a business executive.

Dear Tania,

I read your story in one breath. It made me exited and sad simultaneously. I'm exited because you mentioned some familliar places in the story. My grandfather was born in the collective farm "Serp i Molot" right near khutor Kulikov and stanitsa Jarizhenskaya (Ярыженская). I attached a peace of map. The khutor Amochaev is a bit bellow those places. At that time Cosaks weren't allow to live in ther family khutors and villages because of the collectivization.

But your story also reminds about very dark times in our history. A civil war is the most disgusting thing that can be. My grandfather lived after those events, but there were rough times too: the great famine in the region in 30's and the WWII later. None of his sublings survived and he didn't know much about his father. My grandfather was a very stubborn person. He managed to leave that place, worked and studied hard and become a major in the engineering troops. He served in many places of the Soviet Union and retired in Kharkov, Ukraine where he died 8 years ago. I wish I could ask him more about the family story.

Tania, I think we're related, but just from different branches.

I think that writing a book about your father is a great idea!

Now I'm getting my executive master degree at the Moscow Higher School of Economics. I already have the engineering one and I do believe it will be usefull for my futher career. That's why I'm reading the Economist.

Dear Cousin Artem,

Wow. I'm afraid your note brought tears to my eyes. Thank you so much for sharing your information. And your English is great.

I vaguely remember something about Serp I Molot, but it's been over 40 years since I went back. I guess that dirt road I traveled on is now a highway to Moscow!

And I believe my grandfather—who had 10 brothers and sisters—left khutor Amochaev around the turn of the last century and moved to khutor Kulikov.

My family and I have talked about visiting Russia. We have a dream of following the trail my father's family took—in a телега—when they fled.

Спасибо опять Артём. Thank you again, Artem. It would be hard to say how much joy your letter gave me. Somehow fate concluded that we needed to meet.

Татьяна Анатольевна Амочаева, Or just Tania

Дорогая Татьяна Анатольевна,

спасибо Вам большое за тёплые слова. (Thank you for your warm words.) I am also very pleased with our unexpected acquaintance.

I believe your travelling to Russia is a great idea, as well as visiting the khutor! My father has a dream to drive there for a long time. Now we got a perfect occasion :)

I think you should postpone your idea to repeat the route your ancestors did last century. You have nothing to worry about visiting the Crimean Peninsula if you travel there from the Russian side (by air or via that brand-new bridge across the strait). But if you want to follow the original route, you have to cross the Russian-Ukrainian boundary twice. It might be very tricky. I do not recommend it...

My parents have a lovely dacha (country house) with Russian banya and fascinating nature about 50 miles far away from Moscow and they are happy to invite you there to live.

That final email arrived less than ten days after the first one, and we were on our way. I had been forwarding Artem's emails to my brother and cousin Lena. She shared them with her husband Vitya, as well as her children Katya and Kolya. Their family grew up on fantasies of a lost Russian world and could not pass up an invitation to stay in a *dacha* with a *banya,* or sauna. Sasha said he wanted to go as well, and within a few days of that first email it was all agreed.

We said, "Yes!"

My past was reaching out to me at a critical junction in my life. The book about my mother's Balkan family was launched, and now another culture was demanding to be acknowledged. Russia, my father's homeland and a heritage I had mostly ignored for over forty years, was opening its doors. A month after I met Marina and ten days after that first spam email, we committed to visit Russia and make a pilgrimage to our grandparents' place of birth. I learned that no one in Artem's family spoke English, so only Russian speakers were coming. Incredibly, after all this time that still included all the Amochaev relatives left in America! In May of 2019, one hundred years after Daria and her family left their home in Kulikov, her descendants would converge on what is left of that homeland.

Artem could help us address the mystery of those who stayed behind; people not heard from in a hundred years. He was my first connection to a past that might have been mine but for a twist of fate. I wondered how our families' destinies differed and where our histories crossed. I prepared to delve deeply into the lives of my Russian grandmother, a woman I grew up with, whose character was as hard as steel, and of my father—a man who is still, in many ways, an enigma to me.

Part Two

Chapter 3

Russia, 1910:
A Determined Daria

"I've made up my mind, Papa," Daria repeated. "I'm not marrying that man!"

She really hadn't needed to say it again. Pavel knew that when his daughter stated something so categorically, there was little chance of budging her. That was why at twenty-five she was still single. But Pavel had prevailed upon his good friend Ivan to set up this match. Daria *would* be getting married.

"We'll discuss it later," he said. "Go help your mother."

The noise of arriving horses broke the silence around the ancient *isbas*—mud-walled huts with straw roofs—that lay scattered through the village. Most of the region hadn't changed in generations. The roads were still of packed mud—plenty of dirt to go around in this land—as they had been for years. Gently sloping wheat fields surrounded them far into the distance.

Daria watched in despair as her father stomped out of the house. How could he hand her off to someone called Mikhail, a man he hadn't even met? And Papa's friend Ivan—who could do no wrong in her father's eyes—did he think he could control her destiny? Did they expect her to remain silent? To just

stay in the kitchen and cook? From the kitchen Daria heard her father sitting down at the table with one of the fellows. Through the window she could see the other one putting the horses away. She and her mother were organizing *zakuski*, the starters they always served to guests, and of course the vodka was already on the table.

"Mama, I think they are here," she said, hoping for some support.

"Yes, Daria, they are, and perhaps you should check that tray you are working on," Natalia replied. "You need to make a good impression, you know." Natalia wasn't confident of Pavel's strategy, but she respected her husband and would support him. Their daughter was just so stubborn.

Pavel had no time for a recalcitrant daughter who didn't understand that he was looking out for all their best interests. The spring of 1910 was a crucial time in Russia, and he had to act quickly or be left behind. His family had spent several years working in the Don Cossack region, a fertile farmland on the southern steppes of Russia near Ukraine. The Cossacks had always been independent and had never been serfs. Pavel, from nearby Tambov region, understood the value of that freedom.

The nomadic existence of a migrant worker had never been his objective. Russian peasants—Pavel's ancestors among them—had been freed from serfdom fifty years earlier, two years before American slaves were emancipated. In theory, from that time on, they could hold land of their own. But a variety of laws had prevented that. Now things were changing. Working near *Khutor* Amochaev, he had grown close to young Ivan Amochaev during these years, and they shared their stories. Ivan's family were good employers, treated the workers well, and paid fairly.

"I was just finishing my military service around 1905," Ivan told him. "But it was all far away from here—the Japanese

and Balkan wars, and the protests and violence. I never got involved in any of that."

"Yes, those were hard years," agreed Pavel. "I was grateful that my son Pavelik was too young for service. I know our dear Tsar was threatened, and it looked bad for a time. Then things settled down."

"I'm not sure everyone was satisfied. For some people that revolution in 1905 didn't go far enough," said Ivan. "But it definitely changed things for my family."

"How so?"

"Well, because of it, I now have my own land!" Ivan said, proudly.

In 1906, a man determined to protect the monarchy of Tsar Nicholas II, Pyotr Stolypin, became Prime Minister of Russia. He implemented major reforms in an effort to appease the revolutionaries. The government evolved to a more representative one, with a legislative body called the Duma and a constitution. When land ownership laws were changed, Ivan quickly took advantage of the situation, and now had many acres of wheat.

"But doesn't your community ultimately control what is grown? Isn't it a family plot?" Pavel knew that the Cossacks had long held land under a complex form of communal ownership. But those land reforms had freed Ivan to move to independence from the community and acquire land outside the traditional communal holdings.

"No. It's my land. It is mine!" Ivan punched his hand with his closed fist. "No one can tell me what to do with it."

That sentence stayed with Pavel. Ivan, in his early thirties, was extending his reach beyond just planting and harvesting crops. He expanded from local small-time trade to milling his own grain and doing business with larger markets. Clearly a man with a future, he had his eyes on dealing directly with

Moscow. Now Pavel, for the first time, was also working his own land. Ivan had helped him achieve this independence. Pavel's portion wasn't a big piece, but it would be enough, especially now that his four children were getting older, and, like Daria, would soon be moving away.

It had all evolved quickly. Pavel had mentioned that it was time for his daughter to consider marriage. Ivan told him about his cousin Mikhail Amochaev, who would soon be finishing his military service. One thought led to another, and they both realized there was a match to be made here. Ivan spoke to Mikhail's father, who confirmed his son as a suitor for Daria. Ivan and Mikhail were here to finalize the agreement, and Pavel intended to ensure the success of their mission.

Chapter 4

Daria Meets Her Future Husband

The stranger stood up when Daria and her mother walked in from the kitchen. He was tall, even taller than her father. His face was handsome; there was nothing soft about his features. They seemed carved of stone. His hair was cut short, almost military style, and his mustache made an inverted vee around his lips. He was dressed as if he was going to town: sophisticated, not like the young men in her village. They wore large tunic-like coverings over loose pants that dropped into dirty boots, which tracked the mud from the fields everywhere they went.

This man's white shirt had a smooth round collar that seemed to hold his head high. It was tucked into his pants, which had loops and a leather belt drawn through them. A gold chain crossed his chest, dropping into a pocket, probably ending in a gold watch. She pulled her eyes away as her father performed the introductions.

"I don't believe you have met Ivan Minaevich, Natalia. He is the one who has helped organize the work we have been doing in *Khutor* Amochaev." Her father turned to the gentleman. "This is my wife, Natalia Alexeevna."

"I am most pleased to meet you, Natalia Alexeevna." Even in these remote areas they always used that formal address, a father's name identifying family connections.

"Welcome to our home," said Natalia, before heading back to the kitchen for one more tray.

"And this is my daughter, Daria."

"Yes, yes . . ." Ivan started, but Daria spoke at the same moment.

"*Ochen priatno*, very pleased, Ivan Minaevich," she said, but her glare belied her words. She had heard repeatedly about this man, but he was still a surprise. He certainly knew how to carry himself, head high, with confident eyes that gazed at her unflinchingly. She briefly wondered if his cousin Mikhail would resemble him. "Please sit down, may I pour you a drink?" Hospitality was deeply ingrained in her, and offering the vodka eased the tension in the room.

Something about this woman captured Ivan's attention. She was tall, with long dark hair pulled back in a traditional conservative bun. Her dark eyes flashed, and her mouth was firm. She didn't smile as she poured, but her look no longer seemed forbidding. She was striking in a way quite different from the demure young women he had been presented to back when he was considering marriage. Ivan had not married then, telling himself he was too busy with military service and his budding enterprise. In truth, he just couldn't imagine spending his life with a polite young woman who couldn't keep his attention for even a few hours.

Daria's father observed both of them carefully. He wondered what was going through Ivan's mind.

In fact, at this moment—as Mikhail was about to meet his future bride—Ivan had an instant of doubt about this union for his cousin. The woman Pavel had just introduced him to didn't seem as young as Ivan expected. Mikhail, in his early

twenties, was a fine, handsome lad, and Ivan had been happy to encourage him in this opportunity. But he had to make sure that Daria would match the expectations that had been set in the preliminary talks with Mikhail's family. Pavel knew a little vodka would smooth the way, and as Daria headed back to the kitchen, he raised his shot glass in a toast.

Ivan's eyes followed her as she walked out of the room. He noticed her proud bearing and the way her dark skirt swung against her calves. "That's an attractive woman, my friend. Where have you been hiding her?"

"Oh, she hasn't been hidden. She's as strong as a man and works in the fields as hard as any of them. Then she comes home and cooks dinner or sews me a shirt." He was exaggerating a bit. Daria was surprisingly like a *Cossachka,* as they called Cossack women, of the old school. Her physical strength and skills in the field were unquestionable. The horses knew who was in charge when she was driving the *telega,* the old wooden cart, but her household talents were not something her mother would brag about. She could keep the house neat, and clean the dishes and kitchen, but Pavel easily preferred her sister Claudia's cooking, and his youngest daughter Tania sewed the clothes in the family. However, it was Daria they were presenting at this moment, in the most positive light possible. He was worried that they had waited too long to settle her into a marriage. She hadn't wanted any of the men in their own village and was fortunate in this unique opportunity with Mikhail.

The front door opened again. A light-haired young man turned toward them, hesitating.

"*Mozno?*" he asked politely. "May I?"

"Of course, of course, Mikhail Efimovich. Welcome to our home. Please come in." Pavel stood up in welcome.

Mikhail didn't stride into the room as Ivan had done. He walked in slowly, bowing to Pavel, and shaking hands as his cousin formally introduced them. He was as tall as they were, but his uncertain mien made him seem smaller somehow. He was younger, and handsome, but his features hadn't fully developed and there was openness in them, almost softness. He was visibly nervous. After all, he had come here to woo this man's daughter, to claim her as his bride.

Daria and her mother walked back into the room carrying platters of food. Mikhail stared at the younger woman, surprised at her stature and bearing. She had an unexpected self-confidence, yet somehow kept a distance. She didn't even look his way, seemingly absorbed with her task. He wondered if she was as reluctant about all this as he had been.

It wasn't his idea, this marriage. His family had sprung it on him when he came back on leave. Land reforms had brought change, and acreage was being more widely distributed in their district. His father wanted him settled down. If he was married, he could claim some land, even though he was still serving in the military. This marriage seemed inevitable, so he decided to put on his best behavior and not embarrass his cousin.

"Mikhail Efimovich, may I introduce my wife, Natalia Alexeevna," Pavel said. "And this is my daughter, Daria."

Daria nodded at Mikhail and smiled. But her eyes quickly flew back to Ivan's face. She dropped her head, flustered when she caught his eye, and quickly moved to lay down the dish. Everyone turned far more attention than was warranted to the food.

It was Lenten, as Easter was late this year—on the first day of May. They followed the strictures of the church carefully, and fasted for the seven weeks before Easter, eating no meat or dairy products. Their proximity to the river offered easy

access to fish, and their garden provided greens. There was fresh-baked bread to complement the preserved roast peppers and pickles. Claudia's horseradish added a pleasant zest to the meal, and the requisite marinated fish helped the vodka flow.

To introduce the main courses, Natalia had prepared delicious borscht, a soup whose recipe had been in their family for years. Daria herself had baked the carp, and proudly served the crisply crusted fish. She had a weakness for the eyes and would often eat them before the dish reached the table. But this time she had saved them for the guests. She wondered whether they would appreciate this delicacy and her sacrifice.

The meal went as well as might be expected. The two women sat fairly quietly, listening as the men talked. Then they cleared the dishes and left the room.

Pavel wasn't used to this subdued Daria; it was not like his daughter. To be fair, she had asked a few questions, mostly directed at Ivan, and followed the conversation closely. But she hadn't shared her thoughts very much, as she normally did when the family sat down to meals. Daria and Mikhail had barely spoken to each other, sharing a few brief glances. Mostly, it was Pavel and Ivan who conversed—about the weather, and in praise of Daria's cooking. The men's conversation then moved to politics and farming. Finally, they discussed the future.

Pavel turned to Mikhail and asked, "You are getting some land, I understand?"

"I will be doing that soon," Mikhail replied, speaking more cautiously than the other two. "I am finalizing my military service . . ."

"And your marriage will allow you to acquire the piece we discussed," interrupted Ivan, not understanding why Mikhail wasn't being more forceful.

"Yes, I am looking forward to that." Mikhail was very fond of Ivan, and he looked forward to working with him when he

finished his military service. The men grew more boisterous and optimistic as the vodka went down. By the end of the evening, they had reached a satisfactory conclusion to the primary objective of the visit—the marriage between Mikhail and Daria—and warmly shook hands.

"Natalia, bring Daria and come say goodbye to our guests," Pavel called. When the women came in, he gave his daughter a significant look, which she ignored.

Natalia spoke first.

"It was a pleasure to see you, please know that you are always welcome in our home," Natalia said. Daria didn't reaffirm her mother's invitation, but she did at least smile as the men walked out the door.

All in all, Pavel thought it had gone quite well. Until he turned and heard what Daria had to say.

"You know there's no way I could marry that young man," Daria announced. "He doesn't know who he is or what he wants. I will not spend my life with a man like that."

Pavel decided he would give it a rest for a while. No amount of arguing was going to change her mind. There was time to work on this.

"Your friend Ivan, Papa, he seems like a man with a strong future. I wonder why he is still unwed?" Daria continued.

"It doesn't matter why Ivan is still single!" Pavel roared. "You're about to finalize a relationship with Mikhail Efimovich." In his mind the matter had been settled. He would not let his daughter embarrass him by her denial. She had to understand.

Daria glared at him in a manner he had seen before. She lifted her head and declared, "I've already told you, Papa. I am not marrying that man!"

Chapter 5

Ivan Decides

Outside, Ivan and Mikhail shared few words as they harnessed the horses to their *telega* and started the ride back to *Khutor* Amochaev.

After a period of silence, Ivan finally spoke. "Well, what did you think?" He almost hated to ask, for he could guess the answer from Mikhail's silence.

"I don't know why my father is so determined that I should get married. I still have several years in the military."

"But surely this would be a unique opportunity, Mikhail. A fine woman. We know her family. She is a hard worker. And you could get your own piece of land."

"I wouldn't marry someone just so I could get a piece of land."

"Neither would I," muttered Ivan, almost to himself. "I have passed up many opportunities for marriage myself. But this woman seems unique."

"In what way?"

"Well, she's a woman who knows her mind, I think. She will not be pushed around."

"That certainly seemed true. There was no frivolous chatter. But she hardly smiled. I'm certainly not used to that in our girls."

"That's the thing," said Ivan. "She's not a girl. That Daria Pavlovna is a woman."

"But do you think she would be fun to be around?"

"I think, Mikhail, that a 'fun' girl would get tiresome very quickly."

There was another long pause, as both men sat, wrapped in their thoughts. This time it was Mikhail who broke the silence. "Maybe it's just that she seemed much older than I expected."

"She certainly did seem quite mature."

"How old is she exactly?"

"I think she turned twenty-five not too long ago. Her father mentioned that she was reluctant about this whole marriage thing."

"Well, that's something we have in common!" Mikhail finally smiled. He spoke again after they had passed a few kilometers. "I just don't think I'm ready for this yet. I shouldn't have let father talk me into it. Now I don't know how I can get out of it."

"But, Mikhail, this is a special woman. I have met no one else like her. You should not let this opportunity slip away."

"You might be right, Ivan. But I don't think she is the one for me. In fact, she terrifies me. Even you are calling her Daria Pavlovna. Any other woman would be just Daria." Mikhail seemed to gain strength as he spoke. "No. I cannot do this."

The silence lengthened again. This could be a long trip. Neither man knew what to say at that point. Finally, Mikhail spoke.

"Ivan, I need your help. There has to be a way out of this, and you are a master at thinking your way out of tough spots."

"Are you certain, Mikhail? You might not meet another like her. You may live to regret it. I know I would."

"The truth is, Ivan, I would regret this marriage. I'm not strong and serious like you. I just want some joy and warmth in my life." He paused, then continued. "It's not just that. I am not ready for any of this right now. Our country is troubled, and I need to find my way carefully." He knew the men in his troop didn't think this revolution business was over. He thought he might even stay in the military longer. "None of us knows what's ahead for us."

"You are definitely right, Mikhail. Our future is terribly unpredictable. Our lives could be in turmoil for a long time." Ivan wanted to get serious about establishing himself while things were going reasonably well. He was thirty-five years old already, and he knew this was the moment to create his future.

As they drove on, they spoke about the events of the last several years. There were so many of significance. Summarized in one conversation, it was frightening: the war with Japan, the Revolution, the shifting tides in their country. Even in their remote steppes they were hearing more about other countries as well. There were tensions at their borders, both east and west: with the Turks, with Poland, Ukraine, and Lithuania. The challenges had gone on for years, but rumblings were now coming from far beyond those borders: from Germany, Austro-Hungary, Italy, and, as always, the Balkans.

Tensions with France and Britain seemed to be building too. Ivan had been to Moscow a few times and found the experience unsettling. He couldn't even imagine what it must be like in St. Petersburg, with the Tsar, their *Batyushka*—their little father, Nicholas II—being pressured from inside and outside of his own country. There was an ominous cloud over all of them. And yet there were opportunities, and Ivan knew he had to take advantage of them. Now.

Toward the end of the trip, Ivan turned to Mikhail, and changed the subject back to a more personal one. "This conversation has helped me make up my mind, Mikhail. I've been considering some big changes. I think it is time to implement them."

"What are you talking about?"

"The train from Moscow stops at the train station in *khutor* Kulikov. It's the nearest stop to Amochaev, but it's still several hours by horse-drawn *telega*. I want to expand my business to trade directly with Moscow, and I'd like to be much closer to the train station. I need to move."

"What? Leave our *khutor*? You want to leave Amochaev?"

"I think I have to. I don't want to, but I need to stabilize my future . . . and the future of my children."

"But Amochaev is our *khutor*. It's named after our family."

"I know. That's why I've taken this long to make up my mind. I've known for some time that I needed to make this change. But it's hard."

"I don't know if I could do it. Our *khutor* is everything to me," said Mikhail. "I've grown up knowing that I come from a place that holds my name. My family is there. My grandparents were there. That is where I belong."

"But Mikhail. I'm talking about a move that is no further than what Daria would have to make to come to Amochaev, if she were to marry you."

"Yes, but Daria is a woman. She would expect to move to her husband's home. She will be changing her name to his. It wouldn't matter much. There's no comparison."

It clearly never occurred to him, as it did to Ivan, that Daria might be horrified to hear herself spoken about as such an inconsequential pawn.

"Nevertheless," Ivan mused, "I need to make the move."

"And how can you be talking about the future of your children? You're not even married."

"You're right, I am not. But I think the time is coming for that as well. If I make the move, it should be to set up my future, my *budushnost*. To have children. To build a life. To build a new future in a new home." Ivan repeated the word *budushnost*—an old-fashioned way of referring to the future—as if to cement these thoughts in his mind.

"So, Ivan, Ivan, Ivan! It seems you are the one—and not I—who needs a wife."

"I believe you are right, Mikhail. I think the time has come for me to get married."

The two men looked at each other so long, paying no attention to the road, that the *telega* veered toward the ditch.

"I believe we have a solution to our problem." Mikhail beamed at his older cousin. "I know just the right woman for you."

They pulled over the *telega* and sat, looking at each other for a long time. Finally, Mikhail reached out his hand, as if to shake Ivan's. Instead, Ivan grabbed him in a fierce hug. They sat that way for a moment, then just shook their heads at each other and let the horses move forward.

Now it was Ivan's time to sit silently. But his face wasn't drawn and flat. It was relaxed, and clearly an inner peace settled over him. His future suddenly seemed full of possibilities.

And then the reality of the situation settled in.

"But this is damnably awkward, my good man," Ivan said. "I have reached agreement with her father on your marriage proposal. We left them believing that we were proceeding." He knew they were probably working on the details of the wedding and had most likely shared it with all their neighbors. "I don't know how we will unravel this. Both of our reputations, as well as those of our families, are at stake."

"You are right; it is damnably awkward," Mikhail said. "But you will have to go and make it right."

"I have to go?" Ivan's body reared up in outrage. "You think I am going to explain that you are backing out? You think I am going to go to offer myself as the consolation prize?"

"Well, when you put it that way . . . perhaps not."

"Definitely not. It is not I who shall deliver this news." Ivan was adamant.

Mikhail, for the first time in their relationship, suddenly knew that he himself would take the lead.

"You know, my friend, now that I think back, she seemed to look at you with far more interest than she showed toward me."

"Perhaps."

"I know how we should proceed. Let's go talk to our families and work out the details." Mikhail urged the horses into a trot, and they moved forward toward home. "I will take care of this for you, my dear Ivan. I promise."

Chapter 6

Turnabout

Daria and her father fumed separately as they went about their work, hardly speaking to each other. Natalia left both of them alone, knowing better than to get in the middle of the hopeless battle. The air was electric with their tension. She didn't know how long she could just watch them and do nothing.

One afternoon a few days later, as he was coming in from the fields Pavel heard a *telega*. He turned to look at it, noticing Daria leaving the henhouse with eggs at the same moment. She, too, paused and looked then quickly continued into the house.

But it was Natalia, coming from their neighbor's *isba* where she had been having tea with her friend, who first stopped to talk to the driver. They spoke for quite a while, becoming more animated by the minute. The driver kept shaking his head and pointing back the way he had come. Finally, he nodded strongly. Then Natalia nodded too and headed inside while the horse was put away.

"Pavel, there's someone here to speak with you. I'll bring out the vodka and a few *zakuski*."

"Papa, don't even try!" Daria hissed as he walked by, for she had recognized the driver.

"Daria, leave your father alone. This is men's business." Natalia pulled her daughter back away from the dining room.

"Welcome, welcome, Mikhail Efimovich. It is good to see you." Pavel was nervous in spite of himself and could not imagine what he would say to this young man. He was a little surprised that Mikhail had arrived alone, without Ivan to speak on his behalf.

He poured their vodkas, then both men watched silently as Natalia bustled in with some pickles and peppers. She smiled at Mikhail as she put a few on his plate, then put her hand reassuringly on her husband's shoulder on her way out of the room. The silence lengthened.

"Pavel Nikolaevich . . ."

"My dear Mikhail . . ."

Both men started speaking at once, then stopped again.

"Mikhail Efimovich," Pavel finally broke through. "We need to talk. You need to understand . . ."

"Yes, we definitely need to talk." Mikhail was not letting him continue.

"Oh?"

"I have come to apologize to you and to explain."

"To apologize to me? And to explain?"

"Yes. Please listen."

"Shall I pour us another drink?"

"Yes, please. Definitely. Another drink would help."

Pavel filled the vodka glasses to the brim. This did not sound good.

"Ivan and I have discussed the situation at length with our parents."

"I understand. This is a matter of great import," Pavel said.

"Yes. And I want you to know that everyone would be pleased to join our two families."

"Yes, yes . . ."

"Ivan Minaevich has spoken very highly about you and your family. He has gotten to know you quite well over the last several years. He has enormous respect for you."

"Yes, yes . . ."

"Therefore, he is extremely pleased to ask for your daughter's hand in marriage."

Pavel could barely concentrate, and he sighed. "So, you would like to go ahead with our plans as discussed."

"Perhaps I have not made myself clear."

"I'm sorry? What exactly did you mean?"

"I meant precisely what I said. Shall I repeat it?"

Pavel observed a newly confident young man sitting across from him. If only Daria could hear him now. But Pavel knew it was too late, and there was no changing her mind. He had to muddle his way through this somehow.

"It is Ivan Minaevich who would like to ask for your daughter's hand in marriage," Mikhail said.

As Pavel stared at him in bewildered silence, a crash of breaking glass shattered the stillness in the room. Then his daughter's "*Bože moj*, my dear God," preceded the opening of the door from the kitchen. "What did you say?" Daria burst into the room, her mother following, but unable to hold her back.

"Da... Da... Daria Pavlovna." Mikhail finally got the words out, rising from his chair.

"What did you say?"

"I was just talking to your father."

"I know. I could hear you. What did you say?"

"You know, Daria Pavlovna, I came to talk about the proposal for your hand in marriage."

"Yes, I know," Daria said, glaring at him as he leaned on the chair for support.

"Daria Pavlovna, I may be too young . . ."

"You are definitely too young," Daria interrupted, unflinchingly. "But what did you say? I think I heard you say it twice!"

"Daria. *Perestan*! Stop it this minute!" Her mother reached over and put her arm around Daria's waist. "May we join you?" Without waiting for a reply, Natalia pulled a chair out for her daughter and both of them sat down at the table. The men just stared.

"Mikhail, I believe you told me you had good news to share with us." Natalia set the tone of the conversation easily. She then proceeded to pour vodka for all four of them. She was going to ensure that this would be a momentous occasion, and the women were going to join in. "Pavel, Daria, you both need to let the young man speak. He came a long way to talk to you," Natalia said, giving Mikhail time to collect his wits and remember the advice she had given him a little earlier.

"I am extremely pleased to tell you that I have come to speak on behalf of my cousin, your dear friend Ivan Minaevich."

"Yes?" He was speaking to Pavel, but Daria could not keep still. Would he never get to the point?

Mikhail could feel all of their eyes locked onto his. He forced himself to continue.

"It is he, Ivan, who would like to ask for your daughter Daria's hand in marriage."

"Ivan would like to marry me?"

"Yes, Ivan would like to marry you. He would like it very much."

"Oh. Oh?" Daria gripped the table with her hands as her eyes moved somewhere far beyond the room they were sitting in. She no longer saw Mikhail or her parents. She no longer saw the simple *isba* she had grown up in. She saw a future opening up before her. And she was going to grab that future.

"Pavel Nicholaevich, will you agree to the marriage of your daughter to Ivan Minaevich?"

"Daria, since you are here, what should I say?"

They all looked at Daria. She sat up tall and raised her head.

"What should you say?" she asked.

Her father nodded, relief finally reaching his eyes.

"Oh, I think you can say 'yes,' Papa."

Chapter 7

Married Life

"Rise! Just rise, dammit!" Daria was cursing like a horse trader rounding up a recalcitrant herd of wild beasts. The whole neighborhood heard her last imprecations, but nothing was happening.

Daria couldn't believe that Easter was just around the corner again. Less than one year after she met Ivan, her life had changed beyond anything she could have ever imagined. She greeted most days with anticipation and excitement—but she had dreaded this morning for weeks. She still had a few days. Ivan was away in Moscow but would be returning soon. She had to get this done and get it done right. So far it hadn't worked.

She pulled out her cookbook, *A Gift to Young Housewives*, by that woman, Molohovets. Gift, shmift! She would toss it into the pig's mud if she could, but the truth was, she desperately needed it. Her father had misled her new husband by telling him she was a good cook. While she didn't think that was one of the reasons Ivan had asked for her hand, she was struggling to fulfill his expectations in this area. The dear man had been very gracious and pretended to enjoy her meals. But early in their marriage, on one of his trips to Moscow to

trade grain, he had brought her this gift. This cookbook. This four-hundred-page monster.

Now she was working on the traditional Russian Easter foods—*kulich*, a tall sweetbread, and *paskha*, a cheesecake pyramid. His whole family was coming, and she had to deliver. She knew they would be impressed even if the *kulich* collapsed, for the new house they would soon move into was something to behold. It was the biggest in the village, and the blue-colored spiral framework around the windows pulled every eye to it. The glass was so clear she had almost put her hand through it to wave to her neighbor last week. No more of that mud and straw. The smooth boards had come in on the train, along with the glass and the framing.

But right now, she had to focus on this rising dough. Or stubbornly not rising dough. She turned to the new altar in the corner for inspiration. Ivan had set up a gold leaf icon of the Virgin Mary, a crucifix draped in a piece of white silk, and a framed picture of Tsar Nicholas. The priest would carry all three to their new house when he came to bless it on Easter Sunday. That holy triumvirate would surely get her through the next days.

On top of everything else her belly was so big there was hardly room for her in the little kitchen. She looked around fondly and smiled to herself. This would be her last effort in this old mud *isba*. Ivan was returning with the iron cook stove that would make their new house a home. It was utterly insane to be hosting the Easter celebration days after finishing construction, but her husband was so proud of what they had accomplished. He had the energy of ten normal men and would not be held back.

Of course, she had seen that in him the moment he walked into her father's house. That was what she wanted. And that was what she got.

Once they both acknowledged their desire to marry, things had moved very quickly.

The wedding guests had filled the new church in *khutor* Kulikov. Ivan had nine siblings and Daria three, and the small space echoed with all of their voices raised in prayer. Ivan had asked his cousin Mikhail to hold the traditional crown over his head for the ceremony, and Daria wondered if the best man felt relief when the setting of the crowns on their heads finalized this marriage. The vodka was raised in toasts innumerable times, with shouts of "*Gorko*," bitter. Ivan obliged each one with a sweetening kiss. *Balalaikas* were strummed, accompanied by singing and dancing, and it was late in the night when the *telegi* made their way back home. Loud voices still raised in song filled the air.

And now she was awaiting her first child. They had settled in *khutor* Kulikov, away from both their birth homes, but a few hundred yards from the train station.

There! Finally! The *kulich* was rising. It had filled half the pan. This must be the moment to put it in the oven. She checked the old stove, happy to still be using it instead of the newfangled device Ivan was bringing from the big city. She knew this one would stay hot for the requisite hours it would take for the cake to keep rising as it baked. She could imagine that *kulich* now, tall and gracious and rounded at the top. The eggs from her favorite chicken would give the evenly textured dough a golden color. It no longer mattered that the last one had failed in the oven, turning into solid brick in the center. This one was heading in the right direction.

She would decorate it with the traditional white sugar-cream mixture, and she had some dried grapes to lay out the letters HV on top, for *Hristos Voskrese*, celebrating the rising of Christ, which Easter commemorated. The rising of Christ, a celebration that resonated for her, for she was rising as well. Rising

out of the depths of the Tambov district, rising from being a migrant worker to marrying the man who owned the fields.

Khutor Kulikov was rising as well. They had a train station, a church, and now a new school. Everything was rising, even the damned dough in the oven. It better be rising.

As she paused in her work, she could feel the baby growing inside of her. Of course, it would be a boy. He would be her eldest son and carry on his family name. He would be known throughout the district and even beyond. She could feel him developing into the culmination of all her dreams.

Her horizons had expanded incredibly in the year she had spent with Ivan. His Cossack relatives in Amochaev had advanced far beyond her own people, but Ivan kept breaking new ground with this access to rail travel.

The old Cossack world of theirs was fascinating and full of contradictions. The Don O*blast* or region, halfway between Moscow and the outlying lands of the Russian Empire—surrounded by Ukraine and Kazakhstan—was the heart and soul of the Don Cossacks. They were a fierce breed, evolving from the wild tribes who had plundered this land in earlier centuries and later learned to love it.

When the Romanov royal family came to power in the 16th century, the Cossacks joined forces with the Tsar of Russia. Over the ensuing centuries their connection tightened. The Cossacks became the protectors of their *Batyushka*, the Tsar, their father and beloved leader. They had defended the Tsar and fought to tame Siberia and the borderlands for him. Valiant horsemen, their skills were praised by Napoleon after he failed to subdue Russia. They were definitely still a force to be reckoned with.

Daria had been hearing their songs for much of her life, and the stories were enriched by her new, deeper awareness of their history. They might be remote from the important big cities, but they were a vital part of the Russian Empire.

Even as she came to appreciate their Cossack background and her husband's achievements, Daria was developing a new vision for the future. As she listened to Ivan's tales of Moscow, she knew that was where her family needed to be. The twentieth century was going to be different from all the others. And her family was going to embrace it.

To do that, they needed to be in the city. She would support Ivan in growing his business—she was already developing into a partner—but she would also ensure that there was a path for them to eventually settle in Moscow. Ivan had talked about the university there, and that had set her mind going. Her children would get advanced schooling. Yes. They would attend that university.

Like she had, they would learn to read and write at the local school. They would learn their prayers. They would learn a little bit of history and geography. But she wanted them equipped to become people of means and substance. That was happening in the cities. The world order was being turned upside down. It was no longer just the nobility who could own land and grow their holdings. Her husband was proof of that. But where he used natural cunning, determination, and perseverance, she knew her children would need the added advantage of a complete education. And she would ensure that they got one.

Warm sweet aromas penetrated the kitchen. She opened the oven to find that the perfectly formed dark gold cake had been tamed into submission. She was ready for her family's judgment. She was on her way.

A young Tsar Nicholas II and his sister Xenia with siblings and parents: Emperor Alexander III and Maria Feodorovna.

Chapter 8

The Other Romanov

Life wasn't easy for many of Daria and Ivan's relatives. Ivan had started at the right moment, shortly after the revolts of 1905, which led to a brief easing of autocratic rule. The younger family members like Mikhail struggled with military service and other challenges that would, in the end, become insurmountable. Reforms didn't keep pace, and they suffered under a Tsar who proved unable to lead effectively.

Ivan knew that his wife's maiden name—Romanov—which coincidentally matched that of the ruling family of the last three hundred years, would soon be forgotten. But it gave the younger men an easy way to needle him about moving into what they perceived as a higher class.

"So! Your Romanov—did she turn out to be the real thing? Is she your princess? Or maybe even a Tsarina?" Ivan's brother joked. It was shortly after the birth of their first son, Alexander, affectionately called Shura, and Ivan's brother and his father, Minai, were visiting.

Ivan didn't look amused. "Very funny, my dear brother! I don't need a princess," he said. "I need a partner in life, and that's who my Daria is."

"I do wish our current Tsarina was worthy of being called a partner to the ruler of our country." His brother tipped the vodka shot into his throat in silent toast. He avoided the blasphemy of criticizing the Tsar himself by attacking the Tsar's wife.

Ivan shared his brother's disdain for the Tsarina and her hated acolyte Rasputin but was far more circumspect on the subject. His life was moving in the right direction. He wanted no connection with those who spoke ill of the ruling family. "I will always revere our *Batyushka*, Tsar Nicholas, and his Romanov family," he snapped. "Anyway, my Daria is an Amochaev now, not a Romanov. She is helping me make my future."

"Yes . . . our *budushnost*." Minai stepped into the conversation. His old Russian word for the future—*budushnost*—had a reverent sound. It evoked deep meanings: fate, aspirations, even eternity resonated in that word. "I just hope things stay settled long enough for all of you to *have* a future."

Indeed, as Daria bore Ivan's four children and raised the Amochaev family, the future remained far from certain for them and everyone in Russia. Their destiny was equally unsettled, regardless of what part of the country they lived in, or whether they were Cossacks or royals . . . and the destiny of the royals was to play a huge role in Daria's life.

One royal Romanov—Xenia, the sister of Tsar Nicholas II—had also made her wishes concerning a spouse understood. Xenia Alexandrovna Romanov and Daria Pavlovna Romanov had this one small thing in common. In everything else, the contrast in their lives was overwhelming. Daria knew nothing of Princess Xenia, and she never imagined the parallels that would evolve over their lifetimes.

Xenia was born in 1875, the same year as Daria's Ivan, but to very different circumstances. Ivan was a Cossack, raised to revere a Tsar he knew only as an image gracing

walls everywhere. Xenia grew up calling the Tsar—Emperor Alexander III, a man whose word was law to millions—Papa. Mama was the Empress Maria.

Daria also called her parents—poor peasants, migrant workers with limited education—Papa and Mama. Daria's grandfather had been a serf. Xenia's grandfather, Emperor Alexander II, had freed him, along with all the serfs of Russia.

Both women rode horseback. Neither was an expert in the kitchen. That was where the similarities ended.

Daria married well in the eyes of her family, but her husband was a Cossack who started life with little more than his right to an acre of land and a horse. Xenia's family married into the royal families of Europe. Her other grandfather was the King of Denmark. Her cousins included King George V of England and King George I of Greece. She was meant to carry on the tradition of marriage into the royal families of Europe.

She was born in an enormous palace in St. Petersburg, one of the most beautiful capitals in Europe—an elegantly classical city, with wide boulevards, enormous squares and majestic canals. But she passed much of her childhood in a gloomy remote palace because her grandfather was assassinated, and her father feared a similar end. Her happiest moments were the summers she spent with her grandparents in Denmark, and also on the Black Sea, in Crimea, at the royal seaside palace of Livadia.

Xenia had a lady's education but grew up strong and independent. She skied and skated on the ice that covered the front yard of the palace. She played piano and became a photographer and an artist whose work was auctioned to raise money for charity.

When she was a baby, Xenia lay nestled in the arms of her nurse at Livadia when they met a small boy who introduced himself as Grand Duke Alexander Mikhailovich, the grandson

of Tsar Nicholas I. She would get to know him as her second cousin, Sandro. By the time she was ten, she was madly in love with the tall, handsome, dark haired young man. For her there would be no other partner.

A naval officer, Sandro explored the world. He was very close to his cousin Kolya, Xenia's older brother. And in the end, he fell in love with the persistent Xenia. But her parents didn't approve. And not because the two were closely related. Xenia was simply expected to make a different kind of match.

By the time Xenia was seventeen she had known what she wanted for years. She simply couldn't believe her mother wouldn't agree.

The Tsarina knew that her daughter had to marry foreign royalty, as she had. Xenia was the daughter of the Emperor, and her children were destined to be kings and queens. But Xenia was determined. It was her brother, after all, who would be the Tsar one day. His choice of a wife was crucial, but surely, she could marry her Sandro. She even recruited her grandfather, the Tsarina's father King Christian of Denmark. He had tried unsuccessfully to intercede on Xenia's behalf when they visited him in Fredensborg one summer. Xenia persisted, and finally her parents relented. In 1894, she married her Sandro—and incidentally retained her maiden name, since he too was a royal Romanov.

Both Daria and Xenia had defied their parents to marry the man they had chosen. But there was no comparison between their weddings. Daria and Ivan became husband and wife in the small church of their *khutor* with their families present. There was no discussion of a dowry. After the wedding everything Daria owned was packed into a few bags. Xenia and Sandro's royal wedding was something else again. It took three hours just to dress the bride, and the celebration included the entire royal family, as well as the most wealthy, powerful, and

noble of the land, not to mention ambassadors from around the world. A giant hall was required to hold the trousseau, which included, in addition to an endless quantity of clothes and jewelry, huge tables packed with dozens of sets of linen, a gold toilette set, gold-rimmed glassware, gold-rimmed cups, and gold-rimmed dishes.

This would serve them in their future home, the beautiful Crimean estate called Ay Todor on the shores of the Black Sea, which Sandro had inherited from his mother. It was near the Tsar's palace of Livadia and included gardens and vineyards. The flux of coming historical events was to see the family periodically residing there, sometimes by choice, sometimes not. For much of his life Sandro was a military commander, but during one period of living at Ay Todor—one of the few in which he felt at peace with the world—he even grew to enjoy making and marketing wine.

Xenia and Sandro had set off after their wedding on an extended honeymoon, but it was interrupted by the untimely death of her father. Suddenly, her brother wasn't just Kolya anymore. He was Tsar Nicholas II, the Emperor of Russia. Within a month he married the German Princess Alix, a granddaughter of England's Queen. They would have five children, including one son, the heir Tsarevich Alexei who unfortunately inherited hemophilia from his maternal line. The disease would torture his mother. She enlisted the services of a mystic healer, the mad monk, Grigori Rasputin—evil personified in Sandro's eyes. The Tsarina believed he could cure her son, and because of this, Rasputin had her under his spell, helping fuel her growing unpopularity.

Princess Xenia, now Grand Duchess, had seven children. Her last son, the Prince Vasily Alexandrovich Romanov, was born in 1907. Daria's first son, the untitled Cossack Alexander Ivanovich Amochaev, was born a few years later, in 1911. Xenia's

son was born in a palace; Daria's in a home smaller than one of Xenia's reception rooms. One woman's son was related to the ruling families of the continent; the other woman's had a Cossack father and a one-time migrant worker for a mother.

In those years of the empire and monarchy, neither mother could have imagined that the unbridgeable chasm that lay between their families would dissolve over their own lifetimes.

Worlds apart in their own country, they could not have foreseen a future that would bring their descendants into far closer contact with one another than either of them would ever again have with their own families. Fate tore across all the barriers. Nobles and peasants alike were swept into the funnel of a tornado that swirled over all of Russia and deposited its human debris randomly throughout the world.

Chapter 9

WWI and Revolution

In the years following the birth of Daria's first child she and Ivan grew closer and happier. They developed friendships with their neighbors and became an integral part of their new community in Kulikov.

Daria was pleased that other relatives—Mikhail in particular—planned to move nearby to take advantage of the rich soil and grow their holdings by working with Ivan. She was happy that her children would grow up within that bigger family. But heavy clouds were forming over Russia, and revolutionary groups proliferated. The world Daria was building for her family was threatened in ways she couldn't foresee. Prime Minister Stolypin worked to find a path between the Tsar and the opposition. In some ways it worked. The country's farm production improved astoundingly, and by 1912 Russia's grain exports greatly exceeded those of the United States and Canada combined. Yet the opposition to the monarchy was growing.

The Prime Minister couldn't convince the Tsar to liberalize the political system. He couldn't get him to let the ill-fated Duma—the legislature—legislate. For his efforts, Stolypin was assassinated; it was never clear by whom. Leftists? Conservative

monarchists? Either way, he was but one of many kingpins swept away by the revolutionary tides rising in Russia.

Ivan's cousin Mikhail had stayed in the military, and his career had delayed his marriage. But by 1914 he was ready for a family and a farm of his own. He was temporarily living with Daria and Ivan in Kulikov, and Ivan was helping him acquire some land. Mikhail's bride waited back in Amochaev. The wedding was to happen in just a few months.

It wasn't to be.

One day in August of 1914, two horses galloped up to Ivan's home. Mikhail recognized his father and brother and quickly ran to help them unsaddle. "What are you doing here? It doesn't look like good news. Is Maria all right?" Mikhail was afraid something had happened to his bride.

"No, no. Nothing to do with Maria," said his father. "It is much worse news that we bring. You are to head back to the army. Our country is at war."

World War I had begun. A general mobilization had been ordered, and Mikhail's father and brother had brought his uniform and military kit. He was to head directly to his regiment.

"God bless you, my son. Serve our Lord and your Tsar with honor." His father made the sign of the cross over Mikhail and his horse, holding himself firm so his son wouldn't see how distressed he was.

Mikhail hated going back into the army, but there was no avoiding re-conscription. Serving as a sergeant, he and his troops headed to the Austrian border, which already stretched deep into what would later become part of Ukraine. It was to be the center of a bloody series of battles. Those unfortunate young soldiers were not the only ones taken by surprise. The Russian government had been sure Germany would not launch a war, but they did. The first country targeted was Russia's old ally Serbia, and Russia mobilized in their support. When the

war expanded, Russia was treaty-bound to support Germany's enemy—the Allies. Germany declared war on Russia on August 1, 1914.

Life got hard for Grand Duchess Xenia. Her husband Sandro was disagreeing with almost every decision the Tsar made. He thought that the men put in charge were too old and incompetent, especially Grand Duke Nikolai Nicholaevich, the Tsar's uncle, who was made Commander in Chief of the military. For this reason, Sandro was sidelined from the highest ranks of military leadership. He was, however, allowed to develop a flying school, a field considered harmless by men who had no vision of the future and could barely see beyond their horses. He initiated Russia's Imperial Air Service and ultimately served as the head of Russia's Air Force in the war.

Before the war, Xenia and Sandro had been staying at their home in Crimea, Ay Todor. It was to be their final peaceful stay there. Xenia then traveled with her Mama, the Tsar's mother Dowager Empress Maria, through England and France. When the war broke out, they had a hectic journey home through Denmark and Finland, carefully avoiding Germany. Like so many royal families, the war found them torn between opposing sides. Many of them, including Xenia's sister-in-law the Tsarina, were members of the German aristocracy. Xenia spent most of the war in St. Petersburg, which was renamed to a less Germanic and more Slavic Petrograd, where she ran a hospital for injured soldiers.

In the Don *Oblast*, or Region, the battles took a heavy toll. Don Cossacks like Mikhail fought in World War I not out of patriotism and enthusiasm, but because their government forced them to fight. They had no concept of Germany as an enemy until the press spread stories of terror and massacre. Germany was, after all, not a bastion of infidels, as Turkey or Japan had been, but the homeland of the Tsarina.

Cossacks were expert riders and well trained for military action—in the time of the Napoleonic wars. Their leaders had not kept up with the times. World War I was not to be won on horseback. It was fought and won with artillery. By the end of 1914 Russia had incurred almost a million casualties. The Russian army was severely underqualified for a war of this era. Its weapons were antiques, and the enemy's sophisticated intelligence about Russian military movements stymied many a Russian campaign.

Mikhail was eventually crippled in battle and made his way back to his family's home in *khutor* Amochaev. His father needed help with his small plot, for there were few men left in the *khutors*. While healing, Mikhail married Maria and started a family of his own, but it was a hard time to begin a new life. His plans of living in *khutor* Kulikov near Ivan and his favorite—young Shura—went on indefinite hold. Instead of having his own land to farm, he struggled on his father's. They were near starvation, deprived—by requisitioning—of those few crops they were able to grow. Supplies and animals were scarce. These hardships were to shape their political views in years to come.

Mikhail couldn't believe the government just kept sending the Russian people to their deaths in a war that had nothing to do with them. While fighting, he had watched the morale of his fellow soldiers deteriorate. Some simply abandoned the fighting. He might have joined them if he hadn't been injured. Many now talked openly against the government. His cousin Alexei arrived one day from fighting at the front. He came to the family *khutor*, Amochaev, and told them he was not returning to the battlefield.

"Were you injured?" Mikhail asked.

"No, but I think I would have been killed if I had stayed. It's an awful war, and I don't even know why we are fighting it."

"But you can't just leave!"

"Well, I am on leave and so are many others. Who will make me return?" Alexei was not as confident as he sounded, but the confusion at the front and in the country as a whole made him seriously consider desertion. But return he did, for he had no choice.

Alexei was to grow more disillusioned over the duration of the war. He knew this war had to end, and the government had to change. And it wasn't just Alexei. The country seethed with so many who felt just like he did. This war was not bringing Russians together or inspiring loyalty and nationalism. Instead, as people's needs were ignored and their bodies sacrificed to continuous defeats, the country began to fall apart. By the end of 1915, Russia's casualties had tripled to three million people, the army was suffering through the Great Retreat, and morale was shattered.

The Tsar used the war as an occasion for reasserting full autocratic rule. While Xenia's husband Sandro and many of his closest advisers continually encouraged him to appoint professional military leaders, he loyally retained his uncle as head of the military. When he finally removed Grand Duke Nikolai Nikolaevich, he put someone even worse in his place: himself.

Yes, in 1915 Tsar Nicholas II made himself the Commander in Chief of the Russian Army. It seemed like a very patriotic move at the time, but the Tsar's willingness to die for his country in no way improved Russia's military position in this war. Instead, it only hastened the death of his empire.

Sandro believed the Tsar was growing isolated, that he was increasingly relying on the advice of his wife, Empress Alix, and her spiritual advisor, the infamous Rasputin. Sandro was not alone in his suspicions. This perception disillusioned both the nobility and the peasantry in their ruler. By 1916, the country

was suffering from severe grain shortages. Protests—originally limited to the cities, mostly St. Petersburg and Moscow—now exploded throughout the countryside. Women took the brunt of the pain, as they were left behind while their men went to die. They had been abandoned to work the fields with no men or draft animals, and they were furious. Protesters took out their anger on landowners, including Cossacks who had managed to establish independent farms before the war, a category that included Ivan.

Mikhail and Alexei and their families were swept up in these events, as were many throughout the whole Don *Oblast*. They were angry at the government and blamed the Tsar for the hardships they faced. Ivan continued to urge Mikhail to try and work within the system, but Ivan was now far away, and life in *Khutor* Amochaev had become impossible. It was Alexei whose anti-government arguments were starting to sway Mikhail. Ivan had property and a livelihood to protect. Mikhail felt he had nothing, and therefore had little to lose by protesting. The people just wanted the government to stop stealing their crops and leaving them to starve. Many of the men from the *khutors* were still fighting the war in the far west of the country, and the reports coming back from the battles got worse every day.

In the cities, long lines for bread sparked small-scale riots. To support the war effort, people were brought to work in factories. The population of St. Petersburg had doubled practically overnight, to two million. There was no food and they were expected to work twelve hours a day, six days a week. Women just wanted their husbands back from the war. By early 1917, the women in the city of St. Petersburg—burdened by food shortages, frustrated with the government, and tired of the war—had had enough.

On International Women's Day—March 8—they marched in protest in St. Petersburg, and their march inspired 50,000 workers to strike.

The Russian revolution had begun.

The protestors had no idea what they had set off. By the next day, 160,000 workers throughout the city were participating in work slowdowns and protests. By Saturday, streetcars were stopped, shops were closed, and newspapers canceled. Cossacks, police and soldiers—sent to restore order—were torn between sympathy and obedience. Sympathy largely won.

Tsar Nicholas's advisors and family members, again including Sandro, urged that he endorse a transfer of his power to a new government with the authority to work its way through this crisis: a constitutional monarchy, in effect, similar to England's perhaps. Instead, Nicholas dissolved Russia's legislature—the Duma.

It didn't work out for him. By Monday the whole military was in mutiny. That's when the Tsar's regime crumbled. The Duma ignored him, declared itself the new government, and Tsar Nicholas abdicated. Americans learned of this through journalist John Reed, who gave a famous firsthand account of the events that he called "The ten days that shook the world."

Exactly ten days after the Women's Day March, the three-hundred-year reign of the Romanovs ended.

Sandro could not believe the news. He wrote later of his brother-in-law, "Kolya must have lost his mind. Since when does a sovereign abdicate because of a shortage of bread and partial disorders in his capital? The treason of the St. Petersburg reservists? But he had an army of fifteen million men at his disposal!"

The Tsar, however, didn't know how to lead his country out of this vortex. Winston Churchill, in his reflections about the

man said, "He was neither a great captain nor a great prince. He was only a true, simple man of average ability, of merciful disposition, upheld in all his daily life by his faith in God. But the brunt of supreme decisions centered upon him."

At the time of the revolt, Nicholas had been at his military headquarters, a thousand kilometers south of the capital. In the chaos of the abdication, Sandro took Nicholas's mother to see her son there. They had lunch and Sandro wrote, "I would much rather be burned at the stake than go through that luncheon again. Banalities, soothing lies, exaggerated politeness of the attendants, the tear-stained face of my mother-in-law . . ."

The Tsar was arrested three days later. Xenia never saw her brother again. By the end of March, the new Provisional Government—a struggling compromise between revolutionaries of many persuasions and leading government figures hoping to avoid calamity—had established itself enough to be recognized by the United States. The women had led the way, but what might have seemed like success was only the beginning of a long conflict. The new government struggled to deal with the increasingly unpopular ongoing war, the restructuring of the collapsing army, and a crumbling economy.

The trials of its history continued haunting Russia. A man called Vladimir Ilyich Ulyanov was one of the radicals who didn't think the 1905 Revolution had gone far enough. He had become a revolutionary following his brother's execution for an attempted assassination of Tsar Alexander III, spent some time in Siberia, and then moved to Western Europe, where he headed a Marxist party and campaigned for a proletarian revolution.

He was soon to become the new government's biggest challenge. Arriving in a sealed train traveling through war-torn Germany, he became known to the world as Lenin.

Chapter 10

The Revolution

The history of the Russian Revolution has been written countless times, but the personal consequences to families who were in the midst of it—those who fought and those who fled, those who won and those who lost—were so numerous and individual not all could see the light of day. Americans went through a Revolution and a Civil War, both of which left scars still felt today. But rarely has one historical event caused so much grief to so many as the Russian Revolution, which turned the victors into the greatest victims. Lenin and Stalin unleashed an evil on their country that belied any possible concept of victory.

Grand Duchess Xenia had been in Petrograd through those ten days that destroyed her world. She journaled the events in her diary day by day, and her writing shows how unprepared she was for her brother's abdication. She wrote with horror of those who destroyed him. The next day, she saw her other brother, Michael, for what turned out to be the final time. He had just refused the throne. Unable to get permission to see her brother Nicholas, just weeks later Xenia made the wise decision to join her mother and husband at Ay Todor. They would have all been arrested if not for that flight. The

family, cut off from all their relatives abroad, was to remain in isolation in Crimea, watching the horror that evolved in their homeland.

By the middle of 1917 Lenin was gaining power through speeches and articles that called for a proletarian revolution. His positions gained popularity and in October his Bolsheviks overthrew the Provisional Government with the aid of the newly formed Red Guards, the initial version of the Red Army. He installed a government of Soviets. Soviet means advice in Russian, and these "advisory councils" were established at many levels, from towns and districts all the way to the Supreme Soviet of the Union of Soviet Socialist Republics. Given the far more brutal autocracy that replaced the Tsar's, this very name was cynical in the extreme. But few outside the country understood its intended meaning.

As Civil War started brewing in Russia, the First World War—being fought in the west—grew ever more unpopular in Russia. The first Central Soviet, with its stated objectives of giving voice to the people, passed a law that in effect gave soldiers the right to choose whether or not to obey their commanders. An army with no discipline was a formula for disaster.

It was the Germans who had helped Lenin get from Switzerland to Russia after ten years in exile. They expedited his passage in a sealed train through their own country. Now he decided to consolidate his victory at home by conceding defeat to those same Germans. He had to give up on one war to win what he viewed as a global battle for the rights of the common man.

Lenin's policies vindicated Germany's decision to send him to Russia. In early 1918—only months before the Axis powers were finally defeated by the Allies—Germany was able to declare a victory over Russia and dictate the terms of

the treaty that ended Russia's participation in World War I. In that treaty, Russia gave up the western part of the Empire. As well as ceding Ukraine, it gave up a third of its population and agricultural land, half of its industrial plants, and almost all of its coal mines. Alexei and his fellow soldiers headed home. One week later the Russian government moved to Moscow, as German armies now threatened to reach the old capital in St. Petersburg.

Pulling Russia out of a domestically unpopular battle did win Lenin absolute power. At that point, he had the freedom to create the workers' paradise he preached. Instead he became an autocrat more vicious than any Tsar. Lenin launched the "Red Terror"—a fight against all enemies. The enemies were defined by categories that shifted constantly, but all were brutally attacked. In December of 1917, Lenin established the key Soviet secret police organ, the Cheka, which eventually became the KGB. By the middle of the next year there were hundreds of local Cheka groups under orders to implement Red Terror.

The Bolshevik newspaper *Krasnaya Gazeta*, openly described their goals: "Without mercy, without sparing, we will kill our enemies in scores of hundreds. Let them be thousands, let them drown themselves in their own blood."

The royal Romanovs were portrayed as symbols of the evil to be eliminated and all of them were defenseless targets. Xenia, Sandro, and the Dowager Empress were under virtual house arrest in Crimea. Xenia was no longer the young girl who played lightheartedly with her older brother Kolya and her cousin Sandro in the old royal palace of Livadia. She was now a married woman with seven children, several of them adults. Her youngest, ten-year-old Vasily, joined them in Crimea.

Their family had tried valiantly to prevent the tragic fate of their country. In the most notorious example, it was Xenia's

son-in-law, Felix Yusupov, who had murdered Rasputin in late 1916. But nothing they did helped. By the time Xenia moved to Crimea, her brother the Tsar was on his way to house arrest, in the remote east. A few months later she wrote to him there, "The heart bleeds at the thought of what you have gone through. Sometimes it seems like a terrible nightmare, and that I will wake up and it will all be gone! Poor Russia! What will happen to her?" Not long after she sent that letter, she learned that the Bolsheviks had murdered the Tsar and all his family. She was so worried for her mother that she tried to hide the information from her, but she needn't have bothered. Her mother heard the news, but never believed it. It was too unimaginable.

Fortunately for Xenia and her family, Crimea was to be the last holdout of the "White Russian Army," as the opponents of the revolution were known. The small number of Red Army bodyguards who were based around the Palace had served under Sandro in the Navy. They loyally protected him and the others from specific directives to murder the family. Xenia's last living brother, Mikhail, was not so fortunate. The Bolsheviks shot him shortly after they had killed the Tsar. Ultimately, it was Xenia's maternal aunt, the British Queen mother, Alexandra, who helped them. She compelled her son, Xenia's cousin King George V of England, to send the HMS Marlborough, a British Navy battleship, to the Black Sea to save what was left of the Russian royal family. They finally departed in April of 1919 to begin a life of exile.

Meanwhile, the revolution had turned into a full-scale civil war, with the White Army, composed largely of Cossacks, battling Lenin's Red Army. The odds were not in favor of the Whites. They were outnumbered, outgunned, and outsmarted in propaganda. The Whites also relied on Britain and France, who offered mostly disappointment rather than relief.

Initially many in the Don *Oblast*—certainly Alexei, but all those with little land such as Ivan's cousin Mikhail—welcomed the revolution. But they grew disillusioned when they saw their people viciously targeted. As Lenin's decrees were randomly executed throughout their territories, some followed Cossack leaders into military service against the Bolsheviks. Battles erupted throughout the country, several armies were formed, and the Civil War raged in full force. The *khutors* of Amochaev and Kulikov were on constantly changing sides of that battle. Who was fighting for which side remained confused and fluid to the end. Throughout 1918 and into early 1919 the battle lines reversed incessantly. Sometimes the Whites made gains. But they were spread too thinly along the edges of the country. By the middle of 1919, as Xenia and her family were fleeing Russia, opposition to the revolution was wavering in the Don *Oblast*. It didn't look good for Ivan and Daria and their family. And they didn't have a royal relative abroad to save them.

Chapter 11

Leaving Kulikov

Back in Kulikov, a loud train whistle tore Daria out of her reverie as it pierced the oppressive silence of what had once been a peaceful scene along the nearby pond. Out for a rare moment on her own, she immediately started running and passed the church, nearing her neighbor Kuznetsov's house. She saw his wife step onto the dirt road, curving her hand above her eyes, focusing hard into the distance.

There hadn't been a train for so long that Daria had feared they weren't running anymore. It was the late summer of 1919 and Ivan had been gone for days. And how would he get back if there were no more trains from Moscow? It could take him months to return. And, from what she had been hearing and seeing, they didn't have months.

Daria's mind churned. She was both hopeful and terrified. What if the train didn't stop? What if her Ivan wasn't on it? What if it was just more Red troops heading south? Or worse, troops that would get off here to maraud and pillage? She needed to still her mind, to keep from torturing herself into paralysis.

She could hear the wheels slowing, but that didn't mean anything. Would the train slow further or was it just God's

way of sinking her deeper into the quagmire of unsolvable problems? She stopped then and prayed. There was nothing left to do but pray to a God she was no longer certain existed.

The train stopped. Steam poured out of the locomotive. She heard voices. She heard a door open.

And then Ivan was speeding toward her from the train station. Wait, someone else was running behind him. It was Kuznetsov. They must have met up in Moscow. Had they found buyers for the grain? Had Ivan raised enough funds to see them through the next few months? Two times over the last year, she and Ivan had already packed their belongings and fled, only to return as the tide of battle turned to favor their own White fighters. For a while now it had appeared as if their Cossack army was defeating the Reds. That's why Ivan had risked one more trip to the capital. In the weeks since he had left, however, the war had unexpectedly arrived almost at their doorstep. And victory no longer seemed like a possibility.

People were fleeing in their *telegas*—the four-wheel wooden carts of a size that varied with its owner's holdings had become a mainstay of their lives. They threw their children and possessions into them, put horses between the long bars, aimed their whips at the horses' backs and headed off into the unknown.

Groups of their own soldiers had passed through town, also heading south, warning of the advancing Red Army. In their desperation they stole food and, she had heard, did worse to some women. Daria herself had buried their family silver behind the house and barricaded the doors to protect herself and her family, and so far, this had worked. Just this morning she had packed some clothes and the last of the cellared food and put much of it into their own large *telega*. If the Reds were indeed taking over, she knew her husband would be an immediate target, for he was a man of property.

Ivan had tried hard to avoid choosing between revolutionaries and conservatives. He had finished his military

service as a medic. Carrying bodies, he saw the pain up close and had hoped never to be involved in a battle again. The country needed his skills to raise crops and bring food to the cities. But now, anyone who owned land was suspect. Daria thanked God Ivan had been shipping what remained of the year's crop to Moscow on this trip. Had it been there when the armies sped through, they would have been cleaned out and left with no alternatives. Even troops on their side plundered indiscriminately, for they were starving.

The effects of the first World War had torn through their lands, killing and maiming friends and family. Their small *khutor* alone had lost twenty men. But most of the fighting had happened far from their Don region, and in retrospect, its effects were minimal compared to the gravity of their current situation. Hundreds had already died here in this fighting, this Civil War. And it wasn't over yet. Daria's sons were just infants, but she watched in despair as the young men of all their families fought, and changed sides, and fought some more. No matter which side they were on, it seemed, they died.

When the revolution started, Daria had just given birth to her fourth child, a son—Anatoly, called Tolya. Her father, Pavel, had passed away shortly before that, and her mother Natalia had come to help with Tolya and deal with her own sorrow, away from the home she had shared with her husband. As the intensity of the battles in their region increased, it had become clear that Natalia could not go back home. Resentful, but with no alternative, she had stayed in Kulikov. But now her other daughters—one a widow and one caring for a war invalid—had both given birth and she desperately wanted to go home and help with the new grandchildren.

That was no longer possible. A frustrated Natalia was still with Daria, awaiting Ivan's return.

Chapter 12

Flight

Ivan sped from the train toward Daria.

"Daria, Daria. You are still here! You don't know what I have been imagining. I am so glad you are alive and that the *khutor* seems quiet." Ivan wrapped his wife in his arms and held her close. "It's over. General Wrangel and the White Army have suffered great losses, and the Red Army has been authorized to wipe us out."

"What do you mean wipe us out?"

"There has been a formal government directive. All adult Cossack males are to be killed. All our land will be taken over. Wives and families will be moved away. Pure evil has been let loose."

Ivan talked fast and moved quickly, holding her tight and heading for his home—the beautiful home he would be leaving shortly, perhaps never to see again.

"So, it's not just the soldiers at risk now?" Daria had hoped that her husband's age might protect them.

"No, it's all of us. Every man, woman, and child. Every Cossack. There is a new word out. *Rasskazachivanie*. De-Cossackization. It's serious. But we can talk later. Right now, we have to flee."

"But . . . how will my mother get home?"

"Daria . . ." Ivan realized his words were not sinking in. She wasn't understanding the gravity of their circumstances. He was barely comprehending the situation himself and Daria was hearing of it for the first time. "Your mother has no home. None of us has a home. We are leaving right now, and she has to come with us! Please, trust me. Hurry."

"But where are we going?"

"South! South to the Black Sea! To Crimea! The White army is fleeing, and that is our last chance for escape."

"But Ivan, how will we go?"

"The horse will have to pull us. Have you kept the *telega* packed?"

"*Telega!* But that is over a thousand kilometers, Ivan!" Daria thought her husband had lost his mind. Just minutes ago, she was worried about his return from Moscow. Now this? "It could take months. How will we even find our way? We've never been there. Can't we go to Moscow?"

"I know that has always been your dream, Daria, but you need to understand. It's over. I will be executed if I get anywhere near the military or the authorities."

Daria sped after him to the house. Ivan was shouting at her mother, telling her to get the children ready. He immediately started connecting the horse to the *telega,* which was ready to go. There was no point in any more conversation. Daria rounded up the children and her mother. They loaded up all the remaining food and grain that would fit. They crowded onto that bare wooden cart and headed out, with no idea how long that *telega* would be their only home.

Shura, at nine years old, was the only one of their children old enough to understand anything of what was going on, but they could all feel the intensity of the disturbance. It was not the first time they were leaving the khutor, but this time felt

different. In the past their father had been calm and organized. Now, after being gone for two weeks, he had just raced in and started shouting and telling them to hurry.

"Papa, will we be coming back again?"

"Shura, I don't know. I don't know. This time we might not come back." Ivan looked his son directly in the eyes, determined to keep his own eyes from tearing.

"But Papa how can we leave? All my friends are here. And I haven't said goodbye to my Uncle Mikhail." An improbable but deep affection had arisen between young Shura and Mikhail. But Mikhail was now far away, and there was no way they could find him. They couldn't find anyone.

"We have no choice, Shura. This war is over, and we lost. I don't know if we'll ever come back."

"Papa, Papa. We can't just leave. We have the biggest house in the *khutor*. Who will live in it?"

"I know, dear one. I know. This is the only home you have ever known. But the house is not important right now. You are. You and our family. You are now a man, my son." Ivan knelt in front of his son and made the sign of the cross with his hand over his body, praying that their faith could help them all survive. "You are now a Cossack, Shura. Protect your sister and brothers; take care of them. Take care of your mother and grandmother. We have nothing else left." Frightened, Shura ran to get them organized. He was the oldest son in the family, and he took on that responsibility.

His grandmother Natalia was furious that she hadn't been able to get home to her other children, but finally Daria grabbed her bag and pushed her in with the children. Little Tolya was napping, so she wrapped him in a warm blanket and hugged him to her breast as she climbed into the place next to Ivan at the front. Shura closed the gate—as if it mattered—and they were on their way.

Just a few hours later they joined the small number of others, including the Kuznetsovs, who were also fleeing. There had been no time to communicate with their own families. Thank goodness Ivan had been able to go on that last trading mission to Moscow and had a bit of money with him. And then Daria felt an agonized remorse that filled her mind to the exclusion of everything else. She had left her silver buried behind the back doorstep! How could she have forgotten? Part of her wanted to go back more than anything else. But she knew there was no going back. She had never seen her husband like this, and the others had moved just as quickly. Terror was at their heels. Compared to her life, compared to all their lives, the silver was so insignificant.

And yet, her memory of that family silver, a talisman of a past life, would never fade.

Chapter 13

On to Crimea

In the harrowing fear that filled the early days of their flight, Ivan knew that Daria's stress levels threatened her very existence. He was completely engrossed in coordinating the group that traveled with them, a leader as always. But that didn't leave him much energy to focus on his family, and Daria had to fill in.

She still had a lot of time to worry. What did the future hold for them? Would they ever return? Would they all be killed in this senseless war being fought between brothers? Little Tolya wasn't even two yet, Liza and Kolya at five and seven were too young to understand what was happening. Her mother was of no help. Shura was the only one she didn't constantly have to fret about.

But there was no choice.

Following the rail line, they put the *telegas* on the tracks to speed their flight but had to yank them off whenever they heard a train approaching. They ran constantly and hid when they had to. While Ivan coordinated with the other men, Daria made sure the children were fed and cared for her mother. She had no time to worry about her own health, and she grew so thin that her breasts shrank, and her clothes threatened to

fall off. For the first time in her life, she was not the strong woman in charge of her destiny.

They built fires when they felt safe, but more often than not just ate cold leftover *kasha*. They were hungry all the time, but at least had plenty of water from the streams that flowed throughout the area. The children slept on the back of the *telega*; Daria and her mother wrapped themselves in all their clothes and slept under a tarp that Ivan and Shura would hang from a tree or over a bush. In moments that felt way too brief and rare, Ivan wrapped himself around her and he would feel her heart pounding until she settled into the night.

Finally, they reached a point where they veered off the train line, and the risk of attacks was lower. Over a meal, Ivan decided he had to step in. "Daria, you must take care of yourself. I'll make sure that we have enough food, and we won't move forward until we know there is a path."

"Oh, Ivan, don't we have to just keep fleeing?"

"Yes, *dorogaia*, my dear. But we've moved away from the rails, and for now we've left the majority of the fighting behind." He understood this was going to be a long trip, and they had to rest whenever they could. He was deeply worried about the stress his wife was under and knew it was time for Shura to step up to a new role. "Shura," Ivan turned to his son. "I am going to leave for a few days. You must take care of everyone while I'm gone. There's enough food, and you can collect firewood. Keep everyone well hidden!"

"But where are you going, Papa? Can't I come with you?"

"Son, I can deal with some farmers in the area, and maybe even find us some temporary work. I need to do it alone, and you need to protect your mother. Make sure she eats. I'm worried about how thin she is getting." Making it seem like an afterthought, he turned to Natalia. "And you, my dear, you need to take care of your daughter." He was done with her bullying

attitude toward Daria. She was an ungrateful old complainer, and he was stunned that his wife didn't stand up to her.

Natalia just stared balefully at him. She believed it was her turn in life to be taken care of. She was almost sixty, too old for this. But she kept her mouth shut and let him go on his way. Daria would have taken her home if not for this man.

This was only the first of many times that Ivan had to leave to find food or work. It became the pattern of their travels. He would find a safe spot for the family and leave Shura as the "man" in charge. Then he would search for a farm where they could work, a friendly face to give them shelter for a time, or just an abandoned house.

As soon as he was out of sight, Natalia decided to have it out with her daughter. "Daria, this isn't our battle. I don't even know what this battle is about. Who cares if the Reds or the Whites win?" She insisted. "We need to turn around and head home. We have no idea where we are or where we are headed. This is no future for your children."

"Our future is with my children's father, Mama. If we could go back, Ivan would find a way to do that. We don't have an alternative."

"Ivan is a Cossack, but you are not even a true Cossachka."

"Oh, yes, I am, Mama. I have become a true Cossachka."

"Mama, Mama, how can Baba say you're not a Cossachka?" demanded Shura.

"Hush, Shura. Mama, you're frightening the children." Daria cast a reproachful glance at Natalia.

"Mama, but Papa says I am now a Cossack! What does that mean?" Shura demanded.

"It means you're a part of a proud tribe of people who have protected our country—from Tatar infidels to German invaders—for centuries. It is a force that is fighting even now to keep our country from sinking under these devils, these

brutes who call themselves saviors of the common man but are determined to wipe us all out."

"But isn't Baba a Cossachka?"

"No, she's not. But your Deda Pavel loved your Papa with all his heart and joined our family and our home with the Cossacks. We're all in this together." Daria put her arm around Shura. "You are a Cossack, my dear. But you are so young. I wish our land was at peace so you could be in school instead of here taking care of us. I promise you someday this will all end. I promise you that your *budushnost* still lies ahead of us. In that future you will have time to learn all about your Cossack heritage."

"*Budushnost, shmudushnost . . .*" her mother started again, but Daria didn't have time for more argument.

"Now Shura, go and get some fish. Take Kolya with you; he needs to learn how to fish, and to clean them after he catches them." Daria knew she had to keep them all busy, or they would go mad. She went off to set up their camp, making sure the tarp was secure and slanted to keep the rain out. She would become quite expert at many unexpected new skills, for she had a lot of time to work on them. She called after Shura as the boys were leaving. "Tomorrow you and I will go hunting. I think I heard some wild pigs; they will taste good!"

Ivan came back in a few days, as he had promised, bringing more grain. He made their escape successful with his innate ability to trade and find food, and he still had funds with him, some in the form of gold he had brought from Moscow before their exodus began.

Their home had been in the extreme northern tip of the Don *Oblast*, away from the most heavily populated areas. Since the battles were fiercest in the south, near the capital, Novocherkassk, they had to avoid it. They headed instead far to the west, deep into the Kherson region of Ukraine. In the

beginning, the tracks they followed seemed to lead nowhere. They walked past deserted settlements and untilled fields for days. They didn't really know where they were going. They just kept moving to stay ahead of the conflict.

Ivan remained focused on their goal, even though, as time passed, the group of neighbors they had started with eventually dropped out. Some headed back home, some stayed to work in fields along the way. Others just gave up, slipping away in the night. Soon enough, they were alone. Ivan knew they were safer that way, that their traces were easier to hide, but it was certainly lonely.

There were few cities of any size in their direction. It was a long traverse, opposite from the route to Moscow that Ivan knew well, and much further than even the distance to that capital. They grew used to sleeping wherever the night caught them—by the side of the road, or in an abandoned field. Daria's background as a migrant worker had toughened her up, but Ivan knew that nothing could prepare his family for these months of unsettled plodding. While he did find work for them in fields along the way, few fields were being farmed at that point.

The ravages of war, especially as they headed west, became more apparent. Their Don *Oblast* had been devastated by the Civil War, but the earlier damage from the large artillery of World War I in Ukraine was on a different scale altogether. A terrible blight had spread across these lands. On top of that, the new Soviet leadership was now at war with Poland and Ukraine as well as the Whites.

In the first months of flight Ivan had wondered if things would soon change, if perhaps they might head back home. Now it was the middle of 1920. Almost a year had passed. The White Army's defeats were severe. He learned that the only life left for them in Russia lay in Crimea. The rest of the country was firmly in the hands of the Bolsheviks.

Ivan often thought about all the families who had decided to stay. He wondered about their fate. Had any others left? Were they on this same trajectory? Would they meet up with kinfolk in Crimea? Ivan's father had been ailing—was he even alive? Was anyone alive? Had *khutor* Amochaev been engulfed in the battle? Was the *khutor* where Ivan was born even standing? They had no way of knowing.

He had been very close to his cousin Mikhail, who had named his young son after Ivan. Though Mikhail and Ivan didn't see eye to eye on politics or the future, Mikhail did not feel strongly enough to join the Reds, either. Had Mikhail finally decided which side he was on?

It was hard to imagine how any of them might reconnect. Russia was so big, and Crimea so small. There wasn't enough room for all of Russia's Cossacks on that spit of land. But Ivan knew they had no choice but to find their way onto it. He knew a land-holding Cossack like himself possessed no future in Russia, regardless of the outcome of this war. He'd heard a new word—*kulak*—a derogatory way of talking about farmers who had gained some success in trade. Now he had two strikes against him: he was a Cossack and a *kulak*.

That's why Ivan persisted so doggedly when so many others had fallen by the wayside. His relief upon reaching Perekop, the isthmus that connected Crimea to the mainland, was enormous, although he was still cautious, not wanting to get everyone's hopes up too soon. He herded the little group across a strip of land that was a few kilometers wide at the point where they crossed, with water on all sides. They had reached the Black Sea! It was the family's first time near any sea. As they approached, the air smelled different, a bit salty, and they were ready to see water.

"Can we go in, Papa?" Shura asked, jumping up and down in his excitement.

"Of course, *synok*, little son. Take your clothes off and jump in!" They all knew how to swim, for they had grown up around ponds and rivers, but they had never been in saltwater.

"Mama, look, I am floating!" Liza shouted as she rolled in the shallow water.

For a short time, the children forgot about everything except chasing each other around and splashing in the water.

"Daria," Ivan said when they had a moment to themselves. "Crimea is the final Cossack stronghold. I think we will be safe here. But I need to go check it out, understand where we can live. Will you be all right here?"

"Oh, yes, Ivan. We have some food, the weather is fine, and I think we are well hidden here away from the water. We'll be fine."

Ivan knew that Crimea was held by the White forces of General Wrangel. He believed the city of Yevpatoria, on the west below Perekop, was safer than Sebastopol, further east along the Black Sea shore. Sebastopol was the headquarters of the military. The royal palaces where Xenia and Sandro had lived lay even further east. So, Ivan concentrated his energies on Yevpatoria.

While Ivan was away, Daria and the children camped—once again—hidden and alone, without a horse, with only ten-year-old Shura to protect them, although Daria had become quite expert with the rifle Ivan always left behind.

Just a few years earlier Yevpatoria had been promoted by its mayor as a fashionable resort, a playground for the wealthy. Beaches and hotels lined the bay it sat upon. A city theater had been opened in 1910. Four years later, the first tram ran in the city. But the First World War had transformed it. Now it served as a major center of military hospitals and evacuation.

Ivan's talk of Moscow always excited Daria, but she had never been to a large city. Yevpatoria would be the first. As the

days in this hidden spot passed in relative peace, she could feel some of her fear dissipate. Soon she awaited Ivan's return with more anticipation than apprehension. The children could feel the difference. Tolya, who had turned three on the trip, followed his brothers around like a puppy. Shura, serious far beyond his years, took to heart his father's instructions to be the man of the family in his absence. Sister Liza fetched water from the creek, for Daria was in a frenzy of washing, determined that they would enter the town in clean clothes.

For dinner, they ate mostly *kasha*, the famous Russian porridge made of black dry-roasted grains of buckwheat, their mainstay throughout the trip. A heavily used cover crop, they had found it all along the way. *Kasha* with *borscht*, a red soup—once made with meat, cabbage, potatoes and vegetables—was a favorite meal. But now they made the soup by boiling water with a few roots—a monotonous diet. Daria reminded the children, anytime they complained, to be happy with what they had. Actually, they rarely complained. The real challenge came not from her children but from her mother.

Natalia never reconciled herself to their flight. She grew more despondent as the days crawled on. All she thought about was her daughters, young women who—in her mind at least—needed her and obeyed her. Daria often reminded her that her own husband, Pavel, had adored Ivan and believed in his philosophy of life. But Natalia's other children had been trapped by the war and by a government that continued to reduce their opportunities. They certainly weren't planning to die for that government. Nor did they have any intention of dying for the Tsar. She knew for certain they would never have left their homes on some hopeless flight.

To Natalia, it seemed they would die on this stupid *telega* in the middle of nowhere, for nothing. She told them, but they just wouldn't listen.

Daria didn't know what to say. How could her mother not understand the situation? They would have been slaughtered had they stayed behind in the village. They'd escaped at the last possible moment. They were lucky to still be alive. Instead of being a helper and offering moral support, Natalia was a drain on her energies.

Finally, almost a week after he left, Ivan returned. Daria heard pounding hoofbeats and swore she could tell it was Ivan's horse. Suddenly she heard the children's laughter, and then her husband's voice.

He leaped down from the horse in a way that reminded her of a younger Ivan—the one who had come to arrange a marriage, a lifetime ago. There was a spring in the walk of the man who approached her, and a smile on his face.

"I think you will be happy," he said, wrapping his arms around her. The children ran in circles, only Shura standing a bit to the side, his arms crossed, waiting to hear what his father had to say.

"Shura, take the horse to the field by the creek. I'll wait till you're back to share my news."

Daria put the water on for some tea, and she and Liza finished cooking what she hoped was their last caravanning meal.

"The city seems in relatively good shape," Ivan told them. "And I have found us a place to stay!"

He told them the hospitals were still in operation, and there were a few street cars running. The hotels were all converted to housing, as were many buildings that had been abandoned, mostly by well to do families that had already fled. Because he, Ivan, had served in the medical branch of the military, he had talked his way to a room of their own in one of those buildings. He had stayed long enough to register for a specific room.

"It's a *barskiy dom*, a regal house, right on the water, across a busy street from the sea and the piers. And I was able to set up a small stove, so you can cook special meals," he said, nodding his head to Daria with a private smile.

"I can't wait to have meals to cook!" she replied, happy to be teased.

"Give me some of that so-called *borscht* and *kasha*, Liza," he finally said. He looked at the pale liquid and frowned. "I certainly hope we will be eating something more substantial soon."

Liza laughed in a way he hadn't heard in weeks.

"Oh, you will, Ivan!" Daria said. "We saved the best for last! Show him, Shura!"

Shura glowed as he brought out the large carp he caught, Kolya had cleaned, and Liza had helped stuff. Fresh from the fire, it was a meal they would all remember for a long time. Most importantly, they saved the eyes—for everyone knew it was her favorite part—for Daria.

White Army Departure

*Ships departing Crimea during evacuation of the White Russians
after they lost the Civil War in November of 1920.*

Chapter 14

Leaving a Homeland

Having conquered most of Russia, the Bolshevik Red Army prepared for their final attack against the last stronghold of the White Army in Crimea. The White Army, mostly Cossacks, had some of the best soldiers in the land. Unfortunately, their guns couldn't compete with Bolshevik propaganda, which promised a workers' paradise. The Bolshevik leadership never lived up to those ideals, but for now they owned the minds of all but this shrinking cadre of opponents.

For Daria—after a year of constant flight—their months in Yevpatoria were a moment of relative calm in spite of the chaos. As Ivan had promised, they had a room right on the water, and she could see the docks from her window. She became familiar with the sight of Tatar faces mingling with the Cossacks—and Ivan taught the children the history of this remote corner of the empire.

Crimean Tatars descended from the armies of Genghis Khan, who invaded Russia and dominated the continent for centuries. Cossacks had led the fighting that eventually defeated them over a hundred years earlier. Now those same Cossacks faced annihilation. And in one more ironic twist of history, it would be Tatars watching Cossacks flee. In late 1920, as the

military situation approached desperation, Ivan went to the countryside to trade with the Tatars one final time.

"I'm worried about you leaving, Ivan. What if something happens while you are gone?" Daria tried to keep calm in the face of Ivan's determination to keep them fed, but the situation had felt critical for some time.

"I've been assured we can hold on here for some weeks," he answered. "The Perekop is narrow enough to protect us. There is still time. And we need food if we are to survive the flight."

Daria knew he was right. They needed to replenish the supplies that were keeping them alive. But she worried.

And then an unexpected cold freeze set in. Instead of being surrounded by water, Perekop was now wholly exposed because its shores froze over weeks earlier than normal, creating a passage for the Red Army. The seemingly strongly fortified isthmus fell in a short but vicious battle. The weather had brought on the White Army's defeat. The time Ivan was relying on had evaporated. And he was still gone.

With Perekop breached, General Wrangel directed his army to disengage from the enemy and flee with utmost speed to the ports, where he had planned a major evacuation with his English and French allies. On November 13—one day later—they were under full flight. The primary evacuation port, Sebastopol, had ships from all over the world crowding the docks. Smaller Yevpatoria was fortunate to have any ships at all. Four thousand soldiers, and no one else, were to be taken from that city. But many of them had families, and the men refused to abandon them.

Daria and the children, from high above the street, could see and hear and even feel the intensity of the crowds pushing to get on a handful of ships. At times she feared the noise would shatter the glass in the windows. It didn't help that her mother just cowered in a corner and moaned.

Only a handful of Russian military ships approached Yevpatoria. Three of them were special-purpose ships, mine-sweepers, called Tralschiks. Not deserving even a name, they were numbers 410, 411, and 412. Their mission was to search for, detect and destroy sea mines—not to hold desperate refugees. They were not comfortable passenger liners.

Daria watched tanks and guns being destroyed, then abandoned. Soldiers—to whom horses were like family—had to desert their steeds. Many shot the animals rather than leave them to the enemy. Some even chose to stay rather than surrender their horse.

Still, there was not enough room. Anyone not under major threat was turned away. Only officers and their immediate families—perceived as being at highest risk—were allowed on board.

But Daria was not near the ships. She watched all this from the window of the room they had been living in for months. Ivan was still gone. What was she to do?

Suddenly someone was pounding on the door and shouting. "*Otkroyte! Srazu!* Open the door, immediately!"

Daria pushed the children behind her. She broke out of her catatonic state and went to open it. A wild-eyed Cossack in military uniform stared at her.

"I didn't believe my wife when she told me you were still here! What are you thinking? Everyone is evacuating!"

"Ivan isn't here," Daria said, stoically.

"That can't be. Where is he? Is he down at the docks?" The man kept turning around, staring at the entry, as if Ivan would materialize at his demand.

"No. He's been gone for three days. He'll be back soon. He has gone to trade for some flour. We were running out."

"You are running out of much more than flour!"

"Yes, I know. But what can I do? I have the children. And my mother."

"Of course. I know." The man finally quieted down. While he had been away fighting, his wife had lived next door. Fleeing Perekop, he had immediately taken his family to the ships. "You must leave immediately! And I can't wait for you. My family is already on the ship and it is ready to pull away. I have to go! Please! This is your last chance. You will be executed if you stay."

His worn boots clattered down the hallway as he ran off without a backward glance. He had done his deed.

The stranger's appearance shocked Daria out of her frozen state. She was no longer an observer, one restrained by her mother's fears. She turned away from the door, a reenergized woman. "Mama! Children! You heard the man," she shouted. "*Idem!* We are going."

"But, Daria. How can you leave without Ivan?" Natalia whined back.

Daria would no longer be ruled by her mother. They had to move, and it had to be now. One glance outside the windows showed a Cossack leaping onto a ship that was pulling away from the dock. Most of the ships had already left.

They possessed almost nothing by this point, and it only took a few minutes to get the children ready to go. Daria opened the door and nodded sternly at her mother. "Come with us. We are going."

Her mother grudgingly grabbed her bag and stepped out of the doorway, followed by the children. Daria closed the door—there was no reason to think about locking it.

Outside, indescribable chaos raged. Men pushed each other in all directions, ignoring the risk of shoving people into the water.

Using skills she hadn't lost, Daria wrapped Tolya in one arm, the same one a bag dangled from. Her other hand grabbed Liza's. She told the boys to take their grandmother's arms and not let go.

She then bludgeoned her way to the front of the crowd. They reached the docks and the pier. The intensity of the crowd was easing up, for the last ship was pulling away. Daria stood for a moment, watching it in disbelief. Then, followed by her brood, she pushed her way through the dissolving crowd to the master of the port.

"My husband is an officer; he has passage on the ship. We need to get on."

"I'm sorry, madame. It has left port. There are are no more ships."

"How can that be?"

"The Tralschik T 412 has not appeared. It was the last of the available ships. There are no more."

"But what will we do?"

"The same as all these other people." He gestured at the thousands crowding the quays.

Daria felt her deepest despair. Had all the hardships of the past year been for nothing? Had she sacrificed her children's future? Was it over?

Her mother glowered. "I told you, Daria. You're risking all of our lives. We should not be leaving."

But Daria would not give up. Not now.

She ignored her mother and continued forward, to where the last ship had pulled out. She kept looking toward the water and then back in the direction that Ivan would come from, but he was not to be seen.

All of a sudden there came a loud grinding noise, and then screaming and pushing and shoving. Tralschik No. 412 had appeared out of the icy mist. It was docking.

The level of intensity approached insanity. And still Daria didn't know what to do. But bodies were pushing past her. There was no choice. It was now or never.

"Children, grab your grandmother. Stay together!"

They were at the front and were pushed onto the ship. Daria caught at the railing and stood her ground, staring back into the distance, not believing what was happening. Her mother was still whining, but she no longer heard the old woman.

The ship had no more room, but still the bodies kept coming.

Suddenly, Daria heard a familiar voice shouting. She looked up. One more time salvation was appearing. Ivan jumped off his horse and pushed through the crowds. They pushed back, but his determination was greater. Just as he got to the front however, they started pulling up the gangway. Daria ran out to the middle of the rising gangplank and screamed. "Stop! It's my husband!"

Fortunately, some caring Cossacks manning the process knew Ivan. They slowly lowered the gangway and Ivan ran aboard.

But the horror wasn't over. While Daria and Ivan hugged in unbelievable gratitude, Daria's mother raced along that same gangway in the opposite direction.

They turned, aghast, just in time to see her leap off the ship and onto the dock.

The gangplank continued its way up, and now there was no return. Daria had regained her husband but lost her mother. There was barely time to react.

"*Bože moi.* Dear God." Daria whispered, crossing herself.

As the ship pulled away, they all just stared, helpless. Then a re-energized Natalia waved, as if they were leaving for just a few days. "I'm going home! It will be all right," she shouted as the ship pulled away. There was nothing they could do. And she wasn't the only one. In the chaos of the departure, people had to make final decisions. Many chose not to go. Families were ripped apart.

They were never to see Natalia again. Never. Daria's last view of her mother was of a relieved woman, waving goodbye. As the ship quickly moved out, she and her husband finally

had a moment to talk in relative privacy. "I am so sorry about your mother," Ivan whispered.

"This was all a nightmare. I should have known. She hated the idea of leaving."

"I hate it too. But the alternative is worse."

"For you. But maybe not for her."

"All we can do is hope, Daria. I hope things will go well for her now that she has made her choice."

Daria knew he was just trying to protect her from an unbearable reality. She let go of hope for her mother. There was nothing she could do for her. Daria needed all the hope she had left for herself and her family.

"What happened to you?" She asked Ivan. "I was terrified you wouldn't come."

"I can hardly imagine what ran through your mind," he replied. "I am so grateful you boarded this ship."

"You really cannot imagine. We were told the last ship had left and this one was missing at sea."

"And now it's full to double its capacity. I just hope it doesn't sink."

"Stop that! I can't bear one more worry. I was afraid you hadn't heard about the evacuation."

"Oh, I knew, but so did the Tatars."

"And?"

"Well, they decided they couldn't take our money."

"Why?"

"They were afraid it would be useless."

"Are they right?"

"They could be. We'll soon find out. I have a lot of it."

"You?"

"Yes. Last time they were afraid to take gold. So, I traded some away." Ivan would have a lot of time to regret that choice.

"And now they wouldn't take paper?"

"Yes. And it's the beautiful new currency. The one that was just released."

They would soon hear that the Kornilov, the ship that carried General Wrangel, was full of that newly minted currency. The bills would come in handy, the soldiers later learned—at the field latrines.

Ivan had tried a few other grain sellers in desperation before giving up, paying in gold and swinging that precious bag of flour to open his path onto the ship. He had no idea the evacuation could be so rapid. But once the Perekop fortifications were broken, the Red Army could not be kept out. Now there were hundreds of ships all streaming in the same direction from Crimea to the only outlet of the Black Sea, the only escape by water from Russia. Fortunately, since World War I had ended, Istanbul was in friendly hands. That was where the ships were heading.

But first they had to get there. It was an unusually cold winter, and the fog was heavy. The ship was not only severely overcrowded, there had been no time to put adequate food or supplies on board.

Once more, it was Ivan who saved the day. He had brought only one thing aboard—but that one thing was a large bag of wheat.

Daria learned how to mash it with saltwater and then make patties that she would attach to the hot smokestacks of the ship to bake flatbread. It wasn't much, but they survived. Not everyone was so fortunate. There were many cases of typhoid and other casualties on board, as well as in the months to come.

But the evacuation was, in many ways, successful. A hundred and twenty-six seagoing vessels ended up evacuating some 140,000 people, over 7,000 of them from Yevpatoria. It was a drop compared to the number of those who stayed. White supporters who had been anywhere near the evacuation

were wiped out when the Reds arrived, soon after the ships' departure.

Over the next ten years over one and a half million Cossacks—out of a remaining population of less than twice that—were killed or forcibly relocated. The genocide was appalling.

Daria and Ivan did not then know any of this, but thoughts and memories of their families tortured them. They had squeezed through the veritable eye of a needle to a future—a *budushnost*, as Ivan's father would say—they could only hope would be worth having. They had certainly been saved from annihilation by far more than their share of nearly miraculous events.

Without miracles, there would have been no path away from their destroyed homeland. Countless others were not as fortunate as they.

Years later, Ivan would meet and do some business with Kuznetsov. They would never know what happened to any of the others. In all their years of exile Daria and Ivan never saw another family member nor even anyone who shared their Amochaev name. Not a single Amochaev outside of their immediate family escaped.

They were aware of the royal Romanovs who had escaped, for the Russian émigrés revered the Tsar's family. But—as with Amochaevs—no Romanovs related to Daria—including her mother—would people their future.

Chapter 15

Lemnos 1920

Ivan, Daria and the children, with no other relations, arrived: Nowhere.

They had not found the promised land, or even Istanbul. They were in the Aegean Sea, amid islands still being disputed between Turkey and Greece. It was not a scene of charming white houses and scenic beauty. No, on an overcrowded military ship, they approached the shore of an island that could have been called Purgatory as easily as Lemnos. For this island had been overrun by refugees, and all its natural beauty was invisible to people who had lost everything. But perhaps they would be allowed to land and get shelter; one more pause in a flight whose final destination was unknown.

Wherever they finally landed, Daria knew that this was the beginning of their new life. There was no going back and nothing to go back to. The White Army had been defeated. But Daria Pavlovna also knew she would only stay here until they found the next stop in their passage. She was almost scornful of those who shared her fate, the Russians who thought they would soon re-board to continue the battle. Many of the passengers seemed to believe that this was just a temporary setback. Fools.

Daria might just as well have shouted her thoughts. Her face and bearing showed her every feeling, particularly the dark ones. This tall, strong-boned woman had no time for subtlety. She needed every ounce of her determination to survive the days and years to come. Among the last to leave Yevpatoria, as 1920 ended, they were still on the military transport, the Tralschik T 412—a particularly grueling trip on a ship built to hold a thousand which carried more than twice that many desperate refugees; packed to well beyond bursting point. Storms threatened constantly; the waves tossed them about; empty stomachs churned. The terror of each moment made the present and past disappear into sheer misery.

When they had finally arrived at the docks near Istanbul, an area accepting the fleeing Russian Army, there was a problem. Of course. Cossacks from earlier ships got into conflicts. No one knew what it was all about, but the outcome was clear: Istanbul would accept no more Cossacks. Further through the Dardanelles strait lay Gallipoli. But only active military could disembark there, and her husband Ivan's forty-eight years on the planet made him useless as a fighter. They were again sent on their way.

They ended up docked at this most desolate spot. A barren rock in the middle of the sea was their new home: a Greek Island called Lemnos. Lemnos teemed with crowds. Almost 20,000 Cossack refugees flowed into its confines, and the island didn't have the resources to handle even a fraction of that number. Many would die of starvation and disease while waiting for another destination to open up.

As Daria finally stepped ashore with ten-year-old Shura helping herd the little ones off the boat along the narrow gangway, she realized Ivan no longer walked behind her. Ivan stood on the ship in shock, unaware of his family, focused only on the barren isle; the crowded tents; the chaos; the lack

of anything that would make this future better than whatever devastation had hit their home. He didn't know what the Communists could do that would make his green fields and forests worse than this. He almost didn't care. Everyone and everything he knew was back there. He had family, neighbors, friends. A house. Land. How could he go on? What could he look toward? Surely not this? But he knew there was no turning back. Their ship, already given to the French, was headed for Tunisia where they were fighting another battle. He had to disembark. He looked ahead and saw Daria's determined stare. He gazed into those deep eyes and smiled in spite of himself. If there was a future, she would help him find it. He stepped off to join his family.

The conditions on Lemnos were appalling. Tent camps had been set up for the soldiers of the fleeing White Army. Civilians, including Daria and Ivan, crowded in ragged tents crowded in around the periphery. They were near starvation. That sack of grain that Ivan had held so close to his chest helped them survive the first days.

They waited to learn their future while the whole world, it seemed, debated what would become of them. The French were occupied with other problems and had taken their fill of Russians, who plied the streets of Paris in their taxis. The British wanted to trade with the Bolsheviks and didn't want to jeopardize the relationship by being seen as supporting the White regime.

Yes, the world was tired of refugees—but surely someone would take them in. In that desolate refugee camp, they had no idea when, or who that could possibly be.

Chapter 16

Meanwhile in Russia

While Daria and Ivan and their children escaped what they saw as the nightmare of Lenin's revolution, they were among the few who did. They knew nothing about the rest of their families and friends.

Many of the others had supported the Bolsheviks, the Reds. Cousin Alexei had led the way on this. Ivan still wasn't sure which side cousin Mikhail had finally decided to support. He thought it might have been the Reds. Ivan's success had forced him to join the Whites, and once their cause was lost, and the White Army had fled, he hoped that their support of the Reds would protect those who had stayed behind. He kept wondering who had stayed and who had left; who had survived and who had died. And what happened to his home and land?

Daria couldn't stop missing that home they had left behind. It wasn't just a house. It was the symbol of the life she had created. Her last private moments with Ivan had been in that bedroom, so long ago she could hardly imagine that luxury. Her last moments of feeling in control of her life evaporated with their flight.

The vision painted by young Shura's words—that theirs was one of the finest homes in Kulikov—haunted her. Beautiful

blue trim on the windows, a roof that never leaked, and a stove that kept them warm in the cold winters. A fence of evenly spaced wood strips that Shura had helped his father build. Always knowing when someone approached by the clang of the metal latch on the gate when it opened. She imagined that the *khutor* was now quiet. So many had left when the White Army, most of them Cossacks, suffered defeat. None of them could have imagined a trip of almost a year, with no certainty about the future. Of those who fled, almost no one made it all the way out of the country.

Daria often replayed the moments of their departure in her mind. At first, she thought only about the silver buried under the back doorstep. Ridiculous! With everything at risk, she was shedding sentimental tears over the family silver. But no one in her family had ever owned silver before. Now she might never own any again. She envisioned the sunflowers blooming in her garden. The outside table where they drank tea under a large old tree. The road the house sat on, which ran east from the train station and headed towards the pond where the children had often run to play. It then passed the partially built church, the school, and finally Kuznetsov's house. She could see it all.

And back there, in the heart of Russia, in the late summer of 1919, just weeks after Daria and Ivan's departure, a lone Cossack slowly rode his horse into Kulikov from the southwest. As he passed the train station he kept looking around, as if searching for someone.

It was Ivan's cousin Mikhail, coming from his home in Amochaev. He saw no one.

He approached their house and saw that the horse and *telega* were gone. No clothes hung drying in the wind. No smoke rose from the chimney. He pulled up at the gate, dismounted, and stared at the front door, willing it to open.

He walked up to that beloved home, limping as he had since the war, and knocked. No one responded. No footsteps sounded. No familiar voice told him to come in. Finally, he turned the doorknob. The door opened, and he stepped into the rooms where once Ivan's family had so warmly welcomed him. He all but shivered from the cold that emanated from inside. A pot of what had clearly been water sat on the stovetop, the contents long since evaporated; only a white line remaining. He could see children's clothes scattered on the floor; their beds unmade.

Mikhail stood before the table where he had eaten so many meals and stared at the icon in the corner of the room. The Christ on his cross was gone—probably Daria had taken him; Mikhail knew how much she cared about that cross. But the Virgin Mary still stared balefully back at him. He inadvertently crossed himself. Religion had been demonized by the new regime, but old habits lingered. And what if those priests were right, and hell awaited the nonbelievers?

What, he wondered, had happened to the picture of the Tsar? He was glad it, too, was gone.

He hunted for a note or message of any kind. Surely Ivan knew Mikhail would come looking for them. He found nothing. He had not heard from them in months, and now his worst fears were confirmed. They had fled. Where had they gone? When would they be back? And what about the home they had so loved?

Ivan and Daria and little Shura would stay on his mind for a long time. He hoped they were still alive, but it didn't seem likely. He knew that the battle was as good as lost for the White Army. The Red Army had passed just to the east of both their *khutors*—Amochaev and Kulikov—on their way to the capital of the Don Region in Novocherkassk. The White Army had lost the upper hand, which they held just weeks before. It was almost impossible to tell what was happening,

and the Reds were recruiting everyone who was left behind, whether they wanted to join or not. It was only his injury from the World War that kept Mikhail at home.

Ivan's fields were in better shape than most. Mikhail knew Daria had kept up with the work, for he had sometimes visited and helped out while Ivan traveled to Moscow. He thought of the small harvest of buckwheat which Ivan had interspersed in his fields. His stomach rumbled at the idea of eating *kasha*. He knew some potatoes and beets had also probably ripened since they left. He decided then to bring his family—Maria and his young son—to live here and take care of the property for Ivan in case he returned. Mikhail had planned to move his family to Kulikov before the Great War started in 1914, but the intervening years had defeated that goal. Now, he could prevent the property from being taken over by outsiders. The local Soviets were redistributing abandoned properties, and this one would be a plum, but he would ensure that didn't happen.

He suddenly realized that Kuznetsov's house must also be vacant and decided to check on it.

An idea began forming in his head. He quickly stepped out of the house, turned toward Kuznetsov's place, and almost ran into a woman who had been staring suspiciously at the open door of Daria's house. Fear filled her eyes and she looked about to flee. Then she recognized him. "Mikhail Efimovich! *Eto vi?* Is that you?"

"Yes, yes, it is! I am so happy to see you. I worried there was no one here." Mikhail was very happy to see Daria's friend and neighbor.

"Oh, we're here. A few of us, anyway," she said. "It's mostly just women and children left now. And the old ones."

"Yes, it's the same at our *khutor*."

"What are you doing here? Ivan and Daria have left."

"Yes, I saw. Their house looks abandoned."

"Oh, it is. They had to flee. Along with most of the others. But some of them are back."

"Have you heard from Daria? Or Ivan?" Mikhail asked.

"No."

"You don't know anything?"

"Well, they left with the Kuznetsovs, whose house I am watching over. I keep an eye on Daria and Ivan's, too. Maybe they will come back, so I don't touch anything inside. But I am losing hope that any more of them will return."

She told him a little of what had happened over the last months, with the armies passing through. It was a terrifying time, but most of the battles had happened further to the east, and their *khutor* now enjoyed relative peace. The men had almost all left to fight. She didn't mention for which side.

"So, their family hasn't heard from Daria and Ivan either?" she finally asked.

"I'm afraid not," Mikhail replied. "His brother asked about him, and I came today to see if I could learn where they ended up."

"Well, one of the families who fled with them returned last week. They said they had headed west, following the railroad tracks, away from the battles near here. They planned to head south once they got far enough. The Whites have developed a stronghold in Crimea, people say."

"Yes, we heard the same thing. But no one knows where anyone is. I know Ivan has been identified as a *kulak*. It isn't good."

The term *kulak* kept getting redefined. Originally it meant a peasant who had achieved some success, perhaps entered the middle class. But now it included anyone who hired other workers, owned more than a few acres of land, milled their own wheat, or traded. Ivan definitely qualified, and the Bolsheviks now defined kulaks as enemies of the people.

"Oh lord. But he's a good man; he has helped all of us. He's not some rich landholder."

"I know, but he has traded in Moscow, and that immediately makes him suspect. Anyone with grain to store is a *kulak*." Mikhail knew from Alexei that Ivan would have been targeted and was lucky he escaped.

Mikhail had wavered from the beginning of the revolution in his allegiance. He wanted to support Ivan, but he did not have great faith in the Tsar and his government. And the rest of his family stood strongly against the monarchy.

Back in Amochaev after the Great War, Mikhail grew closer to his cousin Alexei and learned of his dedication to the Bolshevik cause. Alexei's deep belief in some of the Bolshevik aims—especially giving land to the people—coincided with his own, and finally Mikhail began to sympathize with him. He also agreed with Alexei's wholehearted support of the Bolshevik commitment to end Russia's participation in the World War, even in defeat. They had all watched fellow soldiers die in a war that had nothing to do with them and blessed its ending.

Mikhail had always felt trapped between Alexei and Ivan. They were both his cousins—from different branches of the family—but held radically divergent views. He did not possess the confidence either of them had in their beliefs. He just wished to live in peace, farm the land, and raise his children. His wife Maria was pregnant again, and there wasn't enough food in Amochaev to feed any of them. So, Mikhail had finally decided he would not join the White Army. He would stay to develop the future of their country. Alexei applauded Mikhail's decision, and helped him move forward. Now he could help Alexei and learning that Kuznetsov's house stood empty created the perfect opportunity.

He told the woman that he was considering moving to the khutor and inviting his cousin Alexei to join him. She seemed

pleased, for they worried about having random *inogordni*—as they called arriving non-Cossacks—inserted into their lives.

Then he told her that Alexei was a staunch Bolshevik supporter. She sighed, and her face finally relaxed, her lips almost easing into a smile. He learned that it was the Red cause her husband had joined, and he was off fighting. She was relieved that Mikhail understood and supported that. It was so hard, with family members on opposite sides of this battle. Her own sister had fled with the Whites, and she had no idea where they were. With his cousin Ivan so visibly successful, she had worried about where Mikhail might stand. Russia was now Red, and they didn't need any more traces of the conflict arriving in their *khutor*.

A real worry for Mikhail was whether moving into Ivan's fine house would make him vulnerable to the *kulak* accusation. After all, as early as November 1917 Lenin had declared, "If the *kulaks* remain untouched, if we don't defeat the freeloaders, the Tsar and the capitalist will inevitably return." That was another reason to get Alexei to join him. Mikhail needed a strong member of the local soviet on his side.

Mikhail was confident he could talk Alexei into moving here with him. Kuznetsov's house would be perfect for Alexei, with his fifteen-year-old son Dimitry and his younger daughter. In addition, the farmland here was more fertile, and clearly Ivan's lands were available.

He headed back home to make it happen.

Chapter 17

The Ones Who Stayed

The timing of his offer was perfect.

Alexei greeted Mikhail's invitation warmly. He was happy to move from their struggling *khutor* Amochaev, and his Bolshevik handler was pleased at the thought of having dedicated comrades in Kulikov. They would prop up the local Soviets in the area and help in the recovery from the crises. It seemed a great plan. By the middle of 1920 all the White supporters had fled, and the war was finally ending. The Bolsheviks won, and the country needed the farm output of their region.

Mikhail and Alexei settled into the life of the village. At first their wives missed their families, but they had each other, and soon learned to appreciate having their own homes. Mikhail's daughter was born there, and his son ran around the *khutor* as if it had always been home.

"Misha, I am so grateful you didn't leave with the White forces. You'll see, the Bolsheviks care about all our people," Alexei said as they worked their fields outside the *khutor*. They stopped to drink some water; it was hot already, and only June.

"I hope you are right, Alexei. I have made my choice, and I am with you now. Please take care of us, for you have friends in the committees."

"Of course, my brother. I'm glad you had us move here. The land is better, and I confess I like living in my own home."

"And so far, at least, there aren't many *inogorodni,* outsiders, being sent in. I suspect it's because you have such strong ties with the Reds."

There was still that bit of fear in the back of Mikhail's mind. He had thrown in his fate with his cousin, but they were, after all, Cossacks, and tainted with the blood of their brothers. And what if the Soviets decided to take their land?

"You'll see, Misha. They will take care of us. This is about taking wealth and power from the elite, not from us. We are workers, just like the people in the factories." Alexei knew of Mikhail's fears, but trusted his regional leadership to navigate through these tough times.

Alexei's leadership did keep too many *inogorodni* from moving in, although the local Soviets of course continued to redistribute land. There was enough abandoned property that people could feed themselves and pay their constantly increasing share to the government. For a time, in their little *khutor,* it seemed they had perhaps survived the Civil War. They didn't know how rare this was. For Russia was hurting.

Just when peace should have settled on the land, the extent of the Bolshevik government's problems became apparent across the country. Hunger and starvation spread. The wars had destroyed crops, and the subsequent redistribution of lands to *inogorodni* had often created animosity. The new residents generally knew little about farming, and this further reduced output. Then the cities threatened rebellion and the central government started appropriating farm output even more aggressively to feed the urban north and thus tamp down rebellious discontent. But rebellions started again anyway, in both the city and the country.

The government targeted the remaining Cossacks and continued their campaign against them as a class. The Cossack

form of government, down to the lowest level, was a threat to the Bolsheviks. Their *khutors*, a uniquely Cossack form of community with fairly democratic leadership, were declared illegal and converted to normal villages. The leadership of all the districts, called *stanitsas*, was disbanded and replaced wholesale with Soviets composed of outsiders. The Don Cossack Region was formally split up, with most of it going to the Volgograd Region, and the rest to Ukraine.

It didn't matter all that much. Alexei was named to their local Soviet, and they had never been close to the *ataman*, the old Cossack leader. But the changes didn't solve the problem, and in 1921 rumors of unrest started to spread.

"What do you know about these revolts, Alexei?" Mikhail was trying to just stay focused on his family and tend to his land, but it was getting harder.

"They have nothing to do with us, Misha. Just keep your head down and work the fields. I have a meeting of the local soviet next week, I'll let you know."

"I've heard some frightening things, brother."

"Like what?"

"Well, like they don't believe all the dissidents here are gone. They still think the Cossacks are opposed to the government. That people are hiding their crops. I'm frightened."

"Well, we're not part of that. We're doing our share, contributing what we grow."

"I hope the leaders know that, Alexei."

"I'm sure they are working to prevent radical elements from creating problems."

"But what about those others? The revolts we Cossacks have nothing to do with?"

"I hear there are workers, and even criminals fighting. The government has to deal with them."

There were indiscriminate groups all over the country rebelling. They were all starving, all angry. Exhausted and

furious, the Bolshevik leadership fought back just as indiscriminately. Red tribunals arrived in every region and tried thousands, killing many on the slightest pretense. At the time, however, the people on the ground like Alexei still had hopes. He believed he could help the government weed out opponents while protecting the innocent.

Called to a neighboring district to establish new Soviets and initiate tribunals, Alexei worked hard to combat the zeal of the outsiders who thought they were eliminating opposition, even when none existed. He saw many innocent people tried and saved those he could, but his Cossack roots worked against him and his protests were often overridden. He almost gave up in frustration and fear, but he was determined to help his country achieve its aspirations. He still thought he could make a difference. He didn't know, then, that this was the beginning of a genocide of the Cossacks. While he was away, the tribunal arrived in Kulikov.

For the first time, the clanging of the gate outside Mikhail's house didn't indicate friends coming to visit. There had been no warning and he was caught unaware. He opened the door. Complete strangers stood there, asking for him by name. As Mikhail stepped toward them, Maria tried to prevent them from taking him away. They blocked her way and said it was just a normal process. She was no match for their determination. They said he would be back soon.

They lied.

Mikhail was herded with most of the Cossacks of Kulikov to another village. Based solely on the size of Mikhail's house and the envy of some new landholders, he was accused of being an enemy of the people. In minutes—for there were so many of the presumably guilty to judge—he was found guilty. So were all the others.

No one knew what was happening, but suddenly most of the men of the village were gone. Clearly Kulikov, with

its good soil and people who seemed to be doing better than other areas, had been targeted.

The women had tried to stop the removal of their husbands, but they had to protect their children, and, in the end, they could do nothing. Alexei was nowhere near, and the tribunal was not waiting for anyone.

They sentenced Mikhail to death.

Mikhail was shot in front of the people of the village, a fate he shared with most of the other adult male Cossacks of the district. It was a brutal action, directed from the top leadership of the country, and it took place all over the region. Half a million Cossacks were eliminated in a few months. By the time Alexei returned, it was over. He heard what happened and couldn't come to terms with his grief and guilt. He headed home but had no idea how he would live through the aftermath. Before he even got off his horse, Maria sped toward him. "This is all your fault! You let them kill him!" She nearly pulled him from the animal, beating him with her fists, sobbing.

"Maria, *dorogaia*, my dear, it wasn't me! You know how much I loved Mikhail. He was like a brother."

"You did nothing! You let them kill him!"

Alexei tried to apologize, to hold her close, but she was beyond reason.

"It's all your fault!"

"Maria, it wasn't because of me that he was shot. It was because of me that he had a chance of surviving."

It sounded false, even as he said it. He was so distraught he could barely talk, and she didn't want to listen. She blamed him, and deep in his heart he agreed with her. It was his Bolsheviks who had carried out this senseless slaughter. He didn't know how he could live with himself, with what was being done all around him in the name of a movement he had supported.

"No! It was you and brutes like you who shot him. He was a good man!" Maria sobbed in despair.

"Oh, my dear. Yes, he was a good man. He was a great man. I am so sorry." Would he ever be able to look her and his own wife in the eye again? Maria would not let him near her; he couldn't comfort her.

"You could have saved his life!"

"Maria, I did all I could, I promise you." But she simply turned her back on him. Alexei couldn't tell her that he had barely prevented her own removal—and that of her children—to the remote north after they killed Mikhail. By then there were no alternatives. The party members who had arrived from Moscow to deal with the crisis were threatening him at gunpoint too. They implied that he was not different from the other Cossacks, the ones that had fled or been eliminated.

He understood—too late—that they were right. He was a Cossack, no different from the others. He could be shot, right then. But they let him go with a warning. He knew, now, that he had not chosen the "good" side in this war. He saw that no "good" side existed. It was an evil time in his homeland, and it wouldn't end soon.

"I will never forgive you!" Maria shouted.

"I will never forgive myself, either," Alexei replied.

The government had acted horrifically. How could he have supported that evil? If he protested, he would be shot. His wife and children, and Mikhail's, would suffer further. They would either be resettled or simply starve. He couldn't allow that.

Alexei committed himself to finding his way through the disastrous times, because his children and Mikhail's children needed him. He would survive because Russia had to go on. Because someday there would be a Russia to live for, even if he never saw it again. There was no longer room for their beliefs or debates or alternate points of view. There was no

longer any government of the people; there was only the government of terror.

And Alexei was terrified. He knew how close he had come to being eliminated. Who knew what might come in the future? There were no limits on behavior anymore, and there was no one to trust. He would just have to put his head down and try to become invisible.

The next years were terrifying. Hunger grew worse, people everywhere starved. Since the government kept taking the output from the fields, fewer and fewer crops were planted. By 1925 Russia's farm output had fallen to half that of what it had been in 1914, when it ranked among the highest in the world. In desperation, the Bolshevik government devised a new strategy: The New Economic Policy. Since the farms weren't producing, they would be combined into huge plots farmed by new giant machines. The appropriated land created *kolkhozes* or collective farms.

In 1929 some 80,000 hectares of land were combined to launch a big *kolkhoz* just outside of Kulikov, and all the able-bodied adults moved there, mostly without choice. Called Serp I Molot, it was centered about three kilometers from the *khutor*. The words mean hammer and sickle, adopted then as the only symbol on the red flag of the USSR. The authorities clearly saw this way of life as a path into the future.

And the people? The people were given no choice. Beaten down by the brutality of their government, they were far more compliant than in the past. There were no alternatives to doing what the government said. There was no more talk about Cossacks. They had been successfully eradicated. The word itself virtually disappeared.

Alexei decided then that his children would survive and make their way into the future. His son Dimitry married a neighbor, Anna, around the time they moved to Serp I Molot,

where they lived in a form of barracks for a long time. It was an impossibly hard life, but they persisted. It would be their children who made a new life and paved a way to the future. The first two, Faina and Nicholas, stayed there all their lives, but Vladimir, born in 1935, seemed determined from his first breath to leave it all behind. "You are our *budushnost*, our future," he kept remembering his grandfather Alexei telling him when he was just a child. Those urgings of his grandfather's served him well through life, and he became a major in the engineering troops.

Throughout those hard years Mikhail's widow Maria and her children remained in Kulikov. She did not want to remarry, so she stayed with the widows and old people, all of them growing what they could in small backyard plots. Alexei long felt guilt over Mikhail's death and brought them grain when he could. One day he brought a chicken. A neighbor helped Maria start a beehive. Somehow, they survived—among the very few who did. Maria had skills Daria could not have imagined. She baked delicious cakes from just flour, water, eggs and the honey from the bees she raised. Eventually, she started trading her output for meat. Much later, her home became the village teahouse, known for its cakes, and her daughter took it over and ran it.

Shura always remembered that home. In his imagination it grew to have two stories—something that had never existed and never would exist in that *khutor*. But that was the vision Shura carried into his new life.

Ivan eventually learned that one other fact about their home, for someone in the village wrote to his friend Kuznetsov in Serbia. That their house had become a tea shop, a *chayovnya*, was all Daria's family would ever know. Ivan never learned that it was Mikhail's family who was living there, because identities in the Soviet Union were severely protected for years

out of a fear of the government and the spying neighbors all around them.

Those who fled—known as émigrés—were never to learn anything else about the people and homes they left behind. Those who stayed—including Alexei's and Mikhail's families—had no idea that anyone had successfully made it out of Russia to start a new life somewhere far away.

PART THREE

Chapter 18

In Yugoslavia

After their flight from Yevpatoria in late 1920, Ivan and his family were to spend hard times on Lemnos, wondering what would happen to them. Finally, it was Alexander of Yugoslavia who welcomed them and other White Russian refugees. Yugoslavia was then still known as the Kingdom of Serbs, Croats and Slovenes. Alexander had completed his own schooling in St. Petersburg, in the imperial Page Corps, and had wanted to marry a daughter of Tsar Nicholas II—a marriage prevented by the family's assassination. Serbia shared a religion—Christian Orthodoxy—and an alphabet—the Cyrillic—with Russia. The countries had been friends and allies for centuries. It was Russia's entry into the First World War to protect Serbia that eventually led to the Russian Revolution and the refugee crisis.

These close ties between the countries and the two royal families played a key role in the future of thousands of homeless Russian refugees, including the family of Daria and Ivan. Serbia finally offered them shelter. It was believed to be temporary.

"Papa, why are we going to Serbia?" Shura asked his father aboard ship, bound for yet another place they knew little about.

"Because the King of Serbia has invited us to live there. We'll be his guests, Shura."

"Will we go back home?"

"Well, yes, son. It is our intention to go back home to Russia when this is all over."

"Does that mean I will get to see Uncle Mikhail?"

"You will certainly see your uncle when we go home."

"But how long will we live in Serbia?"

"We have been invited to stay until we defeat the enemies of the Tsar."

They were heading for a brand-new country, untested by history. Daria and Ivan were very aware of Russia's role in the First World War, and its eventual separate peace with Germany. But they had hardly paid attention to what was happening in Serbia or Croatia during that time. This lack of awareness would soon change dramatically.

As the First World War was ending, things changed radically for the southern Slavs, many of whom had been part of the Austrian Empire, a big loser in that war. The people in those countries didn't always like each other, but they hated a common enemy more: any outside power that tried to defeat and control them. They overlooked their differences and bonded together, in desperation and fear of what might be done to them if they didn't. For it was the outside powers—the Americans, the English, and the French—who were deciding post-war boundaries.

In December of 1918, before the Treaty of Versailles was finalized, a union of countries with embattled histories was proclaimed in Belgrade as the Kingdom of Serbs, Croats and Slovenes. The United States quickly recognized the kingdom. It was Prince Alexander who had welcomed the delegation that first pronounced this new Union. It was he who launched the birth of this country, which soon became known as Yugoslavia, from *Yug*, meaning south, and *Slav*, or Slavic people.

While this union of Slavs was created voluntarily, many Croats felt they were treated as second-rate citizens. A group of Croats called the Ustaše, under the leadership of Ante Pavelič, would oppose the union aggressively. Their name came from the Croatian word *ustati* meaning "rise up." They were angry at Serbia's assumption of leadership and believed the whole country should have been a greater Croatia. Pavelič was to famously state that assassination was "the only language Serbs understand."

Instead of creating a government that acknowledged the differences in the constituent countries that made up the union, in 1929 Alexander—mirroring the unfortunate Tsar Nicholas— would declare himself the autocratic leader of Yugoslavia. Like his role model, he was murdered. The assassination of Alexander, in October 1934, while on a state visit to France, was actually captured on film, by a news cameraman just inches away from the action. This tortured land—Ivan and Daria's new home of Yugoslavia—was to continue echoing their old country's challenging history for much of its existence. But there was no way to read those tea leaves yet. Their new home, the place where they would raise their family, was the only haven offered. They gratefully accepted the refuge.

Yugoslavia was well served by its welcome of the Russian exiles. Its own population was decimated by World War I, and among those remaining many had little schooling to begin with. The exiles from Russia, mostly well-educated members of the so-called intelligentsia, would help the country as architects, doctors, professors and engineers. But the underlying presumption was that Yugoslavia would take the Russians for only a few years—just until the Bolsheviks were defeated. Russians had fled all over the world. There were thousands of them in China, Japan, France, England, even the United States. The intention was always that they would return to

Russia. They even retained a succession plan for the monarchy, always tracking who would become the new Tsar when
it was all over. Yugoslavia, a strong early supporter of this
vision of the future, welcomed over 100,000 Russians. They
set up schools and military academies for the exiles' children.
The young men trained as soldiers in preparation for return
to their homeland.

Daria's youngest son, Tolya, was barely four when they arrived
in Yugoslavia. A refugee most of his life, he had already spent
a year traveling across Russia in an old wooden cart, and—in
a frequently retold story—almost got left behind when he fell
out, unnoticed. He had spent months in a room overlooking
the sea. Then he sailed on a crowded ship to places where
people were sick and hungry. After more months around old
tents on a rocky island, he and his family came to a country where people spoke in a way he didn't understand. Then
suddenly his family was to be all split up.

He had no bad memories of those early hardships, and he
barely remembered the homeland they all kept talking about—
their *rodina*, their Russia. There had always been someone to
take care of him, and he was way too young to worry about
any of it. Falling out of the cart seemed like a story to amuse
the family rather than something that had happened to him.
But now they were supposed to be happy. He definitely wasn't.

"Mama, Mama, why is everyone going away?"

"Tolya, your brothers are going to school. The King has
set up a Cadet Corpus, a military school just like the one in
Russia that I had hoped Shura could go to. Now they have
agreed to take Kolya as well, even though he is young."

"But why can't they go to school here?"

"The school they are going to is very special, Tolya. They
will speak Russian there, and learn our story. They will learn

to be soldiers. This backwoods town doesn't have the kind of schooling they will get in the Corpus."

"And why don't all the people here speak Russian like we do? I can't understand them."

Daria worried that maybe her youngest took after her mother. Could he be another complainer?

"I want to go to school with Shura and Kolya. I'm not a girl like Liza. I should go to the Corpus!"

"You will, *zolotko*." Her sweet one was just a child, after all, and she needed to be patient. "When you get older you will go to the Corpus as well."

"Well, at least Liza is still with us."

"Oh, Liza is leaving as well."

"What?"

"Yes, she is going to be an *institutka*. She will live at the Russian girl's institute."

Tolya roared in anger. He was not happy that everyone was abandoning him. It really didn't seem fair. But he was soon to make friends in this "backwoods" town of Trebine. Because he was so young, he quickly learned the language, often translating for his mother. Approaching forty, she had never spoken anything but Russian. While Serbian was a Slavic language and used the same alphabet, it was really quite different from Russian, especially as the locals spoke it so quickly. And Daria got terribly frustrated when they couldn't understand her no matter how loudly she spoke.

At first, they didn't even know where they were. They thought it was Montenegro, but soon found out that although they had landed near Kotor, which was in Montenegro, they had ended up in neighboring Herzegovina. It didn't really matter that Daria was confused by this profusion of strange names and places, as they wouldn't stay long. Soon Tolya would again have to make new friends.

Chapter 19

Tolya's New Homeland

Tolya's new friends were Bosnians, for the Yugoslavian government gave them a home near Sarajevo.

Bosnia retained its Ottoman heritage long after that empire collapsed. The Turks were there for four hundred years and had built Sarajevo and the beautiful city of Mostar with its astonishing bridge. Sarajevo, a growing city surrounded by steep slopes, had a center full of both churches and mosques, along with food and clothing markets that drew traders from the countryside all around. You could guess their background by their clothes. Nattily dressed men in Western suits and brimmed hats paced the same sidewalks as Turkic men in skullcaps and ballooned pants. The footwear was a most distinguishing characteristic, however. All the country people wore soft shoes or boots, often with turned up toes. In Serbian this footwear of Turkish origin was called *opanak*.

Ivan found a business opportunity in those shoes. He bought Daria a sewing machine and brought home rope, cloth and leather to make what he called *papuči* or slippers. He knew that with this modern equipment they could create higher quality shoes more quickly than the men sitting in open shops along the street threading rope and leather by hand. Ivan

Daria and Ivan with children in Yugoslavia around 1925. The boys in Cadet uniforms, from left to right, are Kolya, Tolya, and Shura. Liza is on the left, and young Valya in front.

no doubt chuckled over the local expression "*kad se opanak popapuči,*" literally, "when a peasant shoe becomes a slipper." It is an insult about someone pretending to be citified while still obviously from the sticks.

The *papuči* production was only the first in a series of business ventures he was to launch across the country as Ivan tried to ground himself in this strange land. Daria, however, stayed proudly Russian for their entire time in Yugoslavia. She always considered the people she called "*Musulmani*" a race apart, unlike the Serbs who at least prayed in Eastern Orthodox churches similar to the Russian ones back home. She had no problem with Ivan doing business with these infidels, but she didn't want her son running around with them. And these infernal *papuči*. She was always tripping over the strands of rope used to make them, and her eyes were strained from staring at the needle on the sewing machine. She hoped Ivan would come up with a new business idea.

He soon did, for he started talking about crabs, telling her that he was thinking of trading with some Russian in Paris.

Unlike Daria, little Tolya fit right in with his new home. One day as he was running out the door, she stopped him. "Tolya, you cannot go play with those boys."

"What? They're my friends."

"They cannot be your friends, *zolotko*. They are *Musulmani*."

"But we have such fun together. Yesterday we went to the mosque while all the men were praying."

"Oh, dear God. I knew this was a mistake. Tolya, you cannot go to the mosque. You are not a *Musulman*."

"Of course, I'm not, Mama. I am a Russian. I'm a Cossack."

"Well then, you have no business in a mosque. Wait till I tell your father."

"Oh, Papa knows."

"What do you mean?"

"Well, Mohammad's father does business with Papa. That's how we met."

"I cannot believe this. Wait till I get my hands on Ivan!" But Tolya knew he would continue to play with his friends. Once Ivan approved, Daria was likely to shake her head and finally give in. And she had more than Tolya to worry about. She had barely adapted to a new life that included a fixed home, regular food, and a sorting out of the children's schooling when her body told her the news. Now approaching forty, she thought she was done with babies, but with all the new comforts, she had let down her guard, and her husband was irrepressible. Little Valentin—a Yugoslavian citizen—was born not long after their arrival in Bosnia. She could hardly imagine what this would mean as he grew up.

Daria was relieved when Tolya finally went away to school, but Valentin, or Valya, never made it to the Corpus. Long before he reached the age of ten, he was stricken with typhoid and died quickly. Although she rarely talked about it, losing him was a pain that would live with her for her whole life.

Meanwhile, the *papuči* turned out not to be a big success, because the buyers stayed true to their long-time suppliers. Ivan wrapped up the business in Bosnia and they moved to the Serbian part of the country, to a small town closer to the schools the children were attending. During the next years, they moved all over Yugoslavia. Ivan loaded grain on ships at a canal near the Sava River, then started a fishing business, and shipped crabs to Paris. In the summers, the boys would help, for it was arduous work. They built crab cages out of knitted rope and wood hoops, then walked 4 kilometers to the fishing spot. The catch then went around six kilometers to the train station—on a donkey that kept lying down to rest on the job. The boys remembered often having to carry heavy crates full of fish and crabs.

But it wasn't all about trade. Daria's dreams of higher education for her sons were fulfilled, although not in any way she could have imagined back in the *khutor*. The government, in addition to setting up special schools for their Russian language high school education, helped her sons attend the best universities. After the boys finished the corpus, Shura entered Belgrade University and got a degree as an electrical engineer. Tolya attended the Nikola Tesla Institute of Electrical Engineering. Kolya worked on a degree in veterinary medicine. Liza eventually took a job with the postal service in Badjnevac, Serbia, where she met her future husband Mika, a Serb whose family lived across the street from her office.

Like the others, Tolya got his primary education in Russian, and was certainly part of that community. He was fluent in the language, knew its grammar and literature, and learned its geography and history. But he also never forgot which country was his home, the place he lived. He loved Yugoslavia and all its people. To him they weren't foreigners, for he had grown up among them. He didn't remember Russia and needed no other world. After graduating, Tolya took a job with the telephone company and put up telephone wire all over Bosnia, renewing his friendship with that country.

Daria worried because her Ivan never stopped working and striving to make her life better. She wanted to tell him to slow down, that their sons would soon be taking care of them. But he never did. Eventually, the grueling work and those heavy crates killed him. He had a stroke. He struggled to recover but was never the same again. He suffered from low blood pressure, tired easily, and finally died just as World War II changed their world once again. Daria was hit by one more unbearable loss. First her country, then her young son, now her husband. Would it never end?

Then World War II hit. Fortunately, none of the young men were in the military at that time. The battle over their country was over almost before it started. But the consequences didn't end for many years. Like the initial battle of the Russian Revolution, the attack on Yugoslavia lasted around ten days: from a massive invasion by the Axis powers of Germany, Italy, and Hungary on April 6, 1941 to an unconditional surrender of the Royal Yugoslav Army on April 17.

It was a devastating defeat that tore the country up into enemy territories, with Croatia joining the Nazis. Various insurgent groups arose, some fighting the Nazis, but most fighting each other. Books have been written on the complexity of the conflicts between the Axis forces, Serbian Chetniks, Croatian Ustaša and Communist Partisans, which lasted until 1945. They almost defy rational explanation. On top of everything else, many White Russian Cossack emigrés in Yugoslavia became enmeshed with the Germans in a Cossack Army Corps because they believed the Germans would defeat the Communists in Russia. None of the Amochaev brothers joined, wanting nothing to do with the Nazis, but a number of their fellow students at the Corpus fervently believed in the cause.

In the end, what with internal fighting, massacres by competing factions, religious and ethnic exterminations, and aggressive attacks by Fascist forces, the war in Yugoslavia caused over a million deaths.

For Daria and her family, however, the trials did not end when the war was over. The consequences to them were far reaching and long lasting. Like the First World War in Russia had, the Second World War in Yugoslavia led to a Communist takeover, under the leadership of Josip Broz Tito. That Communist takeover eventually led to all of them being swept up in one more cataclysm beyond their control: a flight that made their year-long trip from the Don to Crimea seem short.

At first it seemed they had survived. Toward the end of the war, Tolya, Liza's husband Mika, and Kolya were recruited into the newly reconstituted Yugoslav Army, now under Tito, to drive out the Germans at the time of that country's final surrender in 1945. That action ended with a drive north into Austria, and then they all made their way back to Belgrade. After Ivan died, Tolya was the last son living with Daria in their apartment in Belgrade. Shura and Kolya both married Russian women, and Shura started a company that worked on electrical equipment. Tolya and Kolya joined him in that enterprise, and the business grew successfully in the postwar years.

Tolya met a Croatian woman—Zora Marinovich—while attending his best friend's wedding in Zagreb. That meeting convinced him he was not going to marry a Russian, no matter what his mother said about seeing "foreigners." The attraction was mutual, and they had in common the fact that Zora's father also worried that she was marrying a foreigner. In late 1947, they got married in Belgrade, and Zora moved in with Tolya and Daria. Daria was not pleased that Tolya married a "foreigner" in spite of her imprecations and made no secret of that fact. It made life challenging for the newlyweds. Over the next two years Zora and Tolya had two children—Alexander, or Sasha, and Tatiana or Tania. I was that second child.

Chapter 20

Refugees, Again

Shortly after my birth my family's nightmares started again. Was history in eternal repetition?

Daria and her family had left Lenin's Union of Soviet Socialist Republics, the USSR, under threat of death thirty years earlier, fleeing the Communist Red Army and landing—stateless and with no country to call home—on a godforsaken rocky isle in a foreign sea. When the Communists took over Yugoslavia at the end of World War II, rather than fighting or fleeing, the brothers—Shura, Kolya, and my father Tolya—decided to continue with their lives, not raise waves, and operate within the system. After all, they had grown up and started their families here. They were educated and successful. They were Yugoslavians.

For a time, it worked. Tito's version of Communism was more moderate than his Russian counterpart's, and some initiative was allowed to continue. Their electrical business supported the entire family, and they had friends and a community in Belgrade. Yugoslavia grew stronger. In September of 1947, Tito's aggression toward Italy paid off and the territory of Istria, a part of Croatia near Venice, was returned to Yugoslavia after a thirty-year domination by Italy. That was a

relief to Zora, for her family had been exiled from that part of the country by Mussolini when she was an infant.

When Tito went further and tried to annex Trieste, Stalin dropped his support. Tito then dropped support for Stalin's further expansion in East Europe. It got ugly and Stalin retaliated by throwing Yugoslavia out of the Cominform, or the union of Communist countries. The brothers were at first relieved by this action, for they were not comfortable with the closeness their new homeland had developed with their sworn enemy, the Soviet Union. Unfortunately, things deteriorated from there. Moscow had planted spies in Yugoslavia during the war. Now Tito was seeing spies everywhere. Russian males were eventually stripped of citizenship, no matter how long they had lived in Yugoslavia, or whether they were married to Yugoslav women. Effectively, it ended their lives in that country.

The Amochaev families were again stateless. Again, they had to flee. But where could they go? Europe was already flooded with refugees from the Second World War. The Yugoslav government threatened to send them back to a certain death in Russia. Tito accused them of spying for the very Russians who had eradicated their people and forced their flight. The Cossack fighters who joined the Germans had generated yet more rage against the Cossacks. While sister Liza stayed behind, protected by her husband Mika's Serbian family name, the rest of us escaped. Fortunately, Tito had not succeeded in grabbing Trieste. In 1950 it was still a disputed so-called Free Territory under the administration of the United Nations. A refugee camp called Campo San Sabba had been set up on the outskirts of the city shortly after the end of the war. It was accepting people of East European and Russian origin who found themselves exiled as a result of the wars and revolutions in their lands. That's where we fled.

Everyone hoped that it would be for only a few months. Kolya and his wife Lyolya were thinking of going to South

REFUGEE PRESSURE
APPEARS RENEWED

New York Times July 1950

Western Europe Receives Again
Hundreds Earlier Thought
Settled by the I. R. O.

OTHERS FROM YUGOSLAVIA

Problem of the White Russians
Who Must Move On Anew Is
Among the Most Perplexing

This is the third of six dispatches from a correspondent of THE NEW YORK TIMES who has surveyed in Central Europe the problems presented by millions of refugees from totalitarianism.

By MICHAEL L. HOFFMAN
SALZBURG, Austria

The best current example of why it is hopeless to count on some definite end to the influx of new refugees is the movement of White Russians out of Yugoslavia. As recently as a year ago, no responsible Western official would have dreamed that the White Russians in Yugoslavia would be a refugee class.

Yet, according to some White Russians to whom this correspondent recently talked, from 5,000 to 6,000 of these people who had been settled in Yugoslavia since the time of the Bolshevik Revolution are being expelled by the Yugoslav Government. Everyone must go, even those who married Yugoslav women.

The White Russians interviewed said the expulsion had started in December, 1949. All said that no question of political affiliation was involved—after all these are the people who were the first refugees from Russian communism. They are pitiful victims of the Tito-Cominform split.

No more tragic group of refugees exists. Wholly unassimilable into the Austrian economy, twice forced away from homes they had built in reasonably satisfactory places to raise their children, ineligible for any existing form of international resettlement aid, these White Russians are just about as hopeless cases as can be imagined. Yet there are children among them for whom the elders still have hope.

*New York Times report in mid 1950 about the White Russians
forced to flee Yugoslavia.*

Africa. Shura and Galya were set on the United States, and our family planned to go with them. Daria lived with us, as she had in Belgrade. Conditions were stark. We were part of an unexpected flood of refugees into an already crowded camp. My aunts and uncles were crammed into the only parts of an old rice factory that didn't reek of its horrible past use as a concentration camp during the war. There were no walls, just hanging blankets between couples sleeping on stone floors.

The five of us, my parents, Sasha and I, and Babusia—as I called my grandmother Daria—were housed across the road at the so-called Annex: rows of abandoned U.S. Army barracks. Twenty families crowded each barrack, with thin partial walls and no privacy. The real issue was not the living conditions. They had already lived through far worse. What hurt the most was being robbed of their future again. My father, for one, lost any confidence that life would ever be stable and predictable. He spent the rest of his days making sure his family, and his children, were prepared for the worst. The fear of losing everything again would never leave him.

Little over a year after they arrived in Trieste, Kolya and Lyolya accepted an offer from the Canadian government. They sailed for Halifax, Nova Scotia, and became indentured servants somewhere west of Toronto. They were to work to pay back their fare, and it was expected to take about a year. Many immigrants had great experiences with this Canadian program. Others did not. The people that Kolya and Lyolya joined were abusive and piled on expenses, which they were too naïve to figure out in the beginning. They finally fled to Toronto, where they established a new life and stayed permanently. In the distant future they would welcome sister Liza and then her older son Mima to live with them.

Shura and Galya decided to hold out for America, the dreamland. After another year, they were able to get visas and passage on a ship, the SS Constitution. The men had all

arrived at the camp as successful entrepreneurs, established and with their own business in Belgrade. Shura was a dynamic go-getter like his father Ivan. He was to reinvent himself several more times. He had come prepared with hidden savings from Belgrade. Those were quickly depleted, but it turned out that the items that had the maximum value were not brought for that reason. Shura was a stamp collector. He brought his stamps with him. Decades later, when his daughter Lena was taking the remains of that stamp collection to be assessed, the philatelist looking at the book pointed to the blank spot in the collection of special Russian stamps.

"If you had that stamp, this collection would be incredibly valuable!"

"That stamp," said Lena, "fed my parents in the refugee camp for a year."

Again, decades later I was casually talking to my childhood friend Alek Shestakov, who had also lived in the camps as an infant. "I will never forget your mother trying to teach me to play the piano! I was hopeless," I said. Alek and his parents had gone to South America from the camp, and they arrived in San Francisco when Alek was around ten. His mother had established herself as a piano teacher in the Richmond district of the city and grew very close to my Mama.

"You know," Alek told me, "my mother's piano playing saved us in the camps. I suspect that's why we were able to get away so quickly to South America."

"What do you mean?"

"Well, my father did some work for the YMCA. On a good day he could earn a few hundred liras."

"Oh, I didn't know he worked for the YMCA."

"He did, but that's not what this story is about."

"Oh?"

"My mother played piano in the Symphony Hall in Trieste. She received 5000 lira for a single performance." Alek wasn't

sure of his numbers, but he was confident his mother earned from a single performance what his father could make for a month's hard work.

Tolya worked as a photographer, taking passport pictures. After three years in the camp, everyone had left but our family. The lists of visas kept coming with our names ominously absent. It might have been because my brother and I were small children, but others like our camp friends the Karsanidis had been cleared for New York. It had to be something else.

Tolya knew his children were doing all right and that I loved the Campo, as we called it, and adored our neighbors, elderly Russians called Vava and Zhenya, my adoptive grandfather. But Zora was at the end of her wits, and Tolya's mother Daria wasn't helping the situation. Daria kept complaining and blaming him for their inability to leave. She kept talking about her wonderful oldest son, Shura, who was already making a new life for himself in San Francisco. It grated on Tolya every time she mentioned Shura's name.

Tolya had a vague memory of her complaining about her own mother—his grandmother, Natalia—on that long-ago flight from their *khutor*. As he thought about it, he remembered that his grandmother hadn't joined them on the ship when it left Crimea, but he didn't think his mother would appreciate the parallels in the story.

He didn't know how much more he could take. He had to find out what was holding up the visas. Maybe they had to lower their expectations and go to another country first. He knew Zora was set on America as the place with the best future for the children. So was he, but it might not be possible. They might have to go to Venezuela first, or Australia.

Where will it all end? he wondered. And would he survive to see it?

Galya and Shura boarding a train in Trieste on their way from Campo San Sabba to America. Tolya, Zora and Babusia despairingly seeing them off, as they have no information on how long they will still remain in the refugee camp.

Chapter 21

An Intolerable Interlude

On a day similar to all others, Tolya stood in his makeshift darkroom, his tall frame slightly bent in concentration, counting the seconds. One-o-six, one-o-seven . . .

Soon it would appear. First the bare traces, then an outline, then the gray evolving to an increasing variation in tonality. It was tempting to just let his mind drift in this solitude. His only privacy. His only escape. And this day he needed the escape.

Bang!

The walls shook as a loud curse completed the slamming door ritual and then footsteps receded down the hallway. Tolya's mind leaped back just in time to grab the edges of the developing image and tease it out of its liquid bath. Just in time to save the valuable paper which he doled out by the centimeter, to save the time it would take to start over. But who gave a damn about time? Time was a commodity he had more than enough of. Time was a penalty. Time was something to kill, something to endure, something to tolerate. Time was a grim marker whose passage was destroying his life.

"Damn that woman," he muttered to himself. Of course, it was their neighbor, Vava. Who else would explode through the relative peace and announce the end of quiet time? He

smelled her cigarette and heard her strutting away from the cubicle—so close to theirs—which she inhabited in her amazing, larger-than-life style. He heard his young daughter's joyous shout—for to me that explosion, that opening of the door inches away from our own, meant my dearest friend—the same Vava—was up, and another day could begin.

Tolya's hands continued the delicate dance required to process the images. He stared at the faces that stared back at him from their captivity on the sheet. How long would he go on capturing those blank stares, those images so necessary for escape? How long would he print pictures for the exit visas of others more fortunate, whose immigration papers had been approved? How long could he continue the pretense that he believed life would evolve to a better path? To a future which looked, felt, and smelled different from this camp, this holding block, this displaced persons' nightmare? He had built a good life in Belgrade before it all crashed down. Back then—three long years ago—he was strong and healthy. His career as an engineer was challenging; he had a beautiful wife and two babies; he lived in a happy home in the heart of Belgrade, a vibrant city; his passion for photography filled him with energy. He had even bought a prestigious camera, the Leica he now used to support all of them.

And here he was, sharing a drafty barrack with forty strangers. People who came and went, passing through his life and moving into their own futures while he waited. And waited. And waited.

He had finally accepted that his mother was the stumbling block. She was too old to get a visa to America. If they kept waiting to go as a family, it might never happen. But they had also discovered that there was an alternative. The Tolstoy Fund, supported by the author's writing, had set up a home for the aged in Cannes, France. Families that were already established

in the United States could then bring them over as dependents. Daria was reluctant, but there really was no alternative.

And then his wife's voice penetrated his concentration. "Are you almost done, Tolya?"

He hadn't heard Zora come back from the central kitchen with their breakfast. He hadn't heard his mother head off to the bathrooms in the middle of the barracks building. He hadn't heard a thing since he'd slipped in at some predawn hour, oblivious in his dark hideaway. The walls didn't reach the floor or ceiling, for God's sake. They were barely thicker than cardboard and every noise echoed through the place. But it was his hideaway, his one spot of privacy.

"Another minute, *zolotko*, my sweetheart. I just have this one sheet to finish for the Karsanidis's visas and I'll be right there." One more family—these their closest friends in the camp—with approved visas for America. He had to finish printing their faces, their last records of exile. "I'll be right there."

Zora knew he wouldn't be right there. There was always one more picture to develop. Being in that darkroom was the only thing that gave him peace, that restored him, that brought him closer to the man she had fallen in love with and married in a once hopeful world far from where they were now. He could stay as long as he wanted in the tiny black cave he had created in the corner of the drafty cube that was their home. But she had no more choice. She had to tell him she had reached her limit. It had to end. She had to get away.

As Tolya was wrapping up his work for the day, before it got too light in his makeshift darkroom, he stumbled across a negative that had nothing to do with exit visas or people leaving the camp—an image that he might look at someday in the distant future, shaking his head at a memory that would grow more tolerable as it receded into the past. As hopefully this life would someday recede into the past.

The Risiera at San Sabba, a concentration camp during World War II and the family's home for four years in the early 1950s. This is the picture Tolya took on his final long walk outside the Campo.

He had created it about a week ago. Something had pulled him out and away from the camp. Recently, restrictions had eased, and he could wander with more freedom. Zora would sometimes take the children into Trieste to buy vegetables. They had even gone to the beach. His earnings from photography let them take the tram up to the nearby village of Opicina one time, high enough above Trieste so a cooling breeze relieved the suffocating heat of summer. But he himself rarely left the camp, and almost never alone.

It had been in the middle of the day, the middle of the week. Zora was at the washroom doing laundry; the children were in class. He hung the camera strap on his neck and headed out. He signed his name and walked away from the guard post. Soon the barbed wire fence and the lines of barracks in

the compound receded behind him. He headed north, toward the hills, then veered to the east. He knew if he went the other way, he would have to pass through the gypsy encampments, and he couldn't face even one more person at this moment. He stumbled past the old factory that had housed his brothers before their departure for America—a departure that led to his current state of near despair. He headed toward the old docklands, a derelict industrial center.

He hadn't left the camp in weeks. It felt good to be out. The wind hit his face and he felt it on his body, on the sweat that covered unused muscles. He climbed until he was overlooking the camp. The long red brick building stretched beside the dirt road; a few people walked around. Before him ran the train tracks that led nowhere. Old railcars were filled with the ruins of buildings, probably clean-up from that last war. He was learning all too personally that the consequences of wars went far beyond what the people thought they were fighting about. The chaos at the end of World War I opened Russia to the revolution that forced his family's exile. The end of World War II opened his adopted home, Yugoslavia, to a Communist dictatorship that again forced his family into exile. He could only hope that another war wouldn't come steal his children's future.

That image of the red brick building was now in his hands. As he stared at it he resolved that this would end. He would get away. Another door slammed, bringing his mind back from its turmoil. He looked again at the image of the old *risiera*, the rice factory that now also housed refugees. It had been a relief to take a picture that wasn't a close-up of just another face. He realized this was more than just a picture. This building that might as well have been a jail chronicled the emptiness of their existence. This building was holding their lives in stasis. He could imagine his children looking at

that image someday. Would they have any idea what it had been like for him to be trapped here?

He briefly considered printing that one more image, but he knew Zora was running out of patience. It was time to go have breakfast, to start another day—one that might lead nowhere, just as all the days leading up to this one had done.

No, he decided as he hung the pictures he had been developing up to dry. This day would lead to the future. He would take the steps he had been avoiding. He would do so now. His children's future was in America. If it required his mother to go to France, she would go. They would bring her to America after they were settled. She would just have to understand.

He stepped out of the dark.

Chapter 22

Becoming American

In 1953 my grandmother moved to France, and we got our visas for America soon afterwards. My parents, Sasha, and I ended up on the SS Constitution, the same ship that brought Shura and Galya to America. Interestingly, it was also the same ship that took Grace Kelly on her way to becoming the Princess of Monaco. But in a different class, I am sure. A Greyhound bus brought us to San Francisco, where we joined a large diaspora of Russian refugees from all over the world. It was a community that would permeate every aspect of our lives. My parents' friends were all Russians. Their children went to Russian school and spoke that language everywhere except in "American" school; they prayed in a Russian church; they were part of a Russian scout organization. They were Russians in America, and we melted into that tribe. I became the immigrant child of people who didn't speak the language of my new country. Instead, they insisted I retain Russian.

"*Tania, govori po Russki!*" was my father's refrain, shouted every time I was caught speaking that awful "foreign" language. "*Tut nye govorim po Amerikanski!* We don't speak English here!"

*Tolya, Sasha and Tania on the dock in Genoa shortly
before their departure to America on the SS Constitution.*

Shura repaired small kitchen appliances at Sunbeam Corporation and quickly got my father a job there. Back in the 1950s appliances were a novelty and still got repaired under warrantee, rather than being replaced as they mostly are today.

Shura and Tolya had both been engineers by degree and profession and were successful business owners in Belgrade. Their money was gone after years of refugee camp existence, and those foreign degrees were worthless in America. Their lack of English kept them from passing the requisite exams to be certified engineers. So, they fixed the machines that were moving American kitchens into a new age.

Households of recent refugees didn't brim with appliances in those days. Stars like Lucille Ball advertised waffle-makers while her husband Ricky struggled—on TV programs which I had to go to a friend's house to watch—to make a toaster work. But we were outliers. Products that were too ruined to be repaired under warrantee were discarded—an anathema to my father and uncle. They reclaimed those discards, patched together parts from various units, and rebuilt them for use in our own homes. The furniture in our house came from Bekins Storage auction sales, where you bid low on things labeled "household goods" and then slept on beds people didn't reclaim after moving. But our kitchen had the most modern electric appliances: Mixmasters, frying pans, pressure cookers, percolators, hot water kettles, meat grinders, and egg cookers. I was in high school before I learned to boil an egg, because the electric egg cooker knew what I wanted when I selected "hard boiled" and pushed the button.

In those early days in America, my father and Shura worked together in their free time as well. They bought an old four-unit apartment building in a neighborhood that was going downhill as the middle classes moved to suburbia in an exodus from the inner city. They remodeled it by picking up detritus from

construction projects around the city. Hardwood was being replaced in those days by the new concept of wall-to-wall carpeting, so they brought the old pieces of wood home and made gorgeous floors. Eventually, our extended family from the refugee camp moved into those units.

Babusia, my grandmother, joined us after a couple of years. When she had to go to Cannes, France because it was the only way we could get visas to America, she swore that she would never speak to my mother again. She had never made a secret of the fact that Shura was her favorite child, so we assumed she would move in with them eventually. But when she was able to get her visa—because her sons were living in San Francisco and acted as guarantors—she ended up living with us. Never mind that our apartment only had two bedrooms for the four of us; that poor Sasha had to share a room with his bed-wetting little sister so Babusia could have the living room sofa for a bed; or that Shura and Galya had their own apartment to themselves. She simply moved in.

Like my father had been in Yugoslavia, I was too young for school on arrival in America, so she ended up being my caregiver. Normally a strict figure, Babusia would often loosen up on these walks in the park as I ran ahead and fed the squirrels or sped to the sand under the acrobatics rings in the playground. If I was lucky, I would find enough pennies and nickels that had fallen from the pockets of flipping athletes to earn a merry-go-round ride.

I heard many stories about my grandmother's life in Russia. I learned how she met her husband Ivan, and about cousin Mikhail, the suitor she rejected. I learned about the silver that was left behind. I heard about their flight to Crimea. I heard nothing about the country of my birth.

"But Babusia, you spent thirty years in Yugoslavia."

"*Nu*, well, we certainly did, Tania."

"Babusia, why don't you ever talk about your time in Yugoslavia?"

"*Nu*, it just never felt like home."

"Why not?"

"I guess because we were just waiting to go back home to Russia."

"So, you thought you were going back to Russia?"

"*Nu*, perhaps deep inside I knew it would never happen." When her sentences started with *nu*, meaning "well," I knew she was getting near the end of her patience for questions. But I was a determined little girl.

"So why wasn't it home? It was home to Mama."

"Your mama isn't Russian, Tania."

"You mean she's not a Cossachka, like you, Babusia."

"*Nu, dovoljno uže*, Tania." "Well, enough already," was a phrase I was very familiar with. Daria had become the stern taskmaster once again, intent on getting her granddaughter home in time to clean up for dinner.

She was my nominal caregiver, but a loving grandmother she was not. Quite the contrary. She favored my brother, Sasha, the grandson who would carry on her name. I was just an annoying, stubborn young girl.

My father wanted Sasha to grow up and become an engineer, but Sasha struggled with math as if it were an alien concept sent from outer space to frustrate him. I found math to be my natural language, one I was as comfortable in as all the others that were used in my house: Russian, Serbo-Croatian, English, Math—for me they were ways to communicate that all flowed with ease.

One day, Babusia decided to give Sasha a gift: a dime. Yes, ten whole cents, in a day when a penny could buy you a candy. She handed him the precious gift and turned to me, saying, "*A tebe nichego.* And for you, nothing." Neither Sasha nor I were

particularly surprised; we were used to her behavior. After all, Sasha was her oldest grandson, and I was just a girl. But Sasha decided it wasn't fair and offered to split the dime with me.

"But I don't know how we can do that," he said, holding that tiny coin in his hand.

"Oh, that's easy," I offered. "I have a nickel."

"And?"

"Well, I'll give you the nickel, and you give me the dime," I said, happy with this obvious resolution.

Sasha looked at me, wondering if I was pulling a fast one.

"Then you will have a dime, and I will only have a nickel," he said. "How is that fair?"

I had no way to convince him of the equity of this solution, so he kept the dime. I, however, had a great story for the rest of my life.

My father pushed my brother Sasha to become an engineer for all the years of our childhood, but Sasha would have none of it. While I fought like a banshee against the constraints they tried to wrap me in, Sasha just put his head down quietly and moved on with his life. It was I, and not Sasha, who fought with my father for haranguing him over his math homework. Sasha and I were just as different as day and night.

I had adored my father when I was a little girl in the *Campo*, but as I grew up in America, I was mostly angry with him. My memory of meals at our house were of raging fights about everything. From when I could start dating, to when I could wear a bra. From why Communism was evil, to why no one should vote for that radical Kennedy person. From how bowling alleys were dens of iniquity, to how late I could stay out. My father always thought I was too young to date; but when that time came it would of course be Russian boys. I could continue this list for a long time.

My relationship with my father finally disintegrated one evening when he decided my brother's best friend Val was seducing me in the back seat while we drove home from some party. I was mortified that he was shouting at me and embarrassing me in front of this young lad. I also thought he had drunk too much vodka.

I was still young enough that the two-year age difference with my brother and his friends was significant. To them I was still an annoying little sister. I was trying hard to prove myself an equal partner, but it was an uphill battle.

That evening was one of the first times the three of us were conversing on an almost equal footing in the back of the car. I don't remember what we were discussing, but I was definitely pleased to be part of the conversation rather than just listening in.

Suddenly my father swung his arm back, over the seat and straight at me. It was completely unexpected. The car jerked, and he pulled his arm back to grab the wheel and get it back under control. My mother put her hand on his shoulder to calm him down. Sasha and Val somehow managed to keep me silent and under control. Nobody said a word until we pulled into our driveway, and Val walked up the hill to his house.

My father and I continued the battle at home, but it was to be our last one. I had no more battles left. I gave up the fight and simply stopped communicating with him. I rarely spoke at all to him, and when I did it was about inconsequential matters. If I needed an important decision, I would have my mother put it to him. I was only a teenager, but I had enough. Any softness that might have remained in me dissolved in the backseat of a car on the streets of San Francisco.

It crushed me to realize that he did not have enough faith to just let me to sit in the backseat of a car with my brother's friend. My father didn't trust me, and I could no longer trust

him. It took years for me to forgive, and many more to understand. I concentrated instead on getting free.

The Russian community we grew up in celebrated St. Tatiana and her namesday, January 25. She was the heroine of *Evgeniy Onegin*—Russia's favorite book, opera and ballet. Since that was my name, I couldn't wait to go to the Tatiana Day Ball at the Russian Center. I would wear a long dress and dance the waltzes I had practiced so assiduously. I dreamed of this special day! But of course, my parents decided I was too young to go to the Ball. No amount of arguing—and I do not give up easily—would change their minds. I would wait until I was sixteen to go to a Ball, and that was that. By the time I was sixteen it was over.

By then I had rejected my Russianness and the entire Russian community. I was an American and wanted no part of that foreign stuff. I just wanted to fit in. At sixteen, I graduated from high school, and was about to go to college—for my math brain got me through school very quickly. I had an American boyfriend. I had a job working Sundays in a delicatessen and was a member of the Butcher's Union. I lost interest in all things Russian, and never went to a St. Tatiana Day Ball, the only part of that life I ever regretted.

My determination to be self-sufficient came from that claustrophobic control I thought they wanted over my life. I had a scholarship and held three jobs at a time during my college days so I would never have to ask for permission from anyone ever again. A future boss was to call it a chip on my shoulder, but whatever it was, it drove me relentlessly from those days through the rest of my life.

My math skills were grudgingly acknowledged when I decided to go to Berkeley.

"*Ona tuda poidjet?* She's going to go 'there'?" Shura said to my parents, horrified. To him, that school was a stanchion of liberalism.

"Yes," Papa said. "She has a scholarship and tells me it is the best in the country for mathematics."

"So, she will study mathematics?"

"Yes. Maybe she will teach."

"Well, a few of our young men are going there. Maybe she will get together with one of them," said Shura.

Teaching was the last thing on earth I was likely to do, and I certainly didn't plan to get together with one of their young men. But they didn't know I was listening in and for a change I kept silent.

During my entire childhood, from my first days in America, my battles were fought inside my house and outside it. I did not fit in at my inner-city grammar school of Andrew Jackson. I was too foreign, too smart, and too white. I might have discounted those feelings as normal lack of confidence except for one event. Years later, in that delicatessen in San Francisco, my grammar school friend Sherry Rowland came in with her two infant children. This young black woman was eighteen years old, single, and living in a nearby housing project. Yes, she had fallen into a life I would never want, and one she perhaps regretted. But I still remember feeling like a child lacking in maturity and sophistication compared to this woman finding her way in the world. That episode always reminds me of my continuing lack of confidence and of any sense of belonging in this country.

When I was around eleven, we moved away from a school where I was one of the only white kids to a middle-class neighborhood near Ocean Beach. Things didn't get better very fast. I started making new friends, only to develop new reasons to regret my Russian ancestors. Suddenly these friends included Jews, people I had not really known before. Now my Cossack background brought to mind pogroms and anti-Semitism. How do you apologize for a heritage like that? You can't.

Fortunately, my friends accepted me for myself and not for what my ancestors might have done. But even that guilt still stays somewhere deep inside me.

It took me years to fight my way to self-confidence, seeing ogres and monsters all along the way.

While I pushed my way through the hellhole that outsiders saw as a normal life, Sasha just rolled with the punches. He dropped out of math in high school when suddenly I was with him in the advanced algebra class he had already failed twice. He still tells people that while we shared that classroom, I would correct the teacher, who apparently got confused easily. My brother gave no thought to engineering, knowing from a young age that he wanted to be a psychologist. This was a career path far beyond my father's patience.

"Sasha, you know if you are ever forced to move to another country that *psihologia,* psychology, stuff will be useless!" That was my father's perspective on life, but he just couldn't make his son see reason. To my memory, Sasha never budged. He just ignored all my fathers' advice, while missing out on the gene that pushed me to loudly try and prove him wrong.

Long after I had moved away, and was working at a computer company in Minnesota, I visited San Francisco and spent some time with Sasha, who was finishing his PhD in Neurophysiological Psychology at the prestigious School of Medicine at the University of California, San Francisco. "What is that you're working on, Sasha?" I asked one evening as we were getting ready to go to dinner.

"Oh, just some statistics work I have to get done."

"Statistics?" I asked, amazed.

"Yes, I'll be done in a minute. Let me just finish."

Over dinner, I brought the subject up again. "You're studying statistics?"

"Of course. It's critical for the kind of research I want to do."

"But I thought you couldn't do math?"

"This isn't just abstract numbers, Tania. This stuff makes sense. I can apply it to the effect of . . ." As he talked about his latest project, I realized that my brother wasn't a math idiot. He just couldn't be bothered with that abstract stuff that didn't matter.

My father eventually became an electrical engineer, and Sasha and I both went on to have successful careers. We are as close as you get to the great American immigrant story, the rags to riches variety.

Tolya developed a deep love for fishing, and eventually bought a boat that he took out in San Francisco Bay with his brother and an American friend, a colleague from work. It was his one passion, and he pursued it with dedication. My mother always believed they would travel after he retired, but she was wrong. He mostly fished in his bay and on the Russian River in Sonoma County after he stopped working.

As for me, after graduating from the University of California at Berkeley in mathematics, I joined Control Data, a Fortune 500 computer company. I started as a programmer in what is now Silicon Valley, then moved to France to do technical support work for all of Europe for a couple of years. From there I was recruited to headquarters in Minnesota to take over corporate software strategy at the ripe old age of twenty-five. A couple of years later I was the executive in charge of corporate strategy for supercomputers. That was quite unusual for a woman in those days, and I followed that with several vice-presidential positions at CDC, and then was the Chief Executive Officer of three other technology companies.

In the middle of that progression I decided to go to the Stanford Graduate School of Business to prop up my credentials in a male-dominated world. In the early 1980s I married Harold Hahn, a wonderful man who was also a business executive with a degree from Stanford Business School. I

had spent most of my youth hoping to marry a man with a simple name, to erase the impossible—for Americans—to pronounce, spell or remember, Amochaev. But by then, in my early thirties, I had a successful career and had finally grown used to it. So, I kept it.

Harold had two children, Brad and Beth, from his previous marriage. They were not yet in their teens when we got together. The kids and I became very close through years of joint custody with their mother Lucy, who was unusually supportive of my becoming part of their lives. I loved Harold deeply, and was outrageously fortunate to have spent much of my life with him, until he passed way from cancer almost ten years ago. I savor memories of our time together, and one of my favorite recollections of Harold and my Russian world involved my tall Uncle Shura looking up at my taller husband and giving him a huge bearhug. In spite of the fact that he was an "American," my whole family loved Harold. Sasha lost a best friend when he died.

Harold and I enjoyed traveling, skiing, biking and hiking. In 1987 we spent three weeks on a remote and rugged trek through the Himalayas of Kashmir and Ladakh. It was an extraordinary trip and was to be the last time for many years that Westerners could travel in that disputed territory between India and Pakistan. But my memory of that trip was forever clouded by an event I learned of only upon our return to Delhi.

I wrote my impressions of it in my journal after my return.

Haunting voices echo through the large nave of a cathedral elaborately decorated with holy images. Stained glass windows gently filter rays of midday light. Candles flicker against brass as a regally robed and bearded priest waves streams of incense through the air.

*Tolya's coffin in Russian Orthodox Cathedral of San Francisco,
with wife Zora, son Sasha, and older brother Shura. Tania is
trekking in the Himalayas, unaware of his death.*

*Two tall Russian Cossacks—an honor guard—stand
watch over a coffin lined in white silk and surrounded
by floral arrays. My father, Tolya, his posture as rigid
as that of his protectors, lies directly aligned between
the cathedral's entrance and the altar. Only his head is
visible. The final notes of the haunting hymn "Vechnaya
Pamyat," Eternal Remembrance, signal the end of
Papa's funeral. There, in San Francisco, my brother
Sasha supports Mama; Uncle Shura towers over them;
family and friends stand in widening circles.*

I am asleep, seven thousand miles away, in a tent surrounded by towering Himalayan peaks—remote, unreachable, and oblivious to his passing.

It is 1987, I am in my late thirties, and I am out of time to resolve my relationship with my father.

At least while he is still alive.

Chapter 23

Understanding Tolya

Over thirty years have passed since that day when I lost my father. It took me much of that time to understand the fury I carried deep inside myself for as long as I can remember. I now know it was mostly my father's fears about the future that made me angry, and a lot of that rage was directed toward him.

In the spring of 2018, I published my first book, *Mother Tongue: A Saga of Three Generations of Balkan Women*. It traces the lives of my mother's family through a hundred years. In it, my Russian Papa is just a shadow.

I grew up on stories about family, but the storyteller was my Croatian mother—the only person I could actually speak to in that language, and the only non-Russian in our world. Yet I was raised as a Russian. America and San Francisco played an oblique background role in my young life, which was filled with Russian family and friends, and life as lived in an old Russia that had disappeared except in our community. I knew all about the Tsars and the Cossacks and the saints of the Orthodox Church, but I knew little about the past of my father, Anatoly Ivanovich Amochaev.

It wasn't until 1977, when I was a successful technology executive heading to Russia on business that I learned from my Uncle Shura of a village called Amochaev, a village where my grandfather was born, one of ten siblings. I was oblivious to a hometown named after us. Ironically, I—the one who rejected all things Russian—was the first family member to return to the homeland. But that was more than forty years ago.

During the launch of my book about Mama, as I was answering questions at an event, a friend redirected the discussion from my mother to my father.

"It seems that your father struggled with coming to America more than your mother did."

"That is definitely true," I replied. "My father came here as a refugee and he never grew comfortable here. The only place he ever again felt fully at home was on his fishing boat!"

I didn't duck the issue. I talked about my father's fears. I shared memories that included Papa pushing my brother to become an engineer, believing that this profession could transcend borders, although he—an engineer—was fixing appliances for minimum wages and struggling to learn English. Telling me American boys just had nasty things on their minds and wanting me to marry a Russian. The floodgates to old memories opened.

"I always thought he didn't believe in me," I continued. "Nor in my ability to build a successful life. When I had my first big opportunity for a promotion, he told me that 'people like us' would never be allowed to enter the elite management classes, nor become one of those who led. He told me to just keep my head down, to not make waves."

"'*Oni tebya ne primyat*,' were words he kept hammering me with," I said. "'They' won't let you in, no matter how hard you try.' The famous '*oni*,' or 'they,' described everyone who belonged, as we clearly didn't."

I finally took a breath and looked around the room. Everyone's eyes were glued to mine.

"Did growing up with your father's fears make you fearful?"

"No! It all made me angry." The answer came before I could even think, but the words pulled me deep inside myself.

"Yep, I get that!" My friend replied, smiling at me. Those who knew me the longest know that the deep anger within me would sometimes burst forth—thankfully with decreasing regularity as my life became more stable and successful. It had been so much a part of me that I was almost oblivious to it, only occasionally pausing to cringe at a particularly offensive response to a threat—whether real or perceived. That anger helped make me a successful businesswoman in a man's world, but a lot of my rage had been directed at my father. It isn't a characteristic I am proud of.

"I always knew you were a badass!" my interrogator continued, and the room broke up in laughter, dissipating my concerns in an instant.

Fortunately, being a badass had just become popular. I happily adopted the sobriquet, and that moment launched me on much more than a brief observation about my personality. It embarked me on a search for the world that created my father. It also forced me to acknowledge that if I am, in fact, a badass, it is most likely due to the other badass who helped raise me—my father's mother, Daria.

A hard admission after all these years of being angry with her and with my father.

A few weeks later, on a trip back to the refugee camp I grew up in, I traveled to the industrial back alleys of Trieste and Campo San Sabba. Now, Trieste is in Italy. Yugoslavia— the country where I was born and which we had fled— no longer exists. But the Campo building is still there, a

memorial to the global damage caused by World War II and its aftereffects.

I had visited the campo before, but always saw it in the context of my childhood there, which had been happy. I was surrounded by adults who loved me and had a lot of free time on their hands. I knew no other world, and it was my home—no more, no less.

For the first time, on that trip, I saw the Campo—where I had been happy as a child—through my father's eyes. The rose-colored glasses of my infancy finally dropped away and I imagined what a successful man in the prime of life had to deal with. *Only then did I begin to understand the reasons for his fears.*

Papa rarely talked about his difficulties in life. But I know many of them and started to think about the things he didn't tell me. They were haunting thoughts.

My father fled a homeland twice. As an infant, his family was ensnarled in a bitter Russian revolutionary war that pitted brother against brother. He and his family escaped, but he was raised to believe it wasn't over, that they would soon prevail and return. He grew up in Yugoslavia, and adopted that country as his home, as Sasha and I had done in America. Against his mother's wishes he married a Yugoslavian rather than a Russian woman. He became an engineer and started a company with his brothers. He had two children, a community, and a happy life. He even figured out how to adapt to the takeover of his country by the Communists—his family's most dreaded enemy. Clearly this was a man with strength of character and determination.

And then, in his early thirties—the prime of life—he lost everything. Again.

He was evicted from his country—Yugoslavia—for the simple reason of being Russian by birth. Completely innocent,

he was branded an enemy of his adopted country, possibly a Russian spy. He then spent four years in a Displaced Persons camp in Trieste—waiting for some nation to give him refuge—before heading to an uncertain future in America.

The America he came to was in the throes of Cold War hysteria: it was the McCarthy era. People were being randomly accused of spying for the Russians, of being Communists. It had to be a hard time to arrive as a stateless refugee of Russian birth. As his daughter, I was also a refugee, but I was way too young to understand what that meant or worry about it.

I never knew the strong and confident man my mother married. The father I grew up with knew that the calm present could dissolve overnight into chaos and displacement. He feared America might be just one more temporary shelter, that we would be forced to flee yet again into an unimaginable and uncertain future.

During most of my life this seemed ridiculous to me. I had no empathy for his fear.

By the time I acknowledged my father's pain and the injustices that life dealt him . . . it was too late. Only now am I starting to make peace with Papa. Only now am I acknowledging that his fear and my rage were both caused by global circumstances that heaved us around as if we were toy puppets on a stage balanced on earthquake faults.

And in my journal from that trip to Trieste I wrote the following line:

It is my father's pain I need to heal from.

The house where Tolya was born, in Khutor Kulikov,
when Tania visited in 1977.

Chapter 24

1977—My First Visit to the Homeland

When I made my first trip to Russia in 1977, no one even knew I spoke Russian. I lived in Minneapolis, where there was no such thing as a Russian community. I had moved on, and it simply no longer mattered. Or so I thought.

But in Russia, or the Soviet Union, as it then was, the translators they assigned to us spoke marginal English and understood little about modern computer technology. Suddenly my language skills were key to our continued efforts. I had to step in not just as the head of the supercomputer business unit, but as the coordinator of all our communication.

At that time, Cold War tensions between our countries had started easing very slightly. Russia desperately wanted our supercomputers, but they had no hard currency. Russian Rubles in those days were simply not convertible. The U.S. Government gave us authority to work on alternative ways to fund a machine.

We went thinking we could perhaps reach a technology exchange agreement. That idea failed. But as we toured the Hermitage, the world's second largest museum, and saw the incredible art collections it held, a new idea took hold. We

could organize a global tour of priceless art works the rest of the world had not seen. The funds raised by that tour would more than pay for a supercomputer. Incredibly, the governments of both countries agreed to this plan, and the next two years were spent organizing a tour that included Paris, London, New York and other cities. The plans were being finalized, and a launch organized for early 1980. And then in December of 1979, everything changed one more time.

Russia invaded Afghanistan.

That war lasted almost ten years and became the final Cold War proxy war. The United Nations passed a resolution protesting Soviet intervention. The international community imposed numerous sanctions and embargoes.

Does this sound familiar?

The museum tour was cancelled, and all talk of selling computers to Russia ended. I never went back. Ultimately, it was the collapse of the Soviet Union that ended that war.

Thinking about that earlier trip I took to Russia made me aware of the cosmic changes that happened in the intervening forty years. Communism has finally disintegrated—long after my grandfather's death, and even my father's—but around the time of the birth of Artem Amochaev, the young man I would be traveling through Russia with. There is now a generation that grew up after Russia became its own country again, rather than part of a grand Soviet Socialist experiment.

My connection with Artem has opened the door to discovering this new world, but my mind still holds a strong image of that old Russia.

That trip in 1977 was about much more than business. It was my first trip to my father's homeland, and I was searching for more than ghosts. I remember every moment of my travels to the remote village where my father was born and easily slip into them. . .

I wondered: had I really agreed to fly on a one-way ticket into a remote backwater of 1977 Communist Russia? It was a country repressed by fear and impoverished by incompetent bureaucracy, one my father fled as an infant and couldn't believe his daughter was braving.

My family, Don Cossacks, had lived for centuries on the Don River between Moscow and Volgograd. The Cossacks, although mostly peasants, were staunch supporters of the tsar and represented the last stand of resistance to the Communist Revolution, losing the final battle in 1920.

When I was a child, my grandmother told me stories of that final battle. How the family, following the White Army, repeatedly left their village and returned. How, by the last retreat, there was no time to dig up the silver she had buried under the back doorstep to their house, abandoned to the dust of history. My grandmother was long gone, but in my mind that silver in its dirt grave halfway around the world lived on, my sole keepsake beyond the small gold stars she had always worn dangling from her ears. I wanted to see where our story began. I wanted to retrieve what my grandmother was forced to leave behind. I wanted to dig that dirt.

I flew to Volgograd, and then headed north to a town called Uryupinsk in a ten-passenger WWII biplane converted for commercial use. In front of me a man stared intently into the open cockpit, leaning in as if he would steer from his seat if he could. I had seen him, and the two pilots drink a quick shot of vodka in the cafeteria before departure.

"What are you doing?" I asked.

"I am the observer," the man replied proudly.

The Communist party had observers everywhere. They had broken my camera, pawed through my luggage, read my notes. Now this guy was making sure of what—that the pilots didn't hijack us?

The plane rattled into action and sped down the runway. The noise was deafening. The plane shivered and groaned. Only three hundred miles, it took an interminable three hours, during which the shaking didn't abate. A confident flier who rarely feels queasy, almost instantly I started retching and then vomiting, my head in a bag for the entire trip. Perhaps I should have joined the men for that early-morning vodka shot.

When we finally landed, I couldn't get up. I couldn't think. I could barely breathe. Everyone else deplaned. Finally, holding onto the bag—embarrassed to leave it behind—I crawled to the door.

We were in an abandoned field, dead grass all around. At the bottom of the stairs, a man with a paunch and an official-looking chauffeur's hat waited.

"*Ah, vi Amerikanka!*" he said. You're the American.

"*Kak vi znali?*" I replied. How did you know?

"There was no one else left."

He introduced himself as Yura, the chauffeur for the president of the flaxseed-oil factory, and the proud driver of the only private car in the district. He explained that his boss had loaned him to me for my stay. Did I want to go to my hotel or straight toward the village of Kulikov?

"I have a hotel?" The town had no cars. The airport was a dirty field. My expectations were low.

"Yes," he explained, proudly. "Our town has a hotel because we have a sister city in Czechoslovakia and our visitors need a place to stay."

I decided to head to the hotel. I desperately needed to wash up.

No American had ever visited the modest but clean hotel, far beyond any approved tourist areas. The price for the night was one ruble, less than two dollars at the official exchange rate.

The forms were in Russian. I transliterated my town of Minneapolis into Cyrillic: Минияполис. There was no line for state or country.

The receptionist peered at the form carefully, then said, "That's in the north, right?"

I was impressed with her knowledge of U.S. geography.

"Why, yes. How did you know?"

"I could tell by your accent," she replied. "It is vaguely Siberian."

My father had left Russia as an infant, and I had never set foot here before. All the same, my knowledge of the language was good enough that this woman, who had never been anywhere else, took me for a native. It was an amazing testament to the uniquely powerful Russian concept of *Rodina*, or homeland.

The showers in the hotel were off for the day, and there was no hot water. I washed up in the sink.

Before setting off, I asked Yura if we could buy some water. We stopped in five stores, all empty and deserted. What did these people eat? Finally, he took me back to the hotel, where they gave me a large bottle of apple juice and a chipped glass.

I had been unable to find a map that included the remote village of Kulikov, where my father was born. However, I was fluent in the language, stubborn and determined.

My father's brother Shura was eight when they left, the oldest son and now patriarch of the scattered family. He had sketched a map of the village and proudly pointed out their family home, telling me it was "the only two-story house in the village."

My grandfather, whom I had never met, was a *kulak*, a peasant who took advantage of land reforms passed in 1906 to develop a wheat-trading business and rise above his class. Uncle Shura drew the *ambar*, or granary, on the map. It was across from his aunt's house, near the creek and the church,

and around the corner from the train station. This final detail—that the village was important enough to have a train stop—was the clue that still had me on the hunt.

Yura knew the train station. "The Jarizhenskaya station," he said, "is near your village of Kulikov. Do you know any other details?"

I did. The previous evening in Volgograd I had repeated an act I had performed in countless cities around the world: I had scoured the phone book for an Amochaev. I had never found anyone beyond my immediate family; but Volgograd had two, and I had met one of them: Oleg. While neither of us knew enough about our families to figure out if we were related, his mother lived in our village of Kulikov. I had agreed to look her up and tell her that he was well and would write soon.

"We are looking for Maria Afanasievna Amochaeva at number 6, Gorkii Street," I told Yura.

We quickly reached the outskirts of the city and bounced onto a dirt road.

"This," he said, "will soon be the highway to Moscow!"

"Soon" was a relative term. Weeds abounded. No equipment was in sight. I couldn't help but wonder how soon.

"And what do you think of this car?" Yura asked.

It was a comfortable Volga limousine. I told him how fortunate I felt that his boss let me have use of it.

"Do you own a car?"

"I do."

"Is it like this?"

"Oh, no," I said. "It is much smaller."

"Of course," he nodded, likely visualizing the tin cans of Eastern Europe rather than my late-model sports car. "Did you wait a long time for it?"

"No, we don't actually have to wait for cars."

He mulled this over for a while.

"But you do have shortages, don't you?" He was searching for common ground.

I wracked my brain and remembered a true story.

"Last year," I said, "there was a run on toilet paper. It was started by a rumor that the toilet-paper company was going out of business." I didn't mention that it was a comedy-show gag gone awry.

"Yes, that happens a lot here. But could you buy a truck? Or a bus?"

"If I could afford it, I could."

"Surely that can't be. *Ne mozhet bits.* How would you do that?"

I had never actually thought about it. "I'm really not sure," I said. "I guess I would go to a company that sells them."

"Would you need permission from the powers, *ot vlasti*?"

"Well," now it was I who stretched to find common ground. "I would have to get a special driver's license to operate a large vehicle."

"Ah. They would probably use that to prevent you from buying one," Yura said knowingly, in collusion with me against the bureaucracy.

I found myself torn, as so often happened on this trip, between wanting to share a bit of my life, and not wanting to point out just how desperate theirs seemed to me. It was a fine line to walk. The previous evening Oleg had proudly showed me the latest miracle installed in his family's apartment, to the envy of the neighbors: a sink where cold and hot water merged into one faucet rather than coming out separately. I did my best to act impressed.

As I was leaving, Oleg opened the top of his greatest treasure: a small piano bought with his black-market earnings as a dentist nights and weekends. He withdrew a clear plastic sleeve

with four colored felt pens and offered it with both hands, saying: "This is for you, to take back and remember us by."

"That's . . . those are the ones Cousin Igor brought back from Germany," his wife stuttered, the pain of loss clear in her voice.

He insisted. I didn't have the heart to tell Oleg that at home I had a drawer full of felt pens.

Back in the limousine, my conversation with Yura was interrupted by the appearance of the train station. An elderly man walked along the tracks. We pulled over to ask about our destination.

"Can you tell me, *tovarisch*, how to find 6 Gorkii Street?" Yura asked the man.

"Where do you think you are, Moscow?" came the gruff reply. "We are in the boonies, *mi v derevnye*, not the big city. Who are you looking for?"

"We are looking for Maria Afanasievna Amochaeva," I interjected.

"Ah. Why didn't you say so? She is in her front yard with Efim Ivanovich, as always. Take the first right, it's a hundred *arshins* up the road." I thought *arshins* had died with the Old Testament, but the driver knew it was a measure just short of a yard. We easily found the two friends sipping tea at a table in front of a small house.

Convincing them of my identity was much more problematic.

"What do you mean, you're from America but your father was born here?" said the frowning woman, her gray hair circling her head in a neatly tucked braid. "That's not possible, there's no one in America from here!"

She was almost right. The escape had been a close call. I knew my grandfather had loaded the family, including four children and his mother, onto his horse cart and fled across hundreds of miles of war-torn country to the town of Yevpatoria on the Black Sea. That in late 1920, they boarded one of the last ships taking refugees out of the country.

I started explaining: "Well, his father took his family away during the revolution…"

"Likely story." The old woman spat at the ground.

"Why would I lie to you?"

"Why wouldn't you? And who's he, with the fancy car, driving you around like some kind of princess? What are you doing here? We don't know anything. We have nothing to say."

There was something about her steely strength that reminded me of my grandmother. She clearly assumed I had been sent for some nefarious reason. Was this as far as I would get?

"Marusia, Marusia, wait a minute. Let the young lady tell us what she wants. Maybe she can explain," counseled the man, Efim. Tall and thin and around the same age, which I seriously overestimated as around eighty, he quickly became my ally, loosening up as my chauffeur wisely withdrew.

"Well, all I know is that my grandfather's name was Ivan Minaevich Amochaev," I explained, "and that he had a house and an *ambar* here. When the Red Army defeated the Whites for the last time, they escaped to the Black Sea. Almost forty years later they ended up in America. My uncle was eight when they left, and he drew me a map." I turned to Efim. "Why doesn't she believe me?"

Efim swept his upturned palm across the emptiness that surrounded us. "Well, you see, *dorogaia*, dear, no one survived."

"What do you mean?"

"When the Reds came in they lined up and shot all the men and boys over twelve years old. No one got away. You're the first person in nearly sixty years who ever arrived claiming to be from here."

His words suddenly explained the silence of decades, all the letters gone unanswered. I had trouble grasping the scope of the tragedy, before he continued.

"But you have nothing to gain that I can imagine, so I am prepared to believe you. Do you have that map?"

"Oh my God! Were you here?" I wanted him to keep talking. I needed to learn more.

"We were infants," he said, "but we grew up with stories of the horror. Marusia lost her father, her brothers. She can't bear to think about it all."

I pulled out my map, and we huddled over it.

"Theirs was the two-story house, right here. I was told it had become a tea house, a *chaiovnia*, after the revolution."

"*Milaya*," Efim said, dear one, "there has never been a two-story house in this village, but let me see this. There was a tea shop at that corner. Let's walk over there."

We wandered around with the map. The town hadn't grown since my family left, and the remaining skeleton matched the sketch. I realized that my uncle's little-boy mind had kept a larger-than-life image of his father's home. All the same, we soon found not only the house but even the *ambar*.

The neighboring village became the *kolkhoz* of Serp I Molot, and the young people had been moved there, Efim explained. Most of the homes in Kulikov were abandoned, the church was torn down, and there was no need for a school anymore.

"We're just left with dust and memories," he reflected. "And we don't let the memories go back too far."

Stalin's collectivization campaign, which destroyed the final private ownership of land by peasants and wiped out all kulaks as enemies of the people, became real for me in a way it never had in my history classes at Russian school in San Francisco.

I approached the house, the forlorn and crumbling single-story, brown isba that would eventually disappoint Uncle Shura. I circled the faded wood fence that surrounded it, checked the gate. It was all shut tight. I walked around and shot a few pictures, trying to imagine who I might have been, who my father might have been. The gap was too wide; we simply wouldn't have existed.

"Who owns this now?" I asked.

"No one owns anything, here, *zolotko,*" golden one, Efim said, inadvertently using my father's childhood nickname for me. "No one has lived here in a long time. Everything belongs to the state. We aren't allowed to go inside or touch anything."

I could tell this gentle man would be uncomfortable if I opened the gate and walked up to embrace the house, as I longed to do. People had been beaten into submission by a system that spread fear and terror as a way of life. In an abandoned backwater, miles from anywhere, that authority still controlled their actions, from their fear of strangers to blind obedience to power.

My father, forced to flee a Communist dictatorship yet again as an adult, wore many of those scars. I, on the contrary, had grown up in America—a country that took my family in with little more than the clothes on our backs and allowed me to become a woman unafraid of challenges, knowing how to aim high and break barriers.

I was at the heart of so many memories: my grandmother's, my uncle's, mine. The rough wooden fence with its missing slats, leaning precariously, was no barrier to me. It would be so easy to open that gate or climb over it. To dig a hole at the back-door stoop. To search for my treasure, my grandmother's silver. I had no idea what it really was, just that it was something I had wanted my whole life. But taking liberties unimaginable to these scarred people would rob them of their dignity.

And so, I didn't open the gate.

I just stood there for a long time, quietly memorizing the scene. The dirt lanes. The few old-fashioned Russian houses—the *isbas,* unchanged since Tsarist times. The abandoned train station.

Finally, I had to move on, and we returned to Marusia's house. I drank her tea, ate her apples. I told her about her son Oleg, who had not been back since the train stopped running

several years earlier. Marusia and Efim asked me nothing about America; it was too far removed from their experience. They accepted a few trinkets and, in parting, each one kissed me three times in the familial old Russian way.

As for me, I left Russia with a small bag of dirt, a memento for my father and uncle of this place that once held all we were.

I brought it back to our new homeland.

PART FOUR

Chapter 25

Two Family Trees

Now I am heading back to that old Russian homeland of my father's. The one I rejected so long ago. My remaining Russian speaking family and I are heading back to explore the past and learn about life today for those who stayed when our grandparents fled.

Who are we? Who is heading to Russia to explore the past?

To this day no known relatives of my grandparents Ivan and Daria or their numerous brothers and sisters have been identified, and not for lack of trying. But the years are passing and the likelihood of finding some is growing dim.

Four of their children—Shura, Kolya, Liza and Tolya—survived to adulthood in Yugoslavia. The three boys had to leave when Stalin and Tito had a falling out, as the Cold War got serious. Liza married a Serb and was protected by losing her Russian name. She stayed in Belgrade and raised two sons, Mima and Goga.

My Uncle Kolya, who immigrated to Ontario, Canada, with his wife Lyolya, never had children. Aunt Liza also immigrated to Canada after her husband's death, joining her son Mima in that move. Goga became a successful Dean of Engineering at

the top university of Serbia and raised a daughter who is now raising a child. Unfortunately, he unexpectedly passed away in 2016, soon after Sasha and I had a very special visit with them. Staying in Serbia for all their lives, none of them retained their Russian heritage or language to any visible extent.

The other two brothers, oldest son Shura, by then married to my Aunt Galya, and my father Tolya immigrated to San Francisco, arriving in the early 1950s. Sasha and I were young children at that time. Some years after arriving in this country, Shura and Galya had a daughter, Helen, or Lena.

Lena grew up in San Francisco—her own birth city—was educated here, married here, and had children here. However, she stayed Russian. Her children learned English only when they went to school. Her husband Vitya is Russian; her son Kolya's girlfriend is Russian. But you wouldn't want to sec-ond-guess the implications. Yes, they go to Russian Church and sing in the choir. And Lena's life is full of Russian cooking and supporting Russian organizations. But Vitya was an executive at Wells Fargo before he retired. Daughter Katya is a Summa Cum Laude graduate of Cal Berkeley and Kolya graduated from UC Santa Barbara because he preferred the beach there. Both of them work for startups in the San Francisco area.

Unlike Lena, my brother and I moved away from that Russian world as we entered adulthood, although Sasha's two best friends for many years were Russian childhood friends. We both married Americans—the irony of that specification does not escape me! In most other worlds they would just be people. For our families, they were *Amerikantsi*—foreigners. Our friends know my brother as Alex, not Sasha. Neither of us ever forgot the Russian language we were raised in, but it is getting rusty with lack of use. We lost our father over thirty years ago, and that was our last connection to this community. Sasha and I simply left it behind. I stayed close to Galya, my

favorite aunt, and the only person I spoke Russian with. She also kept me supplied with my favorite tortes!

The six of us making this trip are Sasha, Lena, Vitya, Katya, Kolya, and I. Sounds just like a bunch of San Franciscans, right? We will arrive in Moscow on May 2. We could not arrive even a day earlier. Why? Well, Russian Easter is late this year, falling on April 28, and there is no way Lena and Vitya and the kids could leave before that. Lena will make *kulich* and *pascha,* special Easter treats whose recipes passed down from our grandmothers. Their house will fill with Russian friends, there will be lots of toasts and many shots of vodka. And of course, April 29 is Vitya's mother Irina's namesday—a celebration that for our Russians is more important than a birthday. So, another necessary delay.

In Russia we are joining Artem and his family. What do we know about them? Not too much. Other than Artem, they don't speak English and don't have Facebook accounts. He tells me that Facebook is not a popular social networking platform. In his country it's used more for business, as Russia has its own domestic platforms for social use. It is only because he works for a multinational corporation that Artem has a Facebook account, the miracle link that connected us.

Artem is a twenty-nine-year-old engineer, the same age as Katya. These two young people were born at the same time that the so-called "evil empire" of the Soviet Union—the reason for our family's flight all those years ago—collapsed. His eighteen-year-old brother Roman is studying construction at a college in Moscow. Their parents are Igor, an aeronautics engineer, and Irina, a kindergarten director.

Artem sends a photo of two beautiful blue-eyed blonds on vacation in Tunisia—his mother and brother. From Facebook, I ascertain that Artem is a slender dark-haired young man with a trim beard and mustache. He travels widely on business,

working now for a company that is a subsidiary of Leica, maker of the famous camera that accompanied both Shura and Tolya on their flight to America. While finalizing our trip, Artem emails me that he wants to Skype. He is just back from a ski trip to Siberia, where he also had business travel for two weeks. He has been busy enough to get me worried, but we are back in synch. The trip is definitely on. Skype buzzes on my phone.

"*Zdravstvuy*, hello, Artem!" I say. Silence greets my comment and I can tell it's not the connection; it's the unexpected Russian greeting. As if he had been getting his mind around speaking English.

"Tania, it's Artem," he finally replies. He has a deep voice; his English carries a subtle Russian accent. It reminds me immediately of a kitchen in San Francisco, my Uncle Shura's baritone, those accents which so embarrassed me in my childhood, when all I wanted was to fit in.

"*Nu konechno*, Artem. Of course." I say. "Who else could it be?"

He stumbles through a few more words in English, then realizes that we will be speaking Russian. We work out a few details and I learn his mother Irina is worried about whether we are vegetarians or gluten free. "You're watching too many American videos," I say.

"No, it's started here, too."

"Well, don't worry about us. We eat everything!" Suddenly it hits me that six complete strangers are landing at Irina's doorstep in a few weeks. Strangers from "Amerika!" That must be intimidating.

"Please tell her not to worry. We can even do the cooking!"

He repeatedly assures me it is no problem, and we finish up a few final details. "So, you won't need an English-speaking guide?" he asks at the end.

"No, we're leaving America back here!" I affirm.

His email afterwards is very telling:

Hi Tania,

I'm glad we got a chance to have such talk. To be honest, I didn't expect your Russian would be so fluent!

No matter how often I tell someone we speak Russian, when they learn our ancestors left a hundred years ago, they don't really believe us. But it is true.

Chapter 26

Logistics

During 2018, as we plan the details of this trip, relations between Russia and the United States grow increasingly tense, for the election that made Donald Trump president also launched an investigation into election tampering by the Russians.

In addition, the part of Russia where my father was born is near Ukraine. The eastern part of Ukraine is now nearly a war zone. Crimea is claimed by Russia, but they have been accused of an illegal takeover, and sanctions have been imposed by our country. The trail I wish to trace—my grandparents' year-long flight from their village of Kulikov—now known as Kulikovskiy—in southwest Russia, to Yevpatoria in Crimea—crosses through the conflict zones.

Rational thinking intervenes, and we agree to skip the Ukraine portion of the trip. Somehow, a visit to Kulikovskiy and even to Yevpatoria still seems possible. Incredibly, my seren-dipitously found "relatives"—the family of Artem Amochaev—are welcoming us to their home. We are flying into Moscow and Artem offers to pick us up and take us to the *dacha*, the country home, where—his family assures us—there will be room for all of us to spend a few days. He tells us it is near

the Golden Ring—cities like Rostov, Vladimir and Suzdal— at the heart of medieval Russian history. I can't wait to see it all. We book a hotel in Moscow. Artem and I discuss the meager supply of hotels in the city of Uryupinsk, near Kulikovskiy. He and I have both traveled there and stayed in a hotel that had serious quality issues. We check flight schedules between Moscow and Volgograd, Russian rental car companies, flights from Volgograd to Crimea, flights from Crimea back to the west. It all starts to feel real.

Artem sends great news: His father Igor will definitely also join us on our visit to Crimea.

And then the challenges threaten to overwhelm us.

A few years earlier I had developed a friendship with another Igor, who worked in the Russian Consulate in San Francisco and lived in my building. We talked about their summer home in Crimea, and I had a party to welcome their infant son into our community when he was born.

This relationship could help get Russian visas. But of course, fate steps in. That investigation of Russian meddling into elections was distant and remote. . . until, suddenly, San Francisco's Russian Consulate is closed by the United States with two days' warning.

Russia is outraged, and here is a quote from their web site:

> *"We believe that the decision to close the Consulate General of the Russian Federation in San Francisco is another unfriendly step of the US authorities . . .* <u>*Closure of the Consulate General will create certain difficulties in the preparation of tourist documents for Americans."*</u>

Getting a tourist visa for Russia becomes challenging. And we plan to stay in a private home, not just approved hotels. We are told our hosts will have to apply for approval documents, a long and complicated procedure. My friend Igor disappears, unreachable. But he probably can no longer help.

A friend of Helen's explains to me that the old Cossack Center in San Francisco now boasts a large dining table and chairs—courtesy of the ex-Russian Consulate. Upon learning that the consulate was to be closed, they apparently had about twenty-four hours to clear the place out. They filled a U-Haul with furniture and gifted it to various old Russian Tsarist organizations about town. From the moment of the announcement, streams of smoke were seen from consulate chimneys. Everyone associated with that consulate is gone. Thoughts of presumed Russian spying—and my father's old fears—once more fill my mind.

Sure enough, in early September new headlines hit *The New York Times*:

> "LONDON — *September 5, 2018*
>
> *The two assassins sent to southwest England in March to poison a Russian former spy were active officers in Russia's military intelligence, Prime Minister Theresa May of Britain said on Wednesday, after prosecutors accused the men of attempted murder, the first criminal charges in a case that has driven a deep wedge between Russia and the West.*
>
> *Investigators released a cache of evidence in the case, including security camera images that captured the progress of two husky men from an Aeroflot flight to the scene of the crime, near the victim's home, and from there back to Moscow."*

Tensions between Russia and Ukraine increase. Their navies clash, ships are boarded, prisoners are taken. The United States continues to be enmeshed in its own partisan strife, with the Russia investigations front and center. In November, the Democrats take over the House of Representatives, and things threaten to get a lot more tense as they clash with the Republicans and Trump.

Then there is Russia's arrest of a U.S. citizen on spying charges, reminding me of being detained and questioned in Iran, with veiled accusations of the same thing.

Our travel plans have to be finalized, but Russian visas can only be approved within six months of travel. And visas have to be for specifically approved hotels and dates, and any shifts from those commitments could lead to serious issues. Staying at the private home of people we have never met and whose only connection to us is a common family name and an erroneous email from *The Economist* seems laughable.

Crimea is now firmly embedded in Russia, but Ukraine is not backing off of its claims to it. In December the U.S. state department has the following posted on their website:

Do not travel to:

- *Crimea due to arbitrary detentions and other abuses by Russian occupation authorities.*

Ukraine is a Level 2 risk. Crimea is Level 4. The website continues:

Before You Go to a High-Risk Area:

- *Draft a will and designate appropriate insurance beneficiaries and/or power of attorney.*

- *Erase any sensitive photos, comments, or other materials from your social media pages, cameras, laptops, and other electronic device.*

- *Traveling to high-risk areas puts you at increased risk for kidnapping, hostage-taking, theft, and serious injury.*

Suddenly, instead of planning a trip to the homeland, all I can think about is being trapped in Moscow with an issue about my exit visa many years earlier, during my trip in 1977.

It all feels a bit insane. But I persevere and decide I will think about the challenges another time.

By January of 2019 things ease up on the Russian side and American tourists again enjoy St. Petersburg, Moscow and river cruises. It seems that our visa details can be sorted, without enmeshing Artem and without detailed commitments as to specific travel locations. We are back on track, with only Crimea to worry about.

We are reassured on that issue by the fact that we will be traveling with two Russian citizens, and by our Russian language skills. Also, the Tsarist Russians like us, who fled in 1920, are back in vogue in that country, and Putin supports them wholeheartedly. How much protection could we need? I start poking about the Internet, looking for possible relatives who might still live in the area we will be exploring. I buy DNA measurement kits to take to Russia with me. I wonder if Artem is a descendant of one of Ivan's siblings or cousins. Will we be able to figure it out?

By early April we all have visas for Russia, and I am shopping for San Francisco souvenirs to bring along.

On April 21, a television comedian with no experience in politics wins a landslide election as president of Ukraine. Any comedy show that had forecast this result would have been truly funny. But this comedy has now moved to reality. I am briefly lulled into thinking that perhaps this will lead to an easing of tensions. He is more liberal, less nationalistic, and perhaps Putin will negotiate a settlement. But two days

later, to the outrage of Ukraine, Putin approves streamlining Russian citizenship for Ukraine citizens and I am checking the map again to see how close my home village is to the border.

It's not very far. This is partially because of my Cossack ancestors. When Lenin decided to wipe them out, he erased their Don Region and split it between Volgograd and Ukraine. Now those old Cossack ghosts are haunting his successors. The city of Donetsk, at the heart of the disputed area, lies halfway between our village and Evpatoria, the city in Crimea from which my family departed Russia in 1920.

My medical evacuation insurance lapses and I renew, adding the option that will provide support in case of abduction or other crises! I send the information on who to contact if they don't hear from me to my brother and daughter. I learn that I can temporarily stop all transactions on my financial holdings and how to protect my communications with a VPN—a Virtual Private Network. My passwords are all reset to incredible complexity, double verification is required, all financial apps have been erased from my devices. I know that a determined hacker can still break through my defenses, but I have done my best.

I send the draft version of this book to my publisher, with instructions not to open unless he doesn't hear from me. Then I proceed.

I now have a three-year visa and a one-way ticket to Moscow!

Chapter 27

Meeting the Amochaevs

I walk off the plane in Moscow's Sheremetyevo airport. It looks like any other modern airport, rather than the tired old one I remember from my first trip. But I am oblivious to my surroundings. My mind is in a whirl. Have I really come back to Mother Russia? This is no longer the Soviet Union. This is the land my grandparents had hoped to reclaim, a post-Communist world that took longer than they could wait to arrive. And I will be seeing it with my family, who in some important ways have never left this *rodina*, or homeland. Will I find the key to my father, the man I never really knew? What does this fatherland have in store for us?

Those thoughts are overtaken by the ever-present realities of border guards and government bureaucracy and passport control. What if there's something wrong with my visa? What if Vitya and Lena and the kids are delayed?

What if there's no one there to meet us? How could we come with no back-up plan? That last fear is the deepest one. What compelled me to come to this country at this tense moment in its relations with my own adopted homeland? And how can I be planning to stay with people I have never met and know nothing about?

The drama of this arrival, played out in my mind endlessly, sends me to the ladies' room which is conveniently located along my route. I look myself in the eyes and see the same Tania who has traveled to an endless list of dangerous places. I can do this. It's time to face the bear.

My first fears are overcome as I quickly pass through immigration and Sasha follows mere minutes later. We have no luggage, so there is nothing to wait for. It is anti-climactic to say the least. I am reminded of my mother telling me the same thing about our arrival in America over sixty years earlier. Apparently, all those years ago, we walked effortlessly off the ship, through immigration, and onto shore.

Now, in what feels like the blink of an eye from the landing of the airplane, we are being greeted by a young man in the terminal who laughingly holds up a hand-printed sign that says "Амочаев."

We easily recognize each other without any cues. He matches the image on Facebook, and his voice is the same one as on the call we had, but this time it is accompanied by a gentle smile. That's the word that comes to mind when I think of Artem. Gentle. A gentle young man.

Next to him stands a man in a striped blue long-sleeved polo shirt and jeans. He has short light-brown hair, blue eyes and a smooth rounded face. He could be anywhere from forty to sixty, but I know he is fifty-two years old, for this is Artem's father, Igor. He is gracious without being overly emotional, something that is to define much of his behavior.

Sasha and I cheerfully greet them, and I go off to get rubles from the ATM while they fill those introductory moments when strangers first communicate. Half an hour later, around nine in the evening, the others—Lena, Vitya, Katya and Kolya—arrive, on time, from San Francisco via Norway.

It is all far more comfortable than we could have expected. After all that worry and preparation—the Russian Federation

visa processing and logistical coordination, the U.S. State Department security concerns, the realization that we have no back-up plan if we can't get in or no one is there to greet us—our arrival is anticlimactic, to say the least. They, too, breeze through border control and customs. We quickly greet them and then pile into the van Igor has rented for our stay and take off driving to the *dacha*.

The two strangers—unknown Russians who are to take us to a *dacha* in a location we have never precisely confirmed—don't feel like strangers at all. It is all comfortable and easy, like reconnecting with family after an extended absence.

And yet. It is night, it is dark, and we have no idea where we are heading. Igor drives with a comfortable expertise, avoiding busy roads and circumventing the city. We drive through the darkness and he tells us the *dacha* is about an hour and a half to the east of Moscow.

Except somehow before we get there the road is blocked, and we detour into the remote countryside. Igor takes it in stride, and I confess I don't debate where he might really be taking us or revert to thoughts of my favorite reading material—thrillers of the international crime genre. Well, not completely. A few false heartbeats, but the rest of the crowd is relaxed, and I go with the flow. Until we find a side road and approach a guarded gate. The guys manning it recognize Igor and lift it so we can enter.

A gate? I stare at the guardhouse as we speed inside and take a few hard turns. Then another gate awaits, and Artem jumps out to open it. A wall tall enough to block the view of the property, maybe eight or nine feet, stretches in both directions. Metal, with a double gate that curves and has metal arrows lining the top. Before I have time to react, we have pulled in, stopped, and Artem has locked the door behind us.

We could be anywhere. We could be locked away, waiting for someone to wire money and get us back to America.

The guards could warn the government that strangers have arrived; strangers without detailed permission to stay at this specific house. But my jet-lagged mind drowsily observes the surroundings and doesn't find it very threatening.

I'm about to step out when suddenly the front door opens, light floods out, and I hear a madly barking animal. My head jerks and I freeze in my seat.

The noise is followed by a spinning long-haired dog—the size of a small hairy kitten. The sweet-faced blond woman from Artem's photo of his mother shoos the dog back inside and directs a smile at us that makes clear the source of Artem's gentle style. This is Irina, or Ira. Young enough to be a daughter, she will make us feel coddled and cared for like our own mothers did.

Ira's smile dissipates for good any concerns I have carried. Like excess baggage, I leave them behind, and relax into her world. She quickly hugs us, then rushes back inside and over to the stove, where wonderful aromas greet us. We follow, carrying bags into the warmth and comfort of a large open space. Then Artem's younger brother Roman wanders in from somewhere. He says hello, shakes our hands, and, before we can catch our breath, heads off somewhere else—a normal young man in his late teens, behaving just like his counterpart in San Francisco would. He is clearly mortified that his family has brought complete strangers into the house. Luckily, he has exams to study for and can disappear before it all gets too embarrassing for words.

The *dacha* is a comfortable log-cabin-construction, two-level home with a bathroom on each level and a large open area around the kitchen. The *banya,* a large stand-alone bathhouse, is at the back of the half-acre plot, and an attractively laid out garden gives it all the feel of summer homes around the northern lakes in Minnesota where I once lived. The development houses several dozen such homes, divided by fences, with a gatekeeper—rather than my imagined ominous guard—at the

exit to the country road. A river and the forests nearby also remind me of my time in the upper midwest, where trees are often interspersed with marshes and streams.

The time stamp on our first photo together—at the table in the *dacha*—gives an idea of Ira's commitment to taking care of us. It is after 11:00 pm, we have just arrived from the airport, and she greets us with a delicious meal and her limitless good spirits. Young Roman is getting ready to make himself scarce but takes one picture to memorialize the moment when the Amochaevs meet for the first time.

The relaxed comfort that shows on our faces is real. From the moment of our first meeting, there is not a hint of awkwardness, just ease and familiarity. That is the mood that is to dominate our visit. We aren't here to debate political tensions between our countries. We just want to connect with people whose lives might have been ours in different circumstances. And they have welcomed six complete strangers into their home, as though we really were family.

In one of our first extended conversations, Igor learns that my cousins are avid singers. Igor says that he, too, loves music and is interested in learning what they like to sing.

Vitya talks about retiring from his job as a banker and how he is now free to dedicate himself to developing his voice so he can take lead solos in the choir of the Holy Virgin Russian Orthodox Cathedral in San Francisco. When he and Lena are home with friends, he says, they drink vodka and sing old Russian folk songs reminiscent of the Don Cossack Choir that visited California from the Soviet Union.

"So, what are some of your favorite songs?" I ask Igor as Vitya pauses in his story. "Did you all sing the old Russian favorites when you were young?"

Igor stares at us for a while before finally responding. "Well, no," he says. "I liked Springsteen. And Pink Floyd. And Elton John." Now we all stare at him.

First meeting of the families at the Amochaev dacha at eleven in the evening upon arrival from the airport. Ira and Igor standing, Artem at front left. Around the table starting in front of Igor are Kolya, Katya, Lena, Tania, Sasha, and Vitya.

He tells us he doesn't know any of our old Russian favorites. They weren't part of his growing up. He grew up in the Soviet Union of the 1970s and 1980s, and they listened to the same music that played on our radios and televisions at that same time. Why would he be interested in some prehistoric Russian songs that the old people used to sing in the days before radio and television even existed? More importantly, he wonders, why would we?

Our conversation starts an exploration of the differences in our expectations of each other. Igor is stunned at our Russianness. Artem could not believe we spoke Russian. They are now learning it goes far beyond language. And they have more questions than we can answer in one evening. Or maybe ever. Why, they wonder, is there a Russian community in America that keeps all this ancient history alive? Why are we part of it? I can feel Igor's mind trying to fathom this unusual situation. Perhaps he is also wondering about spending the next few weeks with people who are this weird. What has he signed up for? Who has his son brought into their lives?

Certainly, there were no churches around in the days of his youth, and they didn't have choirs or sing prayers in elaborate harmony. While we had delayed our arrival in Russia because "Russian" Easter was so late this year, it is clear that the Amochaevs in Russia did not join in the rituals of that day. Easter is not an important concept in their lives. Vitya and Lena also celebrated his mom's namesday, and it doesn't escape them that our hostess's full name is also Irina. Again, Ira is oblivious to the event, even though she graciously accepts their good wishes on it as she accepts everything about us. We discover they still don't even celebrate Christmas much, thirty years after religion returned to their country after the fall of Communism in 1989. When we are surprised at that, they tell us New Year's Day is the best holiday and invite us to come visit and celebrate it with them this year.

"But that is in the middle of winter!" Sasha says. Napoleon was defeated by Moscow's winter. Who would dare come visit then?

"Oh, it's not so cold anymore. And it's so beautiful." They sound like my friends in Minneapolis, who tell me the cold I experienced while living there is mostly a thing of the past, that global warming has changed things dramatically.

"We could spend hours in the *banya*; you would love it," Igor rhapsodizes, smiling as he always does when talking about one of his favorite haunts.

That leads us to discussions of the *banya* and we go outside to explore it and check out the *mangal*, the grilling house in the back where Igor will make *shashlik* and other skewered meats for us. Then we come back inside to share more vodka and continue talking.

The next evening, we watch television on the giant screen in their living room, which always seems to be on. It features a long celebratory evening of music, with a big stage, big lights, big sound. There are competitions in every class of music. Singers from Georgia dominate the stage, prize winners in the "over 60" category of music. Then it is time for rap, and Russian Rap music blares from the screen.

"That's Roman's favorite category," says Igor.

Roman perhaps listens to it on Yandex, Russia's social media hub, where streaming has freed teenagers from listening to the government-approved versions, ones that omit mention of drugs, expletives and sexual innuendo.

Igor continues his story, describing his conversations with his younger son.

"'Why do you listen to that?' I ask him about that horrible rap stuff. 'Why do you listen to pop?' he replies." Igor smiles, laughing at himself. "He's right. Rap is what he grew up with. Why shouldn't he listen to it?"

But he shakes his head, obviously not getting the attraction, but also understanding the gap between the music he grew up with and the music we grew up with.

Later that evening I ask how they feel about America.

"You should ask that question while Roman is with us," Ira replies. The younger generation, she says, is much more positive about America. "Roman would say the people are all friendly, and they smile a lot . . ."

It makes me wonder how her generation feels about America, but she doesn't elaborate. I read them a draft of some earlier chapters in this book; ones that lay out the fears the U.S. State Department emphasizes about visiting Russia and particularly Crimea. About the American perspective on Ukraine. Ira is shocked that we would have such a negative view of her country.

I slowly begin to understand the size of the gap in our worldviews.

In my writing I also described the Communist years in a very negative way, using the term *evil empire,* as Ronald Reagan referred to it in a famous speech. I thought it was a common perspective, one that we would all share. But Ira is flustered by these comments and says they don't look back on those years negatively. Before it gets awkward, Igor steps in and points out that everybody looks back on their youth through rose-colored glasses.

Together, we talk about why Communism died, and why it all happened so fast. Igor thinks there were a number of key issues, including the fact that one party was in power for way too long and people were just tired of it. He points out the financial impact of oil prices and other challenges coming at the same time that people started being more aware that those in Western Europe and the rest of the world were better off than they were.

"They believed they could just throw off this yoke and achieve equal status with the rest of the world," he says, "but of course it didn't happen that way."

We are to hear later of all the people who lost their jobs after the Soviet Union collapsed. About engineers and professionals, as he was, with no alternative employment. About the serious financial crisis the country went through from the end of the eighties to the mid-nineties. I start to understand what he might have gone through. Before this moment I mostly had thought about what his father had gone through, living through Stalin. But the challenges for him and his fellow Russians who came after Stalin clearly didn't end with the disintegration of that world.

Igor says there are many in his generation and certainly those who are older who yearn for the old days. "It's a fantasy yearning, but that doesn't make it less real."

"Does your son's generation have the same feelings?" I ask.

"I doubt it."

And for sure his younger son has no interest in talking to us about it.

Igor is really good at smoothing over awkward moments, but I suddenly feel like I have been negative and ungracious about their country. They are so warm and welcoming that it feels churlish, and I resolve to open myself up to their view of the world. It is refreshing to be able to discuss sensitive political subjects without acrimony and blame for a change. Our own political situation at home makes that almost impossible today.

Eventually we talk about the DNA testing that might document our relationship. I hope it will confirm how we are related and how close that link might be. I tell them that there are two sides to the testing: the ancestry or relationship piece, and the medical part that could show potential health risks.

I mention that the medical side had been closed down for a time, telling them some movie star had caused a huge flurry of debate on the subject by having a prophylactic mastectomy as a result of the information.

"Oh, yes. That was Angelina Jolie," Ira says.

I couldn't have come up with her name and am amazed she did.

"That's what our news is all about," she says. "It's romance and Hollywood all the time."

"And ours is always some negative world crisis," I say, intrigued by our contrasting perspectives.

Two days into our trip, and I am thinking that I am not learning fast enough, that there isn't enough time to process everything I want to know about their lives. But that thought gets easily buried in just experiencing life together. Whenever we are home, we mostly sit around the table that links the kitchen and the living room. Ira cooks and serves and cooks and serves, smiling all the time. She pauses to listen a bit, smiles some more, notices an empty plate and fills it again. We sit and talk about this and that and not much. Someone gets up and wanders off, Theodore the dog entertains us with mad swirling and barking, people come and go, and it is always warm and welcoming. We could have been in my mother's kitchen, or Lena's mother Galya's, or even Lena's for that matter. The setting and smells would have been similar. The tablecloth, the nice china, the crystal glasses, the piroshki, the potato salad, the pickled herring, the vodka. It is all familiar.

There are ten of us in this medium-sized home, the six Americans sharing the three bedrooms upstairs, our hosts the one downstairs bedroom. They were right: there is plenty of room for all of us. We have all lived in much tighter quarters at various times in our lives, and it reminds me of the camaraderie that those times engendered.

As the hours and days pass, we begin to feel a bond strengthen, a bond of caring about each other, wanting to spend more time together, wanting to learn about the strangers from two countries who share a very rare and unusual last name. We start morphing into the Amochaev clan, out to explore what it means to be an Amochaev, to have grown up in disjointed universes and to have ended up in this very special moment in time.

Our countries spend a lot of energy trying to make us distrust each other. Much of it is deeply embedded in all of us, and even our mutual skepticism about the media, or governments in general, could not make us oblivious to it. But it doesn't seem to matter.

We do not spend much time debating that cosmic divide. We don't discuss Putin or Trump. When we talk about Ukraine it is in the context of Igor's mother and sister, who live there. When we discuss Crimea, it is about the place where Artem learned to swim as a child, the final place where my parents sheltered when fleeing Russia, and where my friend Marina Romanov's grandparents had their summer palaces and walked between them.

We just talk, as you might with a neighbor who stops by for coffee, or as I do when I walk with my friends in the morning or meet them at the neighborhood bar for happy hour. We just talk.

Chapter 28

Ghenya

"Why do I have to keep apologizing? Why do we Russians have to keep apologizing?"

I am on a walk through the woods, alone, taking a breather from the warm companionship. The man uttering these words meets me on a remote road near *Zadneye Polye*, the small settlement where Igor and Ira's *dacha* is located. The words translate literally to "Last Field," but as I find so often in Russian, the original feels romantic and poetic to me, perhaps as "Hidden Acres," or "Secluded Meadow" might. I have slipped quietly out of the *dacha,* for everyone else is still asleep, recovering from a late night of conversation, food and drink.

In early May of 2019, much of Europe is blanketed in cold rain, but here, an hour east of Moscow, where it should be colder yet, the early morning sun is peering over the pine forests and gentle mists are rising over the wild grasses that surround the ponds. Some hawks circle overhead and a few black birds shout outrage, just like my crows do at home.

Walking restores me, and doing so in the early morning, while life is still slow, lets me absorb the world that surrounds me without being overwhelmed. I often find myself talking to my phone, which helpfully records my impressions for future

rumination. Later, when I am back home, I can reflect and process the thoughts, documenting them as I am now doing.

This is my last morning at *Zadneye Polye*. The previous morning, as I was heading back to the house along the still empty roads, a car slowly entered the lane. A barking dog sped after it, followed by two middle-aged men on foot, one leading a heavy old bicycle. The men teased the dog about chasing wheels, then shared the joke with me. I didn't get it, but grinned and greeted them.

The guy walking the bike, whose name was Evgenii, was drunk out of his mind, but seemed quite happy. His appearance was somewhere between that of an educated cosmopolitan and a vagrant; I couldn't quite place him, but he'd clearly had a long night.

This morning I am just starting out as Evgenii is heading home, this time alone. He is trying to ride the bike but gives up as I approach. He has clearly fallen, as his legs are covered with blood and dirt, but the smile is still present. "Hello again," he says. "Where are you from?"

"I'm American."

"Oh." His eyes briefly focus piercingly, but then return to his country-lad demeanor. We're speaking Russian, as we had the previous day, and he clearly didn't expect my answer. There aren't many American women wandering his neighborhood alone, speaking his language.

"Did you buy a *dacha* here?"

"No, I'm visiting people who live here."

I thought he would ask me about them, maybe learn how long I was staying, or more likely just stumble on, heading for comfort among the *dachas*.

Instead, speaking to me in the gentlest of manners, he says, "Why do I have to keep apologizing? Why do we Russians have to keep apologizing?" It is said in a way that made it clear that

he feels horribly guilty, but also is tired of the burdens of the world landing on his shoulders. "Why do I feel guilty about Ukraine? They were always our people." Without waiting for a response, he continues. "I wish people could all just love each other."

Learning that I am American has given him the opening. He moves to an extended commentary about how his country is being painted as the blackguard, the guilty party. For a time, he almost forgets about me as he searches within himself, exploring his feelings. Midstream, he redirects his view back to me, looking deeply into my eyes. "Are you Christian?" he suddenly asks.

"Yes, I am *pravoslavnaya,*" I answer. The Russian word for the Orthodox faith literally means true believer, but it is the religion I was raised in, so it is a safe answer.

"*Slava bogu,*" thank the lord, he says, relieved, and crosses himself in the Russian Orthodox manner, touching his right shoulder first. It reminds me of the old Russian people I had grown up with in San Francisco and the monastery we walked to on Saturday evenings. I knew that post-Soviet Russia had reverted to the religion Lenin had tried to eradicate, but I didn't expect to find it on a walk in this remote countryside.

We move quickly beyond religion as he asks my age. I round up to seventy and a startled look greets my answer, followed by a smile. Again, any expectation I might have of a response is confounded.

"You look so good I could jump in bed with you!" It takes me a bit to comprehend what he means, as I have not heard flirtation in Russian since I was a young girl, but it was not said in a lewd or unkind way. I understand it as a compliment.

Meanwhile he grins and continues. "You could be my mother," he says, "that's our generation gap. But you look so good, so upright, so confident. I could spend a lot of time with

you." His shoulders straighten, his smile grows wider, and the blood-stained vagrant morphs into a seductive Don Juan.

I am too astonished to say anything, but it wouldn't matter anyway. He is on a roll and keeps talking until he suddenly realizes that he is speaking in an informal way to a much older woman. A woman who could be his mother. This simply isn't done!

He apologizes—not for any comments—but for using the familiar you—*ti*—with me. He switches to the formal you—*vi*—and tells me again that it is all meant as a deep compliment.

He moves quickly beyond the seduction that has briefly distracted him, continuing a wide-ranging conversation nearly solo and requiring little encouragement, which satisfies this writer's wildest dreams. He tells me about how his twenty-three-year-old grandmother had fought and died in the battle of Minsk, one of the largest Russian victories in World War II. His other grandfather, who had two daughters, suffered a radically different fate.

"He earned some money and bought a bicycle," Evgenii says, then points at his own bicycle. "They found it, accused him of earning money illegally, and he was taken away by the NKVD." I remember this was Stalin's secret police. Evgenii then tells me his grandfather wrote his two daughters once from the gulag, saying, "I have lost my teeth; I cannot eat; I will soon die."

As he talks, I realize that his grandparents are the same generation as my father. He could have been describing the fate of my family, had they not fled the country in 1920. These were the stories I had come here searching for, not understanding—yet—that I would hear none of them from people who—not affected as Evgenii was by way too much alcohol—always retain the privacy they so treasure. Tearing up, he tells me no one ever heard from his grandfather again.

I touch his shoulder and tell him he is a good man. But as he looks at me I again see the responsibilities of being the bad guy in this world fall back on his shoulders. Now we are both near tears.

He keeps talking, working on moving to the positive, telling me about what he likes to do. He is going to go home to watch the History channel and learn about the Ancient Greeks. He is going to let his mind get free of all this horrible stuff.

Then he says, "You know, it's only the Muslims we should be afraid of. I am afraid of that. I am terrified." And I wonder if somewhere there is a Muslim man saying, "I am tired of being blamed for all the sins. I just want us to be loved."

I keep reassuring him that he is a lovely man and has nothing to feel bad about, but my heart is breaking. He finally reaches out to shake my hand and then he kisses it, wetting it with the tears that won't stop.

"Goodbye, Zhenya," I say, switching to the less formal name he has asked me to call him, as he pushes his bicycle and stumbles on.

I am more touched by this experience than anything I could have anticipated as I stepped out of a weekend house for a walk. I keep thinking about this man, definitely drunk, but carrying the responsibility of his country's actions on his shoulders. Carrying them not just with the pride Putin is working to instill, but with the shame the rest of the world is pushing on him. I feel ashamed of my country, of myself, of anyone who carries an attitude of their own righteousness with them as they travel through the world. And it is only seven o'clock in the morning.

I wander longer than I had planned, enjoying the warming air, discovering a new row of the traditional *isbas,* the wooden houses I so love. These are similar in construction to the house my father was born in. Typically, they are single-story, square

wooden-slat houses with four or five oblong windows facing the street. A picket fence often serves as a divider. Green, blue and turquoise are the most common colors, and the windows are always elegantly framed, often with white decorative trim.

The roads are again empty until a bus on its way to town passes me, and then traffic starts up. I turn around, thinking about sharing my morning experiences with the group.

As I enter the house, I hear voices and laughter coming from the kitchen. The table is already full of people and coffee and breakfast, and Ira is shaking her head, laughing, but slightly embarrassed.

"What happened?" I ask.

"Well . . ." Sasha starts, and Katya jumps in at almost the same moment, "I was awakened by a lot of noise going on outside our window . . ."

". . . some guy with a bike . . ." Sasha continued.

I hear a story about loud voices, an argument, a bit of pushing, a bottle of vodka, and then life moving on to normal.

"*Toljko shtobi Evgenii ne priehal . . .*" Ira is saying. She holds her head in her hands, shaking it, somewhere between laughter and tears. "I said to myself, if only Evgenii would stay away, it would be so peaceful at the *dacha . . .*"

"*Nu vot,*" now Igor wanders in, a knowing grin on his face. I would learn to enjoy hearing those words, which more or less mean "here we go," for whenever Igor utters them, some funny tale follows. "It was dark last night when we returned, we must have missed the flag." His story of the guards putting up a flag to warn of Evgenii's arrival is greeted with more laughter.

I learn that Evgenii is a neighbor and a character in the community. My brother and cousin had been awakened by his early morning arrival, by the brawl he had gotten into with another neighbor, by their final happy parting with that mysteriously appearing bottle of vodka. I joke about his

flirting with me, but not about the rest. That other Evgenii is my Zhenya, one I want to keep close and private. I also learn that Evgenii has yet another persona.

In another life, in the big city of Moscow, he is a successful attorney, a respected gentleman. I could easily imagine that person, and the considered conversation we might have had under different circumstances. But I will long treasure my uncensored peek under the lowered curtain of the protected stage-set of that more civilized world.

Assumption Cathedral in Vladimir, Russia, consecrated
in 1160, was the largest Russian church for its first 400 years.

The Trinity Lavra in Sergiev Posad is the most important
Russian monastery and the spiritual head of the
Russian Orthodox Church.

Chapter 29

Russia Immersion

The days spent at the *dacha* let us ease into Russia. It's very different from what a tourist would be exposed to. We can hang around and recover from jet lag or go for walks in the countryside. But we also visit some of the most beautiful cities and churches of old Russia. My ancestors hadn't explored these areas, far from their Don Cossack region, but I know they were aware of these testaments to the beauty of their homeland and their culture.

Suzdal and Vladimir are the ancient heart of Russia. They have been restored since the Communists left and live up to any of my possible expectations. But I am not sure what to expect when we head to Sergiyev Posad, although Lena cannot wait to see it. My ignorance is appalling, as this is like Russia's Vatican. But for me, it is much more beautiful.

A large number of churches, all recently restored, are covered with gold and turquoise onion-shaped domes. Maybe a bit over decorated, they cover the landscape as if a photographer had set up a shoot with the world's most beautiful models all in one room. On a small rise, the buildings' height and coloration are exquisitely coordinated against a sky that intertwines white

clouds in counterpoint with deep blue. Soaring birds lend a bit of drama, and a nearby overlook screams, "Take a picture!"

For Lena's family, this is like falling into a world they have lived in vicariously all their lives. Their best friends are Russian Orthodox priests, bishops, choirmasters, icon painters. Every church, every saint, and every battle that has been fought and won to preserve this heritage is familiar to them.

Even for me, someone who left all this behind many years ago, experiencing it brings home the deep nostalgia imbedded in our families' memories of a country that they never stopped considering as their homeland.

But all too soon our *dacha* days are over and suddenly I am in a Moscow that is bursting with life and energy. Remnants of the tired city I visited in 1977 are few. The new Moscow is modern, vibrant and clean: a city I could not have then imagined.

Many of the place names are familiar, but the resemblance goes no further. Red Square, then a fairly ominous place, gleams with bold color. People wander through, and there is no longer a line in front of Lenin's tomb. GUM, Gosudarstveniy Universalniy Magasin, or State Department Store, was then a set of impoverished shops that held mostly empty windows. Now it is a regal mall holding the world's top designers in a manner that matches the best of Paris or New York. But that kind of shopping is not really my thing, and I breeze past those same stores that increasingly fill the streets of my home, San Francisco. Grocery shopping, on the other hand, is something I love to do when I travel.

My memories of food shopping in Russia in 1977 are horrid. Gastronoms, the famous Communist food stores, held faked displays to hide the total lack of food. People lined up and waited for hours hoping fresh milk or, perhaps, a few eggs might show up. No one left home without a bag in case

*Elyseevsky Gastronom, opened in 1901, was restored to
its regal splendor after the fall of Communism.*

of such fortune, and I cannot imagine how many hours were
spent on fruitless searches for bare necessities.

This time the Gastronoms I visit are astonishing in their
vibrant surfeit. The sophisticated Gastronom Number One in
GUM with its caviar boutique doesn't surprise me, sitting as
it does among the Pradas and the Chanels. But the Elyseevski
Gastronom, just a few blocks up Tverskaya street from Red
Square, absolutely stuns me with its opulence. Originally
opened in 1901, it could easily be seen as representing the
massively unfair distribution of wealth that characterized
Tsarist times. Imagine the food court at Harrods in London,
or the Garden Court in San Francisco's Palace Hotel. Or maybe
the palace at Versailles converted to a pastry shop to satisfy
Marie Antoinette's whim.

When I first saw it, in 1977, after sixty years of Communism, it seemed like just one more characterless shell of a world that had been destroyed. The interior still held Grecian columns and elaborate counters. But everything was worn, tired, the workers outnumbering the goods. Back then, just making a purchase involved a mind-boggling series of steps that included getting one server to cut and wrap the item, another to hand you a bill and store your purchase away, a separate counter and staff to handle payment of the bill and produce proof of that transaction, and then a final stop to take possession of your purchase . . . if it hadn't been taken by someone else in the meantime.

Now, back in an age of capitalist abundance and social inequality, this Gastronom's shelves brim over with high-end edible goods. The alcohol section is a stunning collection of vodka and champagne. It has been restored to a royal palace of the early nineteenth century, polished up and filled with mouth-watering delicacies.

In my earlier trip I had missed much of what went on behind the scenes of that old Gastronom. There, the royals of the Communist era, including the wife of Brezhnev—the leader of the Soviet Union during my trip there—were being illegally provided with goods by the manager, Yuri Sokolov. I was as oblivious to that fact as I was to Sokolov's subsequent arrest under the leadership of Andropov, Brezhnev's successor. He was convicted of corruption. Then he was executed.

That's right. A man was executed in 1983 for illegally marketing groceries to the top echelon of leadership in the Soviet Union. It is a strong reminder that, nostalgic memories aside, the Russians have put up with totalitarian governments for generations.

My own nostalgic memories get me thinking about another place I want to revisit while in Moscow. Forty years earlier, I had been standing in front of a tea counter in the old, empty

GUM. It was the only spot that held anything of interest, and I thought about bringing some tea home to my father. A young man approached me and started speaking in very poor English. "I know good tea shop," he said. "I take you."

"I know Russian," I replied. He was shocked, but quickly switched languages and told me he could take me to a very special shop. My personality apparently hasn't changed much in the intervening years, as I had immediately agreed to join him.

Russians did not speak to strangers in those days. Not that there were many strangers in Russia then. But if they saw any, they avoided them. Just being seen with a foreigner could lead to questions which no one wanted raised. This young man was an exception. He and I talked as we sped along the city streets. An innocuous conversation; I knew better than to pry.

We reached an elaborately fronted Chinese-style building in the heart of Moscow, and it did have tea as well as some cheap metal samovars, one of which somehow made its way back home with me and now graces my cousin's house. Eventually, the young man told me he was the first "Moonie" in Russia. That kind of fact sticks with you if you were in Berkeley as I was when this cult religion took off in the U.S. The Moonie told me that Reverend Sun Moon was going to visit Russia and promised to take him away with him. I decided right then that I needed to end the relationship. But, as we approached a larger street, he started walking behind me. I turned around, and he told me not to look at him. "It's dangerous for me to be seen with you," he said.

This worried me even more, but not for long. He suddenly leaped forward and tugged at the scarf around my neck. "Can I have this to remember you?" he asked.

I was about to say "Sure!" when he grabbed it, ran down the street, and jumped on a bus as it pulled away from the curb. He never looked back.

I don't know what happened to that young man, but I am heading back to the store he and I visited. The Chinese tea shop is well known, and I find it easily. It now looks very luxurious and full of an incredible selection of teas. People are lined up to buy them. I stand next to a woman who seems frustrated with the long line. "This store is so beautiful," I say.

"*Normaljno*," she replies. "Normal." After spending time with Igor, this doesn't surprise me. It might mean "I'm fine," or "things are OK," and is just a neutral answer. "Are you from Italy?" she continues, looking at me. My Russian is fluent, but I still have that slight accent that people cannot place.

"No, America." I tell her I was here some forty years ago.

"*Peremenilos*," she says. "It has changed."

"*Da*," I murmur, pointing to the opulence.

She is in her fifties, old enough to have experienced those times. Pale skinned, she is dressed in a sophisticated manner that speaks of improved conditions, so I am surprised at her next words. "*Togda bilo luchshe*," she says. "It was better then."

"Oh?"

"Yes," she continues. "Everything has changed. For the worse."

"In what way?"

"It's all the people who have come."

"The people?" I don't understand what she means. She rolls her eyes and gives me a knowing look.

"The ones who sweep the streets," she says. "Moscow should be for native Muscovites. It should be *our* city." I understand she is talking about the people from the various outlying lands, like Dagestan and Kyrgyzstan. I have met many of them, been waited on by them, smiled at them. I wonder who she thinks would sweep the streets if they left. But I suspect she is not alone in her feelings, and it unsettles me.

This visit to Moscow is quite intense. We are in the lead-up to Victory Day—May 9—which commemorates Russia's victory

in what they call "The Great Patriotic War," known to us as World War II. This is the largest celebration in Russia and an opportunity for an enormous parade that boasts of the country's military might. Russian leaders, like those all over the world, know that focusing on pride and victory pulls people away from their disaffections with their leaders, and Putin doesn't hold back on focusing the county's attention on victory. Because of this, many streets in the center are closed. Preparations include dress rehearsals of the march itself, with thousands of soldiers and tons of heavy equipment moving through Red Square. Police presence is enormous, and crowds of people fight their way through a confusing series of mazes as they try to get to work or whatever tasks they hope to complete. Most of Red Square is closed, but I do finally make it to the back of Saint Basil's Cathedral, that most iconic of churches.

Some men are taking down a truck with a tall crane as I come up. They tell me they have been filming an aerial of the scene and would definitely have hoisted me up to create a unique image of me overlooking the church. But I am too late. They are finishing up. Of course, they all ask questions, and I tell them my story.

"*Pravilno zdelali.* They did the right thing," they say, of my grandparents' decision to flee the country a hundred years ago. I remember hearing this sentence at a Buddhist temple in Sri Lanka, on the streets of Venice, and anywhere in the world where I meet Russians. But I didn't expect it in the vibrant streets of this cosmopolitan city. No matter how critical we Americans might be of our own status in the world, so many people would still trade the dream of America for whatever reality has thrown at them. My trip will test the power of that dream versus the longing for a lost homeland.

Standing under the large sign for Amochaevskiy (Амочаевский in Cyrillic) on the road between Volgograd and Uryupinsk.

Chapter 30

Amochaevskiy Is Real?

Moscow is just the entry point to our quest. We are in Russia to explore our families' homelands, the neighboring villages of Kulikovskiy and Serp I Molot, where our grandfathers were born.

Kulikovskiy is a minuscule spot two-thirds of the way between Moscow and the Black Sea, in the middle of nowhere. There is not one well-known city or town that anyone would recognize within two hundred miles. Heading there from Moscow is akin to going from San Francisco to, say, Elko, Nevada.

Not a simple process.

We can drive eight hours from Moscow, or fly all the way south to Volgograd, and then drive four hours back to the northwest. I can't remember why we chose Volgograd, but I look forward to seeing what has changed in this city where I met my first Amochaev in 1977. There is no chance of finding him, for I changed his name to protect him when I wrote my story about that visit, and I've been unable to recover his real one. Ira and Roman are staying behind, but Igor and Artem are joining us, and we all have airplane tickets to Volgograd. Artem and I are still in the process of organizing this part of

the trip. We have yet to book rooms, as it seems the secondary towns and cities of Russia have lots of availability.

"We should work out the details," I say.

"Well, we could stay the first night in Volgograd and participate in the celebration there," Artem offers as we stare at the map in front of us.

"I don't think so . . ." I reply.

There is a special reason Artem is offering this alternative, for it is not just any city we are flying through, and this is not just any day. We could be in Volgograd on Victory Day.

Volgograd, a city with a long history of names, was known as Stalingrad during World War II, and was the site of perhaps the largest and bloodiest battle in the history of warfare. I have long known of the Battle of Stalingrad, but to read a description of the actual event still staggers me. Almost two million people were killed, wounded, or captured in a battle with the Germans which ended with a Soviet Victory in February of 1943. The city was strategically significant as it protected the Volga River, a key route from the West into central Russia. But it was even more significant from a propaganda point of view to Hitler, as it carried the name of Stalin, the head of the USSR at the time. Hitler had vowed to kill all the men and deport the women upon victory—which fortunately evaded him.

As always on May 9, Putin is presiding over the enormous parade in Moscow. This year there are no world leaders in attendance. In Stalingrad, the day has to be particularly significant. I can imagine the emotions that will accompany the marches. But I can't bear the thought of taking part in this crowded celebration, so I thank Artem but decline his offer. I don't tell him the reason I jump so quickly to this decision. It goes back a long way, to when I was in college. I was at Berkeley during the late 1960s, through the free speech movement,

the Vietnam war, and finally the United States invasion of Cambodia. We protested many things, and certainly there were many marches. I had enough teargassing and being chased by policemen for a lifetime. I wasn't even much of a radical. I was just in a controversial place at a bad time. I've avoided political and military parades ever since.

We also have a limited time at our disposal and want to maximize our time in the *khutor* where my grandparents lived. "Let's stick with our plan of visiting Volgograd after we finish the search for our families' homes," I suggest. Artem, easy as always, agrees.

Upon arrival at the Volgograd airport, we get into the rental van that Igor will be driving, and I reflect one more time how lucky we are that this level-headed and confident man is joining us on this trip. Igor has organized the van rentals in every location. He is the only one who could have taken on this role. It isn't just his driving skills I thank the lord for; it is his Russian nationality and knowledge of the system.

I am a confident driver and have sped along autostradas in Germany and Italy, city streets in Rome and Paris. I have driven in every part of the United States. But I will not drive in this country, where I have no idea of the consequences of being stopped. In Serbia, the closest I have come to such a situation, I was stopped within ten kilometers of passing the border and ended up in an unpleasant confrontation when two policemen confiscated my passport in the middle of nowhere while I headed to the nearest town to get the bribe money that would get it back for me. After that experience, there is no way I will drive in Crimea or in any of the more remote reaches of Russia.

And these areas are definitely remote. As we leave Volgograd and head north, it soon becomes clear that there is almost nothing between Volgograd and Moscow. Nothing.

This is our family's Cossack homeland. In 1910, there had been some two million Don Cossacks. The latest census shows 150,000. After the revolution, the very word Cossack could not be safely mentioned. The abandonment of all that fertile farmland led to the famines of the 1930s, and the eventual creation of the *kolkhoz* form of collective farming, including Serp I Molot, where Igor's father was born in 1935. The decossackization, or annihilation of the people, was completed by Stalin, and the territory was relegated into oblivion.

Aware as I am of this fact, seeing the vast emptiness and the shabby state of the remaining villages in this once vibrant land is still shocking. This highway, which was just a gleam in someone's eyes when I last visited here, starts as a well-paved divided carriageway with two lanes in each direction. Soon, however, the housing on both sides peters out. An occasional rest stop breaks the flatness, a few villages. The road narrows, the quality of the surface decreases. There is nothing to see. We make a rest-stop owner's day when the eight of us swarm her restaurant and order lunch. We are definitely her biggest mob. And the food is surprisingly good, but it seems that she is feeding us the meal she had prepared for her own family.

And then, about 20 kilometers before the turn off for Kulikovskiy, we see a jaw-dropping road sign. Igor quickly swerves off the road, and we jump out. A large blue sign with white print proclaims "Амочаевский" or "Amochaevskiy" next to an arrow pointing left and indicating it is eight kilometers away. It is so large that all eight of us can easily stand underneath it without touching. "But Artem, you said Amochaevskiy no longer has many people," I exclaim.

Artem just stares at the sign and says, "Yes. That is true."

"Well, clearly someone lives there . . ." Lena says. The very size of the sign confounds our belief that this village

is in decline. Perhaps the Amochaevs have already made a comeback, neglecting to notify us of this news.

"Let's stop there on our way back," I say. Everyone agrees, and we pile back into the vehicle. This omen makes everyone excited about the possibilities for the first time on the trip. But when we drive into Kulikovskiy, my brain fogs over as I try to reconstruct my visit from forty years ago. Nothing matches my expectations.

Instead of the chauffeur of an important factory chief, it is Igor and the GPS on my phone directing us to a place that still has not a single street sign, and not much indication of progress. As we weave along country lanes, I stare out the front window, waiting for my "Aha!" moment.

But the road comes in from the wrong side of the tracks. Large new grain elevators dominate the horizon where I think the train station should be. No hints of familiarity tug at me. Nothing approaches "Aha!"

We near what must be the center, and Igor pulls over along what we believe is the road with our house on it. We wander about, fairly aimlessly. We could be in any remote part of this country, among the dirt roads we have been passing for hours. It is all very dilapidated, remote, and deserted. I feel a despair replace my usual optimism. Nothing is familiar, and my mind feels like a vehicle being driven on empty for way too long. There is almost no one around. Finally, we find a couple of men who are finishing a small construction project and tell them about our quest. They don't know any Amochaevs, but tell us if we come back tomorrow, there will be people who know the village well, and they will introduce us to someone who could help us in our search.

Discouraged, but more hopeful due to this final encounter, we head back toward the main road and Uryupinsk.

Chapter 31

Backwater Capital

"We can't stay here! This is in the middle of nowhere!"

The car stops in front of our first hotel in rural Russia; the first one outside of the vibrant city of Moscow. This does not bode well.

I'm not sure who said this, one of the group in the back of the van, but the sentiment seems shared.

"Who picked this place?"

That, of course, would be me. And to me it looks fine. Artem and I look at each other. We know we are in a town that is known for its remoteness, but out family is just starting to figure this out.

I realize we have made a major error. We have driven into Uryupinsk from the back of town rather than from the center. I stare at the hotel. It is a nondescript building on a nondescript street in a nondescript town. Artem and I had originally planned to stay in the same hotel in which he and I had already stayed, but modern technology meant we could look at Trip Advisor reviews. They were quite appalling.

"I don't think Vitya could handle that," was Lena's reaction when we talked about it. She was nervous about hauling her husband to the back of beyond on a mission to investigate

a remote village where there probably was not much to see. "Vitya likes his comfort when he travels."

So, I went online and found this small hotel, which sounded much better. Artem thought it seemed reasonable, and we booked it. But now it looks very depressing. It isn't the quality that is the problem. It just feels so desolate.

"Let's stay in the hotel you stayed in last time, at least it's in the middle of town," someone says.

"I'm not sure you guys could handle somewhere that rundown . . ." I reply.

"There must be somewhere else . . ."

Then Artem remembers there is one more hotel to consider, and he leads us to it. We pass the center of town on the way and finally see a bit of life. But not much. Uryupinsk, a town of less than 40,000 people, is officially known as the backwater capital of Russia.

A blog post I found provides some context, saying:

> *The city's unfortunate reputation among many Russians is entirely undeserved, but for unknown reasons Russians began to use the very word, Uryupinsk, to indicate a dreadful hole, or a backwater where no sane person would ever want to settle.*
>
> *There are many jokes about Uryupinsk, for example: How did Uryupinsk beat Venice, Paris and New York in a competition for best honeymoon destination? It won with the slogan: "There's nothing in our city to give you reason to get out of bed!"*

But this town is where we need to spend the night, so we get rooms in this hotel and cancel the first one. It is very pleasant, clean, and has a common area where locals are having a rowdy wedding celebration. As it is already fairly late, we drive to one of the few restaurants in town and

The population of Uryupinsk marching on Victory Day carrying images of family members who were lost the battles of World War II.

have dinner in a busy eatery that resembles a German beer house, with benches and long tables. It turns out the town is unusually full as families have gathered in preparation for Victory Day. After dinner we wander around, finding a goat monument—number one of two things to do in Uryupinsk according to Trip Advisor—and recruiting as our photographer a young lad who has drunk too much vodka to keep the camera steady.

The next morning, we need to head out to Kulikovskiy, but are distracted by two events. We have learned through a

friend of Lena's whose family lives in Uryupinsk—one of those incredible coincidences that seem to fill my life—about a man called Vladimir who researches family trees. We want to see if he can follow our two Amochaev ancestral paths and find the connection that we are increasingly confident exists. Because it is May 9, however, we can't get to the building where Vladimir has his office. Yes, like Moscow, Volgograd, and—we are to learn later in the day—Kulikovskiy, Uryupinsk has a parade.

As I mentioned, I'm not a fan of military parades. But this parade is made up of the people who live in this town. People of all ages are dressed much as people in a small town in America would dress for the Fourth of July parade. Each of these families carries a poster on a pole, and each poster has the face of someone who had died in the military. I am quite certain that half the population of the town is marching and that every fourth person has an image. This is probably going on in every town in Russia. The level of sacrifice to military action by the people of this country is huge . . . and tragic.

The United States suffered around four hundred thousand deaths in World War II. The Soviet Union lost over twenty-five million, more than any other country. That means that for every American soldier killed, over sixty Soviets lost their lives. I would guess that it represented more than half of the military-age male population of the country, as one out of every six people in the country died. I stand and watch the families and listen to songs that could pull tears out of a statue. It certainly gets mine. Here's an example:

> *Here birds don't sing, and trees don't grow*
> *Here we lie, shoulder to shoulder, and fill the earth.*

The minutes I spend watching these people takes away any cynicism I might have brought with me about this victory day.

We do finally make it to researcher Vladimir's office and agree to provide as much information as we have so he can build our family trees. He warns us that it could be many months before he is done, and that the results are not guaranteed. If we learn anything from our travels or our DNA testing, we assure him, we will let him know.

Chapter 32

Kulikovskiy

The drive from Uryupinsk to Kulikovskiy takes less than an hour. Just before we reach our destination, we pass the turnoff to Serp I Molot and agree we will visit it later. A short time later Lena and I stand at the center of the *khutor* where everything we know of our story in Russia started and ended. The glow of optimism caused by the Amochaevskiy signage on the main road was erased by yesterday's fruitless exploration, and we don't see the men who offered to help us find someone who knew our family.

The village is full of people because Victory Day celebrations are being held in the *Dom Kultury*, or Cultural Center, a small building nearby. We enjoy the dancing and singing of the children, and emerge on the dirt road, ready to finish our search for the house where our fathers were born.

"Maybe it was over there," Lena says, pointing aimlessly toward some scattered houses that don't remind me of anything.

"No, I think it would've been here . . ." I reply, equally unfocused, equally lost.

Lena and I had spent hours in San Francisco going over everything we could find from her father's records or my notes from my last trip here. I have several photos I had taken of

the house where they were born. The photos show a corner building, a wooden *isba* that was brown with blue trim on the windows. We have a map that her father had drawn for me. We found some other maps that were also hand drawn, but we don't know by whom. Unfortunately, they don't match her father's, and none of it reminds me of anything. "Look," she says, staring at the small hand-drawn squiggles that had seemed so clear in her dining room in San Francisco. "On the map it could be that one or this one . . ."

"Yes," I reply, "but that street bends away."

"Let me look at the photograph of our house."

I show her my phone.

"You're right; it can't be this one. Ours was made of brown wood, not gray concrete."

"But then the only similar one is that brown *isba* at that next intersection . . ."

"Yes, the one they said is now the city hall."

We walk back up the road, and stand in front of that brown wooden house, hoping it might be the right one. "Look—on the map the cemetery is behind this house, and our house would be back where that cement house is."

"Or maybe we have it all backwards, and it's that empty space across the street. Maybe they tore our house down."

Lena and I realize our conversation is going nowhere, and only when he speaks up do we realized that Igor has joined us.

"Oh, there's a cemetery here?" he says.

"Yes, it is just down this road."

"I want to go see it."

I jump on this idea, needing to clear my head. I also want to see if I can find any Amochaevs buried there. We walk down the dirt lane indicated on the map, past wooden *isbas* that could all be the one we were seeking—but aren't. Children run by, the road gets more rutted and muddier, and then we see the cemetery.

Igor and I head off to search inside it, and Lena goes back to tell the others where we are. I wander slowly through this expansive scatter of graves that cover a territory almost as large as the center of the village. It lacks any order or structure and is full of crosses and stones in varying stages of disrepair. My search is random—any Amochaev will do, for I have no idea if anyone related to me was ever buried here. This will be a long and probably fruitless search. Many of the wooden crosses are of the same turquoise coloration as the *isbas*. Interestingly, there are bright flowers all around. People come on Easter to visit the graves of their deceased family members, and we are only a week or so past that day.

While I meander, trying to maximize my coverage, I note Igor heading slowly along the back fence, never wavering. Eventually I realize he is no longer moving. I wonder what has happened, and head toward him.

Igor stands, perfectly still, in front of a tall metal marker near the end of the long row closest to the northern edge of the cemetery. He is staring at it, as if at a ghost. I walk up, and he reaches out and rubs his hand on the image at the top of the marker, as if polishing a precious gem. It is a face, super-imposed on a small white lacquer oval which is attached to a tall square tower of rusting metal with a Russian Orthodox cross on top. The photo, too, is starting to show rust stains under the screws that attach it. Three more portraits descend below this one. New plastic flowers sit in the earth at the front of the grave. A foot or so to the right stands an old wooden cross, gray and cracking with age. It is unmaintained and has no labels or flowers.

"This is my grandmother," Igor says, indicating the top oval.

I just stare at him, and then at the image. I see features that are stern, in the way of my grandmother, but not unkind. She is looking at the camera, and I imagine the patience required while the photographer fiddled with focus, got the exposure

*The grave of Igor's Grandmother Anna near
the house where Tolya was born*

just right. She wears a dress with small white triangles, but her head takes up most of the portrait. The photograph shows eyes demanding to be looked at, set in a face wrapped in a white headscarf. "Died on June 27, 1973," it says in tiny print. "Anna E. Amochaeva."

The man standing before me seems almost like the same unruffled Igor I have grown so fond of, but something is different. There is something in his eyes that wasn't there a short while ago. "This is my grandmother," he repeats, as if convincing himself as well as me.

"Did you know her grave would be here?" I hadn't realized he had been to this cemetery before, but he must have been. It seems he knew where to look for the grave, as he had walked slowly but directly to it.

"No, I've never been here before," he replies.

We look at each other, baffled.

"So how did you know where to look?" I break the long pause.

"I can't say, but something told me to head this way, to this spot."

"You sure seemed to know exactly where to go."

"I knew she was buried somewhere nearby, but I haven't been here since before she died."

"Really?"

"My father had been transferred to Siberia by then, and we never went back. There was no reason to."

Igor's father was born in Serp I Molot but left long before Igor was born in 1967. Now I realize that Igor had been but a young child the last time he had visited his grandmother. That reality slowly sinks in.

I already know that he never talks about it, that his own son didn't know until a few days ago that Igor had ever been to the place where his father was born. When he was young Igor probably didn't even know there was a place nearby called Kulikovskiy, let alone that his grandmother might someday be buried there. "But how did you know to come right here, to this very spot?" When walking through the cemetery, I tried to maintain a line parallel to his, but kept getting distracted along the way. He did not waver.

"I don't know. Something brought me right here."

Igor has observed my obsessive search for my ancestors as an outsider might—a tour guide perhaps—but not as someone involved in the quest. Now the search has pushed its way into his consciousness, and he is acknowledging his family in a new way. Anna's is the top face on the stone. Below hers is Faina Nikolaeva, May 1, 1932 to September 2, 1974. "That's my aunt Faina," Igor says. Next to her is Tolik, who died in 1964 at age five.

"Who is that below them?"

Igor looks at the fourth and oldest image, which has no name or date. A smiling woman wrapped in a black head-cloth stares confidently at us. There are no clues beyond the shared marker. "I don't know," he says. "I wish I did, but I have no idea."

I look at him and realize he needs to connect with someone dear to him. "Why don't you call Ira and tell her about this?"

"I tried," he says. "It was the first thing I did the minute I found this. But my phone has no signal."

"Here, use mine." I have just enough signal power for him to reach her. I dial the number, then move away to give him some space. Just as I do, I see Lena and Sasha walking toward me.

"Tania! You need to go back to that last house before this road turns off. We stopped there to see what we could learn." They almost shout the words.

"Why?"

"There's a woman there who needs to talk to you. You'll see."

"What are you talking about?"

"Just go, Tania. Just go," Sasha says, directing his argumentative little sister.

Before I can reply, Igor joins us, thanking me for connecting him to Ira. I step away so he can share his amazing story with the rest of them. I have no idea why I need to go see this person but rush back without further encouragement. As I near the final intersection, one of the men we met the day before, who had agreed to help us find someone to talk to, emerges from the rear of the brown wooden *isba* at the corner—the city hall—and rushes toward me. "The mayor is here!"

"What?"

"The mayor is here!" He escorts me quickly to the back of the building that I still think might be the house where

my father was born. It faces in the right direction; it is brown wood and has blue trim on the windows. But it is too close to this track that leads to the cemetery.

I am directed through the hallway into an office lined with flags. A smiling woman who has to be the mayor greets me. She is here because of the holiday, but there is an added tension in the air; a joyous tension. My guide can't wait for me to hear the other news that he has discovered. The mayor's blond hairdo speaks of a salon, and she wears a dark suit with a white blouse. She is more sophisticated by far than anyone I have yet seen in this remote spot, and her smile welcomes me warmly. "This is Tatiana Danilicheva, the mayor of our *khutor*," says my new friend.

"Hello, I am Tania Amochaeva," I say, warmly holding the hand she holds out.

"Oh, I know who you are!" she says. "I remember!"

I just stare at her. This is clearly not one of the old people I met on my last visit, for they have surely passed by now. "But you are so young . . ."

"I was eight years old," she says, "when a woman from America came to our village, looking for her ancestors. But I remember it well."

My mouth drops open.

"My mother told me about it. The whole village talked about it for years afterwards."

"*Bozhe moy*! Oh my God," I breathe, hardly believing her words.

"Was that you?" She beams at me as I tear up.

"It certainly was me! I can't believe you remember!"

"Of course, I remember. And now you are back!"

"Yes, my family came with me, and I wanted to show them the house where my father was born, but we can't find it."

"Maybe I can help."

Tania with the Mayor of Kulikov, who still remembered the American woman's visit from 1977, on Victory Day 2019.

I leap at this unexpected opportunity. "Look," I say, pulling up the old images on my phone. "I took some pictures the last time I was here, and this was the house."

"Of course!" she says, staring at one of the images. "See, it says FAP on the doorway. I know exactly where that is; I'll take you there!"

I had somehow thought those letters had to do with the teahouse I had heard about, but they actually mean that this was a medical resource for villagers.

"Wait!" Someone calls as she speeds out of the office. "Let's take a picture before you leave." They clearly want to memorialize this moment.

We then walk past the Cossack hall to the exact spot where our home should have been. But the corner is occupied by a bland cement brick house, and not the brown wooden *isba* of my memories. "But that's not it," I say, disappointed. "Ours was a brown wooden house; you saw the photograph."

"Oh, well, I'm afraid this is the right house."

"It can't be!"

"Yes, it can," she says. "And it is. The house has been covered by these bricks. It's often done when a building hasn't been maintained and starts falling apart."

I regard her skeptically, and stare at the house. Can this possibly be it?

"I assure you," she continues. "This is the same house as the one in your photograph."

Dreams and memories fall apart one little piece at a time. Mine are going to have to adjust to reality. And suddenly I understand how fortunate I had been in that earlier return, when the home still stood as my grandfather had left it, and people in the village still remembered those days and shared their stories of what happened after he left. I also understand just how remote a spot this has become, for one stranger from over forty years ago to still be so vividly remembered and excitedly welcomed back.

I thank Tatiana, and make sure I have her contact information. She wanders away as the rest of the family joins us. I explain, and we take pictures and compare the house. The location is right, as is the size. It is the windows that finally convince us. There are exactly the right number, five the long way, three the narrow, and in exactly the right sizes and locations. It has to be our house.

I walk up and knock on the door. It is opened by a tired young man carrying a baby. I tell him who we are, and why we are at his doorstep. Amazingly friendly to this mob of

strangers, he tells me his wife Elena's family has lived here since she was born, thirty-seven years ago. Unfortunately, she and their older son have gone to the celebration in another village. They will be back in about an hour. We confer and tell him we will return. There is nothing more to be done here, and we still have Igor's father's birthplace to explore.

We head off toward Serp I Molot.

The house in Khutor Kulikov where Tolya was born. Built in 1910, by 2019 it was covered in cement bricks because of its decay.

Chapter 33

Serp I Molot

Serp I Molot, where Igor's father was born, really is just a couple of kilometers away. As Artem reminded me in the introductory email he and I shared that started us on this voyage, it was once the collective farm that had been formed during the era of collectivization in the late 1920s after my grandparents left. This was where Igor's grandmother Anna had lived and raised her family. Igor's father Vladimir, "a very stubborn person," according to Artem, had survived "very dark times in the country's history." He left the area and studied to become a major in the engineering troops. He served in many parts of the Soviet Union, leading to a nomadic upbringing for Igor. He finally retired to Kharkov, Ukraine, where he died in 2010. He knew little about his own father but instilled an ethic of hard work in his descendants, as I see in Igor and Artem.

When I visited Kulikovskiy in 1977, the people there told me that after the revolution every able-bodied adult was either shot or had been forcibly moved to the collective farm, and only the old and disabled stayed behind. I know my grandparents fled prior to all this, but still know nothing of their many siblings. Igor knows as little about his ancestors,

and his connection to this area is tenuous. Artem queried his grandmother in Ukraine, trying to learn more, but had failed. We are not likely to unearth a family history here, but we aren't yet ready to stop exploring.

Before I came to Russia, I spent a lot of time online, researching Serp I Molot, which means Hammer and Sickle. In history as I had learned it—including my work while a student of the Department of Slavic Studies at the University of California at Berkeley—the collective farms were created because the Soviets had denuded the countryside of farms and farmers. People were starving. Something had to be done. So, they launched a forced collectivization campaign.

What I knew about these farms was horrific and spoke of stripping identity, individual control, and pride from everything these people had held dear. Not only was their land taken away. People were not allowed to leave them, and most of the food that was grown was taken by the government at fixed low prices rather than given to the members of the farm.

Imagine my surprise, then, to read a document that had been written in 2017 by some high school students who lived there. Again, all my beliefs were upended.

> *The history of the state farm "Serp I Molot" goes back to a distant past, in September of 1929, when workers of the large Moscow metallurgical enterprise "Serp I Molot" decided to help the peasantry in creating a socialist economy. They took over barren land, where no homes existed, and began to build the first dugouts, then some barracks, a workshop for the repair of American tractors with the incomprehensible name "Caterpillar" and other machines. By the following spring, most of the able-bodied adults had chosen to move and work there.*

Slowly the steppe came to life. Where only herds of horses could be seen before, tents were scattered over the farthest corners of the farmland. In the spring, the Moscow factory sent a new leader, who would drive it to success over the next decades . . .

This paper was clearly written with great pride in the history of their village and spoke of the successful development of farming over the years, of the men who went to fight the war, of a local man who became famous for starting another collective farm. When I first read these words, I was stunned that this collectivization—which I had viewed as an act of evil—was being portrayed as a poetic renaissance. Had this been written during the height of Stalin's time, I would have assumed they had been either brainwashed or had no alternative to this glorifying. But these were young people sincerely working to develop an understanding of local history so that future students would have a historic frame of reference about their home. They had done a lot of reading and had interviewed the "oldsters" in their village, drawing on their memories and stories told to them by their own parents. They believed in what they wrote.

As I reflect now on the work of those students, I realize that this is their creation story, and of course it would be positive. Why would they look back and search for the negative? It also helps me understand my own grandparents' creation story. Of course, Daria and Ivan viewed the homeland they had been forced to abandon in a positive light, and those who had forced them out as monsters. These diametrically opposing views of the same history demonstrate that it is the perspective one sees it from that matters.

Before I came to Russia, I wrote an email to the school, hoping to meet with someone during our visit, but I never

heard from anyone. School is now out for the summer, and the holiday almost guaranteed that we would not find anyone with whom to meet. By the time we reach Serp I Molot it is afternoon, and all the celebrations—if there have been any here—are finished. The village feels abandoned.

We drive along a dirt road that seems familiar to Igor. On one side is a pond, lined with houses that seem almost familiar to him, but not quite. We see a spot where Igor fished as a child when visiting his grandmother. We turn in toward the center, but there really is no center. One rotting old cement brick building, three stories tall, might have been the house where his Aunt Faina had lived, in a ground floor apartment. He thinks momentarily that we are passing a store where she worked, or maybe where her husband worked. Or maybe her husband was a photographer? He isn't sure, and it isn't getting any clearer as we drive around.

What is clear is that he doesn't want to go explore and talk to the few people we pass. He found his grandmother's grave, and Faina's grave, and this is enough for him. There is no "there" for Igor here. But even if we see nothing here, we have learned something very significant about the connection between our families.

Igor's family must have moved here when the collective farm was first founded. His father, Vladimir Dimitrievich Amochaev, was born in Serp I Molot in 1935, just six years after the founding, and Faina was born even earlier, in 1932. That means his grandparents were moved here from a nearby *khutor*. We had concluded that Igor and Artem were related to us based on our common last name and the fact that our ancestors were born in villages that were only three or four kilometers apart. But finding his grandmother Anna's grave just steps from the house where my father was born helps us understand that his family did in fact live in Kulikovskiy

before the collective farm was formed—at close to the same time that my family lived there. This is astounding.

Kulikovskiy is a small village, and never had much more than a thousand inhabitants. Igor's great-grandfather, Alexei Amochaev, was close in age to my grandfather, Ivan Minaevich Amochaev, and they had to know each other. They lived in the same tiny village, and near to Amochaevskiy, named after their families. We happily conclude that they had to be kin.

With these thoughts in mind, we turn the van around and head back to Kulikovskiy, which holds their ancestors' remains and my ancestors' home. We stop near the Amochaev house and again, I go to knock on the door. The same man answers, a cell phone in his free hand this time. "I'm afraid they're not back," he says.

"When are they coming?"

"I don't know."

"Oh dear." I so want to talk to his wife, but it is getting late and we need to head back. "Do you mind if I look around?"

"Of course not," he says, and turns desperately to look at the mess inside. He grabs a few dirty baby items, and then gives up. "Come in," he says.

I wander inside, and for the first time, I see the house where my father was born. I wander through, passing the bedroom and thinking that this could be where he had come into the world. I doubt that Daria would have allowed the slightest mess in her house, and for sure she didn't have a fraction of the possessions that fill it now. The wall of the baby's room has large posters of butterfly-winged fairies and red-dotted mushrooms. A small cot has pink flowered bedding, the rug is a red Persian design. I try to see my father in it, but it is a stretch too far.

The living room is another story. It is quite large, three windows on one side, two on the other. Lace curtains cover

those windows, filtering the light as they had in my grand-mother's bedroom in our house in San Francisco. Through the chaos of babies' lives and the smell of their damp diapers I can feel the old gracious elegance that was there when Daria married her Ivan.

Until this moment, I never imagined that something this dignified could have existed in this remote khutor. I had never been inside an *isba* in the countryside and assumed they were simple huts. Now I understand why Ivan ordered special glass for the windows and a stove—all the way from Moscow. One hundred and ten years ago, he had constructed this very special home for his bride. No wonder Daria felt such pride in her husband. Clearly, she had made a wise choice.

My compassion for what they gave up overwhelms me. They had lived here less than ten years when it all fell apart, Daria's dreams shattered. She went from being a migrant worker, to a landowner's wife and partner, then to being a homeless refugee in such a short time. The grandmother I knew was extremely tough, but she earned her right to it the hard way.

As I stand in that house watching a male infant react to my presence, I suddenly realize that my father was this child's age when he left this place forever. I do not expect that baby to remember an American woman invading his home on a day in late spring of 2019. That baby won't remember anything about this day, and surely my father remembered nothing of that house, of that life, or even of that country. Lena's father Shura, on the other hand, was almost ten years old when they left.

When I was eleven my family moved from our first apart-ment in San Francisco to a three-story home out near the ocean. My father got his first job that finally utilized his engineering background, and he wanted his daughter to go to better schools than those in our old neighborhood. But I still remember the old apartment, and the sandbox in the backyard that Papa and

Shura filled with bags of sand illegally gathered at the beach in the dark of night. I remember the family gatherings in the kitchen, the Turkish coffee, the joy we felt every time another member of our refugee family joined our lives. I still feel sad when I pass by now and see that the grocery store across the street is shuttered, or that my backyard is now a parking lot. Shura's map and descriptions of this house confirmed that he remembered all this, just as I did my first home.

Now, seeing this baby in their first house helps me understand why my Papa was able to leave Russia behind in a way his older brother never did. Why Papa married a Yugoslavian woman and regretted the flight from that country much more than he could ever regret Russia. I also understand why Shura's daughter, Lena, raised by a father who carried those memories, is so much more deeply embedded in their Russian world than I am.

That man's wife in Kulikovskiy may never forgive him for letting strangers into a house she didn't have time to prepare for visitors. She may veer between that and regret over not meeting us, as I regret missing her and not learning her family's story, not knowing what it was like for her to grow up in this particular house, then raise her own family there. But I am so grateful I walked through these traces of my heritage. Seeing today's Kulikovskiy and Serp I Molot, I understand how easily the past disappears, and how a trigger can sometimes bring it alive.

Artem didn't know that his father had ever been near Serp I Molot before, for they hadn't talked about it until Artem brought us into his family's world. My father didn't even know that a *khutor* called Amochaev existed, or that his father was born there. He could not have drawn me a map of *khutor* Kulikov, where he himself was born, nor pinpoint the location of their house. But his older brother did, and it led

me there. When I came home from my first trip with photos and stories, that brought this *khutor* back to life for them long after they had left it.

What was the probability of any of this? It wasn't only the mayor of this village who found all this incredible. In retrospect, so did I.

My grandfather's house was built well enough to survive a hundred years of neglect, but it is struggling now. I learn after my visit that the smell I suspected of being wet baby diapers is actually the smell of old *isbas* that are moldy when they are covered by cement bricks. I suspect that if I ever visit there again, it might have rotted away.

Living room of the isba *where Tolya was born, 100 years after he and his family fled.*

Chapter 34

Unlikely Encounters

My talking to strangers and telling them I am from America becomes the family joke. Igor can have us laughing in a moment just by saying a few words.

"*Isvinite, ya Tania*... Excuse me, I'm Tania. I'm from America..."

This has led me to learn many things and meet interesting people everywhere along my path. But sometimes I hear things that just create deeper mysteries. And sometimes there are things that trouble me for a long time, as my conversation with Yevgenii had back at the *dacha*.

Today is our last day in Uryupinsk, our base of operations for the region. Another early morning, another walk. I am on a random street in the middle of nowhere. Well, in the middle of Uryupinsk. I decide to walk away from town rather than toward it, for the street holds many of my beloved *isbas* that still have the traditional old Russian coloration and character.

This morning's walk is accompanied by the wonderful smells of blooming lilacs everywhere, and I pause to take a few pictures. I keep walking until it feels like I have really reached the end of town, and then turn back. I stop in the

middle of a block and snap a picture of the store across the street from me. Sitting in an empty space, it is a white and blue sheet metal construction. The name is one that is an example of signs throughout Russia that confound me. Read phonetically, the store is called Iceberg. But of course, the word is written in the Cyrillic alphabet: Айсберг. When I see Cyrillic, I expect Russian words, so when they spell an English word, it's unsettling.

In Moscow I had photographed a building that said: Беверли Хиллс. I showed it to Katya, who is as fluent in both languages as I am, and she stared for a long time before finally laughing. The phonetics and transliteration are Beverli Heels. It shouldn't take an intelligent person long to get it, but it does, and then it's funny. Cheap laughs, I suppose.

While I am staring at Iceberg, a woman walks out of the yard behind me and starts pulling weeds. Her house is not one I had photographed—it is one of the many such *isbas,* like the one my father was born in, that have been covered with cement bricks. Not to be too critical, suffice it to say they do not tug at a photographer's fancy. I turn and say "Hello." I am running late, and plan to just move on. But unexpectedly, it is she who starts a conversation with me. Really. It is she who starts it all! She obviously knows I am not a local and wants to know where I am from and what I am doing here. I tell her my father was born here and left a hundred years ago. Of course. I tell that to anyone who asks.

She is intrigued. "Where was he born?"

"Not too far from here, in the *khutor.* They were Don Cossacks."

"A *khutor* near here?"

"Yes, it's about thirty kilometers away."

"Do you know what it was called?"

"Yes, I do…" I am still reluctant to continue. I haven't found anyone yet in this town who has responded to the name of Kulikovskiy and am quite sure this will be a dead-end.

"What was it?" She persists.

"It was called Kulikovskiy."

"Kulik?" She says, using a term close to the name my uncle had called it.

"Yes," I respond, finally connecting to her.

"Near Serp I Molot," she continues, with the confidence of one who knows exactly what she is talking about. Which of course she does.

I am floored. "Yes."

"That's where I was born!" She beams.

Now I look more closely, finally acknowledging her. She must have been some years older than I, but our teeth speak of our mutually impoverished childhoods. Mine have been mostly repaired after I reached adulthood and could afford a legitimate dentist. She has a lot of gold ones, with a few gaps in the front, and like many people her age she tries hard to press her lips together when a camera is pointed at her. "You were born in Serp I Molot?" I ask.

"Yes, I was. It's right next to Kulik, you know." She pronounces it Ku-lik, and when she talks about it, she says "*Na Kulikah,*" on the Kulik, an expression I have never heard.

I am stunned. "The people I am traveling with are also from Serp I Molot," I say.

"What is their name?" Incredibly, she has led me the whole way into this conversation. "Their name is Amochaev." At home I wouldn't even bother with the pronunciation, I would just start spelling. Here I can say the name and know it will be heard.

"Amochaev?" she says, peering at me, perhaps acknowledging me for the first time.

"Yes, Amochaev."

"I knew some of the Amochaevs. I knew them well. I knew Faina. She was my friend."

"Oh my God. Faina is my friend's aunt." Something compels me to push the little black button on my phone that will memorialize our conversation. She talks about Faina, about the store she and her husband ran. This woman then tells me that she and her own husband had lived in different parts of the Soviet Union, in the far north, in Indigirka. Her husband had passed away, and she moved back here in 1986. "Just a minute." I say. "Maybe you could help me with something."

"What's that?"

I open the photographs on my phone and find the one of the tombstone of Igor's grandmother.

"Oh yes," she exclaims, peering at the image. "That is Faina. And there is her mother Anna."

"And do you know who the person is in that picture below Faina's?"

She looks at it, thinks about it for a moment, and says, "Oh, yes. That's her grandmother."

"Faina's grandmother?"

"Yes. I don't remember her name."

Igor and I had spent some time discussing who she might be. Now I know that it is his great grandmother. He will be so excited about this conversation, I think. I am thrilled to be recording it. Until her next words . . .

"You know it was so tragic . . ."

"What was so tragic?"

"Anna's death. She died in 1973 . . ."

Her comments are interrupted by the opening of the gate behind us. A younger woman comes out and starts berating her mother for talking loudly enough to wake up her granddaughter. But of course, she joins the conversation, and now

there are three voices to wake the neighborhood. When she learns I am from America, she wants me to come back and talk to her daughter. "She's just started studying English in school!"

"Bring her out here, I'd be happy to talk to her."

"Oh no, we came very late last night from Volgograd. She needs her sleep."

I have to tell them that we are leaving shortly for Amochaevskiy and will not be back. When the daughter asks how our conversation started, her mother replies, "Well, I came out to pull some *travka*, weeds . . ."

"She came out to pick weeds and she picked me up instead!" I laugh, and on that laughter we part.

When I get back, Igor is packing up the car. I regale him with my story, and he looks at me, a bit skeptical.

"You're telling me some stranger that you met out there knew my grandmother?" He laughs, humoring me.

"Yes, she did. She was a good friend of your aunt Faina." Now Igor is alert. This is not a common name, unlike Ira or Anna. I tell him about our conversation and then realize I have to let him listen to the recording. When he hears the part about the tragedy, he just nods. He listens to the end, then stares at me and shakes his head. "Another Tania adventure," I can imagine him telling his wife. "She mentioned something about a tragedy," I say, a bit later. "About your grandmother?"

A distant look comes into Igor's eyes. "Yes," he says, "she died when I was young."

I think about her gravestone and realize Igor had been around seven years old when she passed. I remember the rustic wooden cross in the ground nearby, which he simply said was also a family member's. I think about the fact that he had never before been to the cemetery, that he hadn't know his great grandmother was also buried there until he heard this recording. And that Artem hadn't even known that his

father had been to Serp I Molot as a child. But I also know that if there is a mystery here, it will remain one. No Tolstoyan epic would be shared. There would be no maudlin storytelling followed by a drunken brawl. But there is something almost surreal about my meeting his Aunt Faina's friend on a back street of Uryupinsk—the official nowhere of Russia. Our experience at the cemetery takes on a new perspective as Igor and I look at each other, and we both understand that we are on an unusual journey, one in which the past is reaching out and communicating with us in some unexpected ways.

Igor takes a pass on my offer to take him to meet my new friend. I am not really surprised. This man hadn't persisted in finding the house where his grandmother was born. Unlike me, he isn't searching for his past. It is his past—it seems—that is searching for him.

But it is still early enough that he and I decide on one final exploration in Uryupinsk. I had flown there in 1977 and have since read humorous stories on the web claiming that flying to that "nowhere" is a myth and a joke. But I want to find the airfield that I flew into, which now seems like just a figment of my imagination. Its existence preceded Internet days, but a few people help us with directions to where it had been. Instinct and memory eventually lead us to an old field. In the years since my sickeningly rolling biplane—an Antonov, according to Igor—landed on the grass in front of a round booth the size of a public toilet in Paris, a fairly large airport has been built, abandoned, and left to ruin. It makes me understand, one more time, how long ago that was and how much has changed. The world I flew into no longer exists, and this old rotting building is just one more demonstration. An old world has died, and the new one is still searching for its identity.

I cannot resist wandering through the grass where I first met the driver who was to take me to Kulikov, as it was then

known, and where that journey to my father's birth town started. I even find the rusted metal ring where planes were tied down, not much larger than what might hold a sailboat in a harbor back home. Igor doesn't think it would be wise to bring one of those rings home as a souvenir.

This airport is abandoned and not coming back any time soon, and once again, there is nothing to see or do here. We head back to join the others who are ready to depart for Volgograd, via Amochaevskiy. As I am about to go into the hotel to get my bag, I notice a couple of policemen stopping cars in front of the hotel. There aren't many to stop, needless to say, and I decide to find out what it is all about. "*Normanljno,*" one of them says in response to my query. Igor's favorite response to my usual "How are you?" has taken a while to get used to, but now I like it. So, I burst out laughing when the policeman says it about a traffic stop in the middle of nowhere. He doesn't look happy, but the other cop comes to my defense. "*Isvinite,*" I say, offering my hand, "*ya Tania.*" I apologize for speaking his language poorly, in a feeble explanation for laughing at his partner. He starts asking questions, getting my usual life story. Soon, he and I are laughing and talking and taking selfies . . . until the first guy reminds him that he is still on the job.

"*Kak normaljno,*" I hear Igor say when one of our gang asks him what is going on with me and the policemen. It's a great selfie!

Soon we are off, but we have to visit a church on the way out of town. Vic and Lena have never seen a Russian church they didn't need to visit, but I have seen enough, so Katya and I decide to take a walk.

We drop down by the nearby river, chatting with a local fisherman. I am telling him about the Amochaevs—he knows one—and then Katya is posing with him and the fish. As she and I head back to the car, he is speeding back into town,

shouting, "I met some Americans! I did! They are visiting. We talked!"

I could just imagine his eight-year-old granddaughter, many years from now, telling people about her grandfather, who had met some crazy Americans at the river in Uryupinsk, looking for their Amochaev relatives. But we are on a mission, and Amochaevskiy is our next destination, so we head back down the big road.

Katya with a fisherman on the outskirts of Uryupinsk.

Chapter 35

Amochaevskiy

As we drive toward Amochaevskiy, once again, a nervous anticipation settles in. Imagine finding a large sign with the very unusual name of your family, directing you to the place your grandfather was born, and your ancestors probably spent hundreds of years. A place neither you nor anyone else you know has ever been, a place your father didn't know existed for most of his life.

I look up Amochaevskiy and find a Wikipedia entry, only in Russian. It is brief. I learn that the population dropped from 118 to 30 between 2002 and 2010. I would guess that there were a few thousand people there when my grandfather left as a young man at the turn of the previous century. I find a bit more online. The school, which had been under the direction of teacher Olga S, closed on September 17, 2009. The *khutor* still has a postal index, and someone called Alexander Greshnov is listed as a resident. At one time there was a listing for the sale of some farming equipment, but that entry is defunct. What happened to this homeland where my grandfather was born? How did it come to this?

Not far past the exit for Kulikovskiy, we see an imposing sign for Amochaevskiy on this side of the freeway. Igor takes

the exit. And it all ends right there. There may be a large and modern sign, but there is no surfaced road. The car starts swaying through ruts and rocks, and we grab hold of the seats and the ceiling to avoid hitting heads and shoulders.

"If it should rain," Igor says, "it's over. This road will swallow us."

"*Ostanimsa tam zhitj*. We'll just stay and live there," he continues, his humor never fading.

"Are you kidding me?" Sasha exclaims as we bounce over a particularly deep rut.

A branch of the track takes off to the right, but it looks worse. By the time our road seems almost impassable, we can no longer cross over. It is all flat from a distance, but even seemingly flat land buckles and bends and can break a car if you aren't careful. It takes us a long time to crawl eight kilometers over this terrain, but eventually we spy a house in the distance, then a few more. House is an overstatement. A few abandoned looking shacks appear as the mud road widens and then dips into an open area.

This *khutor* is more remote than Kulikovskiy, which after all had a train station. When the local Cossack population was wiped out by the Communists in the 1920s, there weren't outsiders to infill the population here. And, because no collective farm was formed nearby, the people who survived had to go further away to make their livelihood. With only the old and infirm left, and no resources nearby, they slowly died off and were not replaced. By the time Communism ended, it was too late. Here, we can now clearly see the long-term effects of the extermination of the Cossacks. The land is still fertile. Rain would help crop production. The wide expanse of prairies could be productive. But it is over.

There is one home with a broken tractor toward the end of the trail. Two men are repairing it and point us in the direction

of some ramshackle houses further on. The dirt road splits, and we follow one side toward the river. We search for the village, but just see a few nearly destroyed or abandoned houses. Igor parks in the mud as the road peters out.

We split up, and Katya and I approach a couple of sheds and a house from which we saw a man peering out as we drove by. "*Možno?*" I shout, asking if we can approach. I'm reluctant to barge in uninvited.

Three men slowly emerge from the covered front porch . . . well, from the rotting wood that surrounds a doorway. "*Shto?* What?" someone shouts back.

I shout the question again.

"*Prihodite.* Come on," they call back. We walk up to them. Two younger guys move toward us, wearing several layers of dark clothes. One wears boots, the other plastic slippers over socks. The older man, apparently the owner, sits on the front step, smoking and eating something out of a black cast-iron frying pan. I see the wheel of a bicycle in the doorway behind him but can't see any further into the house. The walls and door were once blue and brown, but now are peeling and cracking.

The older man wears only a pair of black well-worn jeans-type pants with a wide turquoise belt. Extremely thin, he looks in good shape, like he has done substantial physical labor in his life. His teeth are randomly spaced crooked stubs of brown and beige leaning as precariously as his home. His chest is bare except for a silver cross around his neck, and his body is covered with old tattoos. A beautiful woman with long hair graces his left shoulder. Olya, her name, is tattooed below her face. They ask a few questions, then tell us a bit about themselves.

"Aren't there any women here?" I ask.

"Oh, no, they have long left. They are in the towns."

"Why are you here?"

"I was born here. This is my home," the older one replies. "And where would I go? I'm old."

"You're not old," I lie, flirting shamelessly. "You're young and handsome."

He preens.

I learn he lives off his pension, one of the others is getting disability, and the third, who tells us he is Petya, lives off his mother's retirement. He points to the house he lives in.

"Can we visit her?" I ask. "I'd love to say hello."

"She's old, and deaf. She doesn't like visitors." That door seems closed.

The older man has been married three times; his three children live elsewhere. One is in the military, another is married. Petya eyes Katya and says, "Are you married? Spoken for?"

"It's close, so if you're interested you have to hurry," I jokingly reply.

Everyone laughs and we start having a good time.

"What do you do here?" I ask.

"What do you think? There's nothing to do here," says the older man. "Sometimes we find work at a farm nearby. But the farmers are disappearing."

When I share this story with someone later, he says, "You know of course what they do. They drink. What else is there for them to do?"

Before we leave them, I ask, "Do you know any Amochaevs who live here?"

"There used to be several of them, but they've all died."

"No," Petya interrupts. "There is one left."

"Well, she's not an Amochaev; she just married one."

"Still."

They tell me her house is past the cemetery, but they aren't at all sure that she still lives there. It is clear that the population must be down to around a dozen.

One of the very few people still living in Amochaevskiy in 2019.

"Anyway, I think she went to town for the holiday."

"The cemetery is just up that hill?"

They point it out, we thank them, say goodbye, and head back to the others.

The house where Petya and his mother live is on our way. It is rotting in place, and large pieces of cement are falling off the walls. The other few houses we pass are in much worse condition. I travel the world taking pictures of abandoned buildings, and Amochaevskiy would serve as a great base, but I am here to find the living, not to document the abandoned.

We walk on and soon approach a woman working a field. She wears a long vest made of giraffe-patterned velour. A purple skirt peeks out below it. Her legs are covered with

grey tights. Burgundy flats match her headscarf. Three more layers cover her top half, and a thick glove covers four fingers of her left hand. That hand holds an old sickle, the blade of which is a couple of feet long. The handle is taller than she is, and she laughingly shows me how she mows the grass with it and tries to teach me. I'm hopeless. Vitya comes along and is so captivated he needs to try. She teaches him, but clearly thinks he, too, is hopeless. As she is about to take the sickle back and get to work, the handle breaks in two. She kindly laughs it off, saying her husband will fix it. I feel bad, and it sinks in that she is farming using a tool that was the symbol of the Soviet Union in 1917. They may have taken the land away, but they sure didn't get far on technique in this part of the country. She and her husband moved from Dagestan some years ago to a village not far away, and they are clearing this lot and fixing up a house to move into. They plan to retire here, so maybe the place won't disappear. But I doubt any Cossacks or Amochaevs are coming back.

We go to the cemetery and wander through. It is more vibrant and colorful than anything in the area. It teems with graves covered with bright new flowers. Picnic tables are scattered about. I feel grounded, walking here, in a place where my ancestors have surely walked and whose traces might still be lying beneath the ground. For someone who doesn't like churches and doesn't want to be buried, I sure do spend a lot of time in cemeteries. There are a number of Amochaevs, and I take pictures in case they could be useful in our family tree research. I am drawn to Peter Ilarionovich, 1925-1991, a near twin of my father in age. His grave is covered with new plastic flowers, and in his picture, he looks like my uncle. I can definitely see a family connection. Ivan Vasilievich, 1906-1984, on the other hand, doesn't resemble any of us.

None of the Amochaevs have the patronymic Minaevich, as my grandfather's siblings would. I cannot imagine what

happened to them all. My grandfather's nine brothers and sisters—whose names we do not know—seem to have just disappeared. Fittingly, this cemetery is one more dead end. I do get Sasha to take a picture of me hugging a black stone with a large happy Amochaeva etched onto it.

Our trip to our ancestors' homes is over, and our group will now shrink as Sasha leaves us. The rest of us head off to Crimea, via Volgograd and Moscow.

Swallow's Nest Castle in Gaspra, Crimea, overlooking Ay Todor.

Chapter 36

Crimea

My arrival in Crimea fills me with nervous tension and excitement. This was the end of the trail of Daria and Ivan's flight from Russia. This was where a year of rough travel in a *telega*, or horse cart, ended. This was where they spent months in a room on the sea, waiting to learn the next step in their saga.

They knew their story wasn't likely to end in the overturning of the Soviet government. Pretty clearly, the White Army was losing the war. But what could it have been like spending months in the once fashionable town of Yevpatoria, wondering and waiting? I remember hearing about those final tense moments. It was over, the ships were leaving, and my grandfather Ivan was away, trading for grain with Crimean Tatars. Would he arrive on time? I want to see where it happened and try to recreate those moments. I want to see the spot where it all ended.

My grandparents had arrived here by horse cart, traveling almost a full year, following a trail we can no longer replicate because it now weaves between conflict zones in Ukraine and Russia. So, we fly, condensing a year's travel into a few

hours. Still we complain about hours wasted as we detour back via Moscow to do so. We arrive at the new airport in the town of Simferopol and stand around waiting for our van to be delivered. Finally, it arrives, followed by another car. The drivers get out, and within moments I learn that both drivers are Crimean Tatars. In my mind Tatars, descendants of a Turkic people, would look like a younger version of my brother Sasha: Omar Sharif-like, with dark features and dark, mysterious eyes. These young men have blue eyes, and one has a round face and light-brown hair, looking like an average Russian—like Igor, for example.

My gang is no longer surprised that I am making yet another connection to strangers.

"Oh my God! You are really Tatars?" I cry. Within moments I am hugging them. I can't resist.

Instead of being appalled that someone is treating them like exotic beasts, they beam at me, and confirm this identity. Of course, I tell them the brief version of my story: that it was Crimean Tatars who had provided my grandfather, one hundred years ago, with the lifesaving supply of grain just as his family was fleeing the Communists. "Your people saved our lives!"

"Yes, well, those same Communists who sent you away wiped out our ancestors, too," one of them says.

"Are there many of you here? I am surprised to see you," I say, aware of Stalin's removal of these people in 1944, in another act of genocide.

"Yes, many of us returned after the fall of the Soviet Union, although some have moved away in the last few years."

So, they were evicted from their country while it was part of Russia; came back to a Crimea that was part of Ukraine; and now are part of Russia again—a Russia that might not feel all that tolerant to them. It definitely redefines the concept of an unsettled existence. My being welcomed to Crimea by the

very people my grandfather Ivan was trading with prior to departure is a circumstance perfectly fitted to this exploration. Every moment of this journey, it seems, sets me off on an exploration that merges the emotional with the historic—one that there isn't enough time to pursue, as the next moment keeps intruding.

I reflect on the strong historical parallels. Crimean isolation and conflicts with Ukraine one hundred years ago are not all that dissimilar from today's circumstances. In 1920, my grandparents came to a Crimea isolated because it was the last White Russian stronghold in the Civil War. The Soviet military was distracted from final victory in that battle by another war, the Ukrainian-Soviet War of 1917-1921. Russia's success in that battle allowed the Red Army—in November of 1920—to focus intensively on the remaining White forces in Crimea. An unusually early and cold Russian winter froze the Perekop Strait and allowed the troops instant access and success. My family and I, the descendants of that losing White force, are again in a Crimea isolated from much of the world because of another conflict between Russia and Ukraine. Ironically, we are now citizens of a country that has sanctioned Russia over this situation. There seems to be no end of repetition or irony.

There is no predicting how or when the current situation will end. Many of the Ukrainian minority that lived in Crimea has already fled back to Ukraine, and it is the fifth year of the takeover by Russia. An international airport has been built in Simferopol and a highway bridge now connects Crimea to the Russian mainland from the east. Will this land once again stay with Russia? I can't say, but my need to touch this soil could not wait for the world to resolve all these complexities. We part with my Crimean Tatars and head towards Yalta.

I am in Crimea! I have come here in spite of dire warnings by my own country's State Department website, but I have implemented all the cautions recommended. My financial systems are deactivated. My iPhone is free of any incriminating evidence. And once more—just like upon our arrival in Moscow a few weeks ago—the moment is anticlimactic, to put it mildly.

There is no tension in the air, no sense of discomfort, of people looking over their shoulders, of discontent with the Russian "invasion." That doesn't mean that my discomfort disappears immediately. Oh no, it has been deeply implanted, and is just hiding. Its maintenance is helped by one major challenge, having to do with my iPhone, which, in Crimea, is useless. Useless. There is no cell signal. None. And the GPS—which works even when I am offline—is somehow blocked, so if I get lost, I have to find my way on my own. If, as my State Department has warned, I am abducted or held captive, no one would know.

Igor and Artem have cell signals, so there is no technology issue. An American cell phone just won't work. The small piece of good news is that I can't withdraw money either. So, if I am abducted, they can't make me give them money via an ATM! Crimea has taken care of my desire to protect my Internet identity. I am unfindable.

We planned the first few days in Crimea as a vacation. The kids want to play on the beach, party, relax. They are on vacation, after all, and will be heading back to work right after these few days. To them Crimea is a playground. Artem and Katya booked a house on Airbnb, and it overlooks the sea. One more time, the mundane takes over the esoteric, and Crimea starts slipping into another comfortable experience. The house is huge, each of us has our own bedroom, there are baths and showers on each floor. It is also unfinished, as

if someone was preparing a high-end *dacha* for some wealthy Russians and got interrupted. In a sense, that is what much of Crimea feels like. Life, interrupted. Before 2014, it was the playground of the wealthy, much as it had been a century earlier. However, the wealthy had been joined by the middle classes, resort beaches lined the coast, and tourists arrived from all over Europe.

And then came the takeover by the Russians, and the sanctions by the rest of the world. The tourists disappeared overnight. The fancy villas stayed in mid-construction, made to look habitable in case someone dared the challenges, like we have. Things are recovering, but international sanctions keep foreign tourist numbers low, so most of the visitors are Russian. This may sound like the beginning of an assessment of the situation in Crimea in the middle of 2019. But I again learn in Crimea, as I have in many places around the world, that I can't make judgements about such major issues by just traveling through a land. I am neither a historian, nor a political scientist, nor a reporter. I am a traveler. I meet people, talk to them, sometimes connect deeply with them, and get a feeling of the place. But this is not the same as a deep analysis.

The first few days in Crimea are a wonderful replay of our time in Igor and Ira's *dacha*, sadly missing Sasha, Ira and Roman. We have long days and evenings together, filled with exploration and getting to know each other better. After one long day we decide to stay home for dinner. We stop in a small grocery store and stock up on everyday items you can get in any local shop—as long as you are in this part of the world. Delicious *pelmeni*—a uniquely Russian variation on small wontons; *smetana*—a tasty sour cream; chicken stock; salad. Half an hour later we sit in the large kitchen of our house, eating and drinking. The drinking of course leads

to singing . . . and to my understanding that Kolya has one of the most beautiful tenor voices imaginable. Vitya's voice, aided by a bit of vodka, rises to a timber that shakes the building. He and Kolya work to coordinate their keys, and Lena, in addition to a great voice, knows all the words. I still remember most of the songs of my childhood and jump in, knowing my tone-deaf singing will be drowned out.

At first Igor just listens, amazed, not knowing the songs. Then "Moscow Nights" triggers his memory. Soon he, too, is following the words to more songs—having looked them up on his phone—and he joins in. Artem and Katya are drawn in from the sidelines, the house rocks. The evening might not be answering Igor's question about why our close ties to his country could have lasted all these years, but he is pulled deeply into that connection and clearly enjoys it. I realize that he no longer seems like just a disinterested observer.

Eventually, the young people decide they need to go play in town. They call a taxi and disappear. Igor and I sit in the kitchen and talk, sharing our perceptions of perestroika and the end of Communism.

I want to hear what he thinks, and I throw out a simplistic version: the people of Russia finally overthrowing the "evil empire" and starting to control their destiny. His ideas are very different, and he is startled at the naiveté of my view. It is one of the very few times I pierce his equilibrium, and feel I am at the receiving end of his judgement. Yes, they knew back in the 1980s that it was time for that world to end. But it was ended by their leadership with an abruptness that made a move to the future impossibly difficult. There was no transition plan, there was no training, there was no discussion. The leaders just dumped their country into the unknown. One day you knew the government was going to take care of you into the future. Maybe it wasn't very much money. Maybe there wasn't very

much food. Maybe there wasn't very much freedom. Maybe there wasn't very much of anything, but there also wasn't the sudden shock of knowing that you didn't know anything about your future. People were simply told, "now it's up to you." And suddenly jobs were disappearing as industry after industry collapsed. Engineers weren't being paid; they left their jobs to sell goods on the street. And of course, those in power already—the members of the Communist Party—knew their way around the system and figured out how to grab the power and the wealth of the new system, becoming the new oligarchs. For most of the people, this revolution left them at sea as much as the revolution a hundred years earlier had literally left my grandparents at sea.

As Igor and I wrap up our evening and head to sleep, I reflect on getting this deeper understanding of some of their feelings here in the same place where that old Russia bid farewell to my ancestors. Their lives, too, had ended with an abruptness that prepared no one for the future.

The next morning, we continue our exploration. Crimea is certainly a place that calls to be visited, and we explore many of its palaces and sites. We take a boat to Swallow's Nest, a fairytale castle perched on a cliff above the sea, and we scamper about the hillsides like children. Our excursion by funicular to the nearby mountain heights of Ai Petri is stunning, and we climb to the peak with its expansive views of mountainous forests, Yalta and the shoreline.

Bakhchisaray, the capital of the Crimean Khanate until 1783, holds the Khan's palace, a UNESCO site. On a hill outside the town we climb to a monastery built into a cave that they tell us was built in the 800s, before the Tatars arrived.

Another morning I write a few words about my trip for friends:

"I sit on a balcony overlooking the shore of the Black Sea, warm sun mixing with the sounds of birds and crickets. Soon cars will start driving on the steep winding roads that circle around this hillside home near Yalta in the Crimea, music will play from speakers, voices will ring out.

Two weeks have flown by since I set foot in Russia on a voyage that melds the past with the present and reaches parts of me I didn't know existed. My mind is stretched with the challenge of communicating in a language I last used regularly over fifty years ago, and I finally understand that seventy would not be a good age at which to learn a new language.

My emotions tumble over each other like stones in a rushing mountain stream whose waters gently bathe yet unsettle them, as we roam the country—letting chance dictate our path—in seemingly random patterns that evolve moment by moment. What else could drive a trip that so improbably originated from a minor typing error made a year ago by a young engineer in a Moscow suburb?

Now my current location could be described as just what it is: a house on a hill overlooking the sea. But yesterday I visited ancient Greek ruins, then the spot where one thousand years ago Prince Vladimir, who brought Christianity to Russia, was first baptized into the Greek Orthodox faith.

The last three millennia have included wars over possession involving Persians and Scythians, Greeks and Romans, Goths and Huns, Khazars and Arabs, Ottomans and Russians, with Great Britain and France thrown in.

In the early 20th century my grandparents and parents were driven from this land, their final departure point on this very peninsula.

In 1945 Roosevelt, Stalin and Churchill defined the framework of the world I grew up in at a meeting in the town at the bottom of the hill—Yalta.

And of course, the conflict over possession continues to this day.

Just weeks ago, I was still concerned about the safety of traveling here, reading dire warnings on my own country's state department website. Today I wander freely, roaming alone on my morning walks, with no Internet access and no way to contact my friends and family should I get lost.

I start each day wanting to memorialize all my impressions before their intensity dissolves, and then sit staring into space as those same thoughts circle endlessly, floating higher into an unreachable space, intertwining and dissolving, then leaving me spent.

My new family in Russia has welcomed me so warmly that I could write volumes and leaving them will be heartbreaking."

Over breakfast I translate that into Russian and read it to Igor. His humor is awake.

"We're going to make a plaque: *Famous writer worked here.* And the rent will increase immediately." Lena meanwhile shows a picture of us near the Greek ruins. "When they left," Igor continues, paraphrasing Madam Pompadour, "there were only ruins."

We laugh and tell him he's great.

"Oh, yes," he says. "*Ya star. Ya superstar.*"

Star means old, and *ya* means I. It's nonsense, but he's always on a roll. He moves on to describe the roads he has been challenged by driving here, and imagines a conversation:

"You rode on *Americanskye gori*? American hills?" He looks at us expectantly, and we stare back blankly. He can't figure out

why we aren't anticipating the next line. Finally, he clarifies for us that *American hills*, in Russian, means roller coasters.

"After Yalta's streets, *Amerikanskye gori* are boring for me." We finally get it.

It reminds me of another joke he shared yesterday about an overheard phone conversation:

Stalin: "*Nyet, nyet, nyet, nyet, nyet . . .da.*" A stream of "no," then a final "yes."

Surprised colleague: "What was that last answer to?"

Stalin: "Can you hear me clearly?"

I never know what to expect next from Igor, but I always want more.

Chapter 37

Livadia and the Romanovs

While Katya and Artem are in charge of our playtime in Crimea, there are two spots that, for me, are required visits. One is Yevpatoria, and the other is the royal enclave of Livadia Palace, one of the homes of Nicholas II, last Tsar of Russia. These are the places, just a few miles apart, where our ancestors and the surviving royal Romanovs spent their last days in Russia.

Igor's awe at our retention of all things Russian for all these years is starting to rub off on me, and increases my determination to explore a place that, geographically at least, was the closest my family had been to royalty in those distant days. While he is amazed at our link to a foreign culture, I am trying to understand the bond with a royal family. What could have created an attachment to the Romanovs tight enough to force Ivan and Daria to leave their home and their country with no alternative future lined up? How could that tie have sustained them through two exiles and for the rest of their lives?

My time with Marina Romanov at my daughter Beth's home in Colorado started me on this exploration, and I learned that her grandparents, like mine, departed Russia from Crimea. It is but an hour's drive from the palace where the Romanovs

Heading toward the Tsar's Palace of Livadia on the trail from Ay Todor,
the palace of Marina Romanov's grandmother.

spent over a year waiting to learn their future, to the "regal" rooms in Yevpatoria where Daria and Ivan found shelter while waiting to learn their own destiny. I have spent hours reading history books and autobiographies by Marina's grandfather Grand Duke Alexander and her uncle Felix Yusupov, assassin of Rasputin. I feel like I know these places I am now approaching, for they wrote in detail of their time in these palaces. I know that Marina's grandmother Xenia met her future husband as a child while playing at Livadia with her brother. That she later spent time in nearby Ay Todor Palace, her husband's summer home. That they all strolled on a path between those palaces, and also visited the Yusupov Palace, which their extraordinarily wealthy son-in-law called home.

My determination to find my own grandmother's home paid off but took a lot of persistence. Now I want to see the palaces that played such a key role in the lives of Marina's grandparents. It should be easy—after all, no one covers a palace with cement blocks, as they might with an old *isba*.

Livadia is a major attraction in Crimea, mostly because of the Yalta Conference held here in 1945, at the end of World War II. Long after Tsar Nicholas II had been assassinated, Winston Churchill and President Franklin D. Roosevelt met with Stalin here, in sessions that set the global political stage for the rest of that century. Today, wax versions of these men sit at the same table, and tourists wander through, snapping photos. I am sure all traces of royalty were wiped out prior to that event in 1945, but they are back, reinstated in these post-Communist days. Now both worlds can be viewed in concert, and a wax version of Tsar Nicholas II plays a prominent role in the palace as the complex history of this land keeps shifting.

The grandeur of the place is impressive, but subdued. As I wander through, I try to imagine young children running

around, their nannies never far. I try to imagine a childhood of controlled excess, of rigid rules, of a consciousness of responsibility. It doesn't work, I cannot make it come alive. For me, this is like wandering through Versailles when I was a college student in Europe for the first time. It is as impersonal as any other palace I have wandered through in my many travels, although far less elaborate than many Maharaja palaces in India. And I don't need to look that far. I keep remembering the Gastronom and GUM in Moscow, which are far more elaborate and lavishly restored. And then I learn that this palace housed a mental institution between the conference and the end of the Soviet Union. I think of the current conflicted environment it survives in. The place feels unsettled, as if it cannot amalgamate all its past lives: Stalin sharing a room with a tsar and mentally disturbed youth?

I keep wandering, now thinking about Marina's family spending their last years in Russia near here, probably knowing—much better than my family did—that there was no going back. What memories of these years did they bring with them into their new lives? What did they pass on to their children? How did Marina carry that burden? My family held on to that dream for a century. Did hers? I am no closer to answering that question than I was before my arrival here.

But I need to be outside the palace. The real reason I want to explore Livadia has to do with its proximity to Ay Todor, the palace of Marina's grandparents. I ask a few of the guides about it. One of them smiles and walks with me out the door.

"See that trail?" she says, pointing to a neat pathway heading west and a bit south, towards the sea. "That is the trail to Ay Todor." She tells me that this trail has been here since the beginning of the last century, and I realize that this is the path I have been looking for. "Tsar Nicholas's sister Xenia lived there, and she and her husband used to walk that trail and come here for tea!" she says.

At the end of this trail is the story I am seeking. Ever since I learned that Marina will not be coming to Russia in the near future, I have been determined to photograph her family's old palace. Katya joins me and we head off, starting boldly. Vitya and Igor follow, take a few pictures, then get bored and head back. The road wanders for a bit, then the quality deteriorates, and we hit several detours, and then a dead-end. It's clear we won't get anywhere. The distance is theoretically between four and seven kilometers, but no one really knows for sure. And since our phones don't work, we can't call and let the others know what we are doing.

"Katya, you are extremely sweet to be persisting in this, but we need to head back. They will be worried."

"Are you sure, Tania?" Katya wants to support me, but it's not looking good.

"Yes, let's drive the van in this direction and see what we can find."

The others are relieved to see us, and we head off. One more time the roads of Crimea snaggle us. Yes, this is my new word for this particular spot. We wind and roam, and reverse ourselves and roam some more, and hit a dead end, turn around and try again. I ask for directions, and we persist. At last, we see the end of the Tsar's trail that we have been following. But it doesn't lead anywhere. Finally, we know we are not going to get any closer. Igor parks and I set off trying to figure it out on foot.

By now I know that there is no more palace, for Ay Todor, too, is a sanatorium. I'm not even sure exactly what a sanatorium is, except it is a place people live while they try to heal. I keep searching, but any likely opening I find is barred, and I am not allowed entry.

The last time Marina's family was here, they were under house arrest. They weren't even allowed to stay in their own palace of Ay Todor but were moved to the nearby Dulbur

Palace while their executions were debated. Dulbur Palace has now also been turned into a sanatorium, but it still holds an imposing pride of place with its beautiful Moorish architecture. We have passed it several times in our driving. But it is Ay Todor I seek. In 1919 the family was saved by the bizarre circumstance of the Germans appearing after the Soviet government signed a peace treaty with Germany to end Russia's participation in World War I. The Germans protected them from the Communists until Xenia's uncle, the King of England, sent a ship to save her family. Altogether, they spent almost two years on this small spit of land before leaving the country their family had ruled for three hundred years. And after they left, the palaces became symbols of a past better forgotten. It's incredible that there was such a surfeit of palaces that they were mostly converted to sanatoria for the unwell and the insane. Or perhaps for those declared insane by the Communists.

I stop myself one more time from pursuing this channel of thought and am grateful instead that my own ancestral home never shared this fate. What's a bit of cement covering, after all? I have found no reference to Ay Todor on the web that could help me in my search and being on the ground for once doesn't benefit me in the least. I finally concede defeat. I will have to return to Marina empty-handed. And whatever power forged that link between my peasant ancestors and the royal family they sacrificed their futures for, I cannot find it here. I declare failure and we retrace our way through the maze of roads.

Chapter 38

Evpatoria

For almost a hundred years our families carried an icon of Russia within us just as my grandmother had worn a delicate gold cross around her neck. But the average Russian experienced a different reality.

Ours was a Russia preserved through memories and stories, through songs and poems, through religion, through food. It was a vision far more romantic than life could ever have been. Our families had spent a hundred years remembering and recreating that reality. The Russians who had stayed in their country spent many of those years forgetting, or learning a history that was constantly being rewritten. In the Soviet Union, the pre-revolutionary years were considered times of evil and oppression. Why would anyone want to remember its customs and culture? Religion, for them, was a way to perpetuate that oppression. It, along with all other symbols of the past, was eliminated. The Tsar and his family were long forgotten; it was assumed they had all died. The 1920s and 1930s led the way to Stalinist terror and totalitarian rule. The threat of the gulags made any discussion about history life-threatening, so I imagine those who survived learned not to mention the subject. Thus, Russia moved forward and definitively chose to

forget the past that we—the White Russian refugee community around the world—were committed to remembering.

As I consider all this, I cannot come up with a way to explain the long tail of that exile. One hundred years does seem far beyond anything possible. And yet, as I sat in that kitchen above Yalta and joined my family in singing Russian songs, my laughter was tinged with tears. I am living proof of its persistence.

On our final evening in Crimea, we sit in the dining room of a small hotel in Yevpatoria, the same town where Daria and Ivan had spent the last night of their journey into exile. As we enter, a Russian guest starts asking us about our backgrounds. But before we can respond, she says, looking at Igor, "I know this one is Russian, for he has *surovye* eyes." And then she turns toward Katya and says, "and her eyes are *blestyashiye*."

That Katya's eyes glow is easy to translate. "*Surovye*" I am still pondering. It could mean deep, or sad, or cold, or closed off. As so many Russian words are, it is profound and poetic. It makes me think about Igor and our relationship, which in its own way is still evolving. He no longer just watches the family sing; he joins in. He gets out there with his camera and videos, certainly wanting to share it with Ira when he returns home. He smiles a lot more than he did at first, though he still retains that perfect straight face when sharing a joke.

This evening, the hosts join our celebration, their daughter performs American pop songs with Kolya, we fill another room with music, noise and laughter. After dinner, when a fair amount of vodka had gone down, there is a bit of a commotion, and then Lena stands at the front of the room. In her hand she has a tray with a small crystal glass on it.

"We have a custom," she says, "in which we honor those who are very dear to us, those whom we hold in high regard." Vitya and Katya and Kolya join her, and she then asks Igor to

come up. He self-consciously moves from his comfort zone in the rear and stands as far away from her as he can. But Lena is nothing if not relentless, and soon he stands facing her, almost touching, not knowing what to expect.

Suddenly, they burst into a boisterous song we all grew up with, one saved for special moments. A graduation. A special birthday. An engagement. It is an old Cossack favorite called *Charochka Moja*. It basically says: here's a drink on a gold tray, drink it in your honor and health.

As the honoree starts drinking, the group repeatedly shouts, "*Pei do dna*," bottoms up, until the glass is empty, and then a loud "*Oorah!* Hurray!" finishes the toast. As we sing this for Igor, it is clear to all of us and everyone in the room that we are celebrating with deep feelings his role in making our voyage one of such joy.

Igor is not left untouched by this experience. His eyes are definitely no longer *surovye*. Tears appear in many of the Russian eyes that surround us. Like Igor, they are deeply moved by the *charochka*.

We sing more Russian songs. They have heard of some of them, like one about the Black Sea, but they know them only vaguely, and they certainly don't sit around singing them as a family. This in the end is what flabbergasts our hostess to the extent that she cannot stop talking about it. Indeed, she talks on and on. About how amazed and excited she is that this group of Americans has shown up in her hotel to reintroduce an old Russia—one which she had never experienced—to her. To re-introduce a romantic love of a country which those who live here either left behind long ago or never knew. A love for a Russia which must have been killed by the Soviet Union, by a series of leaders who took them on a tortuous path into this present. She is speaking about what my grandparents took with them and re-created everywhere they went. Her words

give me great joy. I begin to understand that we have lived experiences that they never even imagined.

Very early the next morning I walk back through that room, which is again bustling, breakfast preparation underway. I grab a *sirnik*—a roll with semi-sweet cheese inside which Ira got me addicted to—and go explore Yevpatoria. As they would continue to do so for a long time, the moments of that previous evening roll through my mind, haunting me. It's a vision of a world dying before my eyes. The community of Russian descendants of those who were exiled during the revolution, while tight, is shrinking with each passing year. The many thousands like my parents who came to the United States in the aftermath of the second world war have passed or are in their 90s. Their children, like Sasha and I, often married Americans and moved on. Only a handful like Lena and Vitya have passed this deep commitment on to their children. And while Kolya is still deeply immersed in it, it is clear to me that Katya has started moving on, her American boyfriend a first step in that direction. And so that world is shrinking, and it might be the last community that is holding on to a concept of being Russian which is preserved like an old-time photograph, one that is unique and whose loss is heartbreaking.

I watched Igor puzzle over its very existence, as I often have. But during this voyage I have developed a new appreciation for the power of this magical hold, and a gratitude to have participated in it and to have a family who has maintained it so powerfully.

The hotel we are staying in is on a strip of beaches where Igor once brought a young Artem. As I head into town, I try to imagine which hotel they had been in. I am distracted by an old electric tram—whose exact twin runs on the "F line" in San Francisco—suddenly clattering by. I learn that this tram

system was set up before Daria's arrival, but perhaps they were not able to use it as its operation was suspended for the duration of the wars. Entering town, I pass the minarets of an enormous mosque, several churches, a stately old hotel, and a Jewish temple. It reminds me that Tatars are Muslims, and that this is definitely a unique city.

I walk the streets in the glow of my thoughts, accompanied by the songs of starlings and the cooing of doves. An occasional tramcar passes, people buy coffee at shops along the water, and slowly Yevpatoria comes awake. It is a city of 100,000 people, and it feels provincial and innocent. Any possible thoughts of threat tied to Crimea have dissolved for me in the joy of my time here. I feel like a baby who has been dipped in the christening fount and emerged a believer. There are street cleaners all over the city, and it is tidy and swept clean. Yevpatoria starts feeling like a special place, one that connects me to my grandparents.

And I am not just exploring. I am searching for the house where they lived while awaiting their fate.

I pass a theater, then a large movie house, and across from it another area full of trees that looks like the square in my hometown of Healdsburg, but significantly larger. The street widens, there is a walking path through trees in the middle, and 19th century houses line the way. I can easily visualize my grandmother spending those days here with her husband, her children, and her mother. I suspect not much has changed. I imagine her regret at leaving this final shelter.

Deep in the heart of town, I now need to head to the water, where the ships departed. I have researched where the port had been, where the ships docked, and where they spent their last months. When I finally check my map, I realize I have gone past the terminal in my excitement. One dead end after another forces me to retrace my steps, counting the minutes

I still have left before I need to return for our planned 8:30 breakfast meeting. And still this deep joy permeates me.

Three policeman and a policewoman stand on a corner, staring at me suspiciously. I walk up to them, smile, and ask if I could take their picture. They finally say yes after confirming it is not a video. Then I ask if I could take one of me with them. "No," they say. "You cannot be in a picture with us." I move on and enter another large square, with statues and chairs and fountains. I pass more attractive 19th century buildings. "*Could they have lived here?*" I ponder with every distinctive building I pass. But they are either too large, too ornate, or just too far from the water. Somewhere, though, there is a sophisticated old building that had been made available to a refugee family. Could it still be intact?

I pass the site of an ancient Greek excavation. Another museum, another park, more and more beauty. And all somehow preserved through the wars that destroyed so much of this country.

Unfortunately, I hit a dead end after a quarter-mile-long promenade to the water, and there are no turns in the direction I need to head. I walk back toward the main street. I know I will be late. *If only,* I think, *if only I could take a taxi without calling one by phone. If only I could take an Uber. If only my phone worked, and I could call Igor and get him to come pick me up. If only, if only . . .* But to be here wandering in this city so joyously compensates for everything. Almost.

I finally start working my way along the water and understand the issue. The shoreline around the old shipyards is all fenced off, and I can't get near it. My joy dissipates as old metal fencing forces me away from the water. I stumble around, hoping to find a way in, but all the passages here are blocked. I'm ready to give up and head back. Turning in toward the city, I am soon back on the busy road. But I cannot resist and

ask one more person. She kindly tells me I can pass through the churchyard of the cathedral she has just emerged from. It is celebrating its one-hundred-year anniversary, as it opened in 1918. A positive omen.

I exit the churchyard and suddenly I am at exactly the point I have been trying to reach: the old docks are in front of me. I am so close, but now I am seriously out of time. I must run back. This is particularly frustrating as it is my second quest and our last day here. I spent yesterday afternoon searching while the others hung out on the beach, savoring the sunshine, the sand, Igor and Artem's memories of the old lighthearted Crimea. But I am getting so close. I know I am!

I haven't found the one house I am seeking, but my steps are lighter as I head back for breakfast. There, the table bursts with food. They all tease me about my predawn wandering, and about any new friends in the city. "So, did you find it?" Lena asks, going directly to the point.

"No. But I got a lot closer than yesterday."

"You found the pier?"

"I think so. It's all fenced off. There are metal walls all along the harbor." They hang on my every word. "But I found a way in."

This raises the level of suspense, and soon we all wander back together, a chattering crowd.

"See all these fences?" I point. "I wonder if this is because of the current conflict with Ukraine."

"I don't think so, Tania," Igor calmly replies. He is aware of my frustration with the challenges of getting into the ship loading areas. "This is heavy equipment and hard-hat work territory. I'm sure they'd close it off around your home as well." His voice of reason resonates. I think of Hunter's Point and the old dockyards in San Francisco and remember the same complex fencing when I wandered there with Sasha a few months ago.

We walk through the churchyard, somehow avoiding the requisite church visit. We emerge at the piers.

The sea is before us, the town at our backs. We pass fenced-in derelict old boats and some fishermen, and then an old blue building. We learn this is the old customs house, the only building of the old port that is visible. This customs house was the marker we have been seeking. We are at the departure point for the exodus.

We walk out along an old rotting pier and stare out to sea. I try to imagine ships full of jostling people, crowds pushing their way onto them. It doesn't work. It is just a tired and abandoned old seaport. In the other direction there are churches and mosques; a Ferris wheel; greenery, some trees. We take a few photographs and head towards the buildings that edge the city. Then I see it.

Facing these remnants of the old docks where the evacuation of Yevpatoria had taken place in November of 1920 is an old but well-maintained house that is two stories tall and several hundred feet in length. It is pale blue with white windows and is of a somewhat ornate nineteenth century European style, with columns and arches and a domed roof over the central entry. Suddenly I know. I just know. I walk almost robotically towards it, not saying a word to anyone. They follow me, and soon Lena catches up. I suspect we have the same thoughts. We both know. This is it.

This is the house where Daria and Ivan spent months waiting to learn what was next. Like Igor knew to head straight to his grandmother's marker through a cluttered graveyard, I have worked my way through this ramshackle shipyard to arrive at my grandparents' temporary home. I no longer remember precisely what Babusya had told me about it, except that it was directly across from the port where the ships left, and that they lived on the second floor, at the top. But Lena had

Amochaevs in front of the "regal" house where Daria and Ivan awaited the end of their lives in Russia during 1920. From left, Igor, Lena, Katya, Tania, Kolya, Artem.

recorded her father talking about it not long before he died. Shura made a funny comment. "I remember I went to the water and fell in," he said. "My father pulled me out and told me if I fell in from the boat it would be all over." You would not want to fall in from these crumbling cement docks. But his significant statement was almost a throwaway. "We lived in a *barskyi dom*," he said, "which faced the water. It was right near the port." A "baronial house."

This has to be it.

Lena and I check it against our memories of all the stories we have heard. She agrees, this was their house. There

is no other like it in the area. We walk back and forth along the sidewalk that fronts it. We sit before it, pose with smiles, wander about. And finally, I can envision it. Where now a few tired fishermen face some rusted and dirty small boats and water laps on crumbling cement, there was a radically different scene. I imagine that frantic departure. Seven thousand people crowded onto several battleships, families torn apart, chaos, bedlam. The final miracle of my grandfather arriving just as the ship—the minesweeper, Tralschik T-412—was departing, and the friendly Cossacks lowering the gangway for him to board. Their departure, their last view of a country they would love for all their lives. And the final tragedy of my father's grandmother Natalia, who couldn't abandon her homeland, disappearing at the last moment. Never to be heard from again.

Tragedies and miracles.

Life, fully lived.

Chapter 39

Moscow

I am sated with a trip that has established a close link with people who are my family, although I still have no idea how we are related. I have found the house where my father was born, in the same village where Igor has found his grandmother's grave. I have met a woman who knew Igor's aunt and identified his great-grandmother on the gravestone. I have visited a place that shares my last name of Amochaev and saw its decay. Lena and I have sat in front of the house where Ivan and Daria spent their last days in Russia and stared at the port where that final ship departed, with them on it. We are nearly done, and Katya and Kolya have to head home, but I want to re-explore the city of Moscow, which I visited once, forty years ago. I will spend almost a week here, with no schedule or plans, just a desire to revisit a city that has been transformed since that visit.

Before leaving San Francisco, I had unearthed an interesting box of old papers. In 1977, I had gone directly from Russia to studying at the Stanford Graduate School of Business. My mother lived in nearby San Francisco, and I must have left everything from that trip in my old bedroom before heading to my apartment in Palo Alto. In a torn envelope I found a receipt

View of the Kremlin from the suite of the Hotel National, where Tania stayed in 1977 and again in 2019.

that confirmed my stay at the Hotel National, one of the finest hotels in Moscow, with a view of the Kremlin, and learned the astounding fact that I had paid twenty-seven rubles a night. These were old rubles, converted when the Soviet Union fell to new rubles at one thousand to one. And today, there are around sixty of these new rubles to one U.S. Dollar. So today, twenty-seven old rubles are worth an insignificant fraction of one penny. But, as Igor points out to me, while twenty-seven rubles for a room in the finest hotel in Moscow may not have seemed like much to me, an engineer in Russia earned one hundred twenty rubles a month in those days. Reminding me again that everything in life is relative.

Determined to recreate the memories of that stay, this time I book my last few nights in a Kremlin view room for substantially more than twenty-seven rubles. The night before check-in, I receive an email from the hotel welcoming me and asking if I have any special requests. I jokingly ask them to meet the price of my previous stay. They reconfirm the existing reservation for Tania Amochaev.

I am welcomed upon arrival as an old friend, especially when they realize I speak their language. "*Nu, eto Tania*, well, here is Tania," the receptionist says. Several people emerge from behind the reception desk to greet me, and a lovely woman walks me to my room.

When I enter, I have to pause and draw a breath. I stand in a royally appointed ruby-colored salon that faces the Kremlin. Two tall windows with lace curtains frame a round table that holds a bottle of fine iced champagne. To me, the room resembles both the Livadia room that a wax Tsar Nicholas stands in, and a room in an old *isba* that my grandmother moved to in 1910. The only thing they have in common are lace curtains filtering sunlight, but lace curtains play a big role in all my childhood memories. The bedroom next to the

salon is so large it could be another suite in itself. Then I am invited back through to see the other side of the chamber. The hostess smiles knowingly at me. "This is a special room, just for you. We knew you might like to write, and it is a small study."

"How did you know I write?"

"We researched you, of course," she replies. "But is Romanov really your name?"

"Well, it's actually my grandmother's."

"Oh, so you really are a Romanov," she says, in awe.

I suddenly understand why they have so anticipated my arrival: they know I am author Tania Romanov.

"Oh no, I'm not that kind of Romanov," I say, knowing exactly what she has in mind. "My grandmother was far from royal. She was a farmworker, a migrant."

"Oh, I understand," she says. But I'm not sure she believes me, and it doesn't change their attitude toward me. The treatment I receive for the next few days certainly feels royal.

It makes me think of my friend Marina, the real Romanov. She told me she was reluctant to come to Russia, because she is a very private person and is uncomfortable with the publicity her visit might generate. It is easy for her to stay under the radar in her small-town life in America. This visit demonstrates to me that she could not retain the privacy she enjoys if she were to appear here. Russians venerate the life that they rejected one hundred years ago. They romanticize their past in a way that is easy for me to understand, for I grew up with that romantic notion of a fatherland. It is buried deep in my psyche. I am learning that neither they nor I have really let it go. I suspect that is why I travel to remote and abandoned old villages in search of my past; why I carry DNA kits and hope to find that Artem and Igor are relatives; why I seek an expert to research our family trees. It has led me to many explorations, including writing about my experiences. In documenting my

journey, I take individual incidents and see these fragments form an image, like the stones of a mosaic that seem random until you view them from the right distance and angle.

Another incident in Moscow helps shape my mosaic, arranging the past and the present, the familial and the foreign, into a larger image. On a night in a different hotel, I approach my corner room on the seventh floor. A man sits outside my door, wearing an earpiece, a suit, and, I think, a gun. I am a bit surprised, as it reminds me of the keepers that used to sit on each floor of hotels in the Communist era. "Won't they let you in?" I say, somewhat jokingly, in Russian.

"No, it is I who control entry," he replies, quite seriously, pointing to the room next to mine. I smile and enter my room, locking the door behind me.

When I leave for dinner, he is still there, just being replaced by another similarly large and imposing character. I ask the woman at the front desk about them, but she has no idea what I am talking about. A third man whom I had observed on my floor is standing nearby and overhears my question. "We are private guards," he explains.

"Oh, does that mean I will be safe from terrorists?" I persist in my teasing.

"Absolutely," he replies.

"Oh, good, I won't worry about coming home late, then."

"Actually," he backpedals "we just want to be sure he doesn't have a medical problem while staying here." Clearly a reference to the man they are guarding.

When I get home at midnight, this same man is sitting in the hall. I ask him if he has to sit there for eight hours, and he says he doesn't, but that they do provide 24-hour support.

When I check out, I ask the woman at the front desk if she would just tell me the nationality of the man in the room. She agrees to look up his record. Her next words stun me.

"Oh, he's American," she says. I promised I would only ask her one question, and this is all I am to learn, as they had left very early that morning. She and I exchange a conspiratorial smile, but I still scratch my head trying to figure out just who he might have been, and what he feared. I have experienced some trepidations about traveling in my life but have never considered just bringing a private guard with me.

These days in Moscow unfold gently, as I have some social events planned for the evenings, but my days are mine to explore alone. I increasingly need that solo time when I travel, letting my feet drive me along, and my instincts teach me what I need to experience. I step out of the front door of the hotel and say hello to the doorman. He grins at me in a funny way. I smile and give him a questioning look. "I'm the same man who just welcomed you off the elevator," he says.

"And I'm the same woman who didn't recognize you yesterday, either," I tell him, laughing.

"Oh," he says. "That's lovely. We have a saying that if you are not recognized by someone you will have good luck."

I walk off thinking it would take a country of people who can manufacture good luck out of bad news to survive the lives they have been forced to live.

Churches are everywhere in Moscow and they pull me in. The contrast of beautifully painted walls with the scarf-covered women cleaning them gets me hooked on photographs in the style of old Dutch masters. A small church on the other side of the city, near the Kremlin, by a neighborhood called Kitai Gorod, captivates me. It's a tiny place, mostly underground, and I have no idea what first drew me to it. Its intimate rooms weave through passages, and its curved doorways pull me in deeper. Every surface is covered with paintings. Gentle images, with no gold, unlike most Russian icons. Walls, ceilings, doorways, passages—not an inch is untouched. A woman in

*The small church where Tania met Batyushka Nikolai and
her friend Lena. She never found the church again when
she tried to return for Sunday service.*

blue seems in charge and I tell her how lovely the church is.
She smiles and nods.

I walk to the innermost chamber, where the altar is, and
take a few photos. A different woman tells me photography is
not allowed. I put my phone away and keep wandering. The
first woman, however, tells me if I get the father's blessing, I can
take pictures. "*Pozhalyuisto, pomogite,*" I ask her assistance. It's
been a very long time since I have received a priest's blessing.

She walks me over to where a line of women with their
heads wrapped in scarves wait in front of a closed door. They
quickly recognize that I am different and push me to the front
of the line. I wait quietly, then enter when another woman

departs. A small room so beautiful it screams to be memorialized awaits me. A heavyset elderly priest with a bushy beard sits on a bench that lines the left wall. He wears a long black robe and a large cross hangs on his chest. I sit next to him and look into his eyes, wondering what I am supposed to do. He marks the sign of a cross in front of my face. I bow my head briefly. We stare at each other for a few more moments. "Tell me your problems," he finally says, in Russian.

"Oh, I don't have any problems. I am visiting the land my father came from," I say, beaming at him. "I am from America." I share a brief version of my story with him.

He keeps looking at me, then finally tells me to hold God in my heart all the time. Something about him reaches deep into me, and I reach out to hug him.

Suddenly I wonder if this is even allowed. I had abandoned religion after many battles with the priest who taught me in Russian school when I was young. The final straw was when I thought I won the fight about non-believers going to hell. Not quite. "But for sure they will have to come around, in order to leave purgatory," he finished, taking the last word. But I was finished with him. And now I plan to hug a priest?

"*Možno?* May I?" I ask, as my arms stop in midair. A huge grin pushes its way through me as I catch his eyes again. He silently wraps his arms around me and holds me in a deep embrace for a long time. When I pull away and beam at him again, he says, "Bring that joy with you wherever you go. Bring your smile. Make people rejoice. Make them leave happier than before they saw you." And I wonder how this man read my mission in life in that one instant.

Outside, the woman in blue smiles at me, and I head off to take images. The one who told me I couldn't shakes her finger at me again. "I saw the *batyushka*," I say, using a priestly title meant for six-year olds.

"*Batyushka* Nikolai *blagoslovil*?" she asks. Oh yes, I tell her. The father certainly blessed me. After she leaves, I realize I was supposed to get his blessing for taking pictures, not for my soul.

Absorbing that experience takes much longer. It was a Saturday, and the women were waiting for confession so they could go to communion at the service on Sunday. When I was a child, we had to take confession at least once a year, during Easter Lent, a prerequisite for communion. I would invent bad things, for I wasn't going to share my truths with a priest. I never shared my innermost secrets with anyone, and certainly wasn't about to start in church. But of course, I was supposed to tell that *batyushka* my sins, not my stories. The objective of that ritual is absolution. It is about redemption and forgiveness, the very thing I had gone to my homeland in search of. I almost blew it. But I didn't. *Batyushka* Nikolai's *blagosloveniye* will always be with me.

When I describe this scene to Igor and Ira, they can't stop laughing. Igor has watched me hug policemen, Crimean Tatars, total strangers. "Of course, our Tania would hug a priest!" he says.

In that church, as I finish my photography, I again talk to the woman in blue, who tells me her name is Lena. We somehow figure out we are the same age, and both will be seventy in a few weeks. We call each other sister, smile and hug. Of course. She tells me there will be a service tomorrow at nine, that there is a choir and the acoustics are lovely. I plan to return. "Has it always been a church?" She says no, it was a Comsomol, or Communist youth club. It has recently been restored.

The next morning, I decide to go back to this church, to hear the choir sing, to leave some funds, to see it in its Sunday finery. To see my friend Lena, my priest Father Nikolai. I get

up early to find it. And never do. No matter how hard I try, all I run into are dead ends, roads blocked because I am near sensitive government areas. There are military blockades everywhere I turn. The president's government headquarters are very close, making exploring challenging. I just can't find it. And then I find that my photographs have bad GPS locators, and can't help me. I had been told that if you get too close to politically sensitive areas, GPS signals might not work. Now, I am convinced the government has foiled the GPS locators. Eventually, I decide I am falling for conspiracy theories, and remember that the images were taken inside a dense building, and in the lower reaches of the church. That could surely block the location services, right? Either way, I cannot find it. I never see Lena or Father Nikolai again, and I am devastated. I spend a few more hours on Monday repeating my search and fail again.

Later that day I walk down a street and see a woman sweeping, wearing a green vest that has become familiar. The city is full of these sweepers, but mostly in the early morning. I think of Father Nikolai as I give her a big smile and say hello. She looks up. At first, she's completely baffled that a stranger is addressing her, and then a warm smile lights her face. "Hello!" she replies, and steps forward sweeping more brightly.

That evening, Lena and Vitya invite me to join them for dinner with friends. Pavel is an American from the old Russian community, like we are, but he moved to Russia for a job, fell in love and stayed in Moscow. He and his wife Vera welcome us into an apartment teeming with friends and children. A joyful buzz emanates from all the rooms. I talk to Pavel, who tells me he visits San Francisco regularly, wanting to maintain a connection. "This is Tania, from San Francisco," he then says, introducing me to a tall attractive blond woman.

"Hi, I'm Alexandra Tolstoy," she says. I learn she grew up in England, moved to Russia for some years, now lives again in England. Soon we are exchanging stories of traveling in

central Asia. I, who usually have the more intriguing tales, am stunned by this adventurer who has trekked with camels thousands of miles through Mongolia and Siberia. "Oh, I have written a book, also," she says when I tell her of my project. But we quickly divert to her father, who is also a writer.

"Wait," I say, "your name is Tolstoy and your father is a writer?"

"Yes, but we are separated by several generations from . . ."

It turns out there is another famous writer I am familiar with in her family, her step-grandfather Patrick O'Brien. During a challenging time in my own life I binged on his series of novels about a sea captain during Napoleon's time. They were an easier read at that moment than my all-time favorite, *War and Peace.*

I start to pursue her connection with the Tolstoy Foundation that funded my family's ship journey to America, but she has moved on to books her own father wrote about Russians—many of whom had lived in Yugoslavia for years—who ended up in Soviet gulags after World War II due to actions by the British government. This story resonates very strongly with me, as it ties to a movement many of my parents' friends were involved with, and which occupied many hours of debate in our living rooms when Sasha and I were young. I learn that her father was sued for libel. I could talk to her for hours, but someone pulls her away. I end up in a deep discussion with a woman from Australia, who came to Russia seven years earlier as a lawyer for a multinational corporation which has since pulled up stakes. She is now struggling to get her visa renewed, as are many people working in a shrinking foreign sector here. "There are only three ways to get a permanent visa," she explains. "One is to be the son or daughter of someone born in Russia. Another is to request asylum from one's country. And the final one is for the president to grant it to you."

"How do you get that to happen?"

"Well, if there is the slightest hint of royalty in your blood," she says, "you would get it. The Russians have plenty of money, but they want the link to class by birth."

As she talks, I realize I qualify for citizenship in Russia. And not through any royal connections . . .

She tells me the "émigré Russian" expatriate community here is shrinking fast as multinational companies are pulling out. "And the French don't have much time for Australians, you know," she continues. Again, I want to hear more, as her stories are compelling, but we are distracted by the need to get to dinner on time.

Over that meal, in a comfortable nearby restaurant, I converse with Pavel, who explains that Vera will come soon, but she is finalizing a convention of people linked to the White Russian movement from all over the world to be held in the next few days. Lena and I wish we had heard of this reunion earlier, as it sounds intriguing. Alexandra is also heavily involved. The evening continues to be fascinating. I wondered, for much of the trip, how people in Russia view the United States. My Amochaev hosts are so polite and friendly that I hear almost no criticisms. We also hear little of local politics. One Moscow taxi driver casually says, "In your country, if very few voted for a president, could he still win?"

Sasha and I just look at each other. For sure our current president got elected without a majority of the population voting for him, but we're not going there. Someone else tells us Putin probably won't run again when his term expires.

"Who might succeed him?" I ask, surprised.

"*Oni* (my father's famous 'they') haven't decided yet," is the reply. But most people avoid politics as much as they had in my previous visit forty years earlier.

Pavel lets me inside this sphere.

After some polite chitchat, and a few more shots of vodka, I am hearing a worldview that reminds me, in the one-sidedness

of its perspective, of the views held by the Russian refugees I had grown up with. Except these are diametrically opposed to their mindset. With those Russian émigrés, it was always their old homeland—at that time a Communist dictatorship—that was evil; here the point of view reverses. Here are a few perspectives Pavel's experiences in Russia have let him deeply understand:

"Britain is just a stooge—or proxy—for the United States and has always been so. The guy who was poisoned there was certainly not poisoned by the Russians. After all, Theresa May declared fault two days after he died, way too quickly, with no investigation."

"Ukraine's government was overthrown in a coup d'état by the Americans and it led to the Russians facing challenges in Crimea and Donbas. This is even more clear now that it has been revealed that Biden's son was on a Ukrainian company's board of directors."

"An American consul recommended to a small region in Russia—which had oil reserves—that they form their own country, since they were sending much more money to Russia than they were getting back."

"America will not let Russia survive."

"The U.S. stands for a single global force with no individualized personality and Russia is one of the few countries big enough and strong enough to stand in its way. The sanctions in place since 2014 are intended by the U.S. to simply destroy Russia." Pavel has opened the door on a vision of America as the "evil empire"—one that Russia is standing up to. I remember uncomfortably how I had read that label, articulated by Ronald Reagan, to our hosts on our first night in Russia—but about their country's past. And then I understand. Russians would be reluctant to insult my country in this way. They are too polite to offend. But Pavel is an American, talking to another American. He is not offending a foreign country; we

are just discussing politics. We might just be having another debate about Trump.

It is incredibly eye opening, and certainly helps me understand what views are being promoted here. I can imagine hearing an alternate version of this by a Fox news commentator, or their counterpart at CNN, and it is very familiar once I step back far enough to observe it dispassionately. I am grateful that Pavel shared it, but also happy to have avoided political debates while getting to know the people of this land in a different way. Imagine just turning off the news for a few weeks!

Vera soon joins us; we talk about families and the upcoming reunion they will have with old friends. Too soon, the evening ends when Lena accidentally pushes the wrong button on Uber, and we rush out to grab a ride. Moscow and San Francisco are united in this "sharing" and "gig" economy, but we learn that Uber has been bought by Yandex, another sign of the political environment.

The next morning, I plan our final evening in Moscow, which we will share with Artem and his family. I head out to get caviar and *zakuski* and vodka. The National has graciously already provided the champagne! I have one other final detail to take care of that day. I need a repository for the clump of dirt I brought with me from Amochaevskiy. One more time, I could not dig the soil behind Daria's house in Kulikovskiy. I did not find her silver. I was lucky to even find her house, for perhaps the final time. Amochaevskiy provided even less in the way of surviving clues. Its abandoned remnants did confirm the erasure of all traces of their existence by the Bolshevik government, and not much else. I packed that small handful of dirt in a pill container, for I was not about to confirm its presence in my luggage.

In a gift shop in Moscow I find a tiny wooden black enameled box, with a mother of pearl lid. The image on the cover,

a scene out of a dream, could be of Amochaevskiy, with the Panika River burbling merrily along, peaceful and calm. It isn't, but that box will hold a little piece of my grandfather's life—a few grains of soil—and my memories of this trip. I finish my shopping trip with a stop at Elyseevskiy Gastronom and head home from my final exploration of the city. The hotel staff supplies china and cutlery and crystal, and we have a jubilant reunion, with me showing off my luxurious suite deemed worthy of a Romanov. The only sad touch is that Artem's brother Roman has fallen ill and we will miss seeing him before leaving.

The evening is a joy of shared memories, old friends meeting for one more dinner. I am reminded again of my mother's dining room full of noisy Russians, of little Sasha and Tania sitting at the top of the stairs listening to the singing long after we are supposed to be asleep. Of arguments drowned in vodka, an occasional *balalaika* being strummed. Igor is of course gracious and polite, and Ira's smile, which we missed so much in Crimea, lights up the room. Artem and I observe this amazing experience we have masterminded out of thin air, sharing an occasional gleam of the eye with each other. But I really don't know how his parents feel about all this. They have never pried into my life and must now wonder about a woman with this outrageous deluxe living accommodation. I am sure if asked, Igor would reply, "*Normaljno.*"

We finish our *zakuski* and go down to dinner at the hotel restaurant, which is a high-class restaging of Soviet nostalgia. I had considered finding an alternative, but dining in this extraordinary setting is irresistible, and viewing the Kremlin for my final evening in Moscow feels ideal. Sitting at a comfortable table with a perfect view, I sink into myself in a way I haven't for weeks. I do join the gaiety, but not in the same way I have been. I remain a bit removed, observing. Something

about sitting in the glow of a Moscow night and knowing it is my final one has me wondering if I will see it again. After all, it has been forty years since the last time, and I certainly do not have another forty years. These people who have already done so much for us brought us farewell gifts. I will see the shawl Ira picked for me draped over the seat in my living room every time I walk into my apartment.

Incredibly, after all this time together, our farewells remind me of our first meeting in the Moscow airport. Artem, the gentle young man who made all this happen, self-effacingly grins at me and says *dosvidanie*. Russian for goodbye, it actually means until we meet again. We look each other in the eye and without a word acknowledge the power of the events we launched. I hug him; I hug Ira and Igor. They confirm that I don't need a ride to the airport, that Lena and Vitya will find their way to the train for St. Petersburg. And then they walk away.

It is similar to the way Sasha and I part, no matter how long we've been together or how soon we will reconnect. After all, we are family; we are always together.

Chapter 40

The Ties That Bind Us

Recovering from my trip to Russia is a slow process. The experience was gratifying beyond any of my expectations, but I struggle to process all I have learned. I wonder if this is how wisdom finds its way inside us, or if I am perhaps too old to absorb this flow of emotions. But, as I persisted in searching for touchstones in my travels, I am determined to persevere and understand the implications of what I found.

Realizing, for the first time, just how much my grandparents left behind pushes me to try to understand how they could have abandoned everything they knew and owned in support of a monarch—Tsar Nicholas II—who seems like a very remote figure to me. Sasha keeps reminding me that to them the Tsar was inseparable not only from Russia, but even from God. The images of God and the Tsar certainly shared the walls of our homes.

My mind goes to my friend Marina in Colorado. While my own family tree is still a mystery, Marina's is clear. She is the granddaughter of Tsar Nicholas's sister Xenia. And Marina is the woman my stepdaughter Beth introduced me to at her house in the remote Rocky Mountains of Colorado,

Relaxing in Marina's home in Colorado.

where I was launching a book about my mother's Balkan—not Russian—family.

Why did that incredible match-up happen, leading to Marina's inevitable entry into this narrative? I suppose it is no more unexpected than having Artem Amochaev appear in the form of a misdirected email from *The Economist*, but it certainly links reality to fantasy, and the everyday to the truly mystical.

To complete this journey, I need to reconnect with Marina. A few weeks after my return, during a visit with my family in Colorado, she and I meet at The Goat, a simple cafe that she knows. "I want to hear all about your trip," Marina says, and I launch into details about Moscow and the Amochaevs.

"Did you go to Crimea?" Of course, she wants to hear about this part of my voyage. I tell her about the Tsar's palace—Livadia—and about searching for her grandfather's palace of Ay Todor. I tell her about the trail between the palaces and show her an image of myself heading down the trail. "I'm sorry," I say, "I tried so hard to find your grandfather's palace, but I just couldn't. I really searched but hit one dead end after another. It's now a sanatorium, like so many of the old palaces. You have never been there, have you?"

"No, I have not been to Crimea," she says. "But I went to St. Petersburg in the nineties, when they had that funeral for the Tsar and his family."

Of course. It was her great uncle and her cousins who were finally being acknowledged. She watched their burial at the Peter and Paul Fortress. Haunting voices rang through the cathedral, bells tolled, and cannons boomed as the coffins were laid, one by one, in a regal tomb, joining their ancestors. Eighty years after Tsar Nicholas II and his family were executed by Bolsheviks, the president of Russia, Boris Yeltsin, described the murder of the Russian royal family as one of the most

shameful pages in the country's history. He urged Russians to close a "bloody century" with repentance.

Very few family members survived those Bolshevik persecutions. Marina's grandparents and their youngest son—her father Vasily—finally escaped from Russia with the Tsar's mother in April 1919, leaving by ship from Crimea just as my grandparents did the following year.

Marina's father Prince Vasily Romanov, having been born of a royal marriage, was clearly a legitimate successor to the dynasty—a debate I was vaguely aware of during the years that my Russian exile community awaited the fall of Communism and the return of the monarchy. Because Marina is a female, she can avoid all debate about succession. Many Romanovs would have to disappear before a woman was next in line. And Vladimir Putin is the reigning monarch of that kingdom. There is no Romanov in his succession plan, and the woman I am meeting will not be returning to Russia. But who is she, this Russian princess in America?

I told Beth I wanted to compare my life to Marina's, as I had earlier contrasted our grandmothers' lives. She was startled. "Won't that be awkward?"

"Why?" I ask.

"Well, you didn't exactly grow up regal, Tania. You were pretty poor when you came to America, weren't you?"

"And you think Marina grew up like a princess?"

"Well, she was a princess. Her parents were both royals, weren't they?" Beth knew Marina's father married a Russian princess. Surely their daughter's life followed a different trajectory than mine.

For many years, everyone believed that the fleeing Romanovs left the country with great wealth. That could not have been further from the truth. By 1925, Marina's grandmother Xenia was in a desperate financial situation. Her cousin King George V of England—who had saved their lives by sending a ship

to evacuate them from Russia—stepped in and gave her free housing in Hampton Court, near Windsor Palace. She was to stay in that "grace and favor" home for the rest of her life. Her son Vasily left for America. In New York he married his Russian princess, Natalia Galitzina, and soon moved to California. Their daughter Marina was born in San Francisco, perhaps in the same hospital as my cousin Lena. And now *Princess* Marina sits across from me at The Goat—far from a royal setting. It is not the elaborate dining room of the Hotel National; no one here is in awe of the two Romanov women.

A healthy woman who spends a lot of time outdoors, Marina is dressed in casual clothes suitable for a walk in the mountains. Like me, she is busy with family. We savor our time to catch up, and soon the conversation goes to stories of growing up Russian in an American world.

"We didn't have much money when I was young," she tells me. "I went to public schools, of course."

I also attended public schools—in neighborhoods that had seen better days.

Her family moved south of the city for her father's work. My father worked in the South Bay as well, but he commuted from the city.

"My mother worked too," Marina continues. "She worked at Almaden Winery. The owner liked it when she entertained visitors." I am sure he liked having a Romanov princess in that role.

Her father eventually became a money manager, but they always lived a modest life. My mother worked as a seamstress, at home, and my father eventually became an accredited engineer again, just before his retirement. They also lived modestly.

"Did you go to Russian school?" I ask. I resented having to go to Russian school. By the time I graduated I rarely attended; I was really embarrassed about being so foreign by then.

"Oh, yes, of course. But I hated it!" We laugh and acknowledge that we both still speak the language fluently and are finally grateful for that.

Like mine, her parents went to formal balls at the Russian Center in San Francisco—but hers went out of a sense of obligation—a debt to *Matiushka Rossiya*, Mother Russia—and her father served as the head of various organizations. Mine served as the organizers and supporters of those organizations.

As I listen to Marina talk about her childhood home, the parallels keep growing. Her father had lived through fear, which turned to anger and fury.

"He was always talking about the *kashmar,* or mess, the politicians made of things." Like my father and everyone I knew from Russia, he was a Republican—a reaction to Communism, and everything liberal. Like I did, she struggled with the right-wing political stances of our families, the obsessive anti-Communist debates. "Politics were drummed into my face until I was sick of it," she said.

"Me too. I hated that!"

"Yes, I ended up avoiding politics for as long as I could," she continued.

I know exactly how she felt.

Marina had a best friend whose family had money, and in her teens, they took her with them on a trip to Europe, so she could visit her grandmother. I saved enough money to travel through Europe—staying in youth hostels—as a junior in college. Like mine, Marina's paternal grandfather died before she was born. "Were you close to your grandmother?" I ask. My grandmother Daria looks hard in most of her images. There are plenty of pictures of Xenia online, and she looks like a woman who can hold her own as well.

"I spent a year in England with her, in my late teens. I loved her."

I learn that Marina's grandmother was somewhat reticent. She had a gentle sweetness but was hard to connect with. I suspect the world our grandmothers grew up in didn't lend itself to a soft character.

"And did your father want you to marry a Russian?" I ask. This is probably my most important question. My father and uncle wanted that for me more than anything else. It didn't work with me, but my uncle Shura succeeded with Lena.

"No. They wanted me to marry an educated man, one who had character."

I am stunned. That's when it really hits me that their position in the Russian world was a burden and an obligation. People looked upon them with awe and had expectations of them. They were the royal Romanovs, after all. It wasn't easy to just live their lives. They couldn't just blend into the Russian community as my family could. They wanted their daughter to move on, past family obligations, to a future of her own making.

They set her free. Mine kept trying to hold me in.

I exploded out of my constrained Russian world, rejecting it totally. It had to horrify my family when I headed to college in the radical Berkeley of the 1960s. I became financially independent as quickly as I could so no one could tell me what to think, how to live, and, of course, whom to marry.

Marina's family, on the other hand, let her loose. She started by going to college much farther away than I did. She wanted a progressive school and chose Sarah Lawrence, on the East Coast. From there, she became a schoolteacher in New York. She married an American and raised four children. The oldest went to Russian school as a child, near a Russian Orthodox seminary in Yonkers. But that grew too complicated, and the rest of her children didn't really learn the language.

We talk about a book she is reading that includes the story of the birth of her own grandmother, Xenia. I wonder what that would be like, to be surrounded, as she is today, by books and television shows and films about my family. As we talk about the book, I see that she takes it in stride. She enjoys it from a distance, neither rejecting her past nor playing it up.

We share news about our children, and all too soon, our time is up. We hug briefly and head off to grandmotherly activities.

A few weeks later I am back in San Francisco, writing, and remembering my parents as well as Marina's. I decide to commemorate the day of my mother Zora's death with a visit to her gravesite—not something I often do. My parents, Shura, Galya, and Daria are all buried in the Serbian Cemetery in Colma—a suburb of San Francisco populated by twice as many dead bodies as that city has live ones. Marina's parents are in the same cemetery, which I learned only after meeting her in Colorado. I remember nothing about her family and am not sure I had ever heard of them.

I drive south, following Ocean Beach and the sand dunes that line San Francisco. Unusually for that part of the Bay Area, it is sunny, but the wind is picking up and the fog is on its way. I easily find the cemetery, park the car, and start walking. And walking. And walking.

I cannot find my parents' grave. Deep in the heart of Russia, Igor stumbled on his grandmother's grave in an unknown cemetery and yet I just wander in this broad expanse overlooking the Pacific Ocean—which I have visited many times—clueless. This makes no sense. I helped pick the marble headstone after my father died. I spent hours in front of his grave with my mother, supporting her and feeling guilty over how judgmental I had been of him. I was there when she was buried, and when

my aunt and uncle were. There are many familiar names, but I cannot find mine. I decide to see if Marina's parents are easier to identify. I assume theirs will be a large monument, either in the center or anchoring a corner. They are, after all, the most significant connection for most of those who repose here.

It is a large cemetery, but not an opulent one. This is not Père Lachaise in Paris, where tombs are so elaborate you wander in amazement and awe. Here you can see all the thousand or so graves at once, for none is much higher than my shoulders and the land slopes gently. But I cannot find the ones I seek, and I go to the office. A young woman greets me and offers to help. I spell my last name, and she finds my father Anatoly Amochaev and the others. "Oh, that will be easy," she says. "They are next to each other." I ask about a few close family friends as well.

We struggle through the transliteration—the conversion from the Cyrillic alphabet to our own Roman one—of names from my childhood that I only know in Russian. It is the same process that led Artem to accidentally use my email address— he transliterates his own as Amochayev—but eventually she finds the others. Then I decide I will ask for Marina's family burial plot.

"Romanov," I say, a bit self-consciously. I expect a reaction but get none as she turns to her keyboard and starts typing. She gets as far as Romano . . . when she gets her first hit. It is the first in a long list of Romanoffs—an alternate spelling—but there is no Vasily. She registers no recognition of the name; there is no "Of course!" Nothing.

I stand there, thinking again about Marina's comment that Romanovs are as common in Russia as Smiths in America. Certainly, this is the most prolific name we have typed into this registry. But no luck. Finally, I say "Please try it with a 'v' at the end." The French use a double "f" for the Russian

"v", and so those who came through France often finish their name that way. It's also considered more elegant, more noble. Many Russians even add a "D" before their names if they came through France. Again, it's a sign of nobility.

She types in a simple Romanov, as we always did for my grandmother, and exactly two names pop up: Vasily, and Natalia, his wife. "Oh, they're at the far end." She takes a copy of a hand-drawn sketch of sections and plots and marks a spot in an area slightly removed from the central part where the others are.

I wander to my parents' graves and sit, surrounded by their spirits. I remember the remote mountains I was hiking in when each of them departed. I was in the Himalayas when my father died, and in the Dolomites for my mother's passing. I rarely visit them here. For me it's easier to remember my mother's laugh at the redwood grove in my home in Sonoma County. I think of my father when I'm wandering the piers of Fisherman's Wharf, remembering the old boat in which he roamed the waters around San Francisco, fishing.

I have been making peace with my father for some years, and I sense he has forgiven me. But now I feel a new, deeper connection with him. Through my travels in Russia I have gained an understanding of the country of his birth and the complex relationship he and my grandparents shared with it. I relax into this feeling.

My mind goes back to a small church in the heart of Moscow, to *Batyushka* Nikolai, to the absolution he granted me. Transpiring as it did at the end of that journey, it came to a woman who was prepared for it. A woman ready for redemption and forgiveness; a woman ready to be reconciled with her father. A woman now at ease with herself at her father's feet, in a place that commemorates him. One who feels great joy remembering his favorite nicknames for her:

Taniusha. Tanichka. Zolotko. It is my handsome young Papa in that grave, the man a very young Tatiana loved with all her heart. The man I now love again, accepting who he was and acknowledging the pain he went through.

Eventually I get up and wander to the far end of the cemetery. The fog is now rolling in, the wind almost sweeps away my cheat sheet. It is a simple xerox of a messy job, the paper is thin, the sketches ineffective. The plot and section labels marked on the sheet are nowhere to be found in the cemetery itself, so it really isn't very useful.

I had found an obituary of Marina's father written by one of my family's dearest friends, Tolya Joukousky. He had been the head of the Yugoslav national ballet company and was a professor of dance at San Francisco State University. I adored him and was thrilled to find one more connection between Marina's family and mine.

Now, as I search for a large gravestone, appropriate for a royal presence; for the souls that connect this whole community to Russia, I recall Tolya's words:

> *Recently, our Romanovs left us for a better world after living half a century with us.*
>
> *Prince Vasily Alexandrovich was the son of the Grand Duchess, Xenia Alexandrovna, sister of the Sovereign Nicholas II and daughter of the Emperor Alexander III. His father—admiral; founder of Russian military aviation; Grand Duke Alexander Mikhailovich, uncle of Sovereign Nicholas II.*
>
> *The cathedral was full. Russian San Francisco had come to bid farewell to its Prince Vasily. To the ringing of a bell presented by Alexander III, the cadets carried out the coffin of his grandson, Prince Vasily.*

The church he is describing is a few short blocks from my home. The previous Sunday, as I wandered by it, I heard the distinctive sweet sounds of bells that had survived the 1906 earthquake. I was pulled inside, unconsciously searching for my *batyushka* Nikolai. I didn't find him. This service was in English, the priest had a strict appearance, the icons were bold rather than the gentle pastels I had been seeking. But the peace I had been granted in that distant chapel lives deep within me, and I feel it now, in this cemetery with my family.

I continue my search for Marina's father. Nothing pops out, and I determinedly start walking along, reading every gravestone. Finally, I stop before a small white stone cross that I have passed several times.

This cemetery is the burial place of the large Russian diaspora that mostly moved here after World War II. A number of these men fought in the name of the Tsar. Most of the people buried here held the Tsar's family as sacred. And yet, in this very modest cemetery, this one stone does stand out. In its modesty. It is the smallest and simplest by far.

Many of the marble headstones have a cross coming out of them. Some of them have pictures of the deceased, or descriptions of who they were in life. The names are etched in the polished colored marble; sometimes there's an icon or a flag.

Here, there is just a small white stone cross with the word ROMANOV and nothing else. On a small plaque beneath the stone, written in Russian are the names Vasily and Natalia:

Василий Наталия
Романовы
1907 1989

That is all.

*Grave of Vasily Romanov, 1907-1989—nephew of Tsar Nicholas II—
and his wife Natalia, near San Francisco, California.*

I stare at the year of their death, and realize they, like my father, died before it all ended. Before Russia became enamored anew with their family. Before the Cossacks were reinstated in myth. Before I was treated like royalty in Moscow just in case my penname of Romanov was real.

This simple grave must have been what they chose. They did not design an elaborate marker, a testimony to what their family represented. They wanted to just "be."

Marina's father—a true successor to the Tsar—had let it all go.

I sit down at the foot of his grave. I feel surrounded by the world I grew up in—by my childhood—and tears pour down my face. The complexity of my emotions staggers me. I call Sasha and send him a photo of the grave. He too, is stunned, and helps me absorb it all.

My respect for these people and what they went through grows and reaches deep inside me. My respect for all those who preceded us, those who preceded Igor—all those Russians who survived, and those who didn't—has developed through my travels and my thinking about that experience. I have lived a life of ease compared to all of them, and I am grateful for the world they created for me.

I had yearned for the visit to Russia to provide closure on so many issues about my family's history, and it certainly handed up a chalice full of answers. I continue seeking closure on my family's past in Russia. But now I wonder what exactly is closure, and what is family?

Our trip to Russia was borne out of my connection to Artem. Without him and his family, none of this would have happened. The joy of exploring our homeland together was beyond comprehension. The bond we developed, the love we share, convinced us that we are family. We now have a family in Russia—our Amochaev family—where not long ago we only imagined a land our grandparents had fled. But the mysteries abound. Who are Igor and Artem's ancestors and how are they related to us? Did they support the Whites or the Reds? How did they survive through Lenin and Stalin's extermination of Cossacks? What happened to my grandfather Ivan's nine siblings?

We snuck Igor and Artem's spit out of the country, so we could analyze their DNA. The two of them agreed to work with Vladimir in Uryupinsk on defining the Amochaev family

tree, hoping to learn about our two branches, and how they meet. They asked Vladimir to at least find the origin of *khutor* Amochaev if he can find no more about our ancestors or Igor's.

I think again about what happened after my grandparents left Russia in 1920 and imagine Igor as the great-grandson of the man my grandmother Daria refused to marry—Mikhail. It makes me laugh to myself: what if she had agreed? But deep inside I know it is not Mikhail, but his cousin Alexei who launched their amazing family which somehow survived the impossible.

I have spent a lot of time understanding the slim odds my grandparents bucked with their successful departure. But what it took for Igor's family to squeeze through another eye of that same needle is almost unimaginable. Surviving Stalin as a Cossack in those days was definitely a challenge. Surviving and creating a tribe that led to these incredible people I was honored to become so close with is a gift from the universe.

And yet, like so many others in Russia, they know nothing about it all. There was no grandmother sharing stories, no old recordings on 8-millimeter film, no diaries. No one dared talk about any of it, and their history dissolved with Stalin and the threats posed by his annihilations.

But I cannot let go and wait for the DNA results to tell me precisely who these magical Amochaevs are. After all, they appeared out of the ether of random chance to enter our lives and enrich us beyond anything I could imagine. We all know we are closely related! We just need the scientific proof.

A few weeks after our return we get Igor and Artem's DNA results and learn—almost nothing! Sasha and Igor share a tiny percentage of DNA, making him a fifth cousin at best. But this confirms my belief that their ancestor is in fact Mikhail's cousin Alexei. At first a dedicated Bolshevik, he was a survivor who sacrificed his personal needs to support his family.

There is a fine line between truth and fiction. And truths passed down through memories are mostly what we have. I know Igor and Artem are family, and that is all that matters to me. My grandparents' story emerged from tales shared with me by my grandmother Daria and Uncle Shura. Their flight is documented on the Internet, and the adventure of their ship—Tralschik 412—including its delayed appearance through the mists, is historically real. My grandfather Ivan is buried in Belgrade—in an opulent cemetery recently rebuilt with funding from Vladimir Putin to place the stamp of a newly powerful Russia on Serbia.

My grandfather Ivan's cousin Mikhail, whose precise name I am not confident of, existed and was rejected by Daria, from her own stories. There is no question that Alexei, Igor's great-grandfather, was a relative. They share our rare last name, a small bit of DNA, and Igor's grandmother Anna lies in a grave near the house where my father Tolya was born.

Igor marveled at our family's deep connection to his land, but I now see his wonder in a different light. He learned, as we sang together in that kitchen in Crimea, how deep that link to a common past was, and how much joy it could give. I now understand that this connection which so stunned him is my family's creation story. My creation story. They were forced to abandon a land they loved; it was impossible for them to stay. They glorified that world and held its memory close.

Creation stories by definition are myths, and mine is slowly releasing me from old pains and turning into a gift of joy.

My visit to the Serbian cemetery deepened my understanding. It is full of my family; and not just the ones called Amochaev. My family is wide enough to contain the names Joukousky, Ishevsky, Kvasnikov, Mandrusov, Maslenikov, Sluchevsky, Halaj, Klestov, Shestakov, Alexeev, Gerich, and a list I could easily extend for pages. It definitely includes

Romanov, and I am honored that Marina is part of my life, and that her family is part of my daughter's life. The whole Russian community that I grew up with is my family. Lena has known that all her life, and her children do as well. I am just a bit slow catching up.

And the magic that has held them together all these years is their creation myth. In it, a beautiful religious old Russia—symbolized by churches, palaces, and a Tsar who embodied their loss—floats above the sweep of history.

PART FIVE

Glossary of Russian Words and Names

GLOSSARY OF RUSSIAN WORDS

Ambar—granary. At its simplest, a hut that held grain for storage. Its existence in a family was enough to class the owner a kulak, and an enemy of Communism. Tania found Ivan's granary in Kulikov in 1977. It was a rough hut with a straw roof, no windows, less than ten meters long and two wide, maybe two meters tall.

Amerikanskye gori—literally American mountains, but it is the Russian name for roller coaster. When I shared this information with my French friend Martine, she laughed because the French word for roller coaster is *montagne russes*, or Russian mountains.

Amerikantsi—Americans. Male—*Amerikanets*. Female—*Amerikanka*. Tania's boyfriends and her husband Harold were referred to in this way, as her family considered anyone who wasn't Russian a "foreigner."

Arshin—a measure equal to 28 inches, from a Tatar word, and in use for hundreds of years. It was formally discontinued after the revolution and replaced with the metric system, so

Tania was surprised to hear it when getting directions to the Amochaev residence in Kulikov in 1977.

Babusya—Tania's nickname for her grandmother Daria, because she couldn't say babushka, the traditional word children use for grandmother.

Balalaika—a three-stringed instrument with a hollow wooden triangular body. An accompaniment to traditional Russian songs, especially those that men dance to by crouching on the floor and swinging their legs.

Banya—steam bath, sauna.

Barskiy dom—a regal house, perhaps a baron's house. Shura remembered the house where they lived in Evpatoria as such a house, for it was certainly more regal than anything he had ever seen.

Batyushka—father, priest, or an affectionate term for the Tsar.

Blagoslovenie—blessing. Confession is typically required to get a priest's blessing, but the *batyushka* in Moscow blessed Tania in spite of her appalling lack of appreciation for the practice.

Borscht—a soup made by boiling meat and bones with potatoes, carrots, cabbage and onions. It often has beets as well, but the one that Daria made and taught her daughter-in-law to cook did not.

Bože moy—Oh my God!

Budushnost—future, destiny, or fate, but of a positive bent. A deeply romantic word, it was faith in the very idea of a future that Tolya finally lost for good when he was kicked out of Yugoslavia in 1950 simply because he was of Russian birth.

Cadet, Cadet Corpus—In Russia, a military prep school, it was reinstituted in Serbia as a college prep school for all the male

Russian emigrés in the country. There were several of them, and they were mostly boarding schools. A Russian boarding school for girls was also set up, and the attendees were called *institutke*. All of Daria and Ivan's children were educated at these schools, although none of them aspired to a military career. The graduates created an association that functioned around the world, and still exists in San Francisco, although all the original students have died. The schools ceased their existence with WWII and the beginning of Communism in Yugoslavia. The education was of sufficient quality to lead to acceptance to the best universities in the country.

Campo San Sabba (Italian)—a refugee camp in Trieste where the Amochaev brothers fled in 1950, and Tolya and his family stayed in until 1954, when they left for the United States. The *Risiera*, or old rice factory that held many of the refugees, also served as a concentration camp during World War II. Tania's Aunt Galya told her they were never told about this, but "they could smell that it had a terrible past." After more than forty years, the Italians acknowledged its history and made it a Memorial.

Charochka moja—My little silver goblet. An old traditional Cossack song that celebrates the recipient, who must down a silver shot glass of vodka while the singers encourage with "*pei do dna*" or "bottoms up" until the glass is empty.

Chayovnya—tea house, which is what Ivan was told that their house in Kulikov had become after they left. It was how Tania found their home in 1977, because the neighbors still remembered this fact. Tania imagines that it was the family of Mikhail Amochaev, the suitor Daria turned down, who ran it.

Don Cossack—A people who inhabited a part of Russia in the south, near the Don River. They were always independent and

known to be good horsemen. They fought many battles for the Tsars of Russia and were the prime constituency of the White Army which lost to the Bolsheviks after the Russian Revolution. They were largely wiped out after the end of the Civil War that followed.

Cossachka—the feminine gender of the word Cossack. In Russian words have gender, and women's names end with an -a. Tatiana Amochaev in Russian would be Tatiana Amochaeva.

Da—yes.

Dacha—summer house or cabin, an important part of many Russians lives. There are an estimated 60 million *dachas* in Russia, many within a couple of hours drive of a big city.

Derevnya—remote countryside, or small village. Often used insultingly by city folk.

Dosvidanie—goodbye, or literally, until we meet again.

Dyadya—an affectionate term for uncle, often used by children for older men in their lives. *Dyadya* Shura is Tania's uncle. *Dyadya* Zhenya is her adopted grandfather in the refugee camp of San Sabba.

Gorko—bitter. It is shouted at wedding receptions to get the groom to kiss the bride and make it sweet.

Hristos Voskrese—Christ has risen, it is a traditional proclamation at Easter. The reply is *Voistinu Voskrese*, indeed he is risen. It is accompanied with three kisses—on the cheek, except for sneaky young lads.

Imenini—names day, the day of your patron saint, whom you are named after.

Isba—a home in the Russian countryside, from a log hut to an elaborate wood frame structure. Always single story, and

often with decoratively carved window framing. They still line the roads of Russia outside the large cities.

Izvinitje—excuse me. I beg your pardon. So sorry. For some reason, Igor found Tania's use of this word to introduce herself to complete strangers very intriguing. Perhaps she should have been using *požaluysto*, or please, instead?

Kasha—one of Russia's national dishes, this porridge is made with buckwheat groats, most often eaten with borscht. Russians eat an average of 15 kilograms a year, the largest consumption per capita in the world. It is over 1,000 years old, is eaten most often with butter, and has a high nutritional value compared to most other grains.

Kashmar—mess or nightmare.

Khutor—a term for small Cossack villages, almost eliminated during the period of de-Cossackization. The name is used again in Russian.

Kolkhoz—a contraction of *Kolektivnoe Hozaystvo*, or collective ownership, it was a form of collective farm in the Soviet Union. While some early ones were created voluntarily, at the end of the 1920s there was a forced collectivization campaign when all land was requisitioned, and people were forced to live and work on these farms. Tania's family left before these were created. Igor's father was born in one but got permission to attend engineering school outside the area, joined the military, and never returned.

Kulak—a peasant wealthy enough to own a farm and hire labor. They were mostly liquidated by Lenin and Stalin. Ivan was definitely a *kulak* and would have been sent to Siberia or worse had he stayed in Russia.

Kulich—the traditional Easter cake, a tall round sweet bread decorated with white icing. Somewhat like a heavier version of the Italian panettone.

Mangal—an Arabic word for barbecue, both the event and the grilling apparatus. Igor's was a fairly elaborate brick structure with chimney and warming area. I'd never heard of it as a Russian word, but it seemed in common usage. He made a delicious *shashlik* on it.

Musulman—the Russian word for Muslim.

Normaljno—normal. This word was Igor's standard answer that meant anything from "things are fine" to "great" to "what the hell!" depending on the intonation. It seems to be in very wide usage in Russia today. Perhaps like "fine" in the US, or like "cool" used to be.

Nu—well. As an introductory word, it pauses the story. For Igor, this usually presaged a joke. For Daria—as in *nu, dovoljno uže*—"well, enough already," a final warning to stop the current discussion.

Nyet—no.

Oblast—one of 46 Federal entities of Russia. The Don Oblast, where the Don Cossacks lived, was eliminated by Lenin during the period after the Civil War. The land mostly went to the Volgograd Oblast, but some of the far western portion went to Ukraine.

Oni—they. In Russian, this word in effect means "those who control us." Tolya would tell Tania, "*oni*" would not let her become an executive because she was just a foreign girl. In Russia, Tania was told "*oni*" hadn't decided yet who would replace Putin when he decides to step down.

Opanak, papuča (Serbian)—slippers worn in Turkik areas, including much of Bosnia in the early nineteenth century. They often have upturned toes, and Tania has seen them in market-places in the Middle East up to the twenty-first century. Ivan bought a sewing machine and started a business making them, or rather having Daria make them, but it was not successful as the men continued buying from their lifelong suppliers.

Paskha—a traditional Easter dessert to pair with *kulich*, it is a firm sweet cheese custard made in the form of a pyramid, usually around ten inches in diameter.

Pelmeni—a dumpling the size of a small ravioli, filled with meat and wrapped in thin unleavened dough, cooked in a chicken broth. Often called the heart of Russian cuisine, there are fast food restaurants in Moscow that serve them like hamburgers are served in the US, and they come in a myriad of delicious flavors.

Pravilno zdelali—they did the right thing. An expression heard all over the world when a person living in Russian learns that your ancestors left their country many years ago.

Pravoslavnaya—a female of the Orthodox faith, a Christian religion once persecuted by the Communists, but now returned as the State Religion of Russia. To a child, its most distinguishing characteristics are the extreme length of services—three hours is considered short, and the fact that you have to stand all that time unless you are debilitated in some way. There are no pews or seats.

Razkassachivanie—de-Cossackization, or elimination of the Cossacks by Lenin after the Revolution in the 1920s.

Rodina—homeland, the loving term used by Russian emigrés to refer to their country of origin. "*Rossia, Rossia, Rossia,*

Rodina moja" were the words of a song that still haunts Tania and was sung over many campfires at her Russian scout camps in Northern California.

Shashlik—called shish kebab in other languages, these skewered and grilled cubes of meat are a favorite of Russian cuisine—pre- and post-revolution. I am quite sure Ivan and Daria prepared it in Kulikov and in Yugoslavia; Tolya did in San Francisco; and Igor in Moscow.

Sirnik—a fried thick pancake made of farmer's cheese and often eaten for breakfast. Delicious!

Smetana—a sour cream heavier than the traditional one sold in the US and used heavily with Russian cuisine. It is mandatory over *pelmeni*, in *borscht*, on *blini*, and anything else you might think of!

Stanitsa—an administrative district in the Cossack area, administered fairly democratically. These were eliminated by Stalin during collectivization.

Tatar—Russians combine Tatars and Mongols and all Turkic people under this rubric, which basically covers all Islamic people living in Russia. Tania grew up with a myth of Tatars as the evil invaders (think Mongol hordes) who occupied Russia for three-hundred years, until her ancestors helped free her country of them. She was shocked when, on her first visit to Turkey, she met a handsome young man and realized that, not only were they human, but they could be lovable! She still has a talisman he gave her to remember him by, although it happened over fifty years ago.

Telega—horse cart, a common form of transport in the countryside until late into the twentieth century. Daria and Ivan traveled over 1,000 kilometers in one, to flee the Bolshevik armies and escape from their homeland, their *rodina*.

Ti, Vi—Russian carefully divides language between the formal, *Vi*, and the informal, *Ti*, similar to the French Vous and Toi. Because Tania primarily used Russian with family members, she has trouble with the formal variety. Thankfully, she is now an elder, and can *Ti* anyone she likes with impunity. The Soviets nominally gave this all up as everyone became a Tovarisch, or Comrade, but even in 1977 both forms were widely used, and today they are rigorously observed.

Ustaše (Croatian)—a group that originally wanted a greater Croatia rather than Yugoslavia—which it felt was too Serbian—and eventually turned into a Nazi supporting party during World War II.

Vlasti—people holding power or authority. Like "*oni*," it is commonly used to refer to those whose permission is required for every minor action. It would be hard to appreciate its implications for those raised in an American democracy.

Zakuski—starters, served at every formal Russian meal, meant to go with vodka. Often oily, because it was believed that lining your throat would prevent the vodka from making you drunk. Includes marinated herring, smoked salmon, mixed salads, feta cheese, eggplant caviar, and a wide range of mostly cold foods.

Zolotko—little golden one, an endearing term used by Tolya with his wife and daughter.

RUSSIAN NAMES, PATRONYMICS AND NICKNAMES

Russian names consist of a formal name, a patronymic, which is the father's first name, and a family or last name. Thus, Ivan Minaevich Amochaev is the son of Minai Amochaev. If his sister were Maria, she would be Maria Minaevna. Tatiana Anatolievna is the daughter of Anatoly; her brother

is Aleksander Anatoliev. Even in San Francisco, Tania and Sasha were raised to use the formal conventions, and their lives were full of people like Elizaveta Ivanovna and even Ksenia Gregorievna—their Aunt Galya's mother. Even that close a relationship did not allow the informal. Daria Pavlovna retained that name for everyone, including her daughter-in-law, which is why Tania's mother Zora was thrilled when her daughter's attempt at Babushka—Babusya—became her generally accepted name.

Every name in the Russian Orthodox tradition is the name of a saint. My mother's kitchen always had a calendar with 365 pages, and the names of the saints for each day were clearly listed. Your *imenini*, names day, or the day of your saint, was more important than your birthday. If there were several saints with your name, you would be given the one closest to your birthday. There are thousands of Russian saints, and I don't remember a day without at least one.

Alexander—Aleksander, Sasha, Shura
Alexandra—Sasha, Aki
Alexei—Aleksei, Alyesha
Anatoly—Tolya, Tolik
Artem—actually Artyom, as the e is a ë which has a yo sound.
Dimitry—Dima
Eugene—Evgenii, Zhenya
Faina
Helen—Elena, Lena
Igor—Igor
Irene—Irina, Ira
Katherine—Ekaterina, Katya
Minai
Natalia—Natasha
Nicholas—Nikolai, Kolya

Michael—Mikhail, Misha
Tania—Tatiana, Tania, Tanichka, Taniusha.
Vasily—Vasilii
Victor—Viktor, Vitya
Vladimir—Vova
Xenia

TOWN OR VILLAGE NAMES
Kulikov and Amochaev at some time became Kulikovskiy and Amochaevskiy, and now appear on maps this way.

ABOUT THE AUTHOR

Tania Romanov Amochaev is the author of *Mother Tongue: A Saga of Three Generations of Balkan Women* (2018) and *Never a Stranger*, a book of travel stories published in 2019. Born in Serbia, Romanov spent her childhood in a refugee camp and grew up in San Francisco. She is a prize-winning photographer and global traveler as well as an author. In her previous careers, she was the CEO of several technology companies and the founder of a non-profit aimed at helping youths graduate from public school. Tania has a Mathematics degree from UC Berkeley and an MS in Management from the Stanford Graduate School of Business.

CPSIA information can be obtained
at www.ICGtesting.com
Printed in the USA
JSHW021703240920
8218JS00002B/2

9 781609 521950

PUBLISHING IN THE
PUBLIC INTEREST

Thank you for reading this book published by The New Press. The New Press is a nonprofit, public interest publisher. New Press books and authors play a crucial role in sparking conversations about the key political and social issues of our day.

We hope you enjoyed this book and that you will stay in touch with The New Press. Here are a few ways to stay up to date with our books, events, and the issues we cover:

- Sign up at www.thenewpress.com/subscribe to receive updates on New Press authors and issues and to be notified about local events
- Like us on Facebook: www.facebook.com/newpressbooks
- Follow us on Twitter: www.twitter.com/thenewpress
- Follow us on Instagram: www.instagram.com/thenewpress

Please consider buying New Press books for yourself; for friends and family; or to donate to schools, libraries, community centers, prison libraries, and other organizations involved with the issues our authors write about.

The New Press is a 501(c)(3) nonprofit organization. You can also support our work with a tax-deductible gift by visiting www.thenewpress.com/donate.

ABOUT THE AUTHOR

Elie Mystal is *The Nation*'s justice correspondent, an Alfred Knobler Fellow at the Type Media Center, and the legal editor of the *More Perfect* podcast on the Supreme Court for Radiolab. He is a graduate of Harvard College and Harvard Law School, the former executive editor of *Above the Law*, a former associate at Debevoise & Plimpton, and a frequent guest on MSNBC and Sirius XM. He lives in New York.